Praise for the book that started it all,
Tooth and Nail: A Novel Approach to the SAT

"Looking for a way to **augment** your vocabulary? Well, here is a **novel** approach: A mystery story, at once **whimsical** and **elucidating**, filled with hundreds of SAT examiners' favorite test words." —*Los Angeles Times*

"A group of suburban high school juniors is studying for the spring's SAT test by reading a mystery novel that . . . does double duty as a teaching aid.... With a glossary of definitions in the back for quick reference, in addition to entertainment, *Tooth and Nail* is meant to strengthen vocabulary and reading comprehension by placing challenging words in context." —*Chicago Tribune*

"Take a couple of hundred of the words most frequently tested on the verbal portion of the SAT college-entrance exam, set them in boldface, then weave them into a 'mesmerizing mystery' caper and voila—you've got an SAT prep tool that practically spoon-feeds a **plenitude** of **arcane**, yet beneficial vocabulary to a **plethora** of **adroit** high school students." —*Houston Chronicle*

"The most imaginative and entertaining approach to preparing for the SAT that I have ever encountered ... A cracking good plot and absorbing characters."
—Richard Lederer, author of *Anguished English*

TEST OF
TIME

Also by Charles Harrington Elster

Tooth and Nail: A Novel Approach to the **SAT**

Verbal Advantage: 10 Easy Steps to a Powerful Vocabulary

There's a Word for It! A Grandiloquent Guide to Life

The Big Book of Beastly Mispronunciations

TEST OF TIME

A NOVEL Approach
to the SAT and ACT

Charles Harrington Elster

A Harvest Original / Harcourt, Inc.

Orlando   Austin   New York   San Diego   Toronto   London

www.HarcourtBooks.com

"The Broken Tower," from *The Complete Poems and Selected Letters and Prose of Hart Crane* by Hart Crane, edited by Brom Weber. Copyright 1933, 1958, 1966 by Liveright Publishing Corporation. Copyright 1952 by Brom Weber. Used by permission of Liveright Publishing Corporation.

Library of Congress Cataloging-in-Publication Data
Elster, Charles Harrington.
Test of time: a novel approach to the SAT and the ACT/
Charles Harrington Elster.—1st ed.
p. cm.
"A Harvest original."
Summary: An eccentric writer is finishing a manuscript about a rebellious boy named Huck when it suddenly disappears and in its place appears a strange contraption—a college student's laptop that has traveled through time.
ISBN 0-15-601137-9
1. Twain, Mark, 1835–1910—Juvenile fiction. [1. Twain, Mark, 1835–1910—Fiction. 2. College students—Fiction. 3. Time travel—Fiction.] I. Title.
PZ7.E528Te 2004
[Fic]—dc22   2003028214

Text set in Stone Serif
Designed by Suzanne Fridley

Printed in the United States of America

First edition

K J I H G F E D C

To Benjamin G. C. Fincke, my eleventh-grade English teacher, who fanned the flame and taught me to **revere** our **incomparable** language; and to Andrew F. Kay, who gave me the opportunity of a lifetime. Thank you, gentlemen.

Contents

Preface

Mark Twain once said, "The difference between the almost right word and the right word is really a large matter— 'tis the difference between the lightning-bug and the lightning."

If America's foremost writer were alive today and **contemplating** sending his three daughters to college, he probably would have added, "It's also the difference between getting the right answer or the wrong one on that dad-blamed, **farcical hoax** they call the college-entrance exam."

Otherwise known as the SAT and the ACT.

The **amiable** folks in Princeton, New Jersey, and Iowa City, Iowa, who bring you these delightful educational experiences devote their energy to accomplishing two things: making you miserable for several hours on a weekend morning and **devising** questions that require you to choose between the almost right word and the right word.

The book you're holding in your hands won't make taking the SAT or the ACT any less miserable, but it will definitely help you learn the right words for the test. And it will do it without your having to sharpen a No. 2 pencil, fill in any multiple-choice ovals, or study definitions from a word list.

If that sounds like a good way to go, read on.

The "**Novel** Approach" and How It Works

You've probably already realized there's a double meaning in the phrase "a **novel** approach," which is part of the subtitle of this book. That's because *Test of Time* is unusual in two ways.

To begin with, this book isn't anything like all those **didactic** and hopelessly dull test-preparation books on the shelf. It's *not* a textbook, a workbook, or a manual, and it does *not* ask you to memorize and regurgitate some big test-prep company's **arbitrary** list of "hot" or "must-know" words for the test. This book takes an **innovative** and **unconventional** approach to building your vocabulary, an approach that I'm confident you'll find both effective and entertaining.

Test of Time is an actual novel—a comedy-adventure—that uses lots of words you're likely to see in the SAT or ACT. All you have to do is read the book and consult the glossary and you will build your vocabulary, improve your reading comprehension skills, and enjoy a good story all at the same time. In short, the "**novel** approach" says goodbye to boring word lists and **tedious** lessons and lets you read your way toward a stronger vocabulary and a better score on the test.

Here's how it works:

Every boldfaced word in this book (boldface is **dark type, like this**) is an SAT or ACT word (and sometimes both). Boldfacing is a **subtle** way of calling words to your attention without interrupting the flow of your reading. Think of it as a little flag or pop-up window that says, "Hey, I'm a test word! Do you know me?"

For example, of the 471 words you've just read, *contemplating, farcical, hoax, amiable, devising, novel, didactic, arbitrary, innovative, unconventional, tedious,* and *subtle* were printed in boldface. ("**Dark type, like this**" doesn't count because it was just an example.) These and more than two thousand other boldfaced words in *Test of Time* are defined in the glossary at the back of this book. To quickly find out what a boldfaced word means, just flip to the glossary and look it up. Then reread the passage in which the word occurs to reinforce your understanding of the meaning.

Besides giving definitions, the glossary has two other helpful features:

1. *Cross-referencing of synonyms.* Look up **diligent** in the glossary and you'll find two definitions followed by cross-references to four test-word synonyms: **assiduous, industrious, painstaking,** and **sedulous.** Checking the definitions of these and all the other cross-referenced synonyms in the glossary will help you build your vocabulary faster by associating groups of related test words.

2. *Page references showing where each test word occurs in the book.* Each entry in the glossary lists the page numbers where you can find that particular test word. If you're trying to master a certain word, you can easily study every passage where it appears in the book.

For further review and reinforcement, I've also included a section of vocabulary-building exercises. These exercises are not like the questions on the SAT or ACT, and they are not intended to teach you how to take the test. They are designed to solidify your understanding of the words you will learn from reading this book—the words you need to know to **analyze** the questions on the test and answer them correctly.

If you **peruse** *Test of Time*, make **scrupulous** use of the glossary, and do all the exercises **conscientiously,** your vocabulary will be in excellent shape for the test.

What Exactly Is a "Test Word"?

When people think about vocabulary and the SAT or ACT, they usually think about really hard words like *phlegmatic, laconic, egregious,* and *vituperative.* Yikes!

In fact, really hard words—jawbreakers, I like to call them—**constitute** only a small portion of the vocabulary you're going to see on any given SAT or ACT. The **vast** majority of test words are at the high school level, not beyond it. They are the words you need to know to go to college, not the ones you'll learn when you get there.

Yes, you're bound to find a handful of jawbreakers on the test, and it certainly helps to know them. But what matters far more is having a thorough knowledge of the large number of words that come up again and again on the tests, which I call the *essential* SAT and ACT vocabulary. These high-frequency words are the bread and butter of the tests and the words you have to know to get a good score.

Some of them are elementary and fundamental, like *fundamental, interpret, imply, infer, modest, fragile, profound,* and *relevant.* Many are more challenging, like *eccentric, prudent, serene, indifferent, frugal, derive, undermine, substantiate, reprehensible, disdain, inherent,* and *erroneous.* Every high school student who **aspires** to go to college should know these bread-and-butter test words.

There's another **cogent** reason to focus chiefly on this high-frequency essential vocabulary rather than on the low-frequency jawbreaking words. All your efforts to learn the jawbreakers will be **futile** unless you have the essential vocabulary firmly under your belt. That's because words are learned in order of their difficulty. You must know *abundance* to learn *plethora,* you must know *hostility* before you can tackle *antipathy* and *enmity,* and a jawbreaker like *laconic* will never stick to your brain without the easier synonym *reticent* to hang it on. Mastering the essential test words, the ones that come up over and over again, prepares you for the *really* hard stuff.

You may be wondering how I identified the essential SAT and ACT vocabulary and determined which words were "test words," the ones that are boldfaced in this book. The answer is I went straight to the source.

I got my hands on all the available SATs and ACTs published since 1994, including the SAT II subject tests in writing, literature, U.S. history, and world history—more than forty tests in all. I went through them **meticulously,** highlighting words at the high school level or above. Then I typed all these words into my computer and arranged them in order of frequency. In the end I had a **massive** number of high school–level words (the essential test vocabulary) and an **eclectic** selection of college-level words (the jawbreakers). You'll find well over two thousand of these SAT and ACT words scattered throughout the pages of *Test of Time*.

Now, let's face facts. Because English has more than a million words, and because the particular test you take will be different from the tests I examined, I can't guarantee that this book contains every tough word you'll **encounter** on your test. But I can **assert** with confidence that all the boldfaced words in *Test of Time* have a better-than-average chance of appearing on the SAT or ACT, especially words like **assert** and the many other high-frequency test words noted with a ★ in the glossary. So it stands to reason that learning as many of them as you can will **vastly** improve your chances of doing well on the test.

But that's enough about word lists because—I'll say it again—this book is *not* about lists. Lists have no **vitality.** They're **insipid.** No, make that **abhorrent.** And guess what? They're not even effective. It's unnatural to learn words from a list; the normal way to learn them is by reading. If you want to build your vocabulary, reading is the best technique there is (especially reading with a dictionary). And if you want to build your vocabulary for the SAT or the ACT, reading *Test of Time* is the way to go.

Learning Vocabulary in Context

The SAT and the ACT may differ in format and style, but they have one important thing in common: They **assess** your ability to **comprehend** what you read, and they test your knowledge of words in **context.**

Think of **context** (it's in the glossary—check it out) as a word's environment. **Context** is where words dwell.

Studying a word in a vocabulary list is like studying an animal in a cage. You can't **discern** its true nature because it's been removed from its **habitat.** When you study a word in **context**—in the phrases and sentences and paragraphs where it lives—you learn far more than its definition. You see the word in action, **affirming** its existence and **exerting** its special influence on its **environs.** You watch how it behaves and pick up clues about its personality. And as you come to understand how it **clarifies** or **enhances** what you're reading, you discover not only what the word means but also how it works.

Studying a word in **context** involves two things: (1) **scrutinizing** all its dictionary definitions to determine which one is **applicable** and why; and (2) asking yourself some **perceptive** questions: What precisely does this word **imply,** and how does it flavor the passage? Is it positive or negative, **abstract** or concrete, **explicit** or **obscure?** Does it suggest a state of mind or indicate how to **interpret** an action? Does it tell you something about a person or the quality of a thing? How do the words surrounding it provide clues to its meaning? Every earnest attempt to answer these questions as you read this book will help you develop your ability to **ascertain** meaning from **context** and improve your chances of doing well on the SAT or ACT.

I could write a lengthy **treatise** on learning vocabulary in **context,** but don't worry, I won't. Instead I'll be **concise:** Other test-preparation books present words out of **context,** which makes trying to learn them frustrating and boring. *Test of Time* puts the test words in **context** and makes learning them natural and fun.

Now that's about as **succinct** as you can get.

A Few Words to the Wise

You probably will already know some of the boldfaced test words you see in this book. (If so, that's great; you're on your way to a better score.) Many other boldfaced words may seem familiar and you may think you know what they mean, but when it comes to filling in those little ovals on exam day, *thinking* you know the meaning of a word may not be good enough—and it may even come back to bite you.

I know you'll check the definitions of unfamiliar words, but it's also important to look up the words you only *think* you know. Remember, many words can be used in more than one way, and the SAT and ACT specialize in verbal surprises, so don't take the meaning of any bold-faced word in this book for granted. **Analyzing** the **context** for clues, then checking the definition in the glossary, and then reexamining the **context** is the most effective way to gain a clear understanding of a word.

Also, don't simply guess what a word means without **verifying** your guess; that can be **deleterious** to your vocabulary. For example, many people (and I'm talking about adults here too) unfortunately think that *enervated* means "filled with energy" because it looks and sounds like *energized*. In fact, *enervated* means just the opposite: "weakened, drained of strength or energy." The point is, guessing is unreliable; your **conjecture** has a greater chance of being wrong than right. It's always better to know than to think you know, so be sure to check the definition in the glossary (and in your dictionary too) and then reread the **context.**

In short, don't cheat yourself out of the opportunity to learn a new word. And be honest with yourself. If you have the slightest shred of doubt about the meaning of a word, or even if you're 99 percent sure you know it, look it up anyway. It's painless, it only takes a moment, and no one is looking over your shoulder in judgment. Getting into the habit of checking the definition of a word and rechecking the **context** in which it was used is one of the most **beneficial** things you can do for your brain. It will pay you dividends for life. You'll be better prepared for the SAT or ACT, and you'll be building a broad and precise vocabulary that will serve you well through college and beyond.

Extra Credit for the Extra-Serious Reader

Now that we've gotten that **admonition** out of the way, let's talk about how you can do even more to get a great score on the test.

In addition to the hundreds of boldfaced test words in this book, I have also incorporated a great many "extra-credit" words—interesting, useful words that didn't happen to appear in the numerous tests I examined but that may appear in the future. Some of these extra-credit words are high school level, most are college level, and a few—like *hypocorism, demimonde, ululate, contretemps,* and *gibbous*—are well above that. (You can probably stump your teachers with them.)

For example, in just the first few chapters you will come across *fanciful, squalid, respite, impecunious, epithet, unconscionable, stentorian, elephantine, legerdemain, hapless, pejorative, puerile, proprietary, erstwhile,* and *insouciant.* These are just a few of the scores of challenging extra-credit words in *Test of Time.* They're all over the novel, **ensconced** like glistening jewels, waiting for you to discover them.

Keep in mind that these extra-credit words are *not* printed in boldface, which means they're *not* defined in the glossary. As you read and look up the boldfaced test words in the glossary, also keep a **keen** eye out for anything unfamiliar that is not printed in boldface. By keeping your dictionary close by while reading, you can look up the extra-credit words right away. You can also highlight them with a marker and look them up later, after finishing each chapter. (Highlighting gives you an easy way to find these words again just by flipping through the book.) Or, if you can't mark up the pages for some reason and your dictionary isn't handy, just jot down the extra-credit words (with the page number so you can find them later) and look them up as soon as you can.

I have included these extra-credit words to give you more chances to build your vocabulary and prepare for whatever may come your way on the test. If you're **astute** and **perspicacious,** you'll consider them a further opportunity for **edification** and **enlightenment.** (Go on, check the glossary!)

Two Tips for SAT and ACT Success

When studying vocabulary for the SAT and ACT, you will learn more, learn faster, and be more likely to retain what you've learned if you follow these two **precepts:**

1. *Get a partner (or two).* Working with a partner—a "study buddy"—is an excellent way to solidify your knowledge of the words you learn from reading *Test of Time*—especially if your partner is reading it too.

2. *Make it fun.* Preparing for the SAT or ACT doesn't have to be torture. (That's the whole point of this book, remember?) Though taking the test may not be one of life's most pleasurable experiences, building your vocabulary in preparation for that **rite** of passage can be both enjoyable and productive.

Here are some ideas that may help:

• Read *Test of Time* with a friend. When you have someone to help you, and someone you can help, it's a lot easier to stick to a studying schedule and accomplish your goals. Try giving each other a weekly reading assignment, and get together regularly to discuss the book and review the test words you've learned.

• Ask your friend to select a passage at **random** from *Test of Time,* one that has several boldfaced test words, and read it aloud. Listen, and then define the words. Use the glossary to check your answers, and use your dictionary to check pronunciation or to research other definitions. Discuss how the words influence the meaning of the passage. Then reverse the procedure and quiz your friend.

• Try learning the vocabulary in reverse—from the definition to the word. Give your friend a list of the words you want to study and ask him or her to read you the definition, either from the glossary or from a dictionary. Then try to come up with the word that matches the definition.

• Find a convenient place to record your "target words," the ones you find most difficult and the ones you most want to learn. The classic method (which really works) is to create flashcards on three-by-five index cards, writing the word on one side and the definition on the other. Carry the cards with you and test yourself by flipping through them between classes, at lunch, on the bus, or wherever. You can also keep your words and definitions in a small, easily portable notebook. If you have access to a computer, you can create your own database of test words you want to learn or of all the challenging words you find in your reading (starting with the extra-credit words in *Test of Time*). However you decide to set up your list, be sure to review it once or twice a day. Remember also that reviewing doesn't mean skimming. For best results, quiz yourself regularly and keep track of your score.

• Each time you open this book, review the words you learned in the last section you read. Look them up again in the glossary, and keep a dictionary close by so you can read the other definitions, look up the extra-credit words, and— *this is very important*—check the pronunciation. (It would be kind of stupid to learn a new word and then mispronounce it, wouldn't it?) As the **axiom** goes, practice makes perfect, and review is the key to building a lasting (as opposed to a **transient**) vocabulary.

• Remember that test words don't just appear on the test—they can pop up anywhere. Keep *Test of Time* and a dictionary nearby when you're doing your reading for school or recreation. When you come across a challenging word, see if it's in the glossary, then look it up in your dictionary. Also, try to read a newspaper or magazine for a few minutes every day with the goal of finding one or two words you *don't* know.

• Finally, challenge yourself every few days to use two or three of your newly acquired test words in a **pertinent** way, either in conversation or in writing.

As Mark Twain said, "A powerful **agent** is the right word: it lights the reader's way and makes it plain." *Test of Time* is filled with **illuminating** words that will light your way on your journey to a higher score on the SAT or ACT. Give yourself **ample** time to study and absorb them and you will build a powerful, precise vocabulary—one that will stand you in good stead for the test and stand the test of time.

Charles Harrington Elster
San Diego, California

*Irreverence is the **champion** of liberty and its only sure defense.*
— Mark Twain

TEST OF
TIME

Chapter 1

Sam I Am

For once, the newspapers were right. Snow was general all over New England.

The storm had begun quietly in the **mute, impenetrable** darkness before dawn. At first there was almost no wind and only a light, silvery dusting of snow. Then, after a morning in which the sun struggled in **vain** to **assert** itself through an **oppressive** layer of clouds, the wind announced the **impending** blizzard in howling, stinging gusts. Soon after came the heavy snow, falling swiftly and **abundantly** in flakes the size of goose feathers. By nightfall a deep white blanket had covered all. And still the wind wailed and the **incessant** snow swirled and fell.

It fell on **majestic** Mount Katahdin at the northern terminus of the Appalachian Trail in Maine, and on the stony, bald **summit** of Camel's Hump in the Green Mountains of Vermont. It fell on the **dreary, somber** mill towns of western Massachusetts, and on the **opulent, ostentatious** mansions of the **affluent** robber barons in Newport, Rhode Island. It fell on **picturesque hamlets** and villages, on **myriad** farmhouses and barns and **barren** fields, on the crooked crosses and gravestones of countless churchyard cemeteries. It fell and vanished like steam into the dark, **inscrutable** waters of the Connecticut River.

It was falling, too, upon every one of the many gables and dormers and turrets of the fanciful, **eclectic**, and **eccentric** brick house at 351 Farmington Avenue in Hartford, Connecticut, on the western edge of town, where an American writer—the most famous writer in the land—lived with his devoted wife and three young daughters.

This famous American writer was a man approaching fifty, with a slender figure of medium build. The ashes of the passing years had begun to gray the fires of his splendid shock of unruly reddish brown hair. He was dressed in a conservative black serge suit with a starched white shirt and a stiff and **conventional** black bow tie. (Late in life he preferred to wear **immaculate** white suits to **complement** his **luxuriant** and even more **intractable** white hair.) Bushy, **pensive** eyebrows perched over the narrow slits of his piercing blue eyes, which were etched with crow's-feet; an **aristocratic** Roman nose **loomed** over the broad, drooping mop of a mustache that **shrouded** his mouth. At the moment his mouth was also busily engaged in puffing on a short, **pungent** cigar.

The writer bore more than a passing resemblance to another famous American, the twentieth-century scientific genius Albert Einstein. But unlike the **formidable** physicist, who in photographs often appears **bemused** or sad, the writer's **countenance** reflected his **enigmatic** and **mercurial temperament.** One minute he could appear **aloof**; the next minute he would have a trickster's twinkle in his eye that made you wonder whether he was about to tell an outrageous yarn or make you the **credulous** victim of a hilarious prank. He was known and loved for his **prodigious** talent as a storyteller, his **ironic** style, and his ready wit, but there was nothing **jovial** or **jocular** in his **demeanor** right now. That was because the famous American writer was not at all in a good mood.

He was standing in a small booth tucked under the **burnished** walnut staircase in the **ornate** entrance hall of the house. The existence of the booth was disguised by a door whose design blended into the **meticulously** stenciled wooden panels of the wall. To his ear he held a small metal cone, which was attached by a slender wire to a wooden box mounted on the wall. On the box was another small metal cone, and the writer was speaking into it, swearing **profusely.**

"Jeepers creepers, jiminy Christmas, and jumpin' Jehoshaphat!" he roared into the mouthpiece. "Why in tarnation can't this dadgummed thing work properly for once? Central, can you hear me? By criminy, here we go again. Central? Dammit! Are you there? Dagnabit! Can you hear me now? Yes, doggone it. That's right. What? Hello, Central? What? Dammit! Hello! Anybody there? Can you hear me now?"

The writer stamped his foot on the marble floor. "Flamin' hot fireballs of Zephaniah! What in the Sam Hill are y'all doin' down there? Pickin' yer goldurn noses? Scratchin' yer big fat *be*hinds? Can you hear me now, dadblameit? What's that? Hell and damnation! I said: *Can... you...hear...me...NOW!*"

He banged his fist against the **intractable** wooden box. "Well I hope you can hear this: If you don't give me better service you can send somebody up here right now and pull this contraption out. I won't have this thing in the house a moment longer—it's a damned nuisance."

The man who on many occasions had boasted to visitors that his was the first house in the entire country—and perhaps even the world—to have a telephone installed for private use then shoved the receiver back in its cradle, gave the box another sharp cuff, and emerged from the booth, slamming the door behind him. After pausing a moment to collect himself and puff on his cigar, he strode across the entrance hall and into the **sumptuous,** salmon-pink drawing room.

The writer's wife and several guests, with whom he and

his wife had recently dined, were sitting on overstuffed chairs and a matching settee, sipping champagne and brandy and chatting **amiably.** Apparently they had not overheard his **indecorous** outburst. Relieved, the writer took a seat beside his wife and poured himself a snifter of brandy from a crystal decanter. But as he swirled the amber liquid in the glass and brought it to his lips, one of the guests turned to him and said, "Sam, you old devil, was that you we heard using such **disreputable** language a moment ago?"

There was a **lull** in the conversation as everyone waited for the writer's reply. **Unruffled,** he said, "Why, madam, of course not. George, our butler, got to the telephone before me and I heard him swearing into it as I came up. I suppose I shall have to talk to him about it." He paused and then said, "But I daresay I can't blame him."

Out of the corner of his eye the writer saw his wife **suppress** a smile. He took a sip of brandy and went on. "The telephone, my friends, is a time-saving and useful invention. Someday it will be looked upon as one of the great advancements of civilization, ranked on a par with Gutenberg's movable type, Edison's incandescent lightbulb, and the formula for whiskey. But make no mistake about it: The telephone is a device that can strain a man's **tolerance** to the very limits of **propriety.** Why, that thing fairly breeds profanity!" He shook his fist to **emphasize** the point.

"There's been many a time, I must confess, that I've been sorely tempted to cuss into that infernal gadget myself," he continued. "At best, it's **erratic.** On good days, the sound of artillery is **audible** over the line; on other days, it's thunder. And on bad days it's thunder and artillery combined. The telephone may be a miracle of modern science, but most of the time it's nothing but a blasted nuisance."

"Yes," said the writer's wife in a soft but firm voice, "a nuisance is exactly what we heard *George* call it—except that *he* used a different adjective."

The writer nervously fingered his bow tie and cleared his throat. "Well," he said, "as I mentioned, I shall have to have a little talk with him about that. In the meantime, Christmas is almost upon us, and so in the **magnanimous** spirit of that holiday let me say this: It is my heartfelt and world-embracing Christmas hope and **aspiration** that all of us—the high, the low, the rich, the poor, the admired, the despised, the loved, the hated, the civilized, the savage— may eventually be gathered together in a heaven of everlasting rest and peace and bliss, except the inventor of the telephone."

Hearty laughter broke out all around, and as it **subsided** the writer rose and went to the ebony grand piano in the middle of the room. He sat down on the piano bench, stretched his tapered fingers straight out over the keys, and began playing the opening chords of one of his favorite songs, the soulful spiritual "Swing Low, Sweet Chariot."

The others gathered around the piano to listen. The writer threw his head back, gazed up at the elegant, glittering chandelier, and in a confident tenor began to sing:

> I looked over Jordan and what did I see,
> Comin' for to carry me home?
> A band of angels a comin' after me,
> Comin' for to carry me home.
>
> Swing low, sweet chariot,
> Comin' for to carry me home.
> Swing low, sweet chariot,
> Comin' for to carry me home.

As he sang the **mournful** refrain he swayed slowly to the music. He finished the song with a **melancholy** harmonic **flourish** and acknowledged the polite applause with a **modest** nod.

He was about to begin another tune when the sound of

ebullient young voices distracted him. He got up from the bench and saw that his three daughters, dressed in their nightclothes, had entered the room. They were standing with their mother, waiting to wish him good night. Despite the late hour, the three bright-eyed, dark-haired girls were **teeming** with pent-up energy that was impossible to **suppress.**

First the youngest, three-year-old Jean, clambered onto the settee and began jumping up and down. Then nine-year-old Clara and eleven-year-old Susy joined her and the three of them bounced in unison.

"Papa, Papa, Papa!" they cried, bouncing gleefully and disregarding their mother's gentle **admonishments.**

The writer's face lit up with an adoring smile, and anyone could see that these children were the apples of his eye. He spread his arms wide. "Ah, my darlings," he said. "Come to your papa."

They jumped down from the settee and rushed into his arms for a gigantic hug. When he released them they began jumping up and down again and tugging at his sleeves. "Do the dance! Do the dance! Do the dance!" they chanted.

The writer laughed. "Not now, my dears. Can't you see we have guests?"

"We want Papa's crazy dance!"

"Oh, come now," he **chided.** "It's late. Time for bed."

But his daughters would not take no for an answer. They were **persistent.** "We want Papa's crazy dance! We want Papa's crazy dance!"

The writer cast an imploring look at his wife, who merely smiled and shrugged.

The children's voices grew louder. "Crazy dance, crazy dance, we want Papa's crazy dance!" Their **insistent** plea was interrupted by one of the guests.

"Sam, just what is this 'crazy dance' that these young ladies are so **impetuously** demanding of you?" he asked.

"Aw, shucks, it's nothing, really," said the writer. "Just something I used to watch the black folks do when I was a boy down South. One summer at my uncle's farm I asked one of them—a young fella named Jerry—to show me how to do it."

Susy, the oldest, pulled at her father's sleeve. "Was Jerry the slave who used to make those funny speeches to you?" she asked.

"Yes he was, my dear, and I'll never forget him. Every day he would preach a sermon from the top of the woodpile with me for **sole** audience. And everything that came out of his mouth was **impudent** and **satirical** and just plain delightful. To me he was a wonder. I believed he was the greatest **orator** in the United States. I learned a heap about how to tell a good story from listening to Jerry."

The writer paused and looked at the guest who had asked him about the "crazy dance." "Anyway," he said, "I still remember a couple of steps he taught me, and sometimes I entertain the children with them."

"Obviously they enjoy it," the guest observed.

"Crazy dance! Crazy dance!" the girls cried in **affirmation.**

"Why don't you do it, then?" the guest said. "Perhaps we'll be entertained too."

"No, really I couldn't," the writer replied.

"Please do," said another guest. "It sounds amusing."

The writer shook his head. "I don't think it would be appro—"

"Oh, go on, Sam!" a third guest interrupted. "For goodness' sake, why are you so **reluctant**?"

"Because..." the writer began. "Well...I'm not sure you'll..." His voice trailed off. He looked at his wife.

"It won't be the first time you've astonished company, dear," she said.

The writer chuckled and turned to his daughters. "All

right, then," he said, giving them a **conspiratorial** wink. "Let's dance, my lovelies!"

The girls cheered. Everyone rushed into action.

The writer moved several chairs off the large rug in the middle of the room and then motioned for the spectators to be seated. Susy **scurried** through the **adjacent** dining room and into the library, returning a moment later carrying three small tambourines. She handed one to Clara and one to Jean, and then the girls stood in a row in front of the fireplace and began banging a rapid, **vivacious** rhythm on their tambourines. It went like this: *one* two three *four* five six *seven* eight, *one* two three *four* five six *seven* eight.

Meanwhile, the writer shed his suitcoat, bow tie, and vest, revealing a **flamboyant** pair of red suspenders. He slipped off his **supple** leather shoes, raised them above his head, and began slapping the heels together: *one* two three *four* five six *seven* eight, *one* two three *four* five six *seven* eight.

As the children banged their tambourines and swayed to the syncopated rhythm, the writer stepped nimbly forward and backward and side to side, slapping his shoes together in time with the beat. Upon a **tacit** cue from their father, the children chanted a peculiar rhyme:

Juba this and Juba that,
Juba killed a yellow cat!
Juba up, Juba down,
Juba all around the town.

"And then you Juba!" cried the writer, **adroitly** tossing his shoes into a potted plant beneath the **immense** mirror hanging on the wall.

The audience tittered.

"You just Juba!" he cried again, strutting to the end of

the room, on each step lifting his knees high—almost to his chin—and flapping his bent arms like someone imitating a chicken. He tossed his head and strutted back with elbows and knees flying.

The audience tittered some more.

"Juba!" He turned slowly around in a circle with one foot raised. Then he shook his shoulders and swiveled his hips.

The audience tittered **immodestly.**

Suddenly he kicked his legs straight out—one leg forward and one leg back—and dropped to the floor.

The audience gasped.

The writer landed spread-legged on the plush rug with a loud thump. The thump was accompanied by a **vociferous** grunt and the unmistakable sound of a pair of trousers splitting at the seams.

The audience gasped again. The writer **forged** on.

He lay **prone,** with his chin off the floor, and began arching and rocking his body from chest to knees, chest to knees, each time pushing himself slightly forward with his hands. At first he looked like a **gargantuan** fish flopping on dry land. But eventually he gained momentum and lurched across the rug like a **massive, menacing** worm.

Then he flipped onto his side and propelled himself in a circle with his top leg while clawing the air with his free hand. Now he looked like a man **beseeching** onlookers for help while being sucked into a **maelstrom**—except for one **salient** and **ludicrous** difference. From anywhere in the room you could see the gaping hole in the back of the writer's trousers.

The three girls began to giggle, but they continued banging out the **captivating** beat: *one* two three *four* five six *seven* eight, *one* two three *four* five six *seven* eight.

"Go Papa!" one of them called.

"Juba!" he called back, struggling to his feet.

He shuffled to the left and shuffled to the right, patting an **embellishment** to the rhythm on his chest and thighs. Then he flipped around, and with his back to the audience he put his arms akimbo, tossed his head, and wiggled his behind in time to the beat. This **elicited** peals of laughter from the girls and shocked silence from the guests.

He flipped around again and spread, then crossed, then spread his legs, and as he did that he bent over and touched the floor first with one hand and then the other. Then he returned to the floor—less **recklessly** this time—and the next moment he seemed to defy gravity by spinning his legs around his upright torso while holding himself slightly off the floor with his hands. He looked like someone trying to sit and run around in circles **simultaneously.**

He stopped spinning, squatted, placed the top of his head on the rug, and pushed himself up into a headstand. When he got himself securely balanced he spread his legs wide apart. It was an **agile feat** but an unfortunate pose, because through the **breach** in the back of the writer's trousers his rumpled underwear **protruded** like an **inquisitive** prairie dog poking his head out of a hole.

The girls howled with laughter and the rhythm faltered for a moment, but they managed to pick it up again and resume the chant:

Juba this and Juba that,
Juba killed a yellow cat!
Juba up, Juba down,
Juba all around the town.

"Juba!" squeaked the red-faced, upside-down writer. He tumbled from his headstand onto his rear end and, grasping his knees to his chest, spun himself around on his buttocks. As he slowed to a halt and rose to his feet, grinning and sweating **conspicuously,** his three daughters broke into **spontaneous** applause.

"Hooray!" they cheered, **vigorously** shaking and rattling their tambourines. "Hooray for Papa!"

To a **contemporary** observer, this **boisterous** "crazy dance" would not have seemed **alien** or even particularly **unconventional.** Anyone conversant with African American history and culture would have recognized the first part as an enthusiastic but rather clumsy attempt to **portray** two **antebellum** plantation dances: juba, which involves rhythmic hand clapping and body patting, and the cakewalk, a prancing, high-stepping promenade that **mocked** the **genteel** manners of "the white folks in the big house." And anyone even remotely familiar with American popular culture of the late-twentieth and early twenty-first centuries would have recognized the second part as a **primordial**—and comically awkward—version of hip-hop and break dancing.

But the stodgy dinner guests assembled in the **sophisticated** Victorian drawing room that snowy winter evening in 1883 had no such historical or cultural **context** in which to place the writer's **eccentric** performance. Instead, his **uncultivated** "dance" seemed to them to have sprung straight out of a **rustic** religious revival, a backwoods camp meeting where worshipers are possessed by **malevolent** spirits, fall into a trance, **writhe** frantically on the ground, and speak in tongues.

In short, it was the most **bizarre** and disgraceful display of **vulgarity** that these **staid, upright** citizens had ever seen. They were **dumbfounded, flabbergasted,** and thunderstruck. And once they realized they were all of those things, they were **outraged.**

The writer's wife, a sensitive and **perceptive** woman, saw trouble brewing. She hastily ushered her children from the room as the guests began rising from their chairs.

"Utterly tasteless," muttered a fashionable young lady.

"**Deplorable**," muttered a dowdy **matron.**

"What on earth was that, anyway, some kind of bloody fit?" a man with a **dour** expression grumbled.

"You should be thoroughly ashamed of yourself," another man said sternly, pointing an accusing finger at the writer. "Putting on such an **offensive** show in the presence of women and children. It's **reprehensible.**"

Several other men harrumphed loudly in agreement.

The writer pulled a handkerchief from his pocket and mopped the sweat from his brow. "Well, folks, what can I tell you? Usually when I feel the urge to exercise I lie down until it goes away."

The **witticism** met with stony silence.

"And I actually like cats," he added lamely.

At that, one of the ladies fainted dead away and had to be revived with smelling salts fetched by George.

"Was it something I said?" the writer asked no one in particular, a look of **sincere perplexity** on his face.

The question was left unanswered as the guests began a hurried **exodus.** George **deftly** and diplomatically assisted them with their greatcoats and shawls and hats.

"I suppose I'll see you at church on Sunday," the last one said over his shoulder as he stepped out onto the snow-laden veranda.

"Yes, of course," the writer replied with a **feeble** wave of his hand.

George closed the heavy oaken door.

"Or maybe not," the writer mumbled.

"Sir, I'll be retiring for the night now," said George. "Is there anything I can do for you before I go?"

A former slave, George had shown up at the house one day, asking if he could wash the windows. He wound up moving in. For years he had been not only the household's **discreet** and **tactful** butler but also an **ardent champion** of the family's interests and the writer's **trustworthy** and devoted friend.

"No, I don't think so," said the writer. "Unless you happen to have the ability to repair a reputation."

"If I were you, sir, I wouldn't worry myself about it," George said. "Your reputation has an **uncanny** way of repairing itself."

"Well I certainly hope that's true, because I think it just took a mighty fine thrashing tonight."

"I've seen you take far worse," said George, breaking into a grin.

"For goodness' sake," said the writer, "let's not talk about that!"

The two men laughed.

"Sir," said George after a moment.

"Yes?"

"About your 'crazy dance' tonight. May I make a suggestion?"

"Why of course. There's always room for improvement."

"Skip the split next time. I think you're getting a bit old for that."

"Right."

"And one other thing."

"Yes?"

"Would you like me to mend those trousers?"

"Oh, right," said the writer with an embarrassed smile. "No, don't bother with them tonight. You should go on to bed. The maid can do it first thing in the morning."

"Very well," said George. "Good night, then." He turned to leave.

"George," said the writer.

"Yes sir?"

"I'm sorry I had to tell that lie about you cussing on the telephone. I hope I didn't give **offense**."

"Perfectly understandable, sir. No hard feelings at all."

"Thank you, George," said the writer. "Thank you for everything."

The writer extended his hand. George grasped it and the men shook hands warmly.

"Good night, Mr. Griffin," said the writer.

"Good night, Mr. Clemens."

Chapter 2

From Hartford to Hadleyburg

A few years in the future

Suite G-8 of Stormfield College—one of a dozen **stately** residential colleges on the campus of **prestigious** Hadleyburg University—was not the **slovenly** pigsty everyone said it was. At least it wasn't in the eyes of its two male **inhabitants.**

Had anyone bothered to ask, these **sanguine** young men would have cheerfully admitted that their dormitory **domain** was not **immaculate.** In fact, they would even have **conceded** that it was a bit **disheveled** and **unkempt,** and that it could benefit from a little straightening up, some light dusting, perhaps a once-over with a vacuum cleaner. But to them suite G-8 was not the black hole of **chaos** and doom that everyone so often claimed. To them it was simply home—home sweet **putrid** home.

On the outside of the door was taped a handwritten sign: ALL YE WHO ENTER HERE, **ABANDON** HOPE AND HOLD YOUR NOSE. Fair warning, you could say, for the **fastidious** visitor.

It was the week before Christmas—finals period at Hadleyburg. The semester was almost over and the relief of winter vacation was **imminent.** But for now the mood on campus was **frenetic.** Every student at this **celebrated** New England university knew it was time to put up or shut up.

And everywhere you looked—from the dorm rooms to the dining halls to the libraries—they were cramming for exams, slaving over term papers, tapping on laptops, scribbling notes, and skimming **vast tomes** that should have been **perused** weeks ago. They were scarfing **mass** quantities of junk food and energy bars, sipping steaming cups of coffee, and staying up until the wee hours and sometimes the entire night.

In the common room of suite G-8, Orlando Garcia Ortiz lay sprawled on an old stained couch in a **languid** lump. His long, lean, muscular body made the decrepit couch seem **ludicrously** small; parts of him stuck out here and there and other parts dangled to the floor. At six feet six and a half inches, Orlando was an **imposing** sight, even when supine. He had been a star forward on his high school basketball team back in Brownsville, Texas, and he was also class valedictorian—a combination that the admissions officers at Hadleyburg found irresistible. But when he got to college Orlando found himself becoming more interested in poetry than basketball, and after one season he quit the team and devoted himself to a double major of English and biology in preparation for medical school. His secret **ambition** was to be a doctor-poet, like William Carlos Williams.

Across the room from Orlando—on the other side of a makeshift plywood coffee table strewn with papers and books, empty coffee cups, crushed aluminum cans, candy wrappers, fragments of popcorn and potato chips, a pile of peanut shells, an **abandoned** bowl of cereal, a week-old open container of Chinese food, a **rancid,** half-eaten salami sandwich, a **fugitive** remote control hiding under a wet washcloth, several dried wads of gum, a sprinkling of used tissues, a soiled pair of socks, and a few other unidentified festering objects—Henry Louis Morgan, known to his friends as Hank, sat in a battered blue armchair, staring at the screen of his laptop, clicking and typing furiously.

Hank was a computer whiz who excelled at math and whose **aspiration** was to become an engineer. As a New England Yankee, the product of a Vermont dairy farming family, he had been raised to be **industrious, diligent,** and **pragmatic.** But he also had a lighthearted side, and he loved to **indulge** in **innocuous** mischief and practical jokes.

Hank stopped clicking and typing and looked at his roommate. "Hey, Big O," he said, breaking the silence between them, which had lasted for almost half an hour. "You still alive over there?"

When Orlando failed to respond, Hank retrieved a grubby sneaker from the floor and tossed it at his friend. It bounced off Orlando's forehead, ricocheted off the back of the couch, and landed upside down on Orlando's face, covering his nose and mouth like some kind of **bizarre,** futuristic gas mask.

Hank laughed. "Dude, you alive?"

"Unh," Orlando groaned.

"You know you've got a big smelly sneaker on your face?"

"Unh."

"I've heard that inhaling sneaker sweat is **beneficial** for you."

"Unnhh."

"The aroma is supposed to be **therapeutic.**"

"Unnnhhh."

"Sounds like you like it in there."

"Uh-uh."

"Breathe deeply now, and tell Dr. Morgan how you feel."

"Unnnnhhhh."

"Does the odor remind you of anything? Is it **redolent** of something familiar? That lovely **coquette** Brenda, perhaps?"

This **disparaging reference** to Orlando's last girlfriend—who Orlando recently discovered had been seeing *two* other guys behind his back—was the barb that finally hit home and brought him out of his **torpor** and raging back to life. With a **belligerent** roar he tore the sneaker from his face and fired it at Hank. The **reprisal** was so swift and sudden that before Hank could even raise his arms to protect himself the speeding sneaker had slammed into his laptop.

With a **shrill,** offended beep the computer lifted off from the **haven** of Hank's lap and sailed into the air. Both of them watched in shock as the machine seemed to hang in midair for a **protracted** moment, hovering like a sleek gray military spyplane cruising through foreign airspace at high altitude. Then it crashed **headlong** into the wall, **succumbed** to the law of gravity, and dropped to the hardwood floor with a dull thud.

Hank yelped and rushed to the rescue. **Gingerly** he lifted the computer from the floor and **scrutinized** it for signs of damage. He ran his finger gently over the touchpad and tapped a few keys. He studied the screen. "Omigod!" he cried. "Look what you've done, man!"

Orlando sat up and gulped **audibly.** "What? What happened?"

"I've lost everything I've been working on for the last three hours. No, wait…" Hank continued fumbling with the machine as Orlando watched nervously.

"The hard drive is trashed," Hank said, shaking his head. "I've lost everything. All my notes for the semester. My psychology term paper. My project for applied engineering. Even my journal." He made a **despondent** gesture with his hands.

"You lost 'Portrait of the Inventor as a Young Man'?" Orlando asked.

Hank nodded grimly. "Gone. Wiped out. **Annihilated.**"

Orlando's jaw dropped in dismay as he **contemplated** the destruction he had just caused and the **dire** circumstances in which he had **inadvertently** put his friend.

"I can't believe it!" Hank wailed to the ceiling. "I can't believe you did that! That paper was my ticket to an A. And the engineering project is half my grade. That's a whole semester's worth of work down the toilet. And my journal—that was my whole freakin' life! I'm dead, man, I'm dead. Totally slain. Burnt to a crisp. That's me you destroyed, Big O. You just destroyed *me*. Don't you get it? It's over, dude. Over. What am I gonna do now?" He groaned and put his face in his hands.

Orlando stood up, trembling and **contrite.** "Whoa, Hank...I didn't mean to do anything like that. I wasn't even trying to hit it, you know? It was an accident, really." He stepped around the debris on the floor and put his hand on Hank's shoulder. "Hey, I'm sorry. I really am. I didn't mean it."

Hank looked up at his **penitent** roommate. A giant grin spread across his face. "Gotcha, dude! You ate the bait again."

"Hot damn, Hank!" Orlando cried, kicking apart a pile of dirty laundry that had been decaying beside Hank's chair for the past two weeks. "How do you always *do* that to me?"

Hank clapped his hands together and **guffawed.** "Twenty-three times this semester and counting, sucker. You are *so* easy."

"You know what? I think you're some kind of frustrated actor. You should be a theater major, not a computer and engineering geek. Give me a break, will you?"

"I would, but psyching you out is just too much fun."

Orlando flopped back on the couch and rubbed his eyes. "So is your stupid computer okay?"

"Well, it's got a couple of scratches that you'll have to **compensate** me for."

"Get outta here. You should pay *me* for all the misery you cause me with your **inane** practical jokes."

"All right, all right, I'm just kidding," Hank said,

adopting a **conciliatory** tone. "I was just trying to liberate you from the evil clutches of that **soporific** couch. I could see some serious log-sawing coming on and I figured, what with all the studying you have to do, you could use some **stimulation**."

"A scuzzed-out sneaker in my face is **stimulation**?"

"Whatever."

Orlando glared at Hank. "Listen, spudhead. The night before last I pulled an all-nighter finishing my history paper. Then last night I was up till four studying for my biology final this morning, which was a killer. Now I have to prepare for my American lit exam tomorrow afternoon, and I'm totally wiped out."

"Well, if that's how you get staying up for a couple of nights, you'll never make it through med school. Look, dude, you can't be too wiped out for a little break—especially one with the sweet ladies of entryway E. We promised them we'd come by at ten for a bite and some **communal** studying, remember?" He looked at his watch. "It's 9:56 now. C'mon, Big O. Get **animated**. It's time to party."

Outside the Gothic lancet windows of suite E-4 the wind moaned and howled, straining even the most **massive** branches of the ancient elm tree whose canopy filled most of the courtyard. It had been snowing all day, and still the snow continued to fall. It lay in great milky drifts along the bottom of the brick and limestone walls of the building, which were covered with bare, brown vines.

Aimee Gwendolyn Lee stood at one of the lancet windows, gazing up through the clouds at the **luminous** gibbous moon and listening to the **melancholy** second movement of Beethoven's "Pathétique" sonata unfold in her head. She had practiced it that afternoon in a small soundproof room in the basement of Henley Hall, which housed Hadleyburg's music department. It was part of a lengthy program of Romantic piano compositions by Beethoven, Schumann, and Chopin that she was scheduled to perform tomorrow afternoon for her winter recital.

Aimee was an accomplished classical pianist, but she loved all kinds of music—**traditional** and **contemporary,** popular and **avant-garde, indigenous** and foreign. Music had always been not just an **aesthetic** pleasure for her but an essential part of her life, her raison d'être. In a **divisive** and often **hostile** world, she saw music as a **benevolent** and **uplifting** force. It was, she thought, the only **universal** language.

Aimee had grown up in San Francisco's Mission District in an extraordinarily musical family. Her mother was **principal** violist in the symphony, and her father was a professor of music at Stanford. Her two older siblings were **precocious** in their musical development, but Aimee was a **prodigy.** She began playing piano at the tender age of four, and at seven she was already winning sonata contests and performing locally. By the time she was sixteen she was ready for major competition and a concert career.

Her future seemed bright and certain, yet she was **ambivalent.** She loved music with all her soul, and there had been times when she had **immersed** herself in it every waking hour of the day. But was she prepared for the grueling, **single-minded** life of a concert pianist, with its **incessant** practicing and traveling and performing? Or did she need more time to develop other aspects of herself, to experiment and explore and grow?

Despite pressure from her parents, Aimee decided to postpone becoming a concert pianist and attend college instead. In **justifying** her decision, she told her parents that at Hadleyburg she could take advantage of the highly regarded music department and also get a well-rounded education by **cultivating** her **diverse** interests. She **discreetly** failed to mention that in college she could have a decent social life, which there would have been little time for had she chosen to pursue a concert career.

Aimee turned from the window and surveyed her common room. In stark contrast to Hank and Orlando's **squalid habitat,** this inviting space was a **paragon** of **domestic** order. The walls were decorated with attractive prints and posters. Built-in bookshelves harbored academic and extracurricular reading material. A computer and printer occupied a desk in the corner, and a table in another corner **accommodated** a stereo and a microwave oven. The hardwood floor was partly covered with a round hooked rug. There were two comfortable armchairs on one side of the room and a fake leopard-skin sofa with matching pillows on the other. In the center was a tasteful wooden coffee table on top of which sat two steaming mugs of tea and several **aromatic** candles. Everything was neat and tidy, **tranquil** and **serene.**

Aimee's roommate—and best friend since the first week of college—sat on the leopard-skin sofa, composing a term paper for her American history seminar on her laptop. At the moment the laptop lay beside her and she was **perusing** a thick **tome,** twisting a finger in a ringlet of her hair and nibbling at her upper lip as she **scrutinized** some **obscure reference** she wanted to **cite** in the essay.

Angela Tyler McGuinn, as any of her professors would have **readily** acknowledged, was one of the best and brightest students at Hadleyburg. She was also one of the most **amiable.** She exuded confidence, commanded respect, and was **astutely** aware of who she was, where she was headed, and how she intended to get there. You didn't need to be especially **perceptive** to **discern** that this was a woman who was going places—and you had better not mess with her or get in her way.

Angela **hailed** from Baltimore, where her family had

lived for generations. Her mother was a respected judge and her father was a popular member of the city council who was **contemplating** running for mayor. She had always admired her parents and been proud of their accomplishments. But the person she most longed to **emulate** was her great-great-great-grandfather, Warner T. McGuinn. In high school Angela had written an award-winning essay about him, and she knew his inspiring story by heart.

In 1885 McGuinn was enrolled at Yale, where he was one of the law school's first black students. He was a promising scholar, but he had to board with the college's carpenter and work three part-time jobs to make ends meet. Somehow he managed to find time to participate in the Kent Club, the school's debating society, which elected him president that fall. As a historian had described it, one of McGuinn's duties "was to meet the club's guest speakers at the railroad station and introduce them before their lectures. The first speaker that year was Mark Twain."

Twain was so impressed with the young law student and his **eloquent** introduction that on Christmas Eve he wrote to the dean of the law school offering to pay McGuinn's board. Twain's support enabled McGuinn to quit his jobs and focus entirely on his studies. He graduated at the top of his class, winning the **coveted** Townsend **Oration** prize, and went on to become one of the most influential citizens of Baltimore, serving as a member of the city council, helping to found the local chapter of the NAACP, and winning a major civil rights victory in federal court that struck down the city's housing segregation law.

McGuinn was also a **mentor** to a young lawyer who worked in the office next door. That lawyer's name was Thurgood Marshall, who later became the first African American to serve as a justice of the U.S. Supreme Court. As Angela proudly noted at the end of her high school essay, "Thurgood Marshall so **esteemed** my great-great-great-grandfather that he called him 'one of the greatest lawyers who ever lived.'"

Such was the **distinguished legacy** that Angela sought to **emulate**. And from the moment she set foot on the campus of Hadleyburg University she told herself that she was bound for Yale Law School and nothing was going to stand in her way.

"Hey Angela," Aimee said, checking her watch.

Angela looked up from her book and smiled. "What's up, Aims?"

"We'd better go pick up the food we ordered because our favorite nerds are coming over at ten."

Samuel Langhorne Clemens, known to his many readers as Mark Twain, slowly **ascended** the winding staircase of his **capacious** house. One of his hands slid along the polished rail of the wooden balustrade, which had **elaborately** carved columns and arches in the style of a Byzantine arcade. The other hand held a tumbler of hot whiskey (his favorite postprandial libation) and an unlit cigar.

Upon reaching the third-floor landing, he paused. Blast it, he thought, was that the telephone ringing at this late hour? He bent over the balustrade and peered down at the marble floor of the entrance hall, listening.

Nothing, he thought. It was nothing. Probably just Mrs. Clemens putting some hot coals into the metal warming pan she uses to take the chill off the bedsheets. Or perhaps some frozen branches clattering against the house in the storm.

He had just visited the bedrooms of his daughters. All three were sound asleep, no doubt with visions of sugarplums dancing in their heads, for it was well-nigh Christmas. He gently caressed their fine dark hair with the back of his hand and gave each a silent kiss on the cheek. Then he bade good night to his beloved wife, Livy, whom he always respectfully referred to as Mrs. Clemens, telling her he had a little work he wanted to do upstairs and that he would come to bed presently.

"That means you're going to play billiards and smoke another cigar," she had observed with her usual soft-spoken but **frank perspicacity.**

I'll never get anything past that dear old girl, Twain thought, chuckling to himself. She is far too **sagacious.** Her **keen** and **penetrating** vision pierces right through my every **ruse.**

He crossed the hall and entered the billiard room, shutting the door quietly behind him. The large rectangular space was bathed in soft gaslight; a pile of embers glowed in the tiled fireplace nestled along the interior wall. Books and small framed pictures lined the burgundy walls. Elegant wool rugs covered sections of the floor. A plush divan occupied a corner of the room. A **monolithic** billiard table, covered in **lush** green baize, **dominated** the center. Nearby stood a sturdy wooden desk and chair. The desk was littered with books, papers, various writing **implements,** and an ashtray containing several pipes.

He took a sip of his drink and looked around, **contemplating** his surroundings. This room at the top of the house was where he came to escape the **myriad** distractions of **domestic** life. Whenever he entered here he left the **mundane** matters of the world behind. It was his **refuge,** his **haven** for work and play.

He set the tumbler on the desk and lit his cigar, puffing on it lustily until the tip blazed with orange flame. Then he placed a log on the andirons, poked the embers, and gave them a **vigorous** taste of the bellows until the fire was revived. He warmed himself in front of the flames for a minute and then walked over to a window that looked out upon one of the three **lofty** balconies **accessible** from the billiard room. The storm was still raging **relentlessly.** Snow had piled up to the bottom of the window and miniature tornadoes of snowflakes whirled around the balcony, driven by **capricious** eddies of wind.

One of the brightest gems of the New England weather, he thought, is the **dazzling uncertainty** of it. When this **cantankerous** blizzard finally lets up the children will have a grand old time **fashioning** a snowman. I'll give them a **threadbare** scarf to wind around its neck, a rumpled bowler for its head, and an old corncob pipe to stick in its mouth.

Smiling at that image, he turned up the gaslights and went to the billiard table, which differed from a pool table in that it had no pockets. As he chalked his favorite cue, he **pondered** the three polished balls on the table—one white, one pale yellow, and one red—and the **esoteric** geometry of his favorite game, three-cushion billiards, whose object was **deceptively** simple: to shoot the cue ball and hit both of the other balls; doing this would score a point. That may sound easy enough, but there was a catch. Before the cue ball could hit the second ball it had to touch one or more of the cushions at least three times. This requirement made it a game of **consummate** strategy and skill.

For fifteen concentrated minutes he **deftly** practiced the **rudiments** of the game—kick shots and bank shots and caroms—and the **subtle** maneuvers and tricks he had learned over the years, such as putting spin on the cue ball to make it behave in **unconventional** ways. Then, with one **adept** stroke after another, and pausing only briefly to **analyze** each shot, he played a **mock** game against himself, at one point scoring eleven points in a row for player A and fifteen consecutive points for player B—a remarkable **exploit,** considering the modern world record is twenty-eight.

Pleased with this display of **proficiency,** he put away his cue and sat down at his desk. He put his feet up on the desk, took a couple of puffs on his cigar, and looked up at the ceiling, which was **whimsically** decorated with drawings of pipes, cigars, and billiard cues. He raised his tumbler. "To Mark Twain, American writer. May he **gratify** some and astonish the rest." He took a swig and raised his glass again. "And to Sam Clemens, who plays one helluva nasty game of billiards."

Apparently not everyone at Hadleyburg was studying because Ristorante Firenze, a popular campus hangout, was packed. The line for a table went out the door and down the sidewalk, and the unfortunate ones who were stuck outside had to **endure** bitter cold and swirling snow while gazing **wistfully** through the window at the cozy diners enjoying their repast within.

Fortunately, Aimee and Angela did not have to **persevere** with the others in that shivering line. They had called in their order earlier in the evening and were now here to pick it up. Excusing themselves politely, they squeezed through the line and passed through the vestibule into the restaurant, where they were greeted by the **tantalizing** aromas of freshly baked bread and sautéed tomatoes, onion, and garlic. They took a deep breath and **savored** the deliciously pleasant **olfactory** sensation.

Their pleasure didn't last long.

"Hey Aimee, Angela," someone called from a nearby booth. "How ya doin'?"

"Oh, no," Aimee said under her breath. "Not that guy."

"Don't worry," Angela whispered back. "I'll take care of him."

Marty Rocheblatt rose from his seat and **lumbered** toward them. A linebacker on the football team, he was **notorious** on campus for his **relentless** attempts to hit on every woman in sight. His strong, sturdy body was not unappealing, but his face was **repugnant**. He was also

insufferable. As Aimee liked to put it, Marty was just too obnoxious for words.

"What's up, cuties?" he said, curling his upper lip in what he probably imagined was a smile. "You're both looking especially hot on such a cold night."

"Oh, shut up," Aimee said, rolling her eyes.

"Hey, your man Marty—rhymes with *party!*—was just paying you a compliment," he said.

"Wow, I'm glad to see you've learned how to rhyme," said Angela with **mock** admiration. "When did you start referring to yourself in the third person?"

Marty put his hand on the wall and leaned closer to them. "Since I saw you two hotties and started thinking about ménage à trois." He grinned, revealing hideous teeth.

"Oh, gross," Aimee groaned. "You are *so* **vile.**" She inserted her forefinger in her mouth and pretended to make herself gag.

"Marty," Angela said with disgust, "anybody who'd even *think* of doing something **intimate** with you needs medication—fast. Hasn't anybody ever told you you've got a face like Frankenstein? And those teeth, honey. Whew! Like, how many dentists have died working on you?"

Aimee giggled.

"You know what, Aims?" said Angela. "I'll bet if we looked up the word **repulsive** in the dictionary there'd be a picture of Marty in the margin."

Marty seemed unfazed by Angela's verbal **aggressiveness.** "C'mon, give me a break, you guys," he said. "How about joining me in my booth? We can have something to eat and then go back to my room and...talk."

"We wouldn't be caught dead in your room," said Aimee.

"Because even if we *were* dead," Angela added, "you'd *still* try to hit on us."

The girls broke out laughing and exchanged a high-five. As Marty **contemplated** how to respond to that **devastating** putdown, a short, **burly** man with an aquiline nose tapped him on the arm.

"Hey buddy, you here to pick up?" he said. It was Johnny, the seemingly **omnipresent** owner of Ristorante Firenze. Johnny had a reputation for having a short fuse and for not tolerating any nonsense in his **establishment.**

"You bet I am," Marty answered, leering at Aimee and Angela, who looked away.

"So what's your order number, pal?" Johnny said **brusquely.** "I don't got all day."

"Order number? Uh, I was just kidding," Marty said. "I thought you meant—"

"I don't got time for this crap!" Johnny erupted. "I got a business to run here. You wanna kid around, do it on somebody else's dime. Get the hell outta my place."

"Hey," Marty objected, "but I haven't even finished my—"

"Tough linguine," Johnny said. "Check it out." He pointed to a sign on the wall that said WE RESERVE THE RIGHT TO REFUSE SERVICE TO ANYONE—INCLUDING YOU, WISEGUY. Then he stuck two fingers in his mouth and gave a **shrill** whistle. A moment later a giant ponytailed man in a black leather vest appeared. The bouncer Johnny had summoned was a head taller than Marty and his **elaborately** tattooed arms were as big as the young football player's thighs.

"See ya, college boy," Johnny said. "You can leave on your own or Vinny and I can show you out."

Marty looked up at the bouncer, who glared back at him with beady, **menacing** eyes. "Uh, I think I can find my way okay," he said, deciding on the more **prudent** course of action. He took a **tentative** step backward, then turned and pushed his way through the line and out the door.

"Good riddance," Angela said.

"Seriously," said Aimee with a sigh of relief.

"Hey Johnny," said Angela. "We're here to pick up. Can you help us?"

Johnny turned to them with a **congenial** smile. "Certainly, ladies. Your number, please?"

Mark Twain opened the large bottom drawer of his desk. In the drawer lay a thick sheaf of papers bound with string. With a grunt, he lifted the **massive** bundle and set it on the desk. He untied the string and sat there looking at the huge pile of words he had made.

It was the manuscript of his latest novel, over thirteen hundred pages long. He had been working on it on and off for seven years. It had begun with a great outpouring of creativity that suddenly sputtered to a halt after four hundred pages, leaving him in **grave** doubt about the worthiness of the whole **enterprise.** "I like it only **tolerably** well, as far as I have got," he wrote to a friend at the time, "and may possibly pigeonhole or burn the MS when it is done."

For several years he set it aside while he wrote and published other books and took his family on a **sojourn** in Europe. Then, **invigorated** by a steamboat trip down the Mississippi River, he returned to the novel with **zeal.** All last summer he had worked on it feverishly, writing several thousand words a day, six or seven days a week, and by early fall it was finished.

He was now eager to get the book published, but for some reason he just couldn't stop tinkering with it. For weeks he had been **diligently** going over it page by page and word by word, making scores of **subtle refinements** to the novel's intentionally **unrefined diction.**

He had written the novel in seven **distinct ethnic** and regional **dialects,** he explained in a prefatory note he had composed for the book: "the Missouri negro **dialect**; the extremest form of the backwoods South-Western **dialect**; the ordinary 'Pike-County' **dialect**; and four modified varieties of this last. The shadings have not been done in a **haphazard** fashion, or by guesswork; but **painstakingly,** and with the **trustworthy** guidance and support of personal familiarity with these several forms of speech."

By attempting to **elevate uncultivated** speech to the level of art, Twain knew he was taking a calculated risk. And he knew **intuitively** that he had done something truly original and **innovative.** He was certain the book had literary **merit,** and at times he even **entertained** the **notion** that it might be his masterpiece. But he was anxious about how the public would react to a story that was written in a coarse, **rural vernacular,** and one in which the hero-narrator was a shiftless, semiliterate, rebellious boy who thumbs his nose at society and violates its laws and **conventions** at every turn.

He was also worried that the message of the novel would be overlooked or, even worse, misunderstood. For this book was not simply an innocent and pleasant **diversion** for young readers like his earlier *Adventures of Tom Sawyer.* As he wrote in his private notebook, it was a **morality** tale in which "a **sound** heart and a deformed conscience come into collision and conscience suffers defeat." It was a story in which the very people who consider themselves **upright** and **pious** are in fact **hypocrites** and **perpetrators** of evil. And, most of all, with its **poignant portrayal** of a forbidden friendship between a white boy and a black man in the **antebellum** South, it was a ringing **indictment** of the **heinous institution** of slavery and the **entrenched immorality** of racism.

Would people **comprehend** that? he wondered as he gazed down at the foot-high stack of pages on the desk. Would they **perceive** how he was **condemning** humanity's **regrettable penchant** for cruelty, **chicanery,** and **folly**? Or would they accuse him of **impropriety** and dismiss the novel as **vulgar** and **offensive** trash?

He lifted the topmost sheet of paper from the stack and laid it on the pullout writing shelf that **protruded** from the right side of the desk. In the middle of the page was the heading *Chap. 1.* Above that the page was blank. He picked up a pencil and, in **fluent** cursive, wrote the words *Huck Finn* at the top of the page. He took a few puffs on his cigar, then shook his head. After *Huck* he drew a caret and added *leberry,* making it *Huckleberry Finn.* Below that he wrote *Reported by Mark Twain.*

He looked at the opening sentence of the novel: *You will not know about me, without you have read a book by the name of "The Adventures of Tom Sawyer."* In an earlier round of editing he had crossed out *will* and above it he had written *do,* so the beginning of the sentence now read like this: *You do not know about me . . .*

That's still not right, he thought. It's too formal. It should be more **colloquial.**

He scratched out *not* and changed *do* to *don't: You don't know about me . . .*

That's better, he thought, but something's still missing. After a minute or two of **reflection** and cigar puffing it came to him. Quickly he added several words to the end of the sentence, so now it read like this: *You don't know about me, without you have read a book by the name of "The Adventures of Tom Sawyer," but that ain't no matter.*

He set down his pencil and clapped his hands together. "That's it!" he said aloud, pleased with himself for killing two birds with one stone. Now, he thought, anyone who picks up this book won't think they have to read *Tom Sawyer* first, and that'll help to sell more books. And I managed to get *ain't* into the very first sentence, which will surely make the prudes and schoolmarms squirm.

Then another inspiration came to him. With a mischievous grin he pulled a blank sheet of paper out of a drawer, set it on the writing shelf, and grabbed his pen. Just above the middle of the page he wrote the word *NOTICE* in large letters, and below that he wrote this:

> Persons attempting to find a **motive** in this narrative will be prosecuted; persons attempting to find a **moral** in it will be **banished**; persons attempting to find a plot in it will be shot.
>
> By Order of the Author

There, he thought, laying down his pen. Now maybe all the people who will want to shoot *me* after reading this book will think I'm just fooling, while anyone who possesses the rare ability to **discern irony** will **perceive** the truth: that everything about my humor is deadly serious.

He picked up the page and blew on it and shook it a bit to dry the ink. Then he put the **emended** first page and the "Notice" page on top of the pile on the desk and tied up the bundle with the string.

As he reached for his cigar, which was smoldering in the ashtray on the desk, the pen rolled off the writing shelf onto the floor.

"Dagnabit," he muttered.

When he bent over to retrieve the pen he was surprised not to see it anywhere on the rug. Perhaps it rolled under the desk, he thought. He got down on his hands and knees and fumbled under the desk with one hand. The pen was nowhere to be found.

"What in tarnation!" He put his cheek to the rug and peered under the desk, but it was too dark to see anything. He stuck his hand in there and felt around again, but with no success.

"The hell with it," he said, pushing himself up. The back of his head struck the underside of the writing shelf with a sharp crack. He groaned and sank to the floor.

How long he lay there he did not know. It could have been five minutes or five hours or even fifty years. All he knew was that when he awoke and struggled to his feet, he couldn't believe his groggy eyes. The manuscript of *Huckleberry Finn* was gone, vanished from his desk without a trace. In its place was a strange contraption that looked like a tiny, flat typewriter inside a valise.

Chapter 3

Mortifying Moments

Orlando and Hank stepped into entryway E and stamped the snow off their boots.

"Do I smell what I think I smell?" said Orlando as they jogged up the steps to the second floor.

"Oh yeah," Hank said with greedy anticipation, "I think you do."

They knocked on the door of suite E-4 and Angela opened it. "Hey, c'mon in, you two. Aims and I just got back from Firenze."

"I knew it," said Orlando, setting down a **cumbersome** stack of books and notebooks on the floor next to the wall.

Hank laid his laptop on the desk next to the computer. "We could smell that pizza out in the stairwell."

"Well, come and get it while it's hot," Aimee said from her perch on the leopard-skin sofa, where she was sipping soda through a straw. "And maybe this time you selfish **gluttons** can leave a few scraps for us, all right?"

Angela sat down next to Aimee and lifted the top of the square cardboard box on the coffee table. "Dig in, boys. Sausage and onion on one side, pepperoni and black olive on the other. And help yourself to the soda."

Orlando and Hank tossed their coats in a corner, plunked down in the two armchairs, and began to feast.

"You know, Aims?" Angela whispered as she watched Hank devour his first slice in about thirty seconds flat. "There's something about a **voracious** man..."

"That's incredibly disgusting?" Aimee offered.

"No, that makes me hungry," said Angela, picking up a slice and taking a big bite.

"Hey, Angela," Hank said halfway into his second slice. "I just realized your initials are ATM, like the money machine."

"That's right," Angela replied. "Angela T. McGuinn—ATM. I'm a machine, honey. Right now I'm just a straight-A machine, but look out. When I graduate from law school I'm going to be a *real* money machine."

"I bet you will," said Hank. "So if you're an ATM, do you 'teller' like it is?"

"You can bank on that," Angie said, getting into the wordplay. "I have 'teller vision.' And I'm 'tellerpathic,' too."

"Okay, so teller me this. Are you automated?"

Angela laughed. "Only an **automaton** gets auto-*mated*. I am auto-*mobile*. I go with who I want, when I want, and how I want—and don't you forget it, sweet cheeks."

"So do I have a chance with you?"

"Same chance as anybody else who wants to press my buttons," said Angie with a **devious** smile.

"And what about me, Aims?" Orlando said. "Do I still have a chance with you?"

Aimee had had a **clandestine** crush on Orlando since the day they met in the spring of freshman year. They had flirted off and on since then but she could never be sure whether he was **sincerely** interested or **indifferent**. She looked at him and tossed back her long black hair with one hand. "Maybe," she said. "I'll let you know after I see that poem you promised to write me last year."

"I'm still working on it," Orlando said with a **sheepish** grin.

"What is it, an **epic**?"

Orlando's expression grew serious. "No, it's just... **subtle**... and **complex**. Like me."

"I see," Aimee said. "Well, then let me know when you've figured yourself out."

When they had finished eating it was clear that no one was even remotely interested in studying. They needed a **respite** from the pressure of finals period, some brief and pleasant **diversion** to take their minds off all their work.

"We could play 'Mortifying Moments,'" Aimee suggested.

"What's that?" asked Hank, popping the last piece of pizza crust in his mouth.

"It's when you share your most humiliating experience."

"And why would I want to do that?"

"So we can all laugh at you, you dork," said Orlando, and everyone laughed—except Hank, who flashed his roommate a **vindictive** bird.

"Did you know there's a word for **deriving** pleasure from someone else's **degradation**?" said Angela.

"What is it?" said Hank. *"Orlandoism?"*

"How about *hanking*?" said Orlando.

"Sorry, wiseguys," said Angela. "It's *schadenfreude,* from the German *Schaden,* harm, and *Freude,* joy. It means satisfaction gained from another person's misfortune."

"What a lovely **concept**," Orlando said **ironically**. "Who goes first?"

"How about you, dorkface?" said Hank.

"After you, my dear dweeb," Orlando **retorted**.

"Eat me, barf bag."

"You're goin' down, butt lips."

"Sewer breath!"

"Zit brain!"

"All right, you guys," interrupted Angela. "Enough **inane** male **aggression**."

"Yeah," Aimee seconded. "Could you just chill on the sixth-grade **buffoonery**?"

"So who goes first?" said Orlando. "How about you, Angela?"

"No way," Angela replied. "Let's pick straws or something."

"Do you guys have a deck of cards?" said Hank, and Aimee nodded. "We can all draw a card and the highest or lowest goes first."

"Let's make it the lowest," said Aimee, getting up to fetch the cards, "because this game is all about telling everybody how you were brought low."

Aimee spread out the cards facedown on the coffee table. Angela drew the ten of hearts. Hank drew the king of clubs and sat back with a **complacent** smile. "Oh no," said Orlando as he drew the five of spades, but he sighed with relief a moment later when Aimee drew the two of diamonds.

"All right, everybody," she said. "Because you guys are my best friends, and I know I can trust you, I'm going to tell you something I've never told anyone else at college—not even you, Angela."

"Wow, that's brave," Angela said. "You go, girl."

"But it doesn't leave this room. Is that clear?" Aimee added sternly.

"Yeah," Angela said. "That's the rule of the game: complete **confidentiality**."

Orlando and Hank nodded to show their **assent**.

"When I was sixteen, I had my first really big concert," Aimee began as the others settled into their seats to listen to her story. "I guess you could say it was my formal **debut** as a soloist. For months I had been preparing to play the Brahms Piano Concerto number 2 with the San Francisco Symphony. It was a real family affair. My mother was playing viola. My father was guest-conducting. My entire family was in the audience—my sister and brother, my grandparents, all my aunts and uncles and cousins. A bunch of my friends and their parents were there, and my boyfriend at the time was there with his parents. There were some real heavy hitters there too."

"Like who?" asked Orlando.

"Like the mayor of San Francisco and the president of Stanford University. Like Senator Maria Castro, who may run for president next year. And then there were like a gazillion of the city's most **prominent** and **affluent** citizens—you know, the people you always see in the society pages in the newspaper, showing off their face-lifts and jewelry and trophy wives."

"Yeah," said Orlando, "the boring, **conventional** types who give bales of money to the local symphony and opera and art museum but who don't know anything about music and art and don't care."

"But they have a **pragmatic** reason for doing that," Hank said. "**Philanthropy** is a great tax break."

"And let's not forget the socially **pretentious** reason," said Angela. "They do it to **enhance** their image, to see and be seen."

"Anyway," Aimee went on, "I was wearing this beautiful black satin dress that my mother had had custom-made for me by the best dressmaker in Chinatown. It was strapless, and it had a little train. It was soft and kind of slinky but in a totally tasteful way. I have to confess I thought I looked great in it."

"I'll bet you did," Orlando said. "I wish I could've seen *that.*"

"Well, I'm just glad you didn't see what happened later," Aimee said, giggling. "I played the piece and everything went well. All my hard work had paid off. It was a good performance. I was relaxed and confident and totally in the groove. As I played the last few bars of the **finale** I could feel myself starting to glow with pride. This was the beginning of my professional career, and what a great beginning it had turned out to be. I couldn't wait to **bask** in the **resounding** applause of this big and important audience. But it wasn't just their **accolades** that I craved. I wanted them to love me for playing so well for them. I wanted them to shower me with loving, joyous praise."

"Hey, that's a lot to ask of a bunch of middle-aged bankers and plastic surgeons and their twentysomething wives," said Hank.

"Shush up and let her finish," Angela **chided,** leaning over and slapping Hank on the knee.

"So I played the final, triumphant chord and slowly lifted my hands from the piano," Aimee said, "and then something terrible happened. Somehow the train of my dress had gotten stuck under one of the legs of the piano bench, so when I got up to take a bow, I went up and the strapless dress went down. Or maybe I should say it stayed put. Either way, before I knew what was happening I was standing in front of hundreds of people—and my whole family—in a black satin skirt."

"Oh my god, girl!" Angela cried. "You were up on that stage with your boobs hanging out?"

Aimee responded with a **pathetic** nod.

"You must've died of embarrassment," Orlando said.

"**Hyperbolically** speaking, of course," said Hank.

"Well, I certainly wanted to curl up and die," Aimee said, "because the greatest moment in my life had just turned into the worst. Of course I couldn't bow or anything. I just covered myself up as best I could and ran off the stage. For a long time I thought it was some kind of **divine** punishment for being **narcissistic** about my performance."

"What a nightmare," said Angela.

"Yeah, it was a nightmare then," said Aimee, "but I can pretty much laugh about it now."

"I think that shows a lot of maturity," said Orlando. "I would have left town on the next bus and started a new life in Mexico."

"Maybe you should have done that anyway," said Hank.

"Oh yeah?" said Orlando. "Maybe *you* should have—"

"Boys!" Angela broke in. "Please don't **digress,** because it's time for somebody else to relate a tale of disgrace, and that somebody may be you."

"I forgot to tell you guys," Hank said, "that I'm **impervious** to embarrassment."

"Yeah, sure," said Angela. "And you're probably **impervious** to reason and common sense, too." She picked a card from the deck: the queen of hearts.

Orlando pulled the jack of clubs and turned to Hank. "Pick a card, pal."

Hank leaned over and drew the ace of spades. He looked at the others. "Are aces high or low?"

"Low," they responded in unison.

"You guys suck," said Hank.

"Okay," said Angela, "let the **paragon** of self-assurance speak."

"Well," Hank began, "my **mortifying** moment wasn't quite as **devastating** as Aimee's, but I was plenty embarrassed nonetheless. I was taking the SAT and—"

He was interrupted by **vociferous** groans.

"Yeah, talk about one of life's great **calamities,**" said Hank. "Anyway, I had just finished the first math section ten minutes early—"

Everybody groaned again.

"I'm good at math, okay?" Hank said. "Gimme a break. So I've got ten minutes to kill, and I start leaning back in my chair, trying to be all casual and relaxed, you know? I've got my hands behind my head, and I'm kind of tilting the chair back, balancing on the back legs and rocking a little back and forth. There's this girl I've had my eyes on for a while who's sitting two rows in front of me, and I'm kind of checking her out and wondering if I should, like, ask her out after the test."

"Let me guess," said Aimee. "She's not exactly interested after whatever happens next."

"Very **perceptive** of you, Sherlock," Hank replied. "Yeah, I'd say it would be reasonable to **infer** that. Anyway, so then I think, maybe I'll just get really comfortable here and put my feet up on the desk—we're all sitting in my high school gym at these individual desks that are kind of light and portable. I check out the proctor and she's like way up front, writing how much time is left on a whiteboard. I'm way in the back, so I figure it'll be cool, she won't see me. So I tilt back in my chair and lift my legs up to put my feet on the desk and *wham!*—"

"You fall flat on your ass?" said Orlando.

"You got it, dude. They must've waxed the floor the night before or something because that chair just slipped right out from under me. I landed on my butt—which was sore for a week—and I smashed the back of my head on the floor so hard that I had a headache for the rest of the day."

"Ouch," said Aimee. "As if the test alone wasn't enough to give you a migraine."

"Poor Hankie," said Angela, pretending to wipe tears from her eyes.

"Hey, and that's like not even the worst of it," said Hank.

"Pray tell, Mr. Test-osterone," said Orlando.

"Way slick, Big O," said Hank. "About as slick as that dang gymnasium floor. So my chair slips out from under me and goes flying like a rocket. It slams into my desk, then the desk slides forward and bangs into the person in front of me, and she's so surprised by the crash and the bump that she jumps up and knocks over her desk and tosses her number-two pencil in the air. Up goes the pencil, twirling and twirling, and then down it comes, right on the head of the **prospective** object of my affections.

"Next thing I know everybody is staring at me groaning in pain on the floor, the proctor is standing over me with her hands on her hips accusing me of violating 'examination procedures' and intentionally **disrupting** the test, the girl that my desk banged into is blubbering insanely about how I've ruined her score and now she'll never get into her first-choice college, and the no-longer **prospective** object of my affections—who has just been transformed into a giant block of ice—is sitting there shaking her head and rolling her eyes. I mean, it's like there was a big cartoon bubble over her head with the word LOSER! in it."

Everyone burst out laughing, even Hank.

"What a contretemps," said Angela. "I can just picture you on that floor, rubbing your sore butt."

"So what happened with the test?" asked Aimee. "What did the proctor do?"

"She kicked me out. I had to take it over."

"Brutal," said Orlando. "No wonder you're such a twisted psycho beast. You had to take a makeup SAT."

"Well, Orlando, it's down to you and me," said Angela, pulling a card from the deck: the five of diamonds. Orlando leaned forward and drew the seven of spades.

Angela sighed and leaned back on the sofa. "Have I got a story for you," she began. "You all know I've got a strong personality—"

"Uh, yeah," Aimee **interjected.**

"And I'm not too easily embarrassed. But this truly was my most **mortifying** moment. And the sad thing was that it was sort of my own fault."

"Bring it on, baby," said Hank. "We'll help you make reliving it special."

"Gee, thanks for being so supportive," Angela said

ironically. "You're already experiencing schadenfreude and I haven't even told you anything."

"Just imagining you in distress is enough," Hank replied with a grin.

Angela dismissed him with a **contemptuous** wave of her hand. "Enough of your **juvenile insolence,**" she said. "Zip it and let me tell my story. It was my junior year at Putnam Academy and I was running for student body president. My opponent was this stuck-up, superpopular bimbo named Gretchen who excelled in two subjects: flirting and backstabbing. My friends and I called her Retchin' Gretchen because that's what she made us feel like doing and that's how we suspected she maintained her figure. Her campaign manager was a **self-righteous, conceited** little creep named Algernon Percival Sneed, otherwise known as Have Mercy, Percy because he wanted to be a preacher."

"Did everybody in your school have a rhyming nickname?" said Orlando with a chuckle.

"Only the ones my friends and I couldn't stand," Angela said. "Anyway, Percy was a total **sycophant,** a world-class suck-up **toady.** I mean, this guy was incredible. He would give the teachers birthday presents, and every couple of months he would wash and wax the headmaster's car. And he was always giving people **condescending** lectures about their supposedly **immoral** behavior, and ratting on them for **petty offenses** like passing a note or sneaking a call on their cellphone or forgetting to bus their tray in the dining hall."

"What a chump," said Hank. "Why didn't somebody flatten him?"

"Because at Putnam any violent **altercation,** on or off campus, would get you expelled. They had a zero-**tolerance** policy about that."

"Which is probably a good thing," said Aimee, who found violence of any kind **abhorrent,** even in the regulated **context** of sports.

"It turned out to be a really intense campaign, with some serious mudslinging on both sides," Angela continued. "Gretchen had all the jocks and preppies and airheads lined up with her, and all the smart and cool kids were behind me."

"But of course," Hank said.

"Problem was," said Angela, "there were more of them than there were of us, and that worried me. But I didn't let it show. In fact, being the **underdog** made me even more **intent** on winning, to the point where maybe I got kind of **arrogant.**

"So a few days before the election I'm eating lunch in the dining hall with my friends. I'm dissing Gretchen and everybody's cracking up. I'm saying stuff like, 'She's so stupid she thinks a quarterback's a refund,' you know, when suddenly Gretchen walks by with her **entourage.** And when she sees me she stops and gives me this incredibly **supercilious sneer,** and she says, 'Hey everybody, guess what I found out about Angela? She failed her road test last week, so she didn't get her license. How is it possible, Angela, that you can be so smart and not even be able to drive a car?'

"Unfortunately, I was guilty as charged. I had been so nervous taking the test that my legs were shaking. You know how that can happen sometimes when you have a rush of adrenaline? Well, I accidentally stepped on the accelerator instead of the brake and wound up running a stop sign. The inspector freaked and told me to pull over immediately and **relinquish** the wheel, and that was the end of that.

"I look at Gretchen and I see Percy standing behind her, **smirking,** and I just know that somehow that jerk had managed to find out that I'd failed. I don't know how the **deceitful** little sneak did it. Maybe he followed me. I hadn't told anybody except my closest friend, and I knew she would never breathe a word to *him.*

"So now they're all laughing at me, and Gretchen's standing there all **smug** and everything. I can't just sit there and take it. I have to try to save face. So I get up and give Gretchen my baddest whup-ass look and I say, 'You know what, girl? So maybe I did fail my driving test. Well, so what! I'm still in the driver's seat in this election. And I'm driving *you* nuts because you know I'm going to kick your bimbo butt!' 'Oh, yeah?' she whines back. 'And what if I win?' I say, 'There's no way I'm going to lose to you.' 'And what if you do?' she says. 'What will Big Bad Angela McGuinn do when she loses to the best-looking and most popular girl at Putnam Academy?'"

Angela paused and shook her head. "By now we have the attention of the whole dining hall, and before I realize what the **consequences** might be I say to her, 'The day you manage to beat me at anything other than an eyebrow-plucking contest will be the day I lick your shoes.'

"Then she gets this wicked smile on her face and says, 'Really?' And she turns to the **throng**. 'Hey, everybody,' she says. 'What do you think? If Angela loses the election she says she'll lick my shoes. Do you want her to do that?' And then that disgusting little **opportunist** Percy Sneed jumps up on a chair and says, 'Or should she French kiss me for a whole minute right here in front of the entire school?'"

"Uh oh," said Aimee. "This is not looking good."

"No kidding," said Angela.

"I think Percy-poo liked you," said Hank.

"Remind me to kill you later," said Angela.

"So what happened then?" asked Orlando.

"They sealed my doom," said Angela. "They worked that crowd like the king and the duke in *Huckleberry Finn*. Gretchen shouted, 'Who wants her to lick my shoes?' and everybody roared. Then Percy shouted, 'And who wants her to French me?' and everybody roared even louder. Next thing I know everybody's hooting and pounding on the tables and yelling 'French Percy!' 'French Percy!' And Percy and Gretchen are both laughing at me and saying, 'See you after the election!' It was horrible. I was fighting back tears. And then I lost the election."

"So did you have to kiss him?" asked Orlando.

"Are you kidding?" said Angela. "That was his nasty idea to work up the crowd. I just flipped him off."

"But what about licking Retchin' Gretchen's shoes?" asked Aimee. "You said that if you lost you'd do it."

"Yup, that was the rub," Angela said, **paraphrasing** a famous line from the soliloquy in Shakespeare's *Hamlet*. "It was my own **arrogance** that got me in trouble, and I was honor-bound to **debase** myself. At first I considered asking my parents to send me to another school, but I knew that wouldn't be an option. So the day after the election I just walked up to Gretchen in the hallway and told her that unlike some people at this school I was an honorable person who could be counted on to keep her word. Then I took a deep breath, licked her ugly shoes, and did my best to hold my head high and **endure** all the **taunting** and **mockery** until people finally got tired of making fun of me."

"Wow, I think that's worse than what happened to me," said Aimee. "At least my humiliation lasted only a few seconds."

"Yeah," said Hank, "that may be just about as bad as it gets."

"All I can say is thank goodness I'll never have to see those two **malicious** twerps again," said Angela. "So what's your tale of woe, Señor Ortiz?"

Orlando took a swig of soda. "Well, my story involves an old girlfriend, an underdone steak, an **impertinent** sheepdog, a **regrettable** fling, and a pair of hickeys the size of Rhode Island."

"Now that sounds kinky," said Hank.

"Actually it sounds funny," said Angela.

"Not to me," said Aimee. "But don't let me stop you," she added, her curiosity getting the better of her.

"It was the summer between my junior and senior year in high school," Orlando went on. "I was working at my uncle's Mexican restaurant as a prep cook and busboy and I was taking a couple of classes at community college. I was busy and I didn't have much time to hang out, and I was lonely. I craved companionship, especially of the female variety. So when an old girlfriend called me up out of the blue and invited me to her house for dinner that Sunday, I thought, Why not? What have I got to lose?

"Then on Friday a guy I worked with at the restaurant asked me to come to a party at his place the next night. He said there'd be some girls there I might like to meet, and so I thought, Why not? What have I got to lose?

"So I get to the party, which is at a really nice house with a pool on the edge of a canyon," Orlando said. "There's about twenty people there, mostly college age, and nobody I recognize. And the guy who invited me was right: There are definitely some babes there."

"Oh, really?" said Aimee in a frosty voice.

"There aren't any adults at the house," Orlando continued, disregarding the interruption, "and everybody's drinking. They're raiding the poolhouse bar, having beers and rum and Cokes and shots of tequila—whatever. So I open a beer and check out the scene. And the next thing I know I'm talking to this hottie in a pair of shorts and a bathing suit top. We talk for a while, and then all of sudden she's saying everything a lonely, horny dude wants to hear: how cute I am, do I have a girlfriend, so I'm a basketball star, isn't that cool—stuff like that, you know?"

"Yeah, I know," said Hank, who was becoming **captivated** by the story.

"And she says why don't we go someplace more private so we can talk," Orlando continued.

"And you, with your tongue hanging out, say sure," said Aimee.

"Uh...yeah, I guess. And so we wind up on the couch in the poolhouse, and the next thing I know, she's all over me, not kissing and petting but biting and scratching like an animal, clawing at me with her nails and sucking on my neck. It was *way* out of control. After a couple of minutes of that I told her I had to go to the bathroom, and then I got out of there as fast as I could."

"Aw, too bad," said Hank.

"Honey, get your mind out of the gutter," Angela **rebuked** him.

"And when I got up the next morning and looked in the bathroom mirror," Orlando said, "I had two **colossal** hickeys, one on each side of my neck. We're talking totally **immense** black-and-blue splotches. You could even see teeth marks in my skin."

"What was she, a vampire?" said Aimee.

"Seriously," said Orlando. "So then I remember that I had promised my old girlfriend, Muffy—"

"Muffy?" said Aimee, laughing. "You had a girlfriend named Muffy?"

"Muffy the vampire slayer," said Hank.

"So what's wrong with her name?" asked Orlando.

"It's *so* preppie," Aimee said. "Did she wear plaid skirts and knee-high socks?"

"I don't know," Orlando said. "I never saw her dressed."

Aimee stifled a gasp as Hank burst out laughing.

"Just kidding," Orlando said with a **devious** grin.

"That was cold," said Angela.

"Anyway," Orlando continued, "so I remember that I had promised Muffy I'd come for dinner that night and I think, no way. I can't see her with these **grotesque** monstrosities on my neck. I don't want *anybody* to see me. I just want to go back to sleep for a week until they disappear. So I call her up and make some lame excuse and she says, 'Please, you have to come. I really want to see you. I'm going away to college this fall and I don't know when we'll get together again.' And somehow, I have no idea how, she talks me into it. I even tell her about the hickeys and she *still* talks me into it. She says that doesn't matter, that we're just friends, that nobody will care. And like an idiot I say okay."

"Looks like you were a **gullible** pushover in high school too," said Hank.

"Maybe I was," said Orlando, "but at least I wasn't a weasel-faced nerd like you."

"Hey," said Angela. "Will you guys please stop **digressing**? This is getting good and I want to hear what happens next."

"Well," Orlando went on, "all I know is that I must have been out of my mind to go to her house that night."

"Or lonelier than you realized," said Aimee.

"I guess," said Orlando. "Anyway, it's the middle of summer so I can't wear a turtleneck or a scarf or anything."

"How about a neckbrace?" said Hank.

"That would've been cool, except I didn't have one. I did try to cover them with Band-Aids, but you could still see a whole bunch of hickey. So finally I just put on a shirt with the biggest collar I could find and hoped for the best."

"And now the worst is yet to come," said Angela **presciently**.

"So when I get to Muffy's house the first thing that happens is she stares at my neck in astonishment and says, 'You didn't tell me they were *that* big.' Then her smelly sheepdog jumps on me and starts sniffing my crotch, and he won't leave me alone even when Muffy yells at him."

"Maybe it was your vampire woman transformed into a dog," said Aimee, and everybody cracked up, including Orlando.

"So I try unsuccessfully to shrink my neck into my shirt and fasten my chin to my chest. We sit down at the table with Muffy's mom and dad and older sister, who's like twenty-five and visiting from out of town, and after about ten seconds it's obvious that they all think Muffy and I are getting back together. Her sister seems **indifferent** about it, but her dad has this kind of knowing look on his face, and her mom is asking me all these questions."

"Like what are those big ugly splotches on your neck?" said Aimee.

"Well, at first just ordinary stuff like how've I been, how's my family, what've I been doing lately, but eventually, yeah, she gets around to that. Meanwhile, the damn dog gets under the table and starts trying to get between my legs, so I'm **furtively** trying to shove him away while smiling and talking to Muffy's mom."

"Dude, what kind of cologne did you have on?" said Hank. "Canine Passion?"

Orlando, **immersed** in his story, ignored the **affront.** "So as we're finishing our salad she asks me how I got 'those curious marks' on my neck, and I realize what a dork I am because the question was **inevitable** and I hadn't bothered to think of a **plausible** answer. So I'm fumbling around for something to say, and I remember the code phrase my big brother and his friends used to use for hickeys. I look at Muffy's mom and with a completely straight face I say, 'They're muffler burns, Mrs. Benson.'

"'Burns? You burned your neck?' she says, getting all **solicitous.** 'My poor dear, how terrible. How did you manage to do that?'

"Before I can say something like 'Well, I was working on my dad's car,' Muffy's sister butts in. 'Mom, they're hickeys,' she says in this **apathetic,** matter-of-fact way. Then Muffy's mom gets this **perplexed** look on her face, as if she doesn't understand, so the sister says, 'You know, love bites? From making out?'

"'Making out?' says Muffy's mom in this confused voice.

"So the sister says, 'You know, necking?'

"Man, at that point I just wanted to crawl under the table and die, except I couldn't even do that because I was still too busy trying to keep that stupid dog off me. And then Muffy's dad starts to laugh. I can't believe it. Pretty soon he's laughing so hard he starts coughing and his face gets all red and he has to drink some water. When he finally recovers he looks at his wife and says, 'You really don't know what a hickey is, dear?' And he starts cackling again. Then their cook comes in and serves the main course."

"They must be pretty **affluent** to have a cook," said Angela.

"Yeah, they've got big bucks," said Orlando. "They have a cook *and* a full-time maid. Anyway, I can just tell Old Cookie has been eavesdropping. She's checking me out **surreptitiously** as she's going around the table, and whenever she looks at me she has this incredibly **hostile** expression on her face that says, 'Why you miserable lowlife scum, how dare you insult the respectability of this family and my darling Muffy by coming in here with those ugly love bites you got from sucking face with some slut!'"

"Whoa, that's **malevolent**," said Hank.

"I could tell she was totally out to get me," Orlando continued, "and there was nothing I could do about it. Not a damn thing. She sets my plate down in front of me and there's this juicy-looking steak and steaming baked potato on it, and I think, hey, that looks really good. And for a moment I'm actually starting to forget that I have two humongous hickeys on my neck, that the cook would like to cut my throat, and that Muffy's smelly dog *still* won't leave me alone. Then I take my knife and fork and cut into the steak—and it's totally raw."

"Yuck," said Angela.

"I had asked for it rare but not *that* rare," said Orlando. "The cook had browned the outside a little to make it look okay, but the inside was butcher-shop red, and still cold, too. I mean, like, it was mooing at me."

"Gross," said Aimee. "So you tasted it?"

Orlando nodded. "What else could I do? I had to eat it. Muffy's mom said that if it was too rare I could send it back, but I took one look at that bloodthirsty cook and said the steak was just fine. So there I was, exposed as a **despicable** seducer of women before my former girlfriend's whole family, and forced to eat raw meat while the **vengeful** cook glared at me from the kitchen and the family dog nuzzled my privates."

"Oh, **degradation** most foul!" Hank wailed in **mock** sympathy. "Such **egregious** misfortune couldn't have happened to a more deserving guy."

"Get bent, geekhead," Orlando **retorted.**

"Up yours, donkey breath," Hank shot back.

"Anus brain."

"Booger biter."

"Toilet sucker."

"Turd sniffer."

"Sputum licker."

As the boys went at it yet again, attaining new heights of verbal **aggression** and new depths of psychological regression, Aimee and Angela exchanged a weary, **jaded** look. "Forever twelve," Aimee whispered, shaking her head.

"They're **pathetic**," Angela whispered back. "Why do we waste our time with these **boorish, infantile** creatures?"

Aimee smiled. "Because they're kinda cute."

Chapter 4

The Twain Shall Meet

Mark Twain **gingerly** rubbed the large and tender goose egg on the back of his head. A **diligent** inspection of the desk and the billiard room had just **confirmed** that the manuscript of *Huckleberry Finn* had either been **purloined** or had somehow managed to walk off by itself. He earnestly hoped it was the **latter**. With a **bewildered** sigh, he turned his attention to the peculiar contraption on his desk. What the dickens is it, he wondered, and where on earth had it come from?

Twain was constantly on the lookout for some useful new **mechanism** to invest in, for he **entertained** the **notion** that one day an invention he had had the **foresight** to promote would make him rich. **Innovation** had always fascinated him, and he had the highest regard for the power of technology to accomplish **mundane** tasks more efficiently and improve the lot of humanity. Yet, on a philosophical level, he knew that the products of science and technology were not always **beneficial**, and not all progress was forward. Too often, he thought, the things we **devise** to **ameliorate** our lives also have the power to **corrupt** or **devastate** them. And so he was **ambivalent**—**enthralled** by the **lucrative** potential of every new thingamajig that happened to come along, yet **profoundly skeptical** about their tendency to fail, **undermine,** and sometimes harm us.

The gizmo he was now **scrutinizing** looked like a small square valise or traveling bag that someone had left propped open on the desk. The top, upright half appeared to be almost entirely composed of a dark pane of glass. The bottom half had several rows of small keys marked with letters like a typewriter, along with various strange keys with **obscure** markings like "Ctrl," "Alt," and "F9." Below the keys was a mysterious glass pad.

Could this be some kind of newfangled writing machine? he thought. If so, he couldn't **fathom** how you could manage to print anything with the device. To begin with, where was one supposed to put the sheet of paper? There was no roller, no inked ribbon, and no type to strike the ribbon and press the ink onto the page. It was **baffling.**

Extending a **tentative** finger, Twain pressed several letter keys, noticing that they were **concave** and not flat and round like a typewriter's. Nothing happened, at least nothing **discernible.** He picked up the device with both hands and was surprised at how light it was. The smooth gray material of the case was not metal or wood or cloth but something **eccentric** and unfamiliar. He turned the device upside down and swore **vehemently** when the top half closed down hard on his thumbs. Then he examined the sides and noticed what appeared to be a small button marked *Power.*

"All right, whatever you are," he said, setting it down on the desk again and raising the top half. "Let's see if we can make you work." He pressed the button. The machine beeped obnoxiously and gurgled to life.

Twain watched in wonder and awe as the dark pane of glass slowly became **illuminated.** "Well, I'll be damned!" he exclaimed as a message began to roll across the screen: *TEMPUS EDAX RERUM . . . TEMPUS EDAX RERUM . . .*

"Time . . . something or other," he mumbled. "Darnit. If Mrs. Clemens were here, she'd know." He pressed several letter keys and again there was no response. The **cryptic** message continued to roll slowly by. "Okay," he said, eyeing a key in the corner marked "Esc," "let's try this one." He pressed it firmly with his forefinger.

Outside the wind wailed like a banshee and branches clattered against the roof. The gaslights along the walls of the billiard room sputtered and died, then magically roared back to **vivid** life. "What the—" Twain said, but before he could utter the word *devil* there was a loud crack, like the sound of a tree felled by lightning, and he was blinded by an explosion of light.

The great bell at the **summit** of Langdon Tower tolled the hour with a single, **ominous** knell. Outside the lancet windows of suite E-4 the swirling snow had suddenly and inexplicably turned to hail. A **profusion** of glassy pellets tap-danced **recklessly** on the panes to the **mournful** music of the wind.

Aimee looked up from the **soporific gobbledygook** of her sociology textbook, startled into alertness by the staccato rush of sound. It reminded her of a particularly **expressive** passage in the **climactic** conclusion of one of her sonatas.

Orlando looked up from the storm-tossed pages of Herman Melville's **allegorical** masterpiece *Moby-Dick,* in which he had been **immersed** for the past hour, taking notes for his American literature exam. He watched the pellets drumming against the window and thought of the beginning of Edgar Allan Poe's "The Raven":

> While I nodded, nearly napping, suddenly there
> came a tapping,
> As of some one gently rapping, rapping at my
> chamber door.

> " 'Tis some visiter," I muttered, "tapping at my
> chamber door—
>   Only this and nothing more."

Angela looked up from her laptop, distracted from foot-noting a quotation about the **Emancipation** Proclamation in her term paper on the **abolition** of slavery. The sound of the hail made her think about popcorn and wonder if they had any left.

Hank sat at the desk in the corner, his back to the win-dows, **engrossed** in his work and apparently unconscious of the raging hailstorm. He had set his laptop next to the desktop computer, and he was **manipulating** both ma-chines. He looked at one screen and typed in a string of **es-oteric** commands. Then he turned to the other screen, clicked on various icons, and typed in more **cryptic** commands.

He paused and leaned back in his chair. "Whoa..." He **emitted** a low whistle that was barely **audible** over the ulu-lations of the wind outside. "Uh, guys," he said quietly. "C'mere a second, will you?"

"What's up?" said Orlando, noticing the expression of awe and excitement on his roommate's face.

"You've gotta check this out," Hank said.

Aimee, Angela, and Orlando huddled around the desk and peered at the two screens, which were cluttered with **incomprehensible** computer programming **jargon**. "What *is* that?" asked Aimee.

"That," said Hank, "is something only a select few have ever seen. It was created by and for the technological **elite** and not intended for the eyes of mere mortals like us."

"Okay," said Angela. "And?"

Hank gestured grandly, as if addressing **multitudes**. "I have **infiltrated** a place that was heretofore thought to be **inviolable**. My friends, you are looking at the portal to the sanctum sanctorum of **Omniscience**."

There was a **collective** gasp. **Omniscience** was the campus nickname for the **redoubtable** supercomputer housed in a high-security wing of Irving Laboratory on Science Hill. This awesome machine—which was officially called TWAIN, an acronym for Technology With An **Irrelevant** Name—was **allegedly** faster and more powerful than any computer on earth. It was said to be churning out **abstract theoretical** calculations about all manner of **arcane** subjects, from artificial intelligence and quantum mechanics to **chaos** theory and the fourth dimension. It was also rumored to be engaged in a number of top-secret research projects for the U.S. government.

"Get outta here," said Orlando. "Is this another one of your dumb jokes?"

"No way, dude," Hank protested. "I'm not kidding, I swear. I've been working my way into it since last year. I figured if I could ever manage to get this far I might snag one of the department's **merit** awards."

"Or get your hacker butt kicked out of school," said Angela.

Hank grinned. "Well, nothing ventured, nothing gained." He sat up straight and raised his hands like an orchestra conductor about to launch a symphony. "Okay, everybody, now watch this." With the forefinger of each hand he **simultaneously** pressed the "Enter" keys on the two computers. Both monitors crackled and went blank.

Hank's grin disappeared. "What the hell?"

An **enigmatic** message began scrolling slowly across both screens: *TEMPUS EDAX RERUM ... TEMPUS EDAX RERUM ...*

"That's not my screen saver," said Aimee.

"It's Latin," said Angela, who had studied it at Putnam Academy for three **laborious** but rewarding years. "Wait, I can **decipher** this." She **scrutinized** the message for a moment. "Okay, I think it's 'Time, devourer of all things.'"

As if in answer to her translation, the wind howled and a bucketful of hail splattered against the windowpanes. Then both screens erupted with blinding light.

After what seemed only an instant, during which he felt as if he had been hurtling through space at breakneck speed like a man shot out of a cannon, Mark Twain cautiously opened his eyes and realized he was standing on terra firma—or, to be more precise, on a landing in a stairway. A rather cold and drafty stairway.

Where in the Sam Hill am I? he thought, shivering.

He blinked several times and looked around. Above him, a buzzing electric light **illuminated** the landing. To his left was a wooden door marked E-5. To his right was a wooden door marked E-4. In front of him was a recess in the wall containing a slender red canister with a black, horn-shaped nozzle on top. A small round gauge was **affixed** to the side of the nozzle. What could this be? he wondered. Some sort of spraying device?

Beside the recessed canister was a narrow wooden door that had no doorknob and bore a sign **depicting** what looked like a child's simple and **unsophisticated** line drawing of a woman in a knee-length dress. On an actual woman such a short dress would be **flagrantly unconventional** and **shamelessly alluring.** On the other hand, he thought—recalling, somewhat **wistfully,** his freewheeling life as a young, unmarried bohemian journalist in San Francisco—it might not be an altogether unwelcome sight.

He hesitated a moment, then rapped his knuckles on the knobless door: *tap, tap tap tap—tap tap.* He waited for a response, but there was none. He knocked again, more forcefully this time: TAP, TAP TAP TAP—TAP TAP. Again there was no response. He knocked a third time, even harder: *TAP, TAP TAP TAP—TAP TAP.* The sound **resonated** in the empty, **frigid** stairway. No answer. All right, he thought, let's see what's in here. He gave the door a **tentative** push and found it unlocked. He shoved it partway open and poked his head inside.

Suddenly he heard the door on the right fly open. "Yo!" a man's voice bellowed. "What do you think you're doing in the women's bathroom?"

Aimee opened her eyes and stifled a scream. Had she gone blind? Everything was black. And she could barely breathe. Her nose was pressed against something hard.

Something was tickling Orlando's face. It felt like cobwebs, but heavier. He tried to clear it away with his hands and realized it was hair, a big pile of thick, dark hair. He opened his eyes. What was he doing on the floor, and why was Aimee sprawled on top of him with her face on his chest?

Dozens of microscopic **organisms** floated **randomly** across Angela's blurred field of vision. She shook her head but it didn't help. The **organisms** only turned into a meteor shower of **minute** white spots. She rubbed her eyes and blinked hard, and when things gradually came into focus she realized she was lying under the desk looking at the bottoms of Hank's boots, which were inches from her face. What was she doing here, and how did he manage to fall backward in his chair?

Hank opened his eyes and everything was blank. Slowly he became aware of his own legs **looming** before his face. What was he doing sitting in an overturned chair staring at the ceiling? He groaned and gently **probed** a spot on the back of his head where a goose egg was beginning to form. What is it with me and chairs and hardwood floors? he thought. Then, on the desk above him, next to Aimee's computer, he noticed a foot-high stack of paper bound with string.

"Huh? Where's my laptop?"

"What?" said Angela, carefully removing herself from the **proximity** of Hank's **formidable** boots.

"My laptop. Where is it?"

"How would I know?" said Angela, sliding out from under the desk. "Am I **clairvoyant**?"

Hank struggled to **extricate** himself from the chair. "Well, you did manage to **decipher** that Latin message on the screen. What was it again?"

"Time, devourer of all things."

"Yeah, so where's my laptop?"

"Isn't it right where you left it, butthead?" said Orlando, pushing himself up with one arm and helping Aimee up with the other.

"No it's not, goobatron," said Hank, picking up the chair. "It was right here on the desk before that weird blast of light. Now there's this pile of papers in its place."

"What are those papers, anyway?" asked Aimee.

Hank responded with a **rhetorical question.** "How should I know and why should I care? I want my laptop back." He looked around the room in **vain.**

Orlando was understandably **skeptical.** "Yeah, right," he said. "For all we know you hid it in the closet and you're just trying to psych us out."

"Screw you, dude," Hank said angrily. "I'm not kidding this time. Don't you see? Something really freaky happened when we **infiltrated Omniscience.** And whatever it was, it made my laptop disappear."

Realizing Hank was honestly agitated and not faking this time, Orlando raised his hands in a **placating** gesture. "Okay, man. Just take it easy. We'll figure out what happened and we'll help you find it, all right?"

"Are those your papers, Angela?" asked Aimee, pointing to the stack on the desk.

Angela shook her head. "No, I've never seen them before."

"Orlando?"

"Nope."

Aimee approached the desk. "Well, let's have a look at them."

Just then they heard six rhythmic taps.

"Is somebody knocking on our door?" said Aimee.

"It's kinda late for a visitor, Aims," said Angela.

"Maybe it's the pipes," Hank **speculated.**

"Or maybe it's Poe's raven," Orlando said in an **eerie** and **histrionic** voice, "rapping at your chamber door."

Aimee began to untie the string that bound the bundle of paper. "Hey, wow. This looks like a book written by hand. It says, 'Notice: Persons attempting to find a **motive** in this narrative will be—'"

The tapping came again, louder this time.

Hank peered suspiciously at the door. "It sounds like it's out in the stairwell."

"You think those preppie dorks upstairs are messing with us again?" said Angela.

Before anyone could answer that question, there were six more **aggressive** taps.

"Enough of this crap," said Orlando, striding to the door. He yanked it open and saw a man wearing black trousers, red suspenders, and a starched white shirt sticking his head into Aimee and Angela's bathroom.

Yes, thought Twain in the instant after Orlando's **confrontational** words registered in his brain, this is indeed a well-appointed and rather **commodious** women's bathroom—and one that I am definitely getting my damn-fool **inquisitive** head out of *right now.*

Twain turned and **recoiled** when he saw the young man who had **accosted** him. He was a gangling giant, well over six feet tall, with wavy dark hair and fiery blue eyes. Behind this intimidating behemoth, whose head was as high as the lintel of the doorway, hovered another young man and two young women. This bunch ain't no band of angels comin' for to carry me home, he concluded. "I was only..." he sputtered. "I didn't mean to...It was a mis—"

"Who the hell are you and what are you doing here?" Orlando demanded.

"Uh...well, my friend," Twain croaked nervously, "I can answer the first part of your question with **certainty,** but I must confess to a large degree of **uncertainty** regarding the second part."

Orlando took a step toward him. "This is no time for **levity,** pal."

"Please," Twain said, retreating and raising his hands defensively, "there's no need to **resort** to threats or violence. I assure you I'm not here to do any mischief, and I mean you no harm."

"All right, then," Orlando said, crossing his arms. "Then why were you going into my friends' bathroom in the middle of the night?"

"Well, I wasn't exactly entering it. I was just taking a peek."

"Pretty kinky," Hank said from the doorway.

"Weirdo," Angela said.

"Should I call campus security, Orlando?" asked Aimee, displaying her cellphone.

Could they possibly have a telephone here? Twain thought, eyeing the strange device in Aimee's hand. Perhaps I could ring the house and ask George to come and get me out of this mess.

"Hang on, Aims," Orlando said. "Let's find out a little more about this guy first." He studied the slender, slope-shouldered, middle-aged man who, despite the harsh winter storm, had no jacket or coat and wore black leather slippers instead of shoes or boots. Something about his face—with its heavy eyebrows, drooping mustache, and **prominent** hooked nose—was oddly familiar. "Was that you knocking out here a minute ago?"

"Yes, I was knocking on your bathroom door."

"What for?"

"I wasn't aware it was a bathroom."

"What did you think it was?"

"An apartment, or a room in a boardinghouse, maybe. I rightly don't know. I was just looking for help." As he spoke in a croaking, measured drawl, Twain swayed slowly from side to side. It was one of his **idiosyncrasies**, an **ingrained mannerism** that being in unfamiliar and stressful circumstances always **exacerbated.**

Angela crossed the landing and confronted the mysterious stranger. "Hey mister, have you been drinking?"

"Well, I had a little claret with dinner," the swaying stranger replied, "and a little cognac afterward, and then my usual tumbler of hot whiskey before bed...but I never did make it to bed."

"Where did you go instead?" asked Orlando.

"Up to my billiard room and then here, wherever that is. Where am I, anyway?"

"You seriously don't know where you are?" asked Angela.

The stranger shrugged and shoved four fingers of one hand into the pocket of his trousers. "I'm afraid not. And, quite **frankly,** it's a mystery to me how I got here. All I know is that one minute I was in my own house minding my own business—well, sort of minding it—and the next minute I was in this **alien** place."

"Maybe he's an alien," Hank quipped. "Shall we take him to our leader?"

"Zip it, Morgan," Orlando said sternly. "This is no time for **levity** from you, either."

"I don't think you're inebriated," Angela told the stranger. "You seem quite **rational** and **coherent.**"

"Why thank you, young lady," he replied with a **gracious** nod. "Those are **indispensable attributes** in my line of work."

"Maybe he's got Alzheimer's," offered Hank.

"He's too young for that, silly," said Aimee, elbowing Hank in the ribs.

"How about amnesia?" Hank said.

The stranger shook his head. "I don't think I'm **oblivious** because I can remember exactly what happened. I just don't know *how* it happened."

"Okay," said Orlando. "Then why don't you tell us what happened, and maybe we can help you."

"Well, I was sitting at my desk in the billiard room of my house in Hartford, **emending** the manuscript of my new book, *The Adventures of Hu*—"

"Would that be Hartford, Connecticut?"

"Yes, that's right."

Orlando and Angela exchanged a **skeptical** look. Hartford was a considerable distance away, a substantial drive—especially in a blizzard.

"What, you don't believe me? I live at 351 Farmington Avenue, in the community of Nook Farm, and that's God's honest truth," the stranger **asserted.**

"Major loon," Hank whispered to Aimee. "Probably forgot to take his meds."

"I was trying to retrieve my pen from the floor," the stranger continued, "when I struck my head quite badly. I think I lost consciousness..."

Orlando looked at Angela, who raised a suspicious eyebrow.

"And when I recovered, my manuscript had disappeared and there was a most curious contraption on my desk in its place."

"What did this contraption look like?" said Hank, **intrigued** by all things technical.

"I'd say it looked like a small typewriter inside a **diminutive** traveling bag. But it was made of some smooth, hard material I've never seen before, and half of it was a glass window in which moving words—Latin words—appeared."

"Latin?" Aimee repeated.

"Yes. *Tempus* something or other."

"Really," murmured Angela.

"I fiddled around with this dingus a bit because I'm **insatiably** curious about these things, you see. By and by I pressed some button and there was a terrible blinding explosion of light, and the next thing I know here I am under **interrogation** for **blundering** into your bathroom."

"Hot damn!" Hank exclaimed. "Wait a second, guys." He disappeared into the common room and returned a moment later with Angela's laptop in his hands. "Did that dingus look kind of like this?" he asked.

"Why yes, very much so."

"And does this look familiar?" asked Aimee. She approached the stranger cradling the **ponderous** bundle of paper that had mysteriously replaced Hank's laptop.

"Indeed it does," he said, fairly bouncing with delight. "That's my manuscript."

"What did you say your name was, mister?" asked Angela.

"I didn't. I haven't had half a chance to, what with all this confabulation."

Orlando slapped his forehead in sudden recognition. "Oh my god, you guys!" he cried, pointing his finger at the stranger. "It's ... it's Mark Twain."

"Your **conjecture** is correct, young man. Now, would you kindly tell me where I am?"

Chapter 5

A Connecticut Yankee Holds Court

"Well," said Mark Twain, crossing one leg over the other and lounging in the middle of the leopard-skin sofa with Aimee and Angela beside him, "I suppose I should have known that someday, for my sins, I would die and go to hell or Hadleyburg." He stroked his chin. "I was hoping it would be the former."

Everybody laughed. "But isn't it preferable," said Orlando, who was sprawled in one of the armchairs, "to be alive and at Hadleyburg rather than dead and gone to hell?"

A trace of a smile appeared under the bushy mustache. "Whoever has lived long enough to find out what life is, young man, knows how deep a debt of gratitude we owe to the biblical Adam, the first great **benefactor** of our race."

"Why's that?" asked Hank, who occupied the other armchair.

"He brought death into the world."

Hank scratched his head. "Wow, that's heavy."

"Pardon me?" said Twain.

"He meant that was **profound**," said Angela.

"Thank you for the **clarification**," Twain said. "I can see already that my vocabulary has some catching up to do—

well over a century's worth." He patted the pockets of his trousers. "Ah, just as I feared. I have come to the future **bereft** of my vices. Would any of you happen to have a cigar?"

"I'm sorry, Mr. Twain," said Aimee. "None of us smoke, and smoking's not allowed inside any of the buildings on campus. In fact, hardly anyone smokes anymore. It just isn't cool."

A **conspicuous** furrow appeared in Twain's brow. "How could something as ordinary and **innocuous** as smoking possibly be regarded as daring or **insolent**?"

The students exchanged **perplexed** looks. "Is that what *cool* means to you?" asked Orlando.

"Yes. It's a slang word. Where I come from we use it to mean **offensive** or **impertinent,** overly forward or bold."

"Can you give us an example?" asked Angela.

"Be glad to," Twain said. "That *cool* **scoundrel** horn-swoggled me and stole my horse.'"

"Okay, that makes sense," said Aimee.

"So how do you use *cool*?" asked Twain.

"We use it in lots of ways," said Orlando. "For example, it can mean excellent or enjoyable."

"And we also use it to mean fashionable, stylish, **chic, suave, sophisticated, urbane,**" Angela said without so much as a pause.

Twain chuckled. "That's quite an **obstreperous** mob of synonyms you just trotted out there, young lady. You'd better be careful they don't arm themselves and revolt. So, can you give me an example of how you use it?"

"Sure," said Orlando. "'Millions of readers today think that Mark Twain is a totally *cool* writer with a surprisingly **contemporary** voice.'"

"Suck-up," Hank muttered.

Twain looked at him. "What did you say, young man?"

"Uh...I said...'suck-up'?" Hank replied, squirming a bit in his chair.

"That word sounds rather **unrefined.**"

"It is," said Angela. "It's slang for a **sycophant.**"

"I see," Twain said. "Well, my friends of the future, it certainly is **gratifying** to learn that I will have an **enduring** literary **legacy,** but what would most satisfy me right now, quite **frankly,** is a good smoke."

"But Mr. Twain," said Aimee, "don't you know that smoking is bad for your health?"

"So I am told, but it's never been bad for mine."

"It will kill you eventually," Angela said. "There's **indisputable** scientific evidence that it causes cancer, emphysema, and heart disease."

"And let's not fail to mention," Orlando said, "that, on top of that bad news, smoking stinks like hell."

Twain threw up his hands. "Please, enough!" he begged. "You're all going to lecture me to death before I even have a fair chance to kill myself."

"We're just trying to be helpful," Aimee said.

Twain shook his head in **bewilderment.** "Why is it that no matter what century you happen to live in or occupy at the moment somebody is always trying to reform you, trying to take all the pleasure right out of your life and replace it with **dreariness**?" He looked at the four young faces assembled around him. "Ah, don't bother answering that. It's just a **rhetorical question.** Just tell me, please, is there anywhere I can go at this hour where they'll sell me some cigars?"

"There's the 24/7," Hank said. "It's always open."

"But we can't vouch for the quality of their cigars," said Orlando.

"That's all right," said Twain. "Under the present circumstances, I'm not inclined to be particular."

"In fact, they may not even have any cigars," Orlando added.

"For Pete's sake," Twain said, his voice full of **exasperation,** "then does this shop have anything else that I can smoke?"

"Oh sure," Hank said. "They have lots of cigarettes."

"That'll do in a pinch, and I'm feeling the pinch. Can you tell me how to get to this ... what did you call it?"

"24/7," Hank said.

"That's a peculiar name."

"They call it 24/7 because it's open twenty-four hours a day, seven days a week."

"I see. So how do I get there?"

"But Mr. Twain, you'll freeze to death," said Aimee. "You're not dressed for that terrible blizzard outside. You don't have a coat or even some decent shoes."

"And what about money?" Angela said. "Do you have any?"

"Well, I certainly hope so," Twain replied, "because as I always say, the lack of money is the root of all evil." He stood up and patted all his pockets again. From one of his front pockets he **extracted** a rumpled handkerchief and a few coins. "Thirty-two cents," he announced. "How distressing. I'm afraid I've come to the future not only underdressed but also impecunious."

"We could spot you a few frogskins," said Orlando.

"Pardon me?"

"He means lend you some money," said Hank.

"Ah, I see. What an interesting image that **evokes**. My favorite slang term for money is *spondulicks*. At any rate, yes, I'd be much **obliged** if I could borrow 'a few frogskins.' But what shall we do about my inadequate **attire**?"

Twain was still blissfully **oblivious** of just how woefully inadequate his **attire** was, but Aimee and Angela weren't. From their perspective, sitting on the sofa behind him, they couldn't help noticing the long tear down the back of the famous writer's pants that he had sustained during the trouser-rending **exertions** of his crazy dance. To make matters worse, a fluffy portion of his boxer shorts **protruded** from the split, making his rear end look like a cup of latte brimming over with foam. Aimee looked at Angela, who looked at Aimee, and both struggled mightily not to crack up.

Aimee tried to be **tactful.** "Mr. Twain, maybe you should start by borrowing a pair of pants from Hank. The two of you look about the same size." Angela was less **discreet.** She squeezed her nose to stifle her laughter. Twain turned around to respond, and instantly Orlando and Hank **perceived** the cause of Aimee and Angela's **clandestine** hilarity. Orlando clapped his hand over his mouth. Hank snorted.

"Is something the matter with my trou—" The word caught in Twain's throat. A **furtive** grope behind **confirmed** his **predicament:** He had forgotten to change his pants!

His faced turned watermelon red as everyone burst out laughing.

A few minutes later Mark Twain, nursing a wounded **ego,** trudged up the steps of entryway G behind Hank and Orlando. He had one of Angela's blankets wrapped around his shoulders and the manuscript of *Huckleberry Finn* tucked under his arm. "You have seen how a man was made a **buffoon,**" he muttered to himself. "Now you shall see how a **buffoon** is made a man."

They reached the landing for suite G-8. "I want to thank you boys for your generous offer of hospitality during my **sojourn** here," Twain said. "I don't know what kind of trouble I'd be in without your help."

"Hey, don't mention it," said Orlando. "It's the least we can do for a major celebrity from another century."

As Orlando dug in the pocket of his jeans for the key, Twain read the sign on the door aloud. "'ALL YE WHO ENTER HERE, **ABANDON** HOPE AND HOLD YOUR NOSE.' That's not exactly an **auspicious** greeting. Are you trying to scare people off?"

"Nope," said Hank. "Just trying to be honest."

"Let's just say we're not known for our **meticulous** housekeeping," Orlando said, opening the door. "Welcome to our **humble** abode, Mr. Twain."

A faint aroma of decomposition wafted into the stairwell. Twain sniffed and **detected** the mingled smells of mildew and male body odor. There was also a **pungent** smell suggestive of horse urine. He **suppressed** the urge to hold his nose. So how bad could it be? he thought as Orlando and Hank entered ahead of him. He stepped boldly into the room and **assessed** his new quarters.

"Holy mother of . . . codfish!" he cried, letting go of Angela's blanket and clutching his throat. He dropped his manuscript on the blanket, then yanked his handkerchief from his pocket and covered his mouth and nose. "This is the filthiest, foulest, most **malodorous** apartment I have ever had the sad luck to lay eyes upon. Why, a chicken ranch smells better than this place. It looks like a pigsty after a tornado."

"Thanks," said Orlando. "That's the most flattering thing anybody's ever said about it. Hey Hank, maybe we should put that one on the door—**attributed** to Mark Twain, no less. Whaddaya think?"

"I think we should get this guy into some of my clothes, get him down to the 24/7 for some smokes, and get back here for some shut-eye," Hank replied, casting off his coat and flopping into the battered armchair, "so we can all get up early and try to figure out how in the hell to get my laptop back and get his butt back to the nineteenth century where it damn well belongs."

Orlando cast a concerned look at his friend. "Hey, what's eating you, man?"

Hank shook his head. "You can't figure it out, manure brains? Do I have to write it on the freakin' wall for you?"

Writing on the wall would do little to improve the ambience, Twain thought.

"Yo, chill, Morgan," Orlando said, removing his coat and sitting down on the couch. "We've got a gentleman from the Victorian **era** present who's not going to tolerate us swearing and dissing each other."

"On the contrary, young man," Twain drawled through his handkerchief, "the idea that no gentleman ever swears is all wrong. He can swear and still be a gentleman if he does it in a nice and **benevolent** and affectionate way. I'm not offended in the least by indelicate language, provided there is a sufficient and appropriate **stimulus** for it. In certain trying circumstances, urgent circumstances, desperate circumstances, profanity furnishes a relief denied even to prayer. Naturally, I make every effort to draw the line when ladies are present." He paused. "And every effort to cross it when they are not," he added with a wink. He stepped carefully over a flattened fast-food bag **adorned** with ketchup and french fries and laid a sympathetic hand on Hank's shoulder. "What's **vexing** you, my boy? Maybe I can help."

"Aw hell, Mr. Twain," Hank said. "I'm just confused—and upset."

"That much is clear. Can you **clarify** why?"

"This whole business is my fault."

"What whole business?"

"This business of you and your manuscript of *Huckleberry Finn* being in the present and my laptop being in the past."

"And why do you feel **culpable**?"

"Because it was my **arrogant meddling** with **Omniscience** that made it happen."

Twain looked puzzled. "Are you saying you're some kind of **presumptuous** know-it-all?"

Hank managed to laugh in spite of himself. "No, sir. Not at all. I'm saying I'm a **complacent** fool who thought he could take on something a lot more **formidable** than he ever imagined." Hank explained the situation as best he could given the **disparity** in their technical knowledge. Twain was so **enthralled** that he sat down on the couch and, throwing caution to the wind, removed the handkerchief from his face.

"So all by your whippersnapper self," he said, "you figured out how to penetrate the **obscure** workings of this **redoubtable** machine?"

"Well, kind of," Hank replied.

"Using only that little flat typewriter that appeared on my desk?"

"Yeah. It's called a laptop."

"And what did you say it was made of?"

"Plastic."

Twain stroked his chin. "I still can't get over how much smaller and lighter it was than the newfangled typewriter I fell in love with back in 1874. That **cumbersome** contraption cost me a whopping $125. But it proved useful nevertheless, once I could figure out how to punch those damn keys, which had an annoying habit of **congregating** unannounced and refusing to **disperse**—not unlike that typesetter I've been promoting." He ran a hand through his thick shock of graying hair. "But I **digress.** So you're telling me I traveled here through some **intangible realm** called 'the Internet'?"

"Right, as far as I can tell," Hank said. "Except for one problem."

"And what is that?"

"It's totally not possible to send **tangible,** nondigital stuff over the Net. It's, like, right out of *Star Trek.* I mean, meatspace can't interact with cyberspace, at least not yet."

"Please, young man, speak English—nineteenth-century English."

"I'm sorry. What I mean is, we haven't figured out how to send **material** things over the Internet, just things that are in digital—I mean electronic—code."

"Is that anything like Morse code?"

"Yeah, sort of, but a heck of a lot more **complex.** Computers don't just send short, individual messages like telegraphy. They can store **vast** amounts of data on these **minute** semiconductors called microchips, and they can download or upload—I mean transfer—that data to other computers in a matter of seconds."

"By 'data' I assume you mean 'facts' or 'information'?"

"That's right."

"And about how many words would **constitute** 'vast amounts of data'?"

"For the computers most of us use, many millions of words, but for a humongous network of computers or for a **gargantuan** supercomputer like **Omniscience** it would be countless billions, or even trillions, and I'm not exaggerating. In fact, that's probably an understatement. Think about all the books ever written, and then some."

Twain's bushy eyebrows rose sharply, then quickly resumed their normal position. "Why, that's nothing, a mere **trifle,**" he **scoffed,** waving his hand.

Hank and Orlando exchanged an **incredulous** look. "You're kidding, right?" said Hank.

"Not at all," Twain said. "When you said '**vast,**' I thought you meant something *truly* **vast.**" He coughed dryly into his handkerchief. "Not something *half* **vast.**"

It took a moment for the play on words to sink in, then Hank and Orlando groaned: *half **vast**, half assed.*

"You had us going there for a minute, Mr. Twain," Hank said, shaking his head.

"Yeah," said Orlando. "We knew you were a humorist, but we didn't know you were a punster."

Twain pulled at his mustache. "My friends, to succeed in this life one must be a jack-of-all-trades—and a master of pun. But please," he said to Hank, "tell me the rest of the story."

"Well, when I finally plugged into **Omniscience,** I thought it was just going to be sort of a joyride, you know what I mean?"

"No, I'm afraid I don't," Twain replied. "What's a 'joyride'?"

"It's a wild and **reckless** ride in an automobile," Orlando said, "just for a thrill."

Twain looked puzzled. "What's an 'automobile'?"

Orlando laughed and looked at Hank. "Man," he said, pointing his thumb at Twain, "do we have some explaining to do with this nineteenth-century dude, or what?"

"Excuse me, Mr. Ortiz, but I am **decidedly** *not* a dude," Twain said **abruptly.**

The writer's sudden **brusqueness,** his **reproachful** tone of voice, and his lowering expression all took Orlando by surprise. "What's the matter?"

Twain thrust an index finger at him. "*Dude* is one word I *do* know the meaning of, young man, and it's not something I will tolerate being called."

Now it was Orlando's turn to look **perplexed.** "I was just joking around. How did I offend you?"

"You called me a 'nineteenth-century dude,' did you not?"

"What's wrong with that?"

"It's a brazen **affront** to my manhood and self-respect."

"Huh?" Orlando glanced at Hank, who shrugged in commiseration with his confusion. "I don't get it. Calling you a dude is an insult?"

"You bet it is, boyo. That word denotes a fop, a dandy, a **preening** popinjay."

"And what the heck are those?" asked Orlando.

"Yeah, really," echoed Hank.

"They all **signify** a man who is **vain,** overrefined, **pretentious,** and effeminate, and particularly one who is excessively **fastidious** about his clothes and grooming. Out

West they also use *dude* to mean a city person, a tenderfoot, somebody laughably unaccustomed to the **rigors** of **rural** life."

"Yeah, I've heard about that kind of dude," Orlando said, "but I didn't know about the **vain** and **fastidious** one."

"Do you see now why I thought you were being **impertinent**?"

Orlando nodded. "I'm sorry I insulted you. I certainly didn't mean to. That's so weird, how such a simple word can be **ambiguous** and **misinterpreted**. Today we use *dude* to mean just a guy, a man—or as you might say, Mr. Twain, a fellow."

"Well, I'm afraid that in my hopelessly **archaic** lexicon, *dude* is still a pejorative term. You may call each other whatever you like, but please refrain from applying that particular epithet to me."

"I will, sir," Orlando said **sincerely.**

"Thank you," Twain said. He ran his fingers through his hair and looked at Hank. "Now, Mr. Morgan, as you were saying?"

"Saying what?"

"Something about going on a joyride?" Twain prompted.

"Oh, right." Hank cleared his throat. "So anyway, instead of going on a harmless joyride through the **obscure labyrinth** of a supercomputer, I think I wound up accessing the fourth dimension."

"And what, pray tell, is the 'fourth dimension'?" Twain asked.

"Time," Hank replied in a **solemn** voice. "I think **Omniscience** is somehow capable of **conveying** things through time, and it was just my dumb luck to stumble into the transmission room and **unwittingly** push the button marked 'Transport.'"

There was a moment of silence as they **contemplated** the **gravity** of this **hypothesis**. Then Twain jumped up and clapped his hands together. "My boy," he exclaimed, beginning to pace the cluttered room and then thinking better of it, "you are far too **modest** about your gifts. You are going to go down as one of the **paramount** geniuses of the twenty-first century. Just look at what you've done."

"Yeah, I *am* looking. That's the problem."

"Problem? What problem? Why, your **exalted** achievement will outshine the invention of the telegraph, the telephone, and the cotton gin."

"It will?"

"Of course it will. Morse, Bell, and Whitney can't hold a candle to you—and I daresay even Edison would have trouble **illuminating** you with his miraculous lightbulb. Hank, don't you realize what you've managed to do?"

"Yeah, I think so. I've thrown a major wrench in the works."

"Don't be ridiculous, son. You've succeeded in doing something generations of **ingenious** minds have only been able to dream of," Twain said in a **grandiose** croak. "You, Hank Morgan, have **unraveled** the **impenetrable** mystery of time!"

Hank was unimpressed. "With all due respect, Mr. Twain," he said with an **impassive** expression, "I don't know diddly-squat about time, and I know even less about traveling through it."

This **straightforward** admission of ignorance took the wind out of the famous writer's sails. "But surely you must've known that this would—"

"Nope. I had no idea something like this would happen." Hank took a deep breath and let it out slowly. "One of the **fundamental principles** of scientific inquiry—which I'm sure you're familiar with—is that the results of an experiment must be repeatable to be considered **credible**."

"Yes, I'm familiar with that **doctrine**."

"Well, I haven't a clue how to repeat what I did. Hell, I'm not sure I even *know* what I did."

Twain looked crestfallen. "So does this mean I may not be able to . . . get back?"

"To be **candid,** yes."

"C'mon, Hank," Orlando **interjected.** "There's got to be something we can do."

"Like what?"

"You can't hack into **Omniscience** from another unit?"

"Nice try, pal. Problem is, everything I need is on my laptop, which right now is apparently enjoying early **obsolescence** in the nineteenth century. My whole **intellectual** life is on that machine and I don't know what I can do without it—except maybe fail all my courses and alter American literary history."

Orlando wagged a reproving finger at his friend. "So is Joe Cyberjock saying he neglected to make backups?"

"Very funny, fartface. If you weren't such a giraffe, I'd wring your stupid neck."

"Bring it on, butt lips."

"Gentlemen, let us please avoid a violent **altercation,**" Twain said in an **authoritative** voice. "Fisticuffs and dynamite are best left to the low and **unrefined.**"

The **feuding** roommates ignored him.

"Scab sucker," Hank said.

"Toe jam taster," Orlando replied.

"Gentlemen!" Twain repeated, this time in a stentorian voice. "There is nothing so annoying as to have two people go right on talking when you're interrupting."

That got their attention.

"Now," Twain continued, "unless you care to watch me lose my sanity and commit an unconscionable crime, will you kindly make good on your offer to furnish me with some appropriate clothes and take me out to buy some dang cigars?"

Twain emerged from Hank's bedroom, which he had found only marginally less **repugnant** than the common room.

To his surprise and relief, the clothes Hank had offered him were reasonably clean. "How do I look?" he asked, spreading his arms.

"Sort of like me with a mustache and a bunch of gray hair—and that's a scary thought," said Hank with a gulp. "But I think you'll pass for a twenty-first-century dude."

Twain scowled at him.

"*Oops*—I mean 'guy.' Sorry."

Twain turned to Orlando. "What do you think?"

Orlando scratched the stubble on his chin and **contemplated** the curious spectacle standing before him. In the photographs he had seen of Twain the **eminent** writer usually wore a conservative black or white three-piece suit and sometimes an old-fashioned top hat or derby. Now he was dressed in heavy leather work boots, white sweatsocks, baggy black denim cargo pants, and a maroon hooded sweatshirt emblazoned, in the slapdash style of the graffitist, with the words SAPPNIN BRO?

"Well," Orlando said, trying not to grin too **conspicuously,** "in the Linnaean system of taxonomy I think you would probably be **classified** as a member of the **species** *Homo hip-hoppicus.*"

"Do you mean," said Twain, "that I look—as you use the word—*cool*?"

Orlando laughed. "Way cool, my man."

"Good. I don't want to seem like an **anomaly.** It's important to blend in."

"Actually, in that gear I think you may stand out."

"That's all right, I guess," Twain said. "You know that **cliché,** 'Clothes make the man'? Well, it's true. Naked people have little or no influence in society."

Orlando chuckled. "You're a pretty funny guy, Mr. Twain."

"C'mon," said Hank, grabbing his coat, "let's blow this poopsicle stand."

"I really must tell you," Twain croaked as the three-some headed out the door and down the stairs, "that this...this—confound it, what did you call that seam of brass again? Oh yes, now I remember. This *zipper* that you've got to close up your trousers. My, that's a marvelous thing! What an improvement over all those blasted buttons. But you boys should have warned me that operating it can be a rather **hazardous enterprise.** I came damn near to losing an **indispensable** appendage—and I don't mean my finger!"

Chapter 6

Innocence Abroad

It was almost three o'clock in the morning when they hit the street. The storm had **abated**. The hail had **ceased,** the wind was relatively calm, and now only a **continuous** shower of powdery flakes floated gently down.

Mark Twain took a deep breath of the cold night air and exhaled a burst of steam that **dissipated** as swiftly as it had appeared. "You know, it's strange," he said, "but the future *smells* different."

"Really?" said Orlando. "How so?"

"It's not as fresh somehow. Nineteenth-century air has **zest.** You can taste it. Your air seems **insipid,** maybe even a bit **unsavory.**"

They had just passed through the iron gate of Stormfield College—one of Hadleyburg's twelve residential colleges—and were crunching down the deserted, snow-covered sidewalk of Village Road. On their right **loomed** the **imposing** walls of the Gothic revival college. On their left was a line of vehicles parked along the street, their roofs and hoods and bumpers bedizened with a thick layer of glistening snow.

"If the future smells different to you, it's probably because of these," said Hank, pointing to the row of vehicles.

"They're called automobiles or, more commonly, cars. You'll see various **prototypes** on the road as early as the 1890s."

"Really?" said Twain. He approached one of the cars and peered into it. "So this horseless carriage is what you take joyrides in?"

Orlando laughed. "Yeah, but most people use their cars the same **utilitarian** way you use a horse and buggy, to do **mundane** errands and get from point A to point B."

"I wonder if I should invest in them when I get back to 1883," Twain said. "Judging by how many are on this street alone, it seems a **lucrative prospect.**"

"It probably would be," said Hank, "but there's a downside to the automobile that may not sit well with your conscience—at least where **posterity** is concerned."

"And what is that?" Twain asked as they resumed strolling down the street.

"Most cars are propelled by something called an internal **combustion** engine," Hank explained, "and this engine burns a fuel called gasoline, which is made from oil. Since the early 1900s millions of cars have been burning billions of gallons of gas every year, and this has released **innumerable** tons of carbon monoxide and other **noxious** chemicals into the earth's atmosphere. This air pollution is probably what you're smelling. To make things worse, the emissions from cars are gradually destroying the ozone layer."

"What's the ozone layer?" asked Twain.

"A part of the upper atmosphere that absorbs harmful ultraviolet light from the sun. The more damage is done to the ozone layer, the warmer the whole planet gets and the more **vulnerable** to the sun it becomes."

"So are you saying that by driving your cars you are slowly destroying the earth?"

"Basically, yes. And not all that slowly, if you think

about it. Cars have been **mass**-produced for not much more than a century."

"Which is but a scintilla in the **infinite** scheme of time," said Orlando.

"Nice **alliteration**, my boy," Twain said. "You have a natural poetic **diction**." He cleared his throat. "But getting back to these cars. If you'll allow me to **speculate**, I'll bet that people find them such a suitable and **expedient mode** of transportation that nobody cares to work up a solution to the problem."

Hank nodded. "You said it, du—I mean *man*. And it's kind of frustrating because we have the technological capability to manufacture cars that don't pollute—that are powered by electric motors or hydrogen fuel cells, for example—but we seem to be suffering from a severe case of **complacency**."

"Not to mention **avarice**," Orlando said, "because when it comes to protecting profits, the oil interests might as well be a **monopoly**. In the meantime," he added, pointing to an elephantine SUV, "these **gargantuan** beasts of the road keep getting bigger and more **ravenous**."

"Not unlike a lot of the people who choose to drive them," Hank added.

"Such is the human race—**self-righteous, self-serving,** and **self-indulgent**," Twain said, shaking his head sadly. "Often it does seem such a pity that Noah didn't miss the boat."

They came to the end of the block and crossed Charter Road with the **voluble** writer marveling at every newfangled thing in sight: the brilliant, buzzing streetlights; the telephone poles with their tangle of wires; the **autonomous** traffic lights and the monitory, blinking hands of the crossing signals; the **luminous** neon signs glowing above the darkened windows of the stores; a row of parking meters rising like sturdy, metallic stalks of corn.

A **massive** snowplow growled past them, and he marveled at the thunderous sound of it and the swath of paved road that it exposed. He marveled at the pay phone planted in the sidewalk, available for all to use, and marveled even more at its **monotonous** dial tone and the peculiar gray buttons that beeped in the receiver when he pressed them. Somewhat **incoherently,** he marveled at a **gaudy** billboard for women's clothing featuring an **immense,** glamorous woman wearing precious little of it. And when they approached an empty bus kiosk, he marveled at the sea of notices and broadsides that had been affixed to it at **random,** especially the ones advertising concerts by bands with strange and **sensational** names like Strut Yo Stuff, Skanky-Panky, and Onan Up to It. While Hank and Orlando **indulged** him, hopping up and down to keep warm, he studied these messages with the intensity of a dog boldly sniffing out **uncharted** territory. But when it became clear to them that he was not going to **desist** until he had **perused** every last one, they **endeavored** to tear him away.

"C'mon, Mr. Twain," said Hank, grabbing his arm, "wouldn't you rather die from smoking than freeze to death?"

"You're damn tootin'," Twain replied, rubbing his hands together, partly in **expectation** and partly to warm them up. "How far is it to that dadblamed 24/7?"

"It's around the corner," said Orlando, "but first we need to get some *dinero.*"

"Eh?" Twain cocked his head.

"Frogskins," Orlando said. "Just follow us. *¡Vámonos!*"

At the next corner they turned right onto Anchor Street. Twenty yards up they stopped in front of a shiny metal machine **ensconced** in the wall of a brownstone building. The recessed device was **illuminated** from above by a strong floodlight attached to the wall. It had a small glass screen on which were displayed the words Welcome to Hadleyburg Mutual—Please Insert Your Card.

"What is this contraption?" Twain asked.

"An ATM," said Hank. "That's an initialism for automated teller machine."

Twain watched with **keen** curiosity as his companions took turns using wafer-thin rectangular cards to retrieve a familiar cluster of green paper from the machine.

Witnessing this mechanical monetary legerdemain, the writer was **exuberant**. "That's incredible!" he cried. "Mammon at your fingertips in the middle of the night!" But then he grew **pensive**. "Doesn't such easy access to money tempt people to borrow **capriciously** and get mired in debt?"

"With a credit card, yes," said Orlando. "But with these ATM cards we don't have unrestricted access to money. We just can get to what little we have whenever we want. The **innovations** of your century were all about saving time and money, labor and lives, Mr. Twain. The **innovations** of today are all about convenience. The **prevailing ethos** is comfort. People like things easy, fast, and **plentiful**."

Behind his mustache, Twain grinned. "I think I could get used to that."

"I'll bet you could," Orlando said, "but convenience has its price."

"What do you mean?" Twain asked.

"You'll see in a minute," Orlando replied **cryptically**. He turned and strode up the street and Hank fell in beside him.

"Well, isn't that one the **brooding** young social philosopher," Twain said under his breath as he hustled to catch up.

Unlike Village Road, which had been **devoid** of **inhabitants**, Anchor Street **manifested** some **minimal** signs of life. They passed a homeless man curled up in a doorway on a flattened cardboard box, with only a **threadbare** blanket to shield him from the cold. A small group of students hurried past them going the opposite way, **engrossed** in an **obscure** discussion about Marxist economic theory and Social Darwinism. And they passed an all-night greasy spoon called Yankee Doodle Diner where a solitary customer sat at the counter, **avidly** tucking into a steaming plate of ham and eggs.

Several doors down from the diner a **conspicuous** neon sign **protruded** from the wall above a dark, recessed doorway. Twain spied it and immediately his curiosity was **aroused.** ANCHOR BAR, it read in **radiant** green, and below that, in somewhat smaller orange letters, was the blinking message BEER—COCKTAILS—POOL. Now there, he thought, are three of the most **exquisitely harmonious** words in the English language.

"Is this saloon open?" he asked as they approached.

"No," Orlando said. "By law, the bars here close at 2:00 A.M."

"Shucks," Twain drawled. "Why should those danged legislators care what hour the saloons open and close? At this time of night the **virtuous** politician is asleep, and all the rest of 'em are in the brothels."

"This place'll be open again at six," Hank said, "if you feel like getting up early and knocking back a few."

While Hank and Orlando shared a laugh at the risqué **notion** of Mark Twain imbibing in a sleazy bar at dawn, the writer silently **resolved** to visit the place at his earliest opportunity—though not before breakfast, of course. Then he remembered his favorite billiards cue was stuck in the **inaccessible** past. He would have to make do with whatever abused and battered sticks they might have on hand.

They reached the end of the block. Across the street, **basking** in its own **garish** electric glare like a soi-disant celebrity, was the 24/7. This squat, beige building was

notable only for the **nondescript** dullness of its design. As if to disguise this **inescapable** fact, someone had had the **dubious** inspiration to dress up nearly every inch of the drab cinder block walls and the disproportionately large picture windows with a **random** assortment of **vulgar** ads for beer and soft drinks and cigarettes.

From the corner, Twain regarded the building. "Gentlemen," he said, "I can **assert** with the utmost confidence that your 24/7 is the ugliest, most misbegotten **edifice** I have ever seen. It's an **affront** to the very **concept** of architecture."

"Tell me about it," said Hank. "And there are tons more of them scattered all over the country."

"Welcome to modern **urban** America," said Orlando in an **ironic** tone of voice, "proud home of those **epochal** architectural **innovations** known as the fast-food palace, the strip mall, the business park, and the convenience store."

"I think 'business park' may be an oxymoron," Twain said as they crossed the icy street.

At the entrance to the store Hank paused and grabbed Orlando's sleeve. "Hey, shouldn't we give the man some dough?"

"Oh, yeah, I almost forgot," Orlando said. He removed a twenty-dollar bill from his wallet and handed it to Twain. Hank did the same.

"Holy spondulicks, boys," Twain croaked. "Two double sawbucks is downright **munificent** of you. That's more than my butler George makes in a whole month!" This should get me a week's worth of cigars with a few dozen to spare, he thought as he **scrutinized** the two bills. Their design was different and there was a different president **depicted** on them, but they had the unmistakable feel of **bona fide** American money.

Orlando opened the wide glass door and a wave of warm air escaped from the building. "And now for a crash course in **contemporary** American culture," he said, motioning grandly for the writer to enter.

They stepped inside as several piercing beeps from the door's electronic **sensor** announced their arrival. Twain pushed back the thick hood of his sweatshirt and surveyed the brightly **illuminated** room. Everywhere he looked there were shelving units and racks and counters and refrigerated cases displaying an **abundance**—an overabundance, it seemed to him—of everyday items for sale. While Hank and Orlando browsed the magazine rack, Twain wandered the narrow aisles of the store, gawking. He studied the **plethora** of snacks and candy bars and gum. He gave the puffy bags of corn chips and cheese curls a **furtive** squeeze and wondered what these crunchy treats tasted like. He lingered over the pharmaceuticals, examining with wonder the shampoos, hair sprays, styling gels, and deodorants and the preparations for headaches, colds, diarrhea, athlete's foot, and other **commonplace ailments.**

He opened the glass panel doors of a beverage cooler— every one of them in succession, thrusting his head inside each time and peering around for the source of the artificially produced cold air. He lost count of all the different brands of beer and soft drinks on display. He was repulsed by the synthetic appearance of some sandwiches wrapped in shiny, transparent film. He **pondered** the polysyllabic mystery of the word *microwavable,* which he spotted on various boxes of apparently frozen food. One of them, labeled Personal Pizza Pizzazz, featured a picture of something round that looked rather messy and greasy but **savory** nonetheless. And finally he stood in awe before an **imposing** machine studded with colorful buttons, trying to figure out what it was designed to do. **Recklessly** yielding to an **impulse** to experiment, he reached out and pressed one of the buttons.

"Holy smokes!" he yelped as a thick stream of liquid

spewed out of an invisible orifice, splattered off the drip grid, and spilled onto the floor. "Help!"

Orlando and Hank **abandoned** their magazines and rushed to his aid. "You okay?" asked Orlando.

"Yes, I'm fine," Twain said, wiping a wet spot on his sweatshirt with his fingers, "but I'm afraid the floor isn't. That Big Chug machine just vomited Fountain Goo."

"I'll tell the guy on duty," said Hank. He approached the cashier, a pimply-faced twentysomething who appeared to be taking a nap in a chair behind the counter. "Uh, excuse me, but there's, like, a major spill on the floor over by the Big Chug."

The **somnolent** clerk opened his eyes halfway and nodded thoughtfully. "I know. There usually is. Do you want to clean it up?"

"Huh? Are you kidding? That's *your* job, isn't it?"

"Not if I can get away with it. And I can."

"All right, forget it. I'll deal with it." Hank looked around, found a napkin dispenser, grabbed a handful, and returned to the scene of the crime. "Here," he said, tossing the paper on the floor and mopping up the spill with his foot. He picked up the sodden bundle and deposited it in a nearby plastic trash bin.

"Thanks," said Twain. "I'm sorry I made a mess. Everything here is just so...unfamiliar."

"No problem," Hank said. "So can we get your smokes and go now?"

"Of course." Twain looked around. "Where are they?"

"Over by the cashier, I think," said Orlando.

Hank and Orlando returned to the magazine rack as Twain went to the counter. "Pardon me, young man," he said to the dozing cashier. "Do you have any cigars?"

The cashier opened his eyes halfway again and attempted to focus them on the writer. "Sure we do," he said. "What kind you want?" He leaned back in his chair, stretched his arms, and let loose a yawn so huge and **histrionic** that for several seconds Twain had an unobstructed view of the uvula hanging down in the back of his throat.

"What kind do you have?" said Twain. "I usually smoke the six-centers. They're a lot more **tolerable** than the cheap ones. Why, I remember when I was in Hawaii, and the only cigars they had were those **trifling, insipid,** tasteless, flavorless things they call Manilas—ten for twenty-five cents. It would take a thousand of them to be worth half the money."

"Yeah, whatever," the cashier said with another **immense** yawn. He pointed with his thumb to a small display case at the end of the counter. "They're over there."

Twain walked over to the case and examined its contents. Just my luck, he thought, rubbing his chin. It's slim pickings at the slop bucket. There were only two kinds of cigars, both unappealing: individually wrapped stogies— cheap, roughly made cigars—and short, slender cigarillos packaged in boxes of five. He picked up a sample of each and walked back to where the **listless** cashier was sitting, squeezing a pimple on his nose. "How much are they?" he asked, holding them up for the cashier to see.

"Those are a buck-fifty," answered the **lethargic** cashier, pointing to the stogie. "And the box is $4.99." Having supplied the **relevant** information, the cashier crossed his arms, slumped down in his chair with his chin on his chest, and closed his eyes.

For a moment Twain was too **flabbergasted** to speak. "I'm sorry, young man, but did I hear you correctly?"

"Huh?" came the mumbled reply.

"Did you say a *dollar-fifty* and *four-ninety-nine*?"

"Uh-huh."

"Why, that's a staggering sum! An outrageous sum! A mind-boggling sum!"

The **apathetic** cashier yawned and half opened his

eyes. "You don't like the price, don't buy the product—simple as that, pal."

"But how is it possible, or even **conceivable**," Twain said, swaying from side to side, his gravelly voice rising with emotion, "that an ordinary, **humble** cigar—just a **transient diversion**, an **ephemeral gratification**, a transitory scrap of satisfaction in this vale of tears—could be so dear?" He shook his head sadly. "I'm afraid this means I shall have to drastically **curtail** my **indulgence**."

The **phlegmatic** cashier looked **perplexed**. "Mister, have you been drinking?"

"What business is that of yours?"

"Because we don't allow no winos in here. It's management policy."

Twain stiffened. "Are you **implying** I'm an inebriate?"

"What's 'a need be it'?"

"I said *inebriate*. Are you suggesting that I'm a drunk?"

"Yeah—I don't know—maybe," said the **indecisive** cashier, picking absentmindedly at another **prominent** eruption on his face. "Look, mister, you talk funny, you ain't too steady on your feet, and you look like an old fart dressed up in young guy's clothes. To me that says you're probably one of those guys who hang out on the street, get wasted on cheap booze, and toss their cookies outside my store. Working nights here I've seen a lotta messed-up dudes like you."

"I see," Twain said, frowning and fixing the cashier with steely eyes. "Well then, young fella," he drawled, "seeing as you've taken the liberty of **gratuitously** insulting me and **initiating** the name-calling, I am **compelled** to respond in kind, *par pari refero.** You are an embarrassment to the **species** *Homo sapiens,* a worthless, good-for-nothing, low-down, no-account, **despicable, indolent, boorish,** pustulat-

---

*Latin for *tit for tat,* repayment in kind, retaliation; **literally,** "I return like for like."

ing jackass who ought to be **flogged** with a hickory switch from here to kingdom come for your **impertinence!**"

Now it was the cashier's turn to be **flabbergasted.** Before he could figure out how to respond to that **barrage** of **eloquent invective,** or even **contemplate** what it meant, Hank and Orlando were at Twain's side, inquiring and **solicitous.** "What's the matter?" they asked. "Are you okay?"

"Yes, I'm fine," Twain **asserted.** "But this **presumptuous,** suppurating stripling apparently finds it more amusing to offend his customers than to do his job. He made a **derogatory allegation** that he can't **substantiate.**"

"He was bitchin' about the price of the cigars," the cashier protested. "I don't have to put up with that crap at three in the morning. Like, where did you find this guy, anyway? Hanging out in a doorway with a bottle in a paper bag?"

"You see?" said Twain. "There he goes again, **insinuating derogatory** things."

"Dude, this guy is my uncle," Hank said, glaring at the pimply cashier.

"And if you don't like working nights," Orlando said, leaning over the counter, "maybe you should get a day job—cleaning toilets."

Just then the door swung open, the **sensor** beeped **raucously,** and a young woman and a young man swept in. The **altercation** with the cashier was forgotten for the moment as all eyes turned to **assess** the new arrivals.

Chapter 7

Roughing It

The woman was tall and shapely, with a **pallid** face and black lipstick that **complemented** her jet-black hair. She wore a long, furry, black-and-white coat that looked as if it had been assembled from the hides of various hapless skunks. As she stepped inside the warm environment of the store she let the front of the coat fall open, revealing a **taut** white lowcut sweater, a short black leather skirt, and fishnet stockings that disappeared just below her knees into a pair of spike-heeled black leather boots.

The man was another matter. He was nearly as tall as Orlando, with wavy dark hair and eyes, long sideburns, a pockmarked but still handsome face, and a downy, **juvenile** mustache sprouting over a slightly **sinister** mouth. His **extravagant attire** was a mishmash of **genteel** fashion from some bygone **era.** The last owner of his long brown overcoat could have been Sherlock Holmes, for it was an inverness, a flowing woolen cloak with a short, detachable cape. On his head he sported a **jaunty** Scottish tam-o'-shanter, and in his hand he gripped the carved ivory handle of a slender, mahogany walking stick.

Twain took one look at him and said to Orlando and Hank, sotto voce, "Now *that,* my friends, is a *dude.*"

"And *that*," Hank whispered back, "is Big O's ex-girlfriend."

Twain let out a soft whistle and looked at Orlando. "That dame from the demimonde was your gal?"

"For an instant in the wind," Orlando said, staring at his former flame with revived longing. His phrase was an **allusion** to a **stanza** in Hart Crane's poem "The Broken Tower" that Tennessee Williams used as the epigraph to his play *A Streetcar Named Desire*. Once, in a moment of romantic **abandon**, Orlando had quoted the **stanza** aloud in a **vain** attempt to impress his inamorata. The romantic moment had backfired and left him feeling foolish, but the **lush** and lovelorn lines remained fresh in his mind:

> And so it was I entered the broken world
> To trace the **visionary** company of love, its voice
> An instant in the wind (I know not whither hurled)
> But not for long to hold each desperate choice.

The **flamboyant** couple approached the counter.

"Ah, well, well, well, look who we have here, *eh-heh, eh-heh*," said the young man in a raspy, high-pitched voice oozing with **sarcasm**. He stopped in front of Orlando and tapped his walking stick smartly on the linoleum floor. "If it isn't the **formidable** Señor Ortiz, the **virile** vaquero from Brownsville, with his bedraggled band of buckaroos. *Buenas nachos, moo-chachos.*"

Ever since freshman year, when they were thrown together in a suite composed of six **randomly** assigned roommates from **diverse** backgrounds and far-flung places, Orlando had hated Preston Atwater Doolittle III—hated him with a passion that had only grown more **fervent** over time.

He had hated him from the moment they met, when Orlando walked into the room they were about to share for what seemed an **interminable** semester and found Preston

lying on his bed watching videotapes of himself partying
half-naked on his father's yacht in the Hamptons, surrounded by **fawning** bimbettes. He detested him for
his **pseudoaristocratic*** name, his **haughty disposition,** his
unabashed snobbery, and his self-important **swagger.** He
despised him for bragging that the **obscure** armorial bearing that occupied a **prominent** place on the wall of their
room was his family's coat of arms. He **disdained** him for
the bungling, **incompetent** way he played guitar and for
his **supercilious** taste in music. He **abhorred** him for his exceptional SAT scores, which he never failed to publicize,
particularly when women were present.

And that was only the half of what nauseated him about
Preston. There was his ridiculous taste in clothing, especially the pin-striped kimono he liked to prance around in
at night, his pink and buttercup and lime-green polo shirts
with their **pretentious** PAD III monogram, and the sissified
penny loafers that he wore sans socks. There was the **affected** way he had of tossing French words like *sans* into
the middle of a perfectly natural and law-abiding English
sentence, and he had a **myriad** of other **affectations,** too,
not the least of which were his habit of beginning sentences with *Ah* and the annoying, self-conscious little cough-
laugh—*eh-heh, eh-heh*—that **continually punctuated** his
speech. But, most of all, Orlando **loathed** Preston Atwater
Doolittle III for **disparaging** him for coming from a **humble**
home in Texas, and for **mocking** his **heritage** by addressing
him in second-grade Spanish and calling him *Seen-your Ortiz.*

Orlando pulled himself up to his full height, crossed
his arms, and looked Preston straight in the eye. "Go stuff
yourself, *pendejo*," he said.

This **explicit** display of **hostility** failed to **disconcert**
Preston. "Ah," he said with a disapproving shake of his

---

*This compound word unites two test words: the combining form *pseudo-*
and *aristocratic* (see the glossary for definitions).

head, "I see we still have some anger management issues to address, *eh-heh, eh-heh.*" He put a proprietary arm around his female companion and **smirked**. "Señor Ortiz, allow me to introduce my date for the evening, Mademoiselle Brenda Kinkaid."

A muscle in Orlando's jaw twitched **conspicuously**. "We already know each other, and you know it," was his **terse** reply.

Preston shrugged and looked at Brenda. *"Quelle mouche le pique?"** *

Brenda smiled at Orlando. "Hey, how's it going?"

"It's going okay, Brenda," Orlando said. "How you doing?"

"All right," she replied, batting her eyelashes at him a few times more than respectability would **sanction**. Orlando found it **provocative** in spite of himself.

"And who are these fine feathered friends of yours?" said Preston, gesturing at Hank and Twain. "Allow me to introduce myself, gentlemen. I'm Preston Atwater Doolittle the Third, president of the Hedge Club and erstwhile roommate of Señor Ortiz."

"I'm Hank Morgan, Orlando's current roommate," said Hank. "We've met before, actually. And I know Brenda. Hi again," he said to her.

"Hi," she replied with a little wave of her hand.

"Ah, right, Hank," Preston said, touching his forehead in **feigned** recognition. His gold pinkie ring gave off a **vivid** flash in the harsh fluorescent light. "Your face **eluded** me for a second. No doubt the occasion was **memorable**." He looked at Twain.

"And I'm Mark—" the writer began but swallowed his **utterance** when Hank grabbed his arm from behind and gave it a cautionary squeeze. Twain cleared his throat. "I'm, er... Mark Morgan," he said, "Hank's uncle. How do you do?"

---

*French for "What's bugging him?"; **literally,** "What fly is stinging him?"

"I'm doing just dandy," Preston replied.

"I know," said Twain.

"Oh really? How can you tell?"

"By your apparel."

"Oh yeah?"

"Yes, the apparel oft proclaims the man."

"Ah, I see you know your Shakespeare."

"Alas, poor Preston, I know him well."

"Ah, very clever, *eh-heh, eh-heh*. I see you are *un bel esprit*. If you don't mind my asking, what's an uncle doing visiting his nephew during finals period?"

Twain twirled one end of his mustache. "Being avuncular, of course."

"Ah, I see." Preston looked at Hank. "Is he always this **enigmatic**?"

"He's a Connecticut Yankee," Hank said. "We Yankees are naturally **laconic**."

"Well, I'm from New York City where everybody's **garrulous**. I've got the **proverbial** gift of gab, *eh-heh, eh-heh*. So, Mr. Morgan, I'm curious. Just how does one go about being avuncular during finals period at Hadleyburg?"

Twain stroked his chin and rocked on his heels while he **contemplated** the question. "Very carefully," he said finally.

Hank and Orlando laughed. Brenda giggled. Preston scowled.

"He's probably here to give Hank some **moral** support," Brenda suggested.

"That's right," said Hank, looking at Twain, "and... well, a different perspective on things, I guess. He has a more **prudent** and **judicious** approach to life."

Preston looked **skeptical**.

Hank tried again. "It's that older and wiser thing, you know?"

"Yeah. Whatever." Preston pointed the handle of his

walking stick at the **salient** SAPPNIN BRO? **salutation** on Twain's chest. "Mr. Morgan, I have to **commend** you on your fashion sense. *Très chic, mon ami.* It's rare to see a man of your age and **dignified** standing in such youthful and **contemporary** duds, but somehow you manage to pull it off—I guess because you're older and wiser, *eh-heh, eh-heh.*"

Twain seemed **unruffled** by Preston's **subtle derision.** "Well, young fella," he **countered,** "I have a favorite **maxim** that you would be wise to follow: 'Be careless in your dress if you must, but tidy in your soul.'"

"Ah, thanks for the avuncular **counsel,**" Preston said without **conviction.** "By the way, has anybody ever told you that you look like Mark Twain?"

Twain slipped his hands into the pockets of his billowing cargo pants and nodded slowly. "My wife does, occasionally," he drawled. "And my friends have sometimes expressed that **notion.** But I don't take much stock in it. I just let it slide."

Preston's eyes narrowed. "You know, you've got a rather **distinct** southern twang for a Connecticut Yankee, *eh-heh, eh-heh.*"

"Yep, I reckon so. That's mighty **perceptive** of you. Missour*a* was my boyhood home. As a young man I spent some time in California but finally settled in Connecticut to be near the rest of the family. There's nothing like **proximity** to bring people together, that's what I always say."

"Hey, that's just like Twain. He grew up in Missouri, lived in California, and then moved to Hartford." A peculiar light came into Preston's eyes, as if he were on the verge of a **deduction.** "Are you sure you're not related to him or something?"

"Not that I know of. It's just a **fortuitous** resemblance."

"Ah, yes. No doubt. Have you ever heard of a writer named Bret Harte?"

Twain coughed sharply into his fist. "Nope," he croaked. "Never heard of him."

"Ah, then let me tell you who he was. He and Mark Twain were in the **vanguard** of San Francisco's literary scene after the Civil War. At first Harte was Twain's friend and **mentor,** and then they were **collaborators,** but eventually they were **estranged** and Harte became Twain's **nemesis.** One scholar I read **posited** that in spite of Twain's **dominant** nature Harte always had the psychological edge in their relationship and could make Twain feel off balance and defensive. Some people even think Harte was a better writer than Twain, *eh-heh, eh-heh.* Apparently that's why Twain despised him."

Twain coughed sharply again. "Is that so?"

"Yeah, they became bitter **rivals.**"

"So I've heard."

Preston looked puzzled. "I thought you said you'd never heard of Harte."

"I haven't."

"Ah, then why did you say 'So I've heard'?"

"Because you've just told me all about him."

"What? Ah, I get it. You're joking. Well, today everybody knows Mark Twain but hardly anybody remembers Bret Harte, and I think that's a crying shame."

"Why's that?"

"Because I happen to be a descendant of Bret Harte, and proud of it. He was my great-great-uncle."

"Well, I'll be a *monkey's* uncle." Twain ran a hand through his hair. "By the way, has anybody ever told you that *you* look like a young Bret Harte?"

"Really? You think so? I've seen photographs of him and I think I do. Hey, wait a minute, you're pulling my leg again, aren't you."

Twain shrugged. "Not at all. I haven't laid a hand on you."

"Yo Doolittle," Orlando said, "I hate to interrupt this **stimulating** history lesson, but it's late and we've got stuff to do."

Preston looked at Orlando. "Ah, whatever you say, Señor Ortiz. Thanks for **condescending** to chat with us," he **sneered**. "As always, it's been delightful. *Au revoir, eh-heh, eh-heh.*" He turned to address Brenda. "Sweetcakes, I'll be right back. Don't get into any trouble, okay?"

"Okay," Brenda said. "You just do what we came for."

Preston strutted off toward the beverage coolers, tapping his walking stick on the floor. While Hank and Twain resumed negotiations with the cashier, Brenda placed a manicured hand on Orlando's chest. "Aw c'mon, big guy, be nice," she said in a breathy, **sensual** voice, giving him a flirtatious push. "Presty and I are just friends. We both finished our finals today so we're hangin' out."

Presty? Dang, how could she! Orlando thought. Brenda's nauseating hypocorism almost made him wince, but by a superior force of will he remained **impassive**. "Oh, that's nice," he said with a straight face.

"And he's a really great guy once you get to know him."

"I already know him. Quite well. We were roommates, remember?"

"Then you two are old friends. That's cool." She leaned forward and looked up into his eyes with the dreamy, **enticing** expression that had once caused him to fall for her hard and fast. "Hey, it's great to see you again, you know?" she said, and along with the **subtly** fragrant and **tantalizing** aroma of her perfume Orlando **detected** the faint smell of beer on her breath. She was tipsy, he realized. She brushed her fingers gently against his cheek. "Maybe we could get together sometime, have a little fun," she said.

"Sure, Brenda, that would be great."

"Call me?"

"Yeah, sure."

"Promise?"

"Okay."

Brenda flashed him a smile that was so **radiant** and **rapturous** it made his heart race. A tingling wave of warmth surged from his belly to his head, and he felt **compelled** to look away so that she wouldn't see him blush. He glanced over at Hank and Twain. They were standing at the other end of the counter, engaged in an intense conversation with the cashier. "Hey, you guys, everything cool over there?"

Hank looked over his shoulder and gave him a thumbs-up. "Everything's hunky-dory," Twain said, coming down the counter to Orlando's side. He put a hand next to his mouth and spoke in a **conspiratorial** stage whisper: "Peter Pustule has seen the error of his ways. We've **extracted** a **sincere** and heartfelt apology from him, and now we're haggling **amiably** over the usurious price of the cigars. By dint of **persistence** and my remarkable powers of persuasion, I expect to get him to compromise between the going rate in my century and the going rate in yours."

Brenda giggled. "You have a funny way of talking, Mr. Morgan. You actually *sound* like you're from another century."

"Well, young lady, I happen to have been born in a prior century."

Orlando **conspicuously** cleared his throat.

"The twentieth century," Twain said by way of **clarification**. "Don't you remember it?"

"Mr. Morgan," Brenda said, "you know it's not polite to ask a lady to reveal her age." She giggled. "But I don't care. I'm nineteen."

"Why, I remember when I was your age," Twain said, "and I'm sorry I do, for it would be a blessing to forget it. What a hilarious and disastrous combination of **traits** I possessed back then: ignorance, **intolerance, egotism,** self-**assertion, opaque perception,** dense and pitiful chuckleheadedness, and an almost **pathetic** unconsciousness of it all—that is what I was at nineteen and twenty."

"Way back in the **preceding** century," Brenda said, laughing.

Twain smiled. "Or thereabouts. Well, if you'll excuse me, I need to get back to the bargaining table. Those stogies are calling me."

Orlando and Brenda made nervous small talk about **trivial** things until Preston reappeared with a bag of potato chips and a large bottle of soda in his arms. "Ah, how charming," he said, rudely stepping between them and laying his items on the counter. "Catching up on old times, are we?"

"Actually," Orlando said, "I was just telling Brenda what a **proficient** guitarist you are, and how you used to entertain everyone in our suite for hours with your soothing **rendition** of 'Wild Thing.'"

Orlando's **irony** was lost on Preston, or else he strategically chose to disregard it. "Ah, yes," he said, ignoring Orlando and looking at Brenda, "remind me to play something for you when we get back to my room, my pet." He turned and **brusquely** called to the cashier. "Hey, we're ready over here, pal. Can you ring us up?"

"Yeah, yeah, hold the phone, I'm comin'," said the cashier. He **sauntered** over to the cash register squeezing a pimple on his chin. "Let's see, what do we got here? One MegaFizz Junior..." He pressed a plastic panel on the register, which responded with a distressed beep. "And one potato chip." He pressed another panel and the register protested again. "Anything else?"

"That's it," Preston said.

"That'll be $3.89," the cashier announced.

Preston looked at Brenda. "You know, I think I left my wallet back in my room."

"Oh, that's a good one, Doolittle," Orlando said with a **contemptuous** snort. "Right up there with the dog ate your homework."

"That's okay, Presty," Brenda said. "I'll pay." She produced a ten-dollar bill from the **crevice** of a **minute** purse slung over her shoulder.

The cashier took the bill, made change, and put the chips and soda in a plastic bag. As he handed the bag to Brenda, Twain tapped Preston on the shoulder. "Excuse me," he said, "but don't you have some other merchandise to declare?"

Preston looked at the writer as if he were an **alien** being who had just stepped off a flying saucer. "No, I don't think so. What are you talking about?" he said.

Twain put one hand on the counter and the other in his pocket. "I'm talking about the merchandise you have concealed in your coat," he said calmly.

In the space of a few seconds, the expression on Preston's face shifted from surprise and confusion to defensiveness and **hostility.** "What do you mean by that? What the hell are you trying to say, anyway?"

"I'm not *trying* to say anything," Twain replied. "I'm *saying* it. You've got something up your sleeve, young fella, and I mean that **literally.**"

"*Au contraire,* Uncle Remus. I don't have anything up my sleeve, **literally** or **figuratively.** So why don't you mind your own damn business."

"Dude," Hank **interjected**, "that's *my* uncle you're talking to. Have some respect."

"I'd be happy to, dude, except your uncle's talking nonsense."

"I'm not sure how I can make myself any more **comprehensible,** but I'll try," said Twain. "Mr. Doolittle, not two minutes ago I saw you **adroitly** slip something from that cold-drink cabinet into your overcoat. I think you're attempting to pilfer from this store."

"Are you accusing me of shoplifting?"

"Now you're catching on," said Twain.

Preston was **incredulous.** He turned to the cashier. "That's ridiculous," he said, his screechy voice rising even higher. He shook his walking stick at Twain. "This guy's crazy. He's a babbling lunatic. I haven't taken anything."

"If that's the truth," said Twain, "then why don't you simply open your coat and prove me wrong?"

"Yeah," echoed the cashier, "if you ain't lying, open your coat and prove it."

Preston swallowed hard and a look of desperation passed over his face. For a **fleeting** moment it seemed that he would **acquiesce** to their demand. But just as quickly he regained his **equanimity** and tossed his head in **defiance.** "I don't have to do that," he declared. "I don't have to do anything. This is a free country. You want to check out my coat, get a search warrant." He looked at Orlando. A **smug** grin spread across his face. "*Adios, Frito Bandito.* Have fun hanging with your buckaroos." He slipped an arm around Brenda. "C'mon, babe, let's get the hell out of this freakin' dump."

To signalize this **decisive rebuff** of his opponents, Preston rapped his walking stick twice on the floor. *So there,* the sound seemed to say, *get lost.* Then, in a **jaunty** gesture of the utmost **arrogance,** he gave the stick a brisk twirl and turned to leave. But before he and Brenda could take a step toward the door a powerful hand clamped down on his shoulder and spun him around.

"I think you'd better wait up, Presty boy," Orlando said, grabbing the short cape of his inverness with both hands.

"Hey, let go of me!" Preston yelled, trying to squirm out of Orlando's grasp.

Orlando pulled Preston forward until they were almost nose to nose. "You're not goin' anywhere, butt brains," he growled. "What we've got here, in case you hadn't noticed, is something called 'probable cause,' based on eyewitness evidence. Hank's uncle says he saw you stealing. Given all the **clandestine** crap you used to pull when we were room-mates, I'm inclined to believe him. So you can either open up your coat right now or we can call the cops and they'll be happy to do it for you. Your choice, *hombre*. What's it gonna be?"

The two **adversaries** glared at each other.

"Open your coat!" the cashier cried from his safe re-move behind the counter.

"Dude, just do it," said Hank, "or I think you're gonna be sorry."

Preston made no move to **comply.**

"Do it, Doolittle," Orlando commanded, giving him a rough shake.

"Who the hell do you think you are, the Lone Ranger?" Preston hissed. "Get your filthy hands off me, you Texas cowturd."

Orlando's blue eyes blazed with fury. "*¡Cabrón!* I'll break your fat preppie head open on this nice white floor."

As if in slow motion, Mark Twain saw Preston's arm move sideways and the walking stick rise into the air at a steep angle. And as the **pernicious** weapon began its **in-evitable descent** toward the side of Orlando's knee, the writer felt himself lunging into the **fray.**

"*Eeeeeeeyaaaaaah!*" he cried as his feet left the ground and he sailed through the air with his arms outstretched, landing a textbook tackle around Preston's thighs.

Brenda screamed as Preston toppled and thudded to the floor, followed by Twain, then Orlando, and then Hank, who threw himself onto the heap for good measure. Finally, the walking stick, which had been knocked clear out of Preston's hand, clattered on the linoleum at Brenda's feet and lay still. With one hand on her mouth, she bent over and picked it up.

"Okay, that's it, enough of these shenanigans, I'm

callin' the law," the cashier hollered amid the **ensuing** groans of pain and **strife.** He reached for the phone behind the counter. "In two minutes, somebody's butt's goin' to jail."

Preston yielded. "All right, all right, I give up," he wailed from the bottom of the pile of bodies **writhing** on the floor. "Just get the hell off me and I'll open my coat."

Hank and Orlando maneuvered themselves to their feet and then assisted Twain, who stood up and rubbed his shoulder. "Whatever it is you've got in there," he said, looking down at Preston, "it's as hard as a dadblamed rock. It damn near knocked my shoulder out of joint." He extended the hand of his uninjured arm. "May I help you up?"

"I don't need your help and I don't want it," Preston said coldly. He pushed himself up, made a **fastidious** adjustment to the tam-o'-shanter on his head, and then slowly unbuttoned his coat. He spread it open to reveal a navy-blue cardigan over a white button-down Oxford shirt. "Okay, there you are. Take a good look." The coat's lining appeared smooth and seamless. No **illicit** goods were **discernible.** "You happy now? Or are you still going to make me the innocent victim of your vigilante justice?"

"Wow, I coulda sworn," said Hank, shaking his head in **bewilderment.**

"Seriously," said the cashier, putting down the phone and thoughtfully **probing** an **inflammation** on the back of his neck.

Orlando scratched his chin in disbelief and cast Twain a **dubious** look. "Mr. Morgan, are you sure you saw him shoplifting?"

"Oh yes, I'm quite sure," Twain said. He looked at Preston. "Would you mind if I inspected your garment?" he asked. **Reluctantly,** and with a dirty look, Preston **obliged** him. Twain ran his hand lightly down the lining on one side and then the other. "You know, that's a nice piece of clothing you have there," he said.

"It suits me just fine," Preston replied.

"It's got **ample** material," Twain said, patting one flap. "I'd even venture to say it's downright **capacious**," he said, patting the other flap. "And I suppose that's a good thing . . . for a lying, thieving *shoplifter*."

Preston's **countenance** remained **stoic** and **impassive**.

Twain shook his head. "My, what a tangled web we weave, when first we practice to **deceive**." He slipped his hand into an invisible opening in the coat's lining and **deftly** removed a twelve-ounce can of beer. "Well, look what we have here," he said, setting the can on the counter. "And lookee here," he said, slipping his hand into another disguised slit in the lining and **extracting** a second can of beer. Within moments he had retrieved a third and fourth can, the last one badly dented. "Aha," he said, "there's the nasty little devil that collided with my shoulder."

"Wow," Hank exclaimed, "how did you do that?"

"It's that older and wiser thing, I guess," Twain drawled.

Suddenly Brenda, who had remained on the sidelines during the whole **escapade,** burst into tears. "It's not Presty's fault, really," she said, pulling out a tissue from the pocket of her furry coat and dabbing her eyes. "It's mine. I put him up to it. I dared him to steal the beer because I wanted to see if he cared enough about me to take the risk."

"That's bull," Orlando said. "You're just covering his butt, aren't you?"

"No," Brenda said, looking at him with wet and **remorseful** eyes, "that's the truth, I swear. And I'm sorry. I really am."

"Okay, I've heard enough," said the cashier. "I don't care who told who to do what. You guys were shoplifting. I'm calling the cops."

"No, hold on a minute," said Twain. "The merchandise

has been recovered and the offenders are **penitent** and **contrite.**" He looked at Brenda. "Isn't that right?"

"Of course. I never wanted this to happen."

"And you, sir?" said Twain to Preston.

Preston looked back at Twain with a **sullen** expression. "Yeah, I'm sorry," he said with a **notable** lack of enthusiasm. "Actually, I was going to return the beer once I showed Brenda I could lift it."

"*Mentiroso,*" said Orlando. "You were both going to drink it." He looked at Brenda. "Am I right or what?"

Brenda sniffled and looked down at the floor.

Twain turned to the cashier. "Much as I am concerned about this young fellow's **motivation** for committing this **reprehensible offense,** and also this young woman's **motivation** for **abetting** it, I would argue for **leniency.** All young people are guilty of foolish and **impetuous** behavior at one time or another, but as long as no great harm is done they should be afforded another chance. Often a firm **admonition** is sufficiently **corrective.** Wouldn't you agree?"

"Yeah, sure," said the cashier. "Whatever. But somebody's gonna have to pay for that busted-up can of beer."

Twain stroked his mustache. "Well, seeing as I was the one who **inadvertently** damaged it, I'll be happy to pay—as long as you consent to give me that discount on the cigars that we discussed."

"That's fair enough," said the cashier, "considering you were the guy who fingered the creep." He pointed at Preston and Brenda. "Hey, the both of you bozos get out of my store and don't come back. If I ever see you again, I'm calling the cops."

With that, Preston and Brenda hightailed it for the door. But at the last moment Brenda looked back, pursed her lips, and blew Orlando an **ardent** and seductive kiss.

———

"You know," Twain said to his companions as they tramped down Anchor Street, making their way back to Stormfield College, "I'll be ding-busted if that Preston Bilgewater Doohickey the Dadblamed Third wasn't one of the coolest young rapscallions I've **encountered** in my time. Have you ever seen such an **insolent, unscrupulous whelp**? Who in dingnation does he think he is, anyway, stealing what he can clearly afford to buy just to **ingratiate** himself with some **tawdry** gal?"

"Hey," said Orlando, "that's my ex-girlfriend you're **disparaging,** not 'some **tawdry** gal.'"

"I'm sorry, my friend, but it's the truth, at least from my **archaic** and **moralistic** perspective. Trust me. I know her kind, and I'd be **leery** of her if I were you. She's a femme fatale, a **devious** and designing woman bent on practicing her **wiles** upon unsuspecting, chuckleheaded men. Why, I'm telling you, she ought to be wearing a sign that says CAUTION: DANGER AHEAD."

"Yeah," said Hank under his breath, "or maybe CAUTION: DANGEROUS HEAD."

Orlando punched Hank's shoulder.

"Ouch!" Hank yelped. "C'mon, dude, I was just joking."

"Is there something wrong with her head?" Twain asked.

"I doubt it," said Hank.

Orlando cuffed Hank's shoulder again. "Will ya give it a rest, Morgan?"

"Look at it this way, Orlando," said Twain. "Maybe you've got some sense in *your* head. And maybe that's why she's not your gal anymore."

Orlando threw up his hands. "Hey, she was my girlfriend once, and now she's not. It's over, finished, and done with. Can we just drop the subject?"

There was an uncomfortable **lull** in the conversation.

Then Hank piped up. "So I've been wondering, Mr. Twain, about what Preston said about you and his ancestor, that guy Bret Harte. Did you—I mean *do* you—know him?"

"Hell yeah, I know the son of a bitch," Twain replied hotly. "Bret Harte is a liar, a thief, a **swindler,** a snob, a sot, a sponge, a coward, and he is brim full of **treachery** and **machinations.**"

Hank and Orlando laughed.

"That's quite a **litany** of **allegations,**" Orlando said. "But it appears that all those qualities can be inherited."

"Yup," Hank **concurred,** "that sounds like our boy Preston."

"Alas," said Twain, "selfishness, **deceitfulness,** and per-fidy have an **uncanny** way of getting passed down through the generations. **Benevolence,** honesty, and loyalty, on the other hand, have had a harder time of it. They're weaker **traits.**"

They turned onto Village Road and continued walking in silence, each one absorbed in his own thoughts. Despite his sore shoulder, Twain was happy as a clam at high tide. The cashier had proved so grateful for their aid and **inter-vention** that his generosity had exceeded even the writer's wildest **expectation.** Though the air was chilly and the snow continued to fall, in his heart Twain was warm and content, and he strolled down the block with the **sanguine** air of a man who has just come into a fortune.

He was carrying a crinkly white satchel filled with a bulging bag of Treatos, a large bottle of soda, four boxes of cigarillos, and eleven fat and **pungent** stogies, and he was happily puffing away on a freshly ignited twelfth one. And what had he paid for all that wondrous bounty? A mere double sawbucks—or $19.95 to be precise. Granted, that would have been a pretty penny back in 1883, but, consid-ering the probable annual rate of **inflation** over the past century or so, it seemed like a first-rate bargain—manna from heaven, even. Twain took several hearty puffs on his cigar and exhaled with **conspicuous** satisfaction.

Hank coughed and shook his head in disgust. "I'm sorry, but that cigar smells like burning horse manure."

"Or a smoldering pile of garbage," said Orlando, loudly clearing his throat.

"Or maybe," said Twain with a grin, "like the **immaculate confines** of your dormitory rooms."

"All right, touché," Hank said. "All we ask is that you respect the campus prohibition against smoking indoors and that you don't **defile** our place any further with your stinking cigar butts."

"Agreed," said Twain. He took a deep puff and let the **toxic** smoke trail up into his nose. "You know, I've got my own rules of conduct about smoking."

"Yeah? And what are they?" asked Orlando.

"Two simple ones," Twain said. "First, I make it a point not to smoke while asleep. And second, I make it a point not to smoke more than one cigar at a time." The writer stroked his chin. "Boys, as the **adage** goes, one man's meat is another man's poison. I came into this world asking for a light. And I expect to go out of it blowing smoke rings. When they used to tell me I'd shorten my life ten years by smoking, they little knew the **devotee** they were wasting their puerile words upon. They little knew how **trivial** and valueless I would regard a decade that had no smoking in it."

They crossed Charter Road and **lapsed** into silence again. Like a **perambulating** cetacean, Twain puffed away on his cigar and spewed **voluminous** clouds of smoke into the air. Isn't life grand? he thought. One day your time on earth seems **ineffably** dull and repetitive and **pedestrian**, like the **futile** travail of Sisyphus endlessly rolling his **ponderous** stone up the hill, then all out of nowhere it turns into a wild and **unpredictable** adventure, like a **torrid** love affair with a beautiful and **capricious** woman.

He recalled a favorite sonnet by the young and tragically doomed Romantic poet John Keats, in which the poet **yearns** for **enduring** love and spiritual connection in an unstable and **volatile** world where the ultimate and **inescapable consequence** is death.

> Bright star, would I were **steadfast** as thou art—
>   Not in lone splendor hung aloft the night
> And watching, with **eternal** lids apart,
>   Like nature's patient, sleepless Eremite,
> The moving waters at their priestlike task
>   Of pure ablution round earth's human shores,
> Or gazing at the new soft fallen mask
>   Of snow upon the mountains and the moors—
> No—yet still **steadfast**, still unchangeable,
>   Pillowed upon my fair love's ripening breast,
> To feel forever its soft fall and swell,
>   Awake forever in a sweet unrest,
> Still, still to hear her tender-taken breath,
> And so live ever—or else **swoon** to death.

Life, he realized, was a sweet unrest, a mad pursuit, a wild **surmise**. It was a **quest** to obtain the unobtainable in the face of fearsome and **persistent uncertainty**. Anything can happen, he thought, and by Jove it had, for this very night he had made an astonishing transformation from being Samuel L. Clemens, a.k.a. Mark Twain, **esteemed** man of letters and citizen of Hartford, to being an **anonymous** and **anachronistic** traveler wandering through the remote **realm** of the twenty-first century, listening to the poetry in his head and blowing smoke rings at the sky.

Some other man who had plunged **headlong** into the future with but a dim **prospect** of returning to his own milieu would have been **vigilant** and **wary** and, no doubt, **despondent.** Yet Twain felt just the opposite: He was

insouciant and **exhilarated,** eager to explore and experience his new **environs.**

He felt like an **intrepid** steamboat pilot **navigating**
down an **exotic** river in a brave new world, without the
faintest idea of what lay around the next bend. Would
there be deep water and a smooth current, or a **treacherous**
eddy and a concealed shoal?

Chapter 8

River of Words, River of Time

Mark Twain knocked softly on Aimee and Angela's door. It was a few minutes after six in the morning and he was alone. Angela's blanket was tucked under one arm and the bundled manuscript of *Huckleberry Finn* was tucked under the other.

He was **enervated,** worn out from trying in **vain** for two hours to get some rest. Upon returning to suite G-8, Hank and Orlando had retired to their **respective** rooms and Twain, after finishing his stogie and smoking a cigarillo in the courtyard, had retired on the couch. But sleep wouldn't come.

Part of the problem was that his tingling sense of wonder at being a traveler in time had not yet worn off, and his brain was still on fire from all the **stimulation** the evening had provided. Another part of the problem was Hank's damnable, **incessant** snoring, which thundered from behind the closed door of his room and **resounded** throughout the suite like the rumbling **reverberations** of an artillery brigade. Yet another part of the problem was the unbearable uncomfortableness of the beat-up couch, which found new and **merciless** ways to **vex** him with its manifold lumps and sags and springs whenever he changed position. And every time he tossed or turned the image of the

elaborately carved bedstead he and Mrs. Clemens had bought while on holiday in Venice in 1878 would appear before his eyes. It was the most comfortable bedstead that ever was, he thought **wistfully,** with space enough in it for a family, and carved angels enough surmounting its twisted columns and its headboard and footboard to bring peace to the sleepers, and pleasant dreams.

But he could easily have overcome all of these **daunting impediments** to sleep had it not been for the main and irremediable problem: the **profound,** revolting, abysmal stench that **pervaded** the suite and made it nearly impossible for him to take a breath without feeling an overwhelming urge to retch.

Eventually, after repeated attempts to persuade himself that in just another minute he would either fall asleep or die from asphyxia, he decided he had had enough. Anything was better than this rotting rubbish heap of a room. He would be better off curling up on the bathroom floor or even outside in the snow. And he would be far better off, he concluded, if he threw himself upon the mercy of his only other friends in this unfamiliar world, the two tidy **inhabitants** of suite E-4.

Twain heard a rustle inside the room. "Who is it?" came Angela's **muffled** voice through the door.

"It's Sam Clemens," he answered in a hoarse whisper. "Mark Twain."

He heard the click of the lock retracting. Then the door opened and Angela appeared in slippers, gray sweatpants, and a billowy blue T-shirt that said YALE in white sans-serif letters. The thick black corkscrews of her shoulder-length hair were attractively **disheveled.** She gave him a strange look—perhaps because he was wearing Hank's clothes, he thought—then summoned him inside with a wave of her hand.

"Mr. Twain, what on earth are you doing here?" she

whispered, closing the door behind him and turning the lock. "I thought you were spending the night with the boys."

"I apologize, young lady, for disturbing you at this ungodly hour of the morning, when only farm animals and **insomniacs** have any business being awake," he replied. "Indeed, I *was* attempting to spend the night over there, but ultimately it was I who wound up spent and not the night."

Angela looked puzzled. "What do you mean?"

"I mean that over there I was losing enough sleep to supply a worn-out army."

"Why couldn't you get to sleep?"

"Well, to begin with, Hank snores like a cow choking to death on a chicken, their couch would have made a fine instrument of torture in the Inquisition, and the smell of the place...why, the smell of that place beggars all description!"

Angela began to chuckle.

"I have never smelled anything like it, with the possible exception of a beached whale," Twain went on, warming to his subject. "It was **rancid**, rank, and **malodorous** beyond words. It would **incite** rebellion in a gasometer. It made even the foul odors of the great stinking bazaar of Stamboul seem like **aromatic** frankincense and myrrh. I'm telling you, between Hank's infernal snortin' and blubberin' and that sadistic couch and that **intolerable, fetid, lethal** smell, I wouldn't have been able to sleep even with a bucketful of morphine in me!"

Angela clapped her hand over her mouth to **suppress** the cachinnation she felt rising to her lips. "Stop making me laugh, Mr. Twain," she **chided** from between her fingers. "Aimee's asleep and we don't want to wake her up."

"Forgive me," Twain said. "I'm afraid I just can't keep from talking, even at the risk of being humorous."

Angela smiled. "And even after being up all night." She sat down in one of the armchairs with her legs crossed beneath her. "Why don't you set those things down and come get some rest on our sofa. You know, I've been up all night too, finishing my term paper for American history, and I'm still pretty wired from all the coffee I've had. So we could talk for a little while, if you like, until you unwind and feel ready to sleep."

Twain was more than happy to **comply**. "I'd like that very much, young lady."

"May I get you something to drink? Coffee, tea, juice, water?"

"No, I'm fine, thank you," Twain said, laying his manuscript next to Aimee's computer and setting the blanket on the sofa. "Unless you happen to have some whiskey lying around."

"I'm afraid not," Angela said, "but we do have a little brandy stashed away, which Aimee and I keep around for special occasions. Would you like some?"

"Why, don't mind if I do. Will you join me?"

To imbibe or not to imbibe, that was the question. Being a **prudent** person, accustomed to making **rational** and **judicious** decisions about her conduct rather than following every **spontaneous impulse,** Angela **pondered** this unusual invitation to **indulge** in alcohol at such an unlikely hour. Did she have any **inclination** to accept it? Yes, she did. It had been a long night of hard work, her term paper was her last academic obligation of the semester, and she was eager to kick back and relax. Did the current circumstances **justify** such an **extravagance**? It could be argued, without too much of a stretch, that indeed they did.

But what would people think if they saw her slurping brandy at six in the morning? she wondered. Would they regard it as a **decadent** drink taken **surreptitiously** before breakfast, or a celebratory drink taken as a reward for a night of **diligent** and **fruitful** labor? She weighed the arguments for both **interpretations** and came to the conclusion that it was the **latter,** not the former. "Well, okay, I'll have a little," she said, getting up to fetch the bottle and two glasses from the built-in cabinet in the bookcase. "Seeing as I've just finished my term paper, and seeing as my guest is none other than America's most **celebrated** writer, I think this definitely qualifies as a special occasion."

She poured the drinks—making sure the writer's was considerably more generous than her own—and returned with her glass to the armchair. Twain sat down on the sofa and crossed his legs. He saluted Angela with his glass, took a slug of brandy, and let out a long sigh. A mischievous twinkle lit up his tired eyes.

"Y'know, it's a downright curious thing, this **penchant** I have for talking," he said in a quiet drawl. "It seems that I was born to be **loquacious.** Even when I'm dog-tired and run clear into the ground, exhausted from the **rigors** of writing or the **tedium** of handling my business affairs, even when all my **vitality** has been drained and my **stamina** has been wrung dry, somehow I can always manage to scrape up enough of a spark to **discourse** upon a subject— and the **discourse** is all the better if the subject is one that I am quite sure I know little or nothing about. In my experience there is nothing more **fatal** to the successful outcome of a speech than when the speaker sticks **solely** to the facts. You see, I am not one of those who in expressing opinions **confine** themselves to facts. I don't know anything that **mars** good literature so completely as too much truth."

Angela laughed politely, then swirled the brandy in her glass and took a sip.

"Like most men," Twain continued, "I was born **modest,** but it wore off. I like to hear myself talk and, like most men, I find my own words endlessly amusing. The sound of my voice rattling along like a train whistling and clattering down the tracks is to me one of the most familiar and fascinating and **invigorating** things in the world. I also like a good story well told, which is the reason I am sometimes forced to tell them myself. Susy, my oldest daughter, once asked me why I'm not an **avid** churchgoer, like her mother, and I told her that I can't bear to hear anyone talk but myself, but that I could listen to myself talk for hours without experiencing a whit of boredom or fatigue—and she laughed, the little dear, because she thought I was joking. I'm told that I talk even while I'm asleep, which I find **regrettable** because I have to be unconscious during the whole performance and can't properly admire my own **eloquence.**

"Now Mrs. Clemens is too sweet and soft-spoken and well-bred to tell me to put a big fat cork in it, but I know there've been times when she's wished I would—or that somebody else would—because Lord knows when something gets under my skin and I get to flapping my gums about it, I'm likely to talk you all the way into next week. I can become an **oral** machine with a tongue journaled on ball bearings. I can grind and pump and churn and buzz and never stop to oil up or blow out. And when I get that way, my best advice to you is to light out for the territory as fast as you can, before I use up all the oxygen in the room. It's a terrible death to be talked to death, don't you agree?"

"Yes, I do, Mr. Twain," Angela said, pushing several stray ringlets of hair out of her face. "And I think I'm about ready to light out for the territory. The air's starting to get thin in here."

The writer laughed. "Of course you know that was just my **customary hyperbole,** right?"

"Oh no it wasn't," she said, smiling and wagging her finger at him. "I'm not out to become a lawyer for nothing, and I've got a good sense for when people are being **insincere** and when they're telling the truth. So I appreciate your being **frank** and direct with me. Honesty is a quality any woman would appreciate in a man, especially when it's laced with **self-effacing** humor. Your wife is lucky to have a partner who is so gifted with words, and your children are lucky to have you as their father."

"Thank you kindly," Twain replied. "That's a flattering and **gracious sentiment,** and I appreciate your sharing it."

"You're welcome." Angela leaned forward, her eyes gleaming with intelligent intensity. "Y'know, I've always been extremely interested in words," she said. "If I weren't so **intent** on becoming a lawyer I think I'd be a lexicographer, or better yet, a writer like you, although I've heard it's awfully hard to make a living as a writer."

Twain nodded. "The great English literary **sage** Samuel Johnson once said, 'Nobody but a blockhead ever wrote, except for money.' If your **aspiration** is to write, then here's my advice. Write without pay until someone offers pay. If nobody offers within three years then you may **infer** with the utmost confidence that sawing wood is what you were intended for. Or maybe practicing law."

"I'll remember that," Angela said with a grin. She took a sip of brandy and **savored** the fire of it on her tongue and the warmth of it in her belly. "I may be an **aspiring** lawyer, Mr. Twain, but I think I have a writer's love of words. I love the stories of words—their **etymology**—and I'm fascinated by the **breadth** of the English language, how **comprehensive** its vocabulary is. There seems to be a word for almost everything. It's just a matter of finding it."

"Or of making it up," said Twain.

"And I can tell you the word for *that,*" Angela said.

"Oh, really? What is it?"

"*Neologism,* from the combining form *neo-,* new, and the Greek *lógos,* word."

"Well done," Twain said. "You've taught me a new word, and learning a new word is always a cause for celebration." He lifted his glass and took a healthy swig of brandy. "So you think there's a word for everything," he mused, stroking his mustache. "That's an interesting **thesis.** Can you give me some examples?"

Angela nodded enthusiastically. "Sure, I can give you plenty—or even a **plethora.**"

Twain chuckled. "If you give me a **plethora,** my dear, the words will be spilling out of my ears. Just a few will be sufficient, I think, to **substantiate** your point."

"All right, here's one I'll bet you can use: *philodox.*"

"Fill a what?"

"*Philodox.* From the Greek *philo-,* loving, and *doxa,* opinion. It means someone in love with their own opinions, a person who's **dogmatic,** who makes **categorical assertions.**"

"Now there's a useful word!" Twain exclaimed. "I'll have to add it to my characterization of that **pontificating rascal** Bret Harte. Give me another one."

"*Horbgorbling.* It's from English **dialect.** It means the act or habit of puttering around, occupying oneself in an aimless and ineffective manner."

"Another excellent word. I daresay the human race spends three-quarters of its time horbgorbling. Keep going!"

"*Lucubration,* from the Latin *lucubrare,* to work by candlelight. It means **laborious** study, especially burning the midnight oil, as I did tonight writing my paper."

"That's fascinating—no, make that **illuminating.**" He took a drink of brandy and raised his glass. "Give me one more!"

"Okay," Angela said, "this one, I think, is my all-time favorite. *Resistentialism.*"

"Now there's a mouthful of a word. What does it mean?"

"It means **hostile** or **malevolent** behavior **manifested** by **inanimate** objects. Resistentialism is a philosophy founded on the **concept** that things are against us."

A look of wondrous **revelation** slowly spread across the writer's face. "That is stupendous!" he cried. "Simply stupendous!"

"Sshhh!" she **admonished** him with an index finger across her lips.

"I'm sorry," he said in a hushed voice. "But Angela, do you realize what you've just done?"

"No, what?"

"Something remarkable."

"Really?"

"Oh yes. Yes, indeed. On account of knowing that word, I am a changed man."

Angela looked **skeptical.** "You're kidding, right?"

"Not at all, my dear. You have uplifted an entire category of my experience—and a **universal** category of human experience—from the **shrouded,** veiled, Cimmerian **realm** of the Inexpressible into the clear, comforting, **lucid** light of the Known!"

"Wow," Angela said, impressed with the writer's impassioned **rhetoric.** "Hey, what does *Cimmerian* mean?"

"Look it up," Twain replied **evasively.** "At last I have a word for something that has **plagued** me for as long as I can remember, ever since my unfortunate **confrontation** with a rake on my uncle's farm when I was a boy. I had let my guard down for a moment—I think because I was **coveting** a prize watermelon that was sunning its fat rotundity in the garden behind the house—and that evil, **insidious implement enticed** me to step on it so it could spring up and smack me in the face. Thanks to you, Angela, I finally have a word for the insubordinate behavior of Hank and Orlando's couch and the drunken and **disorderly** conduct of that refractory telephone I installed in my house in

Hartford. And I finally have a word that explains the countless **insolent** acts of things—the vicious razor that nicks
and scrapes my face, the buttons that heartlessly **abandon**
my shirts, the burglar alarm that goes off at all hours
simply to amuse itself, the rug that **furtively** curls up so it
can snag my toe, the **wily** piece of toast that **eludes** my
grasp and always hits the floor butter side down."

"Maybe you're buttering the wrong side of the bread,"
Angela suggested, smiling and taking another sip of brandy.
"Or maybe it's rye toast, as in *w-r-y*."

Twain laughed. "Very punny, young lady. Well, that bit
of casuistry might explain the behavior of the toast, but it
doesn't explain all the rest of the **recalcitrant phenomena**
we are forced to **endure** every day."

"What's *casuistry*?"

"Look it up."

"Oh, c'mon, tell me," she pleaded. "Please?"

"All right," he acceded. "It means specious reasoning,
argument that is overly **subtle, deceptive**, and misleading.
It's an **indispensable** word for a lawyer." He spelled it out
for her. "Look it up—and don't forget to check the
pronunciation."

"Okay, I will."

"Promise?"

"Yes, I promise."

"There's something else I think I should tell you about
resistentialism," she said after a pause.

"What's that?"

"When you get back to your own time, you can't use it."

"Why not?"

"Because it wasn't coined until 1948."

"That's no fair," Twain said. He drained his glass and
set it down on the coffee table with a smack. "A word that
serviceable can't come around after I'm dead." He paused
and stroked his chin. "By the way, when did I die, anyway?
Did I make it to the twentieth century?"

"Yes, you did. You lived until 1910."

A faraway look came into the writer's eyes. "Until I'm seventy-five, when Halley's comet comes around again." He looked at Angela. "I came in with that comet in 1835, you know, and I think it makes perfect sense for me to go out with it."

Angela smiled. "I suppose it does, Mr. Twain. After all, you are something of a force of nature."

Twain cleared his throat. "Well anyway, as I was saying, I'll just have to take the law into my own hands and coin that word *resistentialism* when I get back."

Angela shook her head. "I'm afraid it doesn't work that way, Mr. Twain. You can't change the history of the language—or maybe I should say that you can, but you shouldn't. As much as you and I might be tempted to do that under the present circumstances, we'd be crazy to try. It could backfire and have **unpredictable** and possibly dangerous **consequences.** At the very least, for you to coin *resistentialism* wouldn't be **ethical.** You'd be making a false claim and stealing the word from its rightful creator, and that's an **offense** punishable by ten years of writer's block."

Twain chuckled. "You'd put me in the literary hoosegow for word-rustlin'?"

"Damn straight I would. I think it's best just to treat this whole conversation as an **aberration,** a **chronological** mistake. Consider it **memorable** but not repeatable."

"Okay, you're right, I give up," Twain said. "You can bet I'll remember it—especially whenever I see a rake. But I'll refrain from using it."

"Promise?"

"Yes, I promise."

They were silent for a minute. Angela sipped the last of her brandy and set her glass down on the coffee table next to Twain's. "It's so incredible to sit here and talk with you," she said, "but I really do hope we can get you back where you belong soon."

"So do I," he said, a note of **nostalgia** creeping into his voice. "Christmas is coming and I want to be with my family and watch my darling daughters open their presents. I miss my wife—who right now probably thinks I've been kidnapped and is worried sick about me, poor thing. I miss my billiard table. And my pipes and **savory** six-cent cigars. And my own clothes, clean and pressed. And a million other things."

"You'll also be missing my great-great-great-grandpa if you don't get back," Angela said.

"Is that so? Do I know him?"

"Not yet, but you will. Or at least you're supposed to." She told him the story of Warner T. McGuinn, how he had graduated from Yale Law School at the top of his class and had a **distinguished** career because of Twain's **altruism** and **philanthropy.** "So you see, I have an ulterior **motive** for getting you back to 1883," she said. "Because if you don't get back, you won't become my great-great-great-grandpa's **benefactor,** and then he might not graduate from Yale. And if he doesn't graduate from Yale he won't become a lawyer. And if he doesn't become a lawyer he won't be able to shape the history of civil rights in Baltimore and become a **mentor** to Thurgood Marshall. And if he doesn't do all that, just as he's supposed to, then the history of my whole family will be altered, not to mention the history of Baltimore and even the United States. And then my life will be changed too, probably for the worse, because I won't **aspire** to **emulate** my great-great-great-grandpa. I'll be somewhere else, doing something else, who knows what? I might even be *someone* else. Or maybe I won't even get born. And if I'm not born then—"

"Whoa, hold your horses, young lady," Twain said, raising his hands palms outward to arrest Angela's verbal cascade. "That's quite a **pessimistic scenario** you're **concocting** there."

"But that's what could happen if you don't get back. Anything could happen. I mean, the fact that Mark Twain is sitting in my room at six thirty in the morning and I'm telling him how he's going to meet my great-great-great-grandpa in 1885 *proves* that anything can happen. And I don't want *anything* to happen. I want what's *supposed* to happen."

Twain sighed. "I do too," he said. "I just wish I didn't have such a **vague notion** of what that might be." He glanced over at the window and saw the **pallid** light of dawn beginning to **suffuse** the sky and seep into the room. "Look, the sun's coming up already," he said. "We ought to get some sleep."

"Yes, I know," she said, standing up and going to the window.

"You know what else I miss?" he said after a moment.

"What?" she said, gazing out the window at the wavy carpet of snow that had covered the courtyard overnight. The storm was over. The sky was quiet and the wind was calm.

"I miss the simple beauty of the sunrise on the Mississippi River."

Angela turned around. "What was it like?"

"There's nothing like it, Angela. It was **unparalleled. Incomparable.** For a young boy, it was the most **serene** and sublime thing on earth." Suddenly his eyes filled with dancing light. "May I read you my description of it?"

"Yes, please do," she said, settling into her chair again. "I'd like that."

Twain rose and retrieved his manuscript from the desk, then returned to the sofa and sat down with it on his lap. He flipped through the pages. "Here it is," he said, removing several sheets and setting the rest of the pile beside him. He looked at Angela. "Now, this may sound a bit strange to your modern ear because it's written in southern **dialect,** but I think you'll understand it. This is the voice of an intelligent but uneducated fourteen-year-old boy from Missouri in about 1840 or so." He cleared his throat and began to read in a slow and curiously **juvenile** drawl.

"We set down on the sandy bottom where the water was about knee deep, and watched the daylight come. Not a sound, anywheres—perfectly still—just like the whole world was asleep, only sometimes the bull-frogs a-cluttering, maybe. The first thing to see, looking away over the water, was a kind of dull line—that was the woods on the t'other side—you couldn't make nothing else out; then a pale place in the sky; then more paleness, spreading around; then the river softened up, away off, and warn't black any more, but gray; you could see little dark spots drifting along, ever so far away—trading-scows, and such things; and long black streaks—rafts; sometimes you could hear a sweep screaking; or jumbled up voices, it was so still, and sounds come so far; and by-and-by you could see a streak on the water which you know by the look of the streak that there's a snag there in a swift current which breaks on it and makes that streak look that way; and you see the mist curl up off of the water, and the east reddens up, and the river, and you make out a log cabin in the edge of the woods, away on the bank on t'other side of the river, being a wood-yard, likely, and piled by them cheats so you can throw a dog through it anywheres; then the nice breeze springs up, and comes fanning you from over there, so cool and fresh, and sweet to smell, on account of the woods and the flowers; but sometimes not that way, because they've left dead fish laying around, gars, and such, and they do get pretty rank; and next you've got the full day, and everything smiling in the sun, and the song-birds just going it!"

The writer set the pages in his lap and looked at Angela. "Well, what do you think?" he asked, tugging at his mustache.

"I think it's pure American folk poetry," she said. "It's so simple and graceful and mellifluous—and so full of **vivid imagery.** That's from *The Adventures of Huckleberry Finn,* isn't it?"

"Yes it is," he said. "How did you know that?"

"Because I've read that book twice, once on my own in sixth grade because I was curious, and then again for English class in tenth grade."

Twain looked puzzled. "But I haven't published it yet. I hope to do that early next year." He patted the stack of paper beside him. "You see, this is the manuscript right here. I was putting some finishing touches on it when it **abruptly** changed places with Hank's... what did he call it again? Oh yes, his laptop."

Angela gasped. "That's the... the original manuscript of *Huck Finn*?"

"Yes," he replied, looking at her. She was covering her mouth with one hand. "Angela, is something wrong?"

"Uh, no, well, maybe, oh I don't know," she stuttered. "It's just that... I forgot that it wasn't just *you* that had to get back to 1883." She shook her head in disbelief. "This is crazy. Do you have any idea what an **invaluable commodity** that is?" she asked, pointing at the manuscript.

"Are you telling me the book will be successful?"

"I'm telling you it will be incredibly successful, assuming you can get that manuscript back to 1883 and publish it. Mr. Twain, that's a **compelling** book you wrote. A truly great book. I loved it, and millions of other people have read it too, and not just in America but around the world, in dozens of other languages. Do you know what Ernest Hemingway said about it?"

"No. Who's Ernest Hemingway?"

Angela smiled. "Oh yeah, that's right. He came after you. He was a famous American novelist in the first half of the twentieth century. He said that 'all modern American literature comes from one book by Mark Twain called *Huckleberry Finn*. There was nothing before. There has been nothing as good since.'"

Twain let out a **subdued** whoop. "You know, I think I might have liked this Hemingway fellow."

"Mr. Twain," Angela went on, "American literature came of age with *Huck Finn*. Unfortunately, America itself hasn't managed to grow up, or isn't willing to."

"What do you mean by that?"

"I mean that you changed American literature but you couldn't change America. You knew that America had to change itself. I think that was your **motivation** for writing *Huck Finn*. And I think that's why, from the very beginning, the book has been **controversial**."

Twain leaned forward and rested his chin on his fist. "**Controversial**? How so?"

"Well, you may not like to hear this, but at one time or another it's been **banned** from public libraries and schools in practically every state in the nation. At first it was challenged as **morally offensive**. Later it was accused of being racially **offensive**. Even today there's lingering **controversy** over the book's **alleged** racism. Now, as I see it, the people who criticize your book for that are judging it unfairly, not on its own **merits** as a work of art but by their own **arbitrary** standards or **subjective** experience.

"First, they fail to **comprehend** that it's a deeply **satirical** novel. Then they fail to **comprehend** the historical **context** of your story—the **antebellum** South, when slavery and **overt** racism were the social **norm**. And finally they fail to **comprehend** the historical **context** in which you wrote it—post-Reconstruction America, when de facto, **institutionalized** racial **oppression** replaced de jure slavery. In other words, the people who want to **ban** *Huck Finn* fail to see that it's society, not the book, that was and still is the problem.

"But here's the good news: Although it continues to be challenged as an **insidious** book, it continues to be read and respected by millions. Year after year it's taught in thousands of classrooms, where it **stimulates** young minds and **provokes intellectual** inquiry. Despite all the challenges to its reputation and **misinterpretations** of its message, *Huckleberry Finn* is considered one of the greatest works of American literature. It has **endured,** Mr. Twain. It has stood the test of time."

"This is an extremely **enlightening commentary,**" Twain said, his **keen** eyes ablaze. "And why do *you* think *Huckleberry Finn* has stood the test of time?" he asked.

"Because you told the truth," she answered, returning his gaze with a steady and confident one of her own. "And it wasn't just 'the truth, mainly.' It was the plain truth, the kind that makes people squirm. This wasn't just some yarn you spun for the fun of it. Your book has a **moral** message that comes through loud and clear to anybody who's willing to pay attention—that slavery and racism warped our **collective** conscience and **stupefied** our humanity.

"Mr. Twain, you told America to stop lying for once and look in the mirror. You **ridiculed** our **superficial** piety and our **hypocritical self-righteousness** and exposed the false gods we worship: **avarice,** selfishness, cruelty, and power. You told us it was high time to make good on that bold promise of liberty and justice for all, or we would someday come to regret it. And you told us to listen to our hearts and be willing to learn from our mistakes, like Huck Finn, not to live in some stupid fantasy world like that

egotistical and **condescending** Tom Sawyer, who treats people as if they existed merely for his own amusement.

"Most of all, Mr. Twain, people love your book because of the sensitive way you develop the friendship between Jim and Huck. Both of them are social **outcasts**, one a rebellious runaway slave and the other the white-trash, no-account son of an ornery town drunk. Your **portrayal** of their relationship shows us that all human beings, even the lowliest and least regarded members of society, have an **innate** dignity and worth and deserve to be treated with respect. And it shows us that we all are capable of being good and decent and fair and loyal and honorable and even heroic, regardless of our class or the color of our skin, if only we can cut through all the lies and nonsense and **disingenuous** crap that society throws at us in the **spurious** name of authority and truth. That, to me, is what your book is really all about."

Angela sat back in her chair and folded her arms. Twain looked at her silently for a moment, then slowly rose from the sofa. He stepped around the coffee table and stood in front of her chair.

"May I please have your hand?" he said.

She extended her hand and he took it in his. It was a surprisingly fine and delicate hand for a man, Angela thought, and it **quivered** as he spoke.

"Thank you, my dear girl, for that soaring **affirmation** of my work," he said quietly, looking into her eyes. "I will **cherish** it always." Then, with the elegance and grace and formality of a Victorian gentleman, he bowed and gently kissed her hand.

Angela beamed. But then her expression turned **solicitous.** "You see why we've got to get you back as soon as we can, Mr. Twain?"

"Yes I do," he said, turning away from her and wiping a tear from the corner of his eye. "I truly do."

Chapter 9

A **Harangue** and a **Dilemma**

"I knew it, dadfetchit, I just knew it!" said Mark Twain, striking his fist on the heavy wooden table hard enough to make the plates and glasses rattle. His four dining companions—Aimee, Angela, Orlando, and Hank—could tell from that **spontaneous** gesture, from his tone of **exasperation,** and from the **vivid** pink spots appearing all over his face that he was damn well **riled** and on the verge of a humongous **harangue.**

They were sitting together at a refectory table in a remote corner of the Rotunda, Hadleyburg's only **communal** dining hall, which was open to all members of the university. They had chosen to eat lunch in these **capacious** surroundings rather than in the more **intimate** atmosphere of the Stormfield College dining hall because they thought that here, amid the **raucous** hustle and bustle of the noisy Rotunda, their mealtime conversation would be more private. At the moment, however, that **assumption** was proving to be false.

"I knew that infernal, profanity-breeding contraption would never **cease** to be the **perpetual** botheration of the human race," Twain thundered. "Why, just look at everybody here. Look at 'em!"

"What about 'em?" Hank asked with his mouth full of food.

"Wuddabowdum?" said Twain, **mimicking** him. He looked around the table, an **incredulous** expression on his face. "You mean to tell me y'all can't see?"

Aimee wiped the corner of her mouth on her napkin. "See what?"

"See what everybody's doing," said Twain, waving his hand at the huge, crowded room with its **myriad** people standing in line for their food, eating at long dark tables, busing their trays, and otherwise mingling under the **lofty** domed **vault** of the Rotunda.

"So what are they doing?" asked Orlando. "I mean, besides eating their lunch or getting it."

From somewhere nearby there came a jangling, **dissonant,** metallic sound, as of some hopelessly out-of-tune instrument making a **ludicrous** attempt to be musical. Angela reached into her purse and retrieved her cellphone.

Twain struck the table again. "Practically every single person in this entire place—including *you,* young lady," he said, pointing an accusing finger at Angela, who had just answered her call, "is talking like there's no tomorrow into one of those **diminutive** doohickeys you call . . . what in tarnation are they called again? Oh yes: 'cellphones.'"

"Hey, I'll call you back later," Angela said into her phone, then stowed the object of the writer's **imminent invective** in her purse.

"Just look around this place," Twain went on. "Look at how many people have one of those blasted cellphones glued to their ear. They're talking into the dang thing while they're standing in line for chow, they're talking into it while they're walking around the room, they're talking into it while they're sitting at the table chewing and swallowing their food—and it's a wonder they don't choke what with all the words coming out and all the food going

down. Why, they're even talking into it while they're talking to somebody else, and then that somebody else is talking into one too! I honestly don't know how you folks can
stand being smack-dab in the middle of the **din** of all these
one-way conversations. I don't see how you can be so **indifferent** to all this **cacophony.** I've never *seen* such **incessant** yippin' and yappin' and yammerin' in all my life. I've
never *heard* such an **intolerable,** damn-fool racket. What
man in his right mind would want to live in the midst of
such a blimblammin' all the time?"

"Or *woman* in *her* right mind," Aimee **interjected.**

"Er, uh, sure," Twain said. He was momentarily derailed,
but he got himself back on track. "Well, I'll be ding-busted if
y'all don't have an **epidemic** of elbow tendinitis or laryngi-
tis, or **succumb** from a suffocating **effusion** of bad breath, or
drown yourselves in a river of molten cerumen."

Hank leaned over and whispered to Angela. "What's
cerumen?"

"Earwax," she whispered back.

Twain clattered right along. "'Cellphones' you say you
call 'em? Well that's not what *I'd* call 'em. Nosirree. That's
not an appropriate appellation for them at all. Why, I think
you ought to call 'em 'cell-fish,' and you can spell that
s-e-l-f-i-s-h. And that applies not only to that devilish little
phone you've invented but also to the **self-absorbed**
people who are constantly talking into it. Look," he said,
pointing to a **corpulent** older man wearing a herringbone
sports jacket with leather patches on the elbows. He was
lumbering through the Rotunda with a tray of food in one
hand and his cellphone pressed to his ear with the other.
His **sonorous** baritone voice **resonated** across the hall.

"Objective correlative, my arse!" the man bellowed.
"If that's an objective correlative then I'm a **pathetic** fallacy. And who is this **presumptuous** nitwit who dares to
impugn the **illustrious** and **venerable** T. S. Eliot? Aha, I

should have known it would be that lemon-sucking twit from Harvard! *Ne supra crepidam sutor iudicaret.*"*

"Listen to that highfalutin galoot," said Twain. "He's lost in his own **loquacious** world, **oblivious** of the effect he's having on others and **indifferent** to the fact that anyone can eavesdrop on his conversation. And look at her," he said, indicating a **garrulous** woman a few tables away whose bleached hair was so full of spikes that her head looked like some **bizarre species** of echinoderm, perhaps a mutant sea urchin. She was chattering lickety-split into her cellphone and **punctuating** her **verbose torrent** of words with **emphatic** thrusts of the fork she held in her free hand.

Twain shook his head. "How would you like to sit next to that babbling Medusa? I'll bet you wouldn't last a minute. First she'd stab you with that fork, then she'd impale you on that hair, and then she'd **flog** you to death with her tongue. And I suspect it would be a welcome **demise.**" He raised a forefinger in the air. "You know what I think all these public prattlers are? I think they're verbal exhibitionists. They *want* other people to overhear them because it makes them feel important. They crave attention, and they don't care how **insufferable** they have to be to get it."

"You know, I think he's right," Orlando said, addressing his friends. "It's, like, totally out of control. Our whole society has gone haywire over the cellphone."

"Dude, we're a hay-wireless society," Hank said with a grin that was **grotesquely amplified** by the food stuffed in his cheeks.

Aimee and Orlando groaned.

"*Hey, wire* you doing this to us?" said Angela, joining the pun.

---

*"Cobbler, stick to your last"—a Latin **idiom** that in **contemporary** English means "Don't be **presumptuous**; don't offer an opinion on something you don't know anything about."

Aimee and Orlando groaned again.

Hank swallowed **audibly.** "I'm just **concurring** with Big O," he said. "I think everybody's 'celling out.'"

"Nice one," said Angela. "I like that: 'celling out' with a *c,* equivalent to 'selling out' with an *s.*"

"Thanks," Hank said. He shoveled the last of his lunch into his mouth, swallowed it all in one **voracious** gulp, and washed it down with about a pint of milk.

"What gets me," said Aimee, "is that there's no **prescribed etiquette** for using your cellphone, or if there is, nobody seems to know about it and nobody cares. Some people use them in a legitimate and courteous way, while other people are unbelievably inconsiderate. You know what I mean?"

"I know what you mean, Aims," said Angela. "It's kind of a free-for-all."

"Yeah, seriously," said Orlando. "Sometimes you just want to say, 'Hey, you moron, could you take your asinine conversation and your stupid self somewhere else? You're not the only person on the planet. I'm trying to have a life here too.'"

"That's right," said Angela. "I can't believe the stuff some people think they can get away with. Like, they're standing in a movie-theater line cussing or dissing somebody, saying the F-word this and the F-word that, or they're walking around a mall talking about all the **lurid** and **sensational** details of their last date, who did what to whom and how and whatnot. I mean, give me a break. I don't need that."

"What's the F-word?" Twain asked with a **naive** smile.

Aimee giggled and Hank let fly with an uncouth snort.

"Oh, c'mon, Mr. T," Angela said, dismissing his **feigned** ignorance with a wave of her hand. "You are such a naughty boy!"

Twain just grinned and pulled at his mustache.

"The other thing that bugs me about cellphones is the

strident way they sound," Aimee went on. "All those awful nerve-racking beeps and squeaks and squeals. It's like they've got miniature android mice on drugs stuck inside. Maybe their **shrillness** doesn't bother you guys. Maybe it doesn't even register. But I'm a musician and I've got sensitive ears, and it just drives me nuts—especially when they go off in the library or during a movie or a concert."

"Or while you're simply trying to enjoy a civilized meal," said Twain as the piercing jingle of a cellphone erupted from an **adjacent** table.

"I'm totally with you, Aims," said Orlando. "And it's not just cellphones. I mean, when you think about it, the whole dang society has become one big beep. Everywhere you turn something electronic squawks at you. We're beeping ourselves to death. It's a bleeping mess!"

"And who exactly is to blame for this sorry state of affairs?" asked Twain. He looked around the table with an icy, **perceptive** stare. "Who **endowed** all these devices with the ability to jangle you into a bowlful of nervous jelly? Who are the tin-eared, **cantankerous rascals intent** on **tormenting** us with all this **vexatious** noise?"

Everyone was silent for a moment. Everyone, that is, except for Hank, who was playing with his PalmPirate, which **emitted** a **muffled** beep whenever he pushed one of its tiny buttons.

Suddenly Aimee cried, "I know! I know who's responsible!" She looked at Hank. "It's engineers. It's a **vast conspiracy** of software programmers and engineers."

They all turned and glared **contemptuously** at Hank.

"Huh?" he said, glancing up at them innocently. "Did you say something about engineers?"

Nobody spoke. They just glared.

Hank laid his PalmPirate on the table and threw up his hands. "Hey, don't go blaming me, you guys. I'm not responsible for a bleeping thing. Really. All I did was take an **inadvertent** trip to the fourth dimension and exchange one famous writer and his **invaluable** manuscript for a beat-up laptop with my whole life on the hard drive."

"And if you can **rectify** that mistake," said Twain, "then we'll be happy to **exonerate** you from any **culpability** for your brethren's **heinous** crimes against humanity's eardrums."

"Yeah, well I'm trying," Hank said grimly, picking up his PalmPirate and punching a few buttons. "Believe me, I'm trying."

"Speaking of **invaluable** manuscripts," said Angela, "check *this* out, you guys." She held up a copy of the *Hadleyburg Herald-Tribune,* which an earlier diner had left on the table, and pointed to a **prominent** headline on the front page.

"Oh my god!" Aimee said.

"Wow, that's weird," said Orlando.

"Read it to us," said Hank.

"Sure," Angela said. She laid the newspaper over her tray and began to read.

MARK TWAIN MANUSCRIPT MISSING

"Huckleberry Finn" disappears from library collection; authorities **baffled**

by Melanie MacGuffin

CANARD NEWS SERVICE

BUFFALO—When Artemus Ward, a security guard at the Buffalo and Erie County Public Library, went on his **customary** rounds last night at 2 a.m., checking to see that all the doors and windows were secure and the alarms and video cameras were in proper working order, he made a startling discovery.

Upon entering the library's **commodious,** wood-paneled Mark Twain Room, he was stunned to find that the 1,361-page manuscript of Twain's classic 1885 novel "The Adventures of Huckleberry Finn" was no longer inside its **hermetic** glass case. Ward had seen it there when he checked the room only an hour earlier. But since then it had somehow managed, like the **mercurial** Huckleberry Finn himself, to "light out for the Territory."

A **cursory initial** inspection by authorities revealed no evidence of forcible entry into either the sealed glass case or the building, and library officials and local police were at a loss to explain how this priceless manuscript, which has been the pièce de résistance of the library's collection since 1992, could vanish without a trace.

"Right now I'd rather not engage in **speculation,** but if I had to **speculate** I'd say it looks like an inside job," said Detective Joe Twitchell of the Buffalo Police Department, who is in charge of the investigation. Today detectives will conduct a **diligent** search of the premises and dust the room for fingerprints, he said. The library will be closed to the public during the investigation.

Mary Fairbanks, director of the Buffalo and Erie County Public Library, which is one of the most important **repositories** in the country for Twain's literary **artifacts, scoffed** at the **notion** that a library **curator** or employee could be **culpable.**

"Very few people have access to that manuscript, and those who do are highly **competent** and **trustworthy** professionals who take great pride in serving as the caretakers and guardians of our precious literary **heritage,**" she said. "The idea that they would violate the **solemn** duty of their stewardship is unthinkable, and to suggest that any of them would **jeopardize** their careers and risk going to jail for such a **reckless** and **foolhardy** crime is so **preposterous** as to be almost risible."

What makes this mysterious disappearance even more **perplexing** is the intriguing and **convoluted** story of the manuscript of "Huckleberry Finn," half of which was **deemed** lost for nearly a hundred years.

The story begins with a **civic**-minded attorney named James Fraser Gluck, who served as a **curator** of the Buffalo Young Men's Library Association, the predecessor of the Buffalo and Erie County Public Library. One of Gluck's **aspirations** was to establish a collection of manuscripts of books by important authors so that their original handwritten work could be preserved for the **enlightenment** and **edification** of future generations.

In the late 19th century, book manuscripts were not valued the way they are today, and manuscript **acquisition** for historical preservation or commercial gain was a **novel concept.** "Until then, authors' literary manuscripts were often misplaced or casually discarded shortly after the publication process," said Victor Doyno, professor of English at the State University of New York at Buffalo and an **eminent** Twain scholar. "In that **era** manuscripts were seldom valued for their own sake as **inherently** special."

In 1885 Gluck wrote to Mark Twain, inquiring whether he would be interested in donating the manuscript of one of his books to the library. Twain liked the idea, and wrote back praising Gluck for establishing the collection and promising to send him the second half of the manuscript of his recently published novel "The Adventures of Huckleberry Finn." In his letter Twain explained that he couldn't send the first half because he suspected it had been lost or destroyed by the printer. Soon two packages containing 696 pages of the manuscript arrived at the Buffalo library.

Two years later, the missing first half of the manuscript magically reappeared, and Twain dutifully packed up these 665 pages and sent them to Gluck. According to Professor Doyno, Gluck's legal work and various other **civic** duties distracted him from properly attending to this half of the manuscript. "After [Gluck's] unexpected death in 1897, his family sorted and packed his papers," Doyno said. "Some unknown person put the neatly wrapped and labeled 665 sheets of extraordinarily valuable manuscript into a trunk." The trunk was put away and forgotten, and the first half of "Huckleberry Finn" was lost again.

Nearly a century passed, during which Twain's novel gained both worldwide fame and **notoriety.** "Then one day in late 1990 a granddaughter of James Fraser Gluck living in California decided to look into her grandfather's trunks," said Doyno, and she rediscovered the long-lost pages. Experts **verified** the **authenticity** of the manuscript, and the remarkable discovery was formally announced and reported in the press.

Then the **inevitable** legal battle began, a long and **complex** contest over who owned the manuscript and controlled the literary rights to it. When the **litigious** dust finally settled, the disjoined halves of "Huckleberry Finn" were reunited—"as Twain had intended," said Doyno—in July 1992 in a ceremony at the Buffalo and Erie County Public Library.

That was the happy ending to a **long-standing** literary mystery until the sudden and disturbing disappearance of the entire manuscript last night. Now it remains to be seen whether authorities will recover this **elusive document** yet again—and if they do, will it be **intact**?

Angela looked up from the newspaper. "That's it," she said.

Hank let out a soft whistle.

"That's incredible," Aimee said.

Orlando looked at Twain, who had been listening **intently**, a puzzled expression on his face. "I guess this means, as far as the police are concerned, that you are now in possession of stolen property—extremely valuable stolen property."

"And we're all **accessories** after the fact," Angela added.

"I'm afraid I don't understand," Twain said, scratching his head. "How can there be two copies of my manuscript when I've made only one—unless, of course, the copy the library had is a **forgery**?"

Hank leaned forward. "It's not a **forgery**," he said, looking around the table. "Here's my **hypothesis**. Both copies of your manuscript are genuine and **bona fide** because they're one and the same. The library's copy is your copy, just a heck of a lot older. Now, as the **cliché** says, you can't be in two places at once, so when your copy arrived in the future the library's copy **ceased** to exist as an **artifact** from your time. Your copy **supplanted** it, and theirs disappeared."

"But disappeared where?" Twain asked, stroking his chin.

"Into the **intangible domain** of the fourth dimension, I guess," said Hank.

"So how can the library get its copy back?" Aimee asked.

"Good question," Hank said. He looked at Twain. "Probably only by getting his copy back where it belongs."

"And what are the **prospects** of that at the moment?" asked Orlando.

"That's another good question. I've been messing around with some stuff on my PalmPirate, and if everything goes right I may be able to get it to talk to my laptop over the Net. That would at least be a start." He paused and looked down at the table. "And I'm also thinking about talking to Merle," he said in a low voice.

Orlando frowned. "Merlin the Magician? The crazy troglodyte?"

"Uh-huh."

"You mean that **eccentric** computer geek who's supposed to know everything about **Omniscience**, even stuff the professors don't know?" said Aimee.

"And who's **infamous** for being an **antisocial** weirdo?" said Angela.

Hank nodded. "Yup. Him."

"Can we trust that guy with this?" Orlando asked.

Hank shrugged. "I don't know. But I'm kind of running out of options."

"I don't think this is a good idea," Aimee said, shaking her head.

"Neither do I," said Angela, "**Disclosure** is too risky, especially now that the missing manuscript is all over the news."

"Yeah," Orlando said, "we could get ourselves into some major *caca* if we don't keep this whole business secret. I mean, do you want to wind up in jail, dude?"

Hank slammed his fist down on the table so hard the trays and dishes jumped, and so did everybody else. "What the hell do you want me to do, then?" he growled through clenched teeth. "If you've got any good ideas about how to get us out of this stupid mess then please let me know, because guess what? I don't have the answer. You're all expecting me to figure this out and formulate a plan, but I'm sorry. I'm only a gearhead. I'm not **omnipotent.** I can't just flip a switch and fix everything. I don't think I can solve this problem on my own. I'm going to need help. And Merle is the only person I know who can help me—and us."

There was a long silence as everyone **brooded** over Hank's **proposition.** Finally Twain cleared his throat, leaned forward, and spoke in a voice just loud enough for them to hear him over the **clamor** and hubbub of the Rotunda. "What we've got here, it seems to me, is a classic **dilemma.** Hank's saying that he can't fix things by himself; he needs help and he thinks this Merle fellow can provide it. The rest of you are saying that to let anybody else in on things wouldn't be **prudent,** that the best course is to keep our eyes open and our mouths shut. Well, there's nothing wrong with being **circumspect**; I'm all for staying out of trouble, especially when it may involve being **incarcerated.** But if we don't do something soon we'll remain at an **impasse**; we'll be stuck where we are now, with no **probability** of change or hope for **amelioration.** So I suppose we're damned if we do and damned if we don't, and that's why I say we're on the horns of a **dilemma.**

"Now, my friends, I'm going to share a bit of cornpone wisdom with you," he drawled. "After nearly five decades of **fretting** over a great many decisions of this nature I have **devised** a rule of thumb for **resolving** them, which I have expressed in a kind of **maxim** or **aphorism.** This is how it goes: 'When faced with a choice between equally undesirable **alternatives,** choose the one that's more *interesting.* That way, at least you'll be entertained by the **consequences.**'" He paused and looked around the table. "I've never gone wrong following that advice."

"Really?" said Aimee.

"Really," said Twain. "Of course, I've never gone right much either, but that ain't no matter."

Orlando scratched his head. "So what exactly are you suggesting here?"

"I'm suggesting that necessity is the mother of taking chances," Twain said. "We should do what's more interesting, and seeking help is more interesting than sitting tight. I think Hank should talk to his man."

"So it's settled then?" asked Hank. "I'm going to see Merle?"

"Yes, it's settled," said Twain. "Let's see what sort of magic your wizard can work." **Reluctantly,** Aimee, Angela, and Orlando **deferred** to his decision.

"Hey guys," Angela said as they began gathering their stuff and getting up to bus their trays, "has everybody forgotten that tonight's the Winter Bacchanal?"

"Omigod, that's right," said Aimee. "I've been so busy with finals and my recital and everything that I haven't even thought about a costume."

"Neither have I," said Orlando. "I guess we've all been too **preoccupied** lately."

"No kidding," said Hank. "Especially since 'Uncle Mark' came to visit."

"I take it this Winter Bacchanal is some sort of **revelry,**" said Twain.

"You bet it is," said Orlando. "It's the biggest party of the year, even bigger than the Spring Fling, and it's a lot of fun. The whole campus participates, everybody's blowing off steam, and things can get pretty rowdy and **boisterous.**"

Angela explained that the bacchanal was a time-honored Hadleyburg **tradition,** an annual **rite** celebrating the end of the fall semester and the grueling demands of finals period and the beginning of winter vacation. People dressed up in silly costumes, there were banquets and dances in all the dining halls, and the merrymaking went on deep into night. Right after sunset the president of Hadleyburg, Jane Addams, would **initiate** the festivities by ringing the bacchanal bell in the courtyard outside the Rotunda.

They all agreed to **reconvene** that evening at six and attend the bacchanal together. Then they **dispersed.** Orlando went off to face the **trials** and **tribulations** of his American literature final; Angela left to deliver her history term paper and then go to her part-time job in the **bursar'**s office; and Hank set off to seek out Merle. As she got up to leave, Aimee handed Twain a spare key to her suite.

"You're not going to get into trouble without us, are you?" she asked in a sweetly **solicitous** voice that Twain found charming.

"I doubt it, young lady," he replied with a tug at his mustache. "Unless I'm suddenly possessed by the daredevil spirit of adventure."

"Well, let's just hope you're not." She flashed him an **amiable** smile and headed off to prepare for her recital at Henley Hall.

Twain leaned back in his chair and gazed up at the **stately neoclassical** architecture of the Rotunda. He took a deep breath, and as he slowly let it out the realization came to him that for the first time since arriving here he was on his own, left to his own devices. He wondered what **diversion** he should pursue—besides smoking, of course—in the several hours that lay ahead. But he hardly had a moment to **relish** the possibilities before he was rudely interrupted by someone pulling at his sleeve.

"Sir, excuse me, but can I ask you something?" said an unfamiliar voice. It was not a pleasant voice, he thought. It was an **insistent, officious,** squeaky voice, filled with tension and **tenacity,** as if all it had ever done and all it knew how to do was nag, complain, **vex,** pester, **harass,** buttonhole, and bore.

Twain turned and saw that it was the **voluble** woman from the nearby table, the sea urchin with the spiky bleached hair who had been jabbering on her cellphone while thrusting her fork in the air. Her **proximity** now also enabled him to notice, with no small amount of shock and **repugnance,** the silver stud in the middle of her lower lip and the **meandering** green snake tattooed around her exposed navel.

"Excuse me, sir, but did you hear me? Can I talk to you for a minute?" Now it was her index finger, rather than her fork, that poked **random** holes in the air.

"Yes," Twain said, already weary of her voice, "if you must."

"I must. I absolutely must. Because it's so incredible."

She pulled up an empty chair and plopped down in it backward. Then she opened the floodgate of her mouth and released a roiling river of words. "I was sitting at that table over there like talking to a friend on the phone about how Mark Twain's manuscript of *Huckleberry Finn* has just disappeared from a library in Buffalo—isn't that terrible? like, what a tragic day for American letters—when I happened to look over here and see you, and I thought, like, wow, I can't believe it, this is amazing, there's this guy over there who looks exactly like Mark Twain, and is that freaky or what? Because guess what? You're not going to believe this, but it's true, I'm not kidding. I am like totally into Mark Twain and I'm writing my senior **thesis** on him! Can you believe that? Is that weird or what? I mean, like, talk about **serendipity.** So what I want to know is, like, who are you, anyway? Are you some kind of Twain impersonator who visits college campuses and freaks people out? Because I mean it's just **uncanny** how you resemble him. Or maybe you're an **obscure** relative of his or something? Or—and I can't help thinking this—could you possibly maybe somehow—and I know this is going to sound crazy, but I'm not wacko, okay?—could you actually be the real Mark Twain doing some Connecticut Yankee–style time-traveling and making a special guest appearance at Hadleyburg so I can interview you for my **thesis**?"

She paused for breath or, it seemed to Twain, to pant. "What did you say your name was?" he asked in the brief **hiatus**.

She jabbed her forehead with her finger. Then the floodgate opened and he was **inundated** again. "Oh, didn't I tell you that already? No? Stupid me, I forgot to introduce myself. Can you believe it? Like, how did I manage to do that? You know, it's like totally weird but sometimes I think and talk so fast I forget what just came out of my mouth, or didn't come out in this case, or whatever, you know what I mean? Anyway, my name's Isabel Lyon. What's yours? Wait, let me guess. Is it Samuel Langhorne Clemens?"

Chapter 10

The Mysterious Stranger

Hank sped up High Street toward Science Hill as fast as his legs could carry him. He had a good idea of where to look for the man he wanted to see, and he didn't think he would be too hard to find.

The man he sought was **renowned** for being irritable and **capricious,** but Hank knew he had one **trait** that you could always count on. He worked. In fact, he was such a tireless and obsessive worker that the words *assiduous* and *sedulous* simply did not do him justice. The man was the **personification** of **diligence,** Hank thought. He would almost certainly be holed up in his solitary cell, toiling away.

They called him Merlin the Magician, the Techno-Wizard, and the Hermit of Science Hill, but his real name was Merle Paige. He occupied a windowless office in the basement of Irving Laboratory, which, rumor had it, he rarely left except to visit the bathroom that was conveniently situated across the hall. Merle was something of a campus legend, an object of curiosity for the student body in general and a mysterious, **mythic** figure to the inner circle of hardcore nerds, geeks, and wonks who frequented Science Hill. He was **notorious** for his **misanthropy** and feared for the **irascibility** with which he sometimes **mani-**

fested it. His technological **exploits** were the stuff of tall tales and **anecdotes** breathlessly **recounted** in the hallway on the way to class. The extent of his **prodigious** genius was a matter of **continual** debate, but his **intellectual** superiority—like the military **supremacy** of the United States—was simply taken for granted. Nobody was smarter than Merle.

Little was known about his past. It was said that he had come to Hadleyburg some years ago as an **ambitious, precocious** twenty-year-old doctoral candidate in physics, math, and computer science. He had turned down generous offers from Harvard, the University of Chicago, and UC Berkeley and chosen Hadleyburg instead because he wanted to work on an exciting new project: the creation of a giant supercomputer whose databases and applications and speed would dwarf all others and whose potential capabilities were, if not unlimited, then impossible to **circumscribe.** This magnificent **feat** of technology came to be known around campus as **Omniscience,** but its formal name, which was rumored to be Merle's **facetious** invention, was TWAIN—an acronym for Technology With An **Irrelevant** Name.

After two years he was awarded his Ph.D. He might have gotten it in one if he hadn't been expelled from the university for **inflicting** a **malicious** onslaught of malware upon various **intellectual rivals,** including several professors. He was quietly reinstated when it became clear that he was the only person who could undo the damage caused by the **debilitating** string of viruses he had created and **disseminated.** This incident established his reputation as a brilliant antihero and earned him the lasting **enmity** of his **peers**—in particular Gideon Reisenzeit, an **esteemed** professor of physics and computer science whose recently published research Merle had boldly **debunked** and shown to be suspiciously **derivative** of his own.

The following year, the university **exacted** its **vengeance.** Merle was not granted the assistant professorship he **coveted,** and the only person who was surprised was Merle. He blamed it on departmental politics and **resentful colleagues** who publicly **derided** him but privately envied his gifts. The university administrators, however, were not stupid. They knew he was **indispensable** to the success of their **incipient** supercomputer; they also knew he was emotionally wedded to the machine. So they offered him a position as a researcher and programmer for the TWAIN project on one condition: that if he ever again violated the university's Code of **Ethical** Conduct he would be subject to criminal prosecution. Merle accepted, and from that point on he **literally** went underground.

He **embraced** his solitude and **cultivated** his **haughty disdain** for others the way some people **nurture** a grudge. So rarely did he emerge from the gloom of his **subterranean** hideaway that he became a kind of spectral being, showing up in strange places at odd hours and startling people with his wild eyes and **shabby** clothes and long, stringy, **unkempt** hair and beard. People began talking about "Merlin visitations" with mingled awe and **dread**—the kind of awe that a biologist would feel upon finding a member of a **species** believed to be **extinct,** and the kind of **dread** that anyone would feel upon being invited by an **extraterrestrial** lifeform to go for a ride in a spaceship.

No one could agree whether witnessing a Merlin visitation was **auspicious** or **ominous,** but they could all agree on one thing about Merle: You definitely wouldn't want to mess with him because he was one big, ugly, creepy-looking dude.

The ground began to rise. Hank clomped steadily up the hill, leaving an **obscure** trail of bootprints in the **hodgepodge** of other footprints embedded in the shallow layer of snow covering the sidewalk. As he **ascended** he passed some of the most **imposing edifices** on campus. They were all so different from each other, so **diverse** in their architecture, that to anyone observing them for the first time they would have seemed almost laughably **incongruous.**

There was the sleek, tall, **antiseptic** chemistry building, with its smooth concrete **facade** and **embellishments** of steel. There was the durable brick biology building, a **paragon** of **colonial** architecture with its ivy-covered walls, **stately** porticoes, and white mullioned windows. There was the **neoclassical** physics building, which, with its fluted Doric columns and **elaborately** sculptured pediment, looked like a cross between a mausoleum and the Parthenon. And then there was the **abstract, amorphous** blob of the geology building, a bold modernist experiment in rough-**hewn** granite that sadly went **awry.**

Finally, at the **summit** of the hill stood Irving Laboratory, the home of the engineering and computer science departments and the most **imposing** and **eccentric** structure of them all. It was built in the shape of a majuscule I in honor of Miles "Cosmo" Irving, a **prosperous** computer chip **magnate** and Hadleyburg **alumnus,** and the **benefactor** whose **munificence** had paid for its construction. A **critic** attempting to characterize the building's architectural style might have described it as Big-Box meets the Big House. It was **austere** and plain and purely **functional.** It managed to combine all the **forbidding** aspects of a factory, a fortress, and a prison. The **unadorned** walls were grim, gray geometric planes. The windows were thin vertical apertures—like the **loopholes** and machicolations in the battlement of a castle—that seemed better suited for defending the building from a **siege** than for admitting light and air.

The only ornament in the whole design was a **massive** cinder-block pyramid on the roof, situated in the middle of the stem of the building's I, directly above the main entrance. At the **apex** of the pyramid was a horizontal oval window with a dark circle in the center, which made the window look like a huge, **vigilant** eye staring down High Street at the heart of the Hadleyburg campus.

Gazing up at this giant, glassy eye, and squinting as it glinted in the **feeble** winter sunlight, Hank recalled how Orlando had once **expounded** brilliantly on the various things it symbolized, peeling off layer upon **convoluted** layer of meaning.

First he had **postulated** that the eye occupied the highest spot on campus because Hadleyburg is an **institution** devoted to higher learning and the **elevation** of the mind.

Then he had engaged in some quasi-Freudian **analysis** and said that because the pronoun *I* is a symbol or representation of the self or the **ego,** and because the **ego** is one's conscious mind, the eye, **metaphorically** speaking, is thus a window to the mind—the eye through which we **perceive** the *I* and through which the *I* **perceives** us.

Next he had theorized that if the *I* shape of the building stands for *Irving* then it is reasonable to assume, because *I* and *eye* are homophones, that *eye* and *I* are equivalent and that the eye also stands for *Irving.* And when you have an *eye* for an *I* and an *I* for an *eye,* then it stands to reason that you also have an *I* for an *I,* the self-centered **doctrine** of **egoism,** and an *eye* for an *eye,* otherwise known as *lex talionis,* the **principle** of **retributive** justice famously **articulated** in Hammurabi's Code.

Finally, if you look at the back of a dollar bill you will see, on the lefthand side, a pyramid with a glowing eye at the top that looks just like the pyramid on the roof of the building. This, he had said, was the key to putting the whole thing into perspective.

As Orlando saw it, Irving Laboratory was not an idle piece of architecture; it was architecture for an **idol.** The building was a thinly veiled **tribute** to the presumed great-ness of Miles "Cosmo" Irving, billionaire captain of indus-try. It was a **monument** to his **monumental ego** and a window through which to view the **conceited** workings of his mind. By placing his I—the symbol of his **ego**—atop Science Hill, Irving **elevates** himself above all others. And by placing his eye—the outward symbol of his mind's eye—atop the entire campus, he ranks his **intellect** and his **perception** above all others. He **glorifies** self-interest and the philosophy of look-out-for-number-one (an *I* for an *I*), he **endorses** the code of revenge and retaliation (an *eye* for an *eye*), and he makes **manifest** his faith in the almighty dollar and his **creed** that money is, quite **literally,** life's **ideal** (as in *I deal*).

"Which makes the guy, in my **humble** opinion, an un-believably stuck-up and unbelievably humongous dork," Orlando had concluded, and Hank had heartily agreed, adding a few **vigorous** expletives of his own.

The five bleak stories of the **somber** building **loomed** before him. He strode up to the entrance, slid his photo ID card through the slot, and punched in his numeric pass-code. There was a **strident** beep and the automatic glass doors opened with an almost **imperceptible** whoosh. He passed through them, nodded to the expressionless secu-rity guard at the desk, and headed for the stairs. The sound of his heavy footfalls echoed in the cavernous lobby.

Hank knew Merle's office was in the basement, but he didn't know where. He **surmised** that it would most likely be somewhere near **Omniscience,** which was housed in the west wing of the building—either the capital or the pedestal of the majuscule I, depending on which end you **perceived** as the top and which the bottom—and **acces-sible** only to an **elite** handful of Hadleyburg's most **distin-guished** professors and scientists. So when he emerged from the stairwell Hank turned left, toward the west, and walked down the brightly **illuminated** hallway.

The hallway was empty and quiet except for the faint buzzing of the fluorescent lights. He passed room B-3 on the left, which was labeled OPERATIONS, and B-4 on the right, labeled FURNACE. Then came B-5, ELECTRIC, B-6, AIR CONDITIONING, B-7, CUSTODIAL, and B-8, STORAGE. Why would anybody intentionally **isolate** himself down here in the mechanical bowels of the building? Hank wondered. Why **willfully dissociate** yourself from the **stimulating** and **rarefied** scholarly **discourse** going on above your head?

He came to a T intersection and stopped. He looked left and right down the hall and saw the same thing both ways: more smooth white walls occasionally interrupted by a dark blue door, more bright fluorescent lights buzzing over speckled linoleum floors. Instinct told him to turn right, and he yielded to its **visceral impulse.**

The first door on the left was a men's bathroom. The first door on the right was room B-9. Its label was advisory rather than descriptive: PRIVATE—KEEP OUT. Hank noticed there were two deadbolt locks above the doorknob. The other doors he had passed had only one. This door also had a peephole. The other doors didn't.

Hank's **intuition** told him this had to be it. He put his ear against the door and listened **intently.** He heard a **continuous** clickety-clacking sound, as of someone typing rapidly on a keyboard. Could that be Merle? Suddenly the clickety-clacking **ceased** and the room was silent. His heart began to beat harder and faster. He swallowed and realized that his mouth was quite dry. Here's hoping, he thought as he raised his hand to knock, that the occupant of room B-9 turns out to be like the room: **benign.**

He knocked on the door three times and listened. Something moved inside. He was certain of it. It was just a small, **indistinct** sound, perhaps of a chair creaking, but he had heard it. He waited about thirty seconds and then knocked again.

"Hello?" he called through the door. "Merle?"

Hank listened for a full minute this time. There was no answer and no other sound from inside the room. He knocked a third time.

"Merle, I need to talk to you," he said. "I need your help."

The appeal met with silence.

Hank knocked again, this time more **aggressively.** "Dude, I know you're in there," he said, almost shouting through the door. "I heard you typing." He paused. "C'mon, Merle. I know you're in there and I need your help and I'm not going anywhere until you open this door and talk to me."

There was another long silence. Then Hank heard something stir inside the room.

"Who the hell is it?" asked a deep, gruff voice.

"My name's Hank Morgan. I'm an engineering and computer science major. I need your help."

"I don't teach, you dim bulb. If you can't pass your courses, get a tutor."

"I don't need a tutor, Merle. I need to talk to you about **Omniscience,** I mean about TWAIN. I need your help fixing something I did with it, or maybe *to* it."

There was a pause. "No you don't," the voice grumbled. "I'm busy. Get lost."

"Maybe I could come back later when you're not so busy?" Hank pleaded.

"Forget it," the voice growled. "I'm always busy, and I'm even more busy when some damned idiot has the **arrogance** to interrupt me. Now get the hell out of here and leave me alone."

Hank took a deep breath and silently **exhorted** himself not to be disappointed or **deterred** by this stern **rebuff.** Merle was his best hope of straightening things out, his only hope—if he could just persuade him to open the door and talk. He fumbled in the **voluminous** pockets of his **bulky** coat and retrieved the small spiral notepad and pen that he always carried.

He flipped open the notepad to a blank sheet of paper, laid the pad against the wall, and scrawled this message:

> Last night I hacked into TWAIN and **inadvertently** accessed the fourth dimension. Some **crucial** stuff got transported, including somebody famous. I don't know how to fix things. Will you please help me?

Hank pounded on the door with his fist. "Hey Merle, this is serious!" he shouted. "I'm not kidding. Something totally weird happened with TWAIN, something I did. I need to tell you about it. I can't say anything out here in the hallway. Somebody might be listening. I'm going to slip a note under your door. Read it and you'll understand. Okay, here it comes." He tore the message from the notepad and slid it under the door.

There was no response. Hank bit his lip and held his breath. Finally, after a silence that seemed **eternal,** he heard the **muffled** sound of steps approaching the door, then the faint crinkle of paper as the person inside picked up the note from the floor. Then there was silence again.

Hank rapped softly on the door. "Merle, will you please help me? This is an emergency...Merle? Are you there?"

There was another **interminable** silence, during which Hank had the **distinct** sensation that he was being **scrutinized** through the peephole.

"How do I know this isn't a practical joke?" the voice snarled **abruptly,** and Hank flinched with surprise. "'Cause if this is some stupid undergraduate prank," the voice continued, rising to a roar, "I swear I'll break every damn bone in your body and kick the ass of anybody else who's hiding out there with you. I've got a baseball bat and you don't want to give me an excuse to use it."

Hank's heart sank as he realized that his **secretive** approach had backfired. He should have been more **candid.** He had seemed too **surreptitious** and **deceptive,** which had only **exacerbated** Merle's **paranoia.** Now he would have to find a way to **mollify** him, but how? What could he say or do that would convince Merle he wasn't being **deceitful?** He needed something, and he needed it fast.

Then, mercifully, the answer came to him. The access code to TWAIN. That's what he would give him. That would prove he was telling the truth.

Knowing the access code to TWAIN was like having security clearance to enter the Pentagon or Fort Knox. The code unlocked the otherwise **impenetrable** door to the supercomputer, enabling the user to explore its **multifaceted** contents and capabilities. It was like a PIN, only far more **cryptic** and **complex.** After months of **fruitless** attempts and frustrating failures, Hank had finally managed to **decipher** it, and when he did he had promptly memorized it.

"Hey, take it easy," Hank said in his most **placating** voice. "I'm not joking and this is not a **hoax.** I swear it isn't. This is totally on the level and I can prove it. Hang on a second."

He opened his notepad and scribbled the **abstruse** code on a fresh page. Then he tore out the page and slipped it under the door. "There, I think you'll know what that is," he said. "I figured it out myself," he couldn't help adding with unconcealed pride.

Hank strained his ears to listen. He heard the crinkle of the paper being lifted from the floor. Then silence. Then a low grunt, as of recognition.

"Are you alone?" the deep voice asked.

"Yeah. I'm alone. I swear."

There was another long silence.

"All right, let's talk," the voice said finally.

Hank heard the scrape and click of the two deadbolts sliding back. The doorknob turned and the door drew back partway, just enough to allow him to enter sideways, with one shoulder first. Then a shockingly hairy, thick-fingered hand appeared from behind the door and summoned him in.

Chapter 11

Mark Twain in Eruption

"C'mon, Mr. Morgan, I know you're not really Mr. Morgan, you're really Samuel Langhorne Clemens, a.k.a. Mark Twain, so like you might as well admit it because you can't fool me," said Isabel Lyon in her impossibly rapid, **shrill**, and **vexatious** voice.

Mark Twain zigzagged through the maze of tables and chairs and people in the **teeming** Rotunda, heading for the main exit. It was a desperate and **erratic quest** for **egress**, a mad dash for freedom. For the past five minutes—the five most **insufferable** and **interminable** minutes of his life—he had been badgered, **coaxed, harassed,** wheedled, and hectored by this strange and detestable woman. Never had he witnessed such **relentless cajolery** and **remorseless coercion.** Never had he been so **mercilessly** bedeviled and miserably importuned. He knew there was no hope of fending off this deranged chatterbox. She was a verbal train wreck, **catastrophe incarnate.** His only hope for survival was to **flee.**

Isabel had grabbed her coat and backpack and followed him like an **assiduous** hound pursues the **elusive quarry.** "You can try all you want to hide it," she squeaked, "disguising yourself in those **contemporary** clothes and telling me stories and lies—boy were you a famous fibster—but it won't do any good. No way. Not in a million years. Because I just know you're the real deal, mister, and I'm going to find a way to prove it."

"I never tell a lie," said Twain, "except for practice." He yanked an empty chair behind him to block her path, but that did little to **thwart** or **deter** her. She clambered over this **inconsequential hindrance** and continued pummeling him with words.

"Hey, wait up for a minute, will you? C'mon, I'm not going to bite you, I just want to talk to you, I'm your friend, I can help you if you just let me. You can trust me, really. This is just between us, okay? I'm not going to tell anybody else who you are, I swear. I'm like your biggest fan, your most **ardent advocate**. I have nothing but **esteem** for you. I've read almost every word you wrote and probably over half of the mountain of criticism people have written about you. Didn't I tell you my **thesis** is all about you?"

"Yes, unfortunately you did," Twain grumbled.

"Don't you want to know what it's called?"

"No thank you."

Isabel was **undaunted** by his **indifference**. "It's called 'Individualism, Duality, and the Significant Other in the Fiction of Mark Twain.' How do you like that? Pretty cool title, huh? It's a Freudian **analysis** of how your **subliminal preoccupations** and **motivations manifest** themselves in your characters and plots. Oh yeah, stupid me, I forgot to mention I'm a double major in American studies and psychology, which is why it's a Freudian **analysis,** but that probably doesn't mean anything to you anyway because good old Siggie didn't achieve **renown** until the last years of your life, so you probably don't know who he was and why he's significant. But I still think you'd find my **thesis** really interesting and I'd love to discuss my theories with you if you've got a minute. Hey, can you just slow down for a second? What's the big rush, anyway?"

Twain's head was throbbing and he was breathing hard. He **yearned** for a long, soothing smoke but he vowed then and there that he would joyfully part with the habit if only a stray lightning bolt would strike Isabel dead. He realized that his **aversion** to her wasn't **rational**; it was **spontaneous** and **visceral.** He had **conceived** it from the moment he heard her **odious,** ugsome voice. Who in the world, he wondered, could bear to listen to such hideous gobblings?

"Hey c'mon, Mr. Clemens," Isabel squawked, "take it easy, lighten up, chill out. What's the matter, anyway? Was it something I said? Don't you like me?"

Twain stopped dead in his tracks. Slowly he turned around and scowled at his **tormentor.** It was a **withering, forbidding** scowl, all raging eyebrows and grim lips. "Young lady," he said, his voice filled with **indignation** and **contempt,** "I do not believe I could ever learn to like you except on a raft at sea with no other provisions in sight."

"Omigod, I can't believe it, this is so amazing!" Isabel announced to no one in particular, waving her hands in a manner not unlike the **frenzied** flapping of a startled chicken. "I mean, can you believe I'm like talking to the writer that I **revere** above all others and he's just **reviled** me with one of the wittiest lines in his autobiography? That's awesome! I am like *so* flattered."

Twain was momentarily taken aback. "What autobiography? I haven't written an autobiography."

"Aha! You see? I told you you couldn't **deceive** me," cackled the **frenetic** fowl with the spiky crest. She thrust her finger at him. "You just repeated a **memorable** put-down from your autobiography practically **verbatim.** If you'd known it was from your own writing you wouldn't have repeated it because you want me to believe you're not Mark Twain. But you didn't know it was from your own writing because you haven't written it yet. You won't write your autobiography until you're an old man."

"Very clever, young lady, but **patently** false. I once heard someone say those very words and I repeated them just now because they were so **apt**."

The sea urchin–chicken creature laughed, although the laugh was really more of a **modulated** shriek. "Now that's a stretch, and from like the king of the stretchers no less," she said. "You can stop being so **evasive** now, Mr. Clemens, because I'm just not buying it. I mean, that was like totally **credible** evidence that you're the real McCoy."

The **vivid** pink spots began to appear again on Twain's face. "I don't know who or what 'the real McCoy' is, but I'm telling you I ain't it—and that's that!"

"Double aha!" Isabel crowed, jabbing her finger at him again. "'The real McCoy' is a **commonplace idiom**. Like, everybody knows it, you know? But you just admitted you didn't and that can only mean one thing: that you've never heard it before because the expression didn't come into the language until you were . . . well, you know—whatever. Anyway, that's **corroborating** evidence to **substantiate** my case."

"Hell and damnation, woman, that's enough!" Twain exploded, clenching his fists and stamping his foot. "Your dadblamed blimblammin' would make a preacher swear! Why, I'd rather suffer **eternal** fire and brimstone than **endure** another minute of your **unremitting** and **diabolical persecution**!"

This **vehement** outburst did not shock Isabel. Instead she grinned, affording Twain a glimpse of her pearly white fangs. "This is, like, *so* cool," she said, regarding him with curious amusement. "I can't believe I'm witnessing Mark Twain in eruption."

The **harried** writer noticed that heads were beginning to turn in their direction. Their **confrontation** was attracting an audience. Not good, he thought. He drew the hood of Hank's sweatshirt over his head and hightailed it for the exit.

But the chicken of the sea was right behind him again, hideously gobbling away. "Okay, okay, I can see you're like not really in such a good mood right now. You seem kind of stressed out and I guess I can't blame you—coming to the future must be really freaky, now that I think about it— but maybe you could just take a second to, like, give me your autograph?"

Having fallen once for her **subtle deceptions,** he wasn't about to be **duped** by this more obvious **subterfuge.** "Sorry, but I'm **illiterate,** just like my pap and his pap before him," he drawled. "Can't read or write a lick."

Isabel reacted to this **stratagem** with **skepticism.** "Oh yeah, sure, like I'm really supposed to believe that," she quacked. "Since when does an **illiterate** person use **cultivated diction** like 'unremitting and **diabolical persecution**'? And how would an **illiterate** person even know the word *illiterate,* anyway?"

Twain didn't answer. He maneuvered around several tables and **forged** on. The exit **loomed** ahead.

"You know, Mr. Clemens," Isabel continued, "I can be pretty **persistent,** in case you hadn't noticed..."

Make that **willful, dogged,** and **tenacious,** Twain thought. As **tenacious** as a **recurring** nightmare.

"And the fact that all of a sudden you show up here at Hadleyburg—by whatever means I can't even imagine, but we can talk about that later—it's just so intense. I mean, it's the most amazing thing that's ever happened to me. So you can refuse to talk to me right now, and that's cool, like whatever, and you can ignore me or shine me on, and I can deal with that, no problem, but I want you to know that

I'm not going to give up. I'm going to follow you wherever you go and I'm not going to leave you alone until you sit down and talk to me and admit that you're the man that I admire and the writer I adore."

The squawking sea urchin's words hit him like a brick. What an odd mixture of blandishments and threats, he thought. Clearly, her **bizarre** obsession with him, her **mania** for Mark Twain, had made her demented. He wondered if he might have to **resort** to the **indecorous** use of a blunt instrument to effect his escape. Then he spied what appeared to be his salvation.

"Pardon me," he mumbled, ducking into the men's room **adjacent** to the foyer of the Rotunda. She can't follow me in here, he thought. At least let's hope not.

He looked around for an escape route, but there was only a small window high up on the wall. He'd just have to kill some time and hope that the foul creature would **forsake** her insane pursuit and go away.

After a few minutes of pretending to urinate he was painfully self-conscious. After another few minutes of pretending to groom himself in front of the mirror he felt like a **buffoon**. And after an **excruciating** fifteen minutes more spent hanging out in a stall amid a variety of **unsettling** sounds and smells he was so **disconcerted** that he was ready to surrender himself to the sea urchin's clutches, confess all, and beg forgiveness for his sins. Had he possessed a **contemporary colloquial** vocabulary he would have thrown open the stall door and shouted, "Yo, baby, I'm outta here!"

But he didn't throw open the door and he didn't shout. Instead he ran back into the foyer, gasping. Isabel was sitting on the marble floor with her back against the stone wall, calmly waiting for him. She stood up and slipped on her backpack.

"I knew you wouldn't last long in there," she said, following him out of the Rotunda. "You're, like, too **fastidious** for that sort of **crass ploy.**"

"And *you* are a raving lunatic the doctors **regrettably** failed to **diagnose** and commit to an **asylum**," Twain replied as he strode briskly across the busy, snow-covered court-yard. How was he going to get this maundering maniac to let him alone? he wondered. He could try to give her the shake, but that tactic might require **inordinate exertion.** He could seek out the police, but that could **unduly** complicate matters, what with the manuscript of *Huck Finn* missing from the library in Buffalo. He could knock that fellow off his odd-looking bicycle and speed away to safety, but that would surely get him in trouble with the law. No, there just wasn't an easy way out of this **quandary.**

A harsh squeal from Isabel interrupted his **ruminations.** He glanced at her and saw that she was stabbing her fore-finger wildly in his direction.

"Omigod," she cried, "this is *so* unbelievable. You even *walk* like Mark Twain! They say he had this **undulating** way of walking and his head would tilt from side to side. The way you walk perfectly matches that description. That's like totally freaky!"

Twain immediately tried to modify his **gait,** but his legs wouldn't listen to his brain. He felt like a kangaroo trying to dance the polka. "Young lady," he said, resuming his natural stride, "your **manipulation** of the evidence is noth-ing short of astonishing. I daresay you would have made a **commendable** prosecutor for the Inquisition."

The **inquisitor** stabbed her finger at him again. "Aha! *Daresay.* Nobody uses *daresay* anymore. It's **archaic.** It's like a totally nineteenth-century word."

"Actually," Twain said, "at the risk of sounding **pedan-tic** I must insist you are mistaken about that. *Daresay* is not a nineteenth-century word; it is a thirteenth-century word. So I guess I am slightly more ancient than you claim."

Unable to come up with an **alternative** course of action, Twain found his legs carrying him back to Stormfield College with the gobbling and cackling Isabel Lyon in tow. He didn't know what else to do; she had driven him to the point of **consternation**. He decided he would lie down on Aimee and Angela's sofa and take a nap, and hope that when he awoke the prattling lunatic at his side would prove to be only a chimera.

"You're staying here?" Isabel asked as Twain produced the key to suite E-4 that Aimee had given him. "This is a women's floor. Where did you get that key?"

"I'm visiting my daughter," he said, unlocking the door. "She gave it to me."

She snorted **grotesquely.** "Oh yeah sure, that's a good one."

"Good-bye, blatherskite." He pushed open the door.

"Hey, can I come in and, like, just talk to you for a minute?"

"It would **gratify** me deeply if you would **contrive** a way to disappear. Permanently." He slipped inside the room, shut the door **emphatically,** and locked it.

Isabel called through the door. "Hey, you can stay in there as long as you like, you know? But I'm going to be right here when you come out." She banged on the door. "You hear me, Mr. Clemens? I'm not going anywhere until you grant me an interview."

Twain peeled off his sweatshirt and threw himself down on the couch. Then he ran his hands through his hair and sighed. Maybe being a famous writer isn't all it's cracked up to be, he thought. Far better to live and die **anonymously** and in peace than to have some blathering **fanatic** all over you like horseflies on a meadow muffin. If this deluded **devotee** is representative of my future admirers, then while I'm here I hope to God I don't meet any of my future **critics**!

For the next hour he tried every technique he could think of to **compel** himself to forget about the **nemesis lurking** in the stairway and go to sleep. But nothing worked, not even trying to **comprehend** the **arid, tedious prose** of Aimee's sociology textbook, with its **vague** and **ponderous abstractions** and bloated, **bombastic** words like *implementation, utilization,* and *methodology.*

He got up from the couch and began to pace the room. He hadn't had a cigar since before lunch, and he hungered for a smoke. A draft of ale or a spot of whiskey wouldn't hurt either, he thought; his jangled nerves could use a sedative. But every so often he could hear the crackpot clucking and scratching around out there, waiting for a chance to peck and jab at him again. It was hopeless, he concluded. He was stuck here, cooped up for the rest of the afternoon until his friends could return and rescue him.

Then he remembered the **luminous** orange sign he had seen the night before on the way to the 24/7 and the three **exquisitely harmonious** words it had proclaimed: BEER—COCKTAILS—POOL. A broad smile spread across his face. The Anchor Bar.

Yes, that's where he could go. That's where he would find **deliverance,** with a glass and a cigar in one hand and a billiard cue in the other. And if the Lyoness pursues me, he thought, so be it. What harm can she possibly do in the **sociable** and **convivial** atmosphere of a good saloon? They'll probably figure she's crazy, same as I do. I'll just play billiards and ignore her, and if that babbling barnacle commits any **impropriety** I'll **incite** the bartender and the **patrons** to give her the bounce.

There was even a **distinct** possibility, he thought, that the **establishment** would be for gentlemen only and not admit the fair sex—although he was **skeptical** whether Isabel, with her spiky hair and lip stud and ophidian tattoo, qualified as a member of the fair sex. But that warn't no matter, as Huck Finn would say. It was settled. He was on his way to the welcome relief of billiards and beer at the Anchor Bar, and to hell with Isabel Lyon.

"Where are we going, anyway?" asked Isabel as Twain surged up Village Road and she hurried alongside. The sky had grown overcast and the air was biting cold.

"*We* are not going anywhere," was the writer's **brusque** reply. "I am on my way to a place where, if luck has it, *you* will not be welcome."

Five minutes later—the second most **insufferable** and **interminable** five minutes of Twain's life—they arrived at the Anchor Bar. The entire way the **indefatigably garrulous** Isabel had peppered him with an **exasperating** blend of questions, **inferences,** and accusations, while he had done his best to disregard the **interrogation** and focus on what **palliative** relief he could **derive** from smoking a cigar and exhaling in her face.

The snub didn't bother her in the least. "Omigod," she had cried when he lit up his stogie, "you smoke cigars! See, Mr. Clemens, that proves that you're Mark Twain."

Affixed to the door of the saloon was a sign he hadn't noticed the night before. NO ONE UNDER 21 ALLOWED, it read.

Twain looked at Isabel. "I know this is an **impertinent** question to put to a lady," he said, "but since your **status** in that regard is **dubious,** I believe I am **justified** in taking the liberty of asking it. How old are you?"

"I'm twenty," Isabel answered. "I'll be twenty-one in March—March 15."

Twain nodded **gravely** while silently rejoicing. "Of course, I should have known. Beware the ides of March. No wonder you have that lean and hungry look."

The slender sea urchin gave him a look that was **decidedly predatory** and **ravenous.** "Mr. Clemens," she rasped, "are you going in this bar so you can ditch me?"

Ditch? Now there's a colorful verb, he thought, firing a smoke ring at her nose. Come to think of it, he'd heard it before. It was low slang. Tramps used it to mean to put someone off a railroad train, usually by force. Well, he thought, I guess that's about what I'm fixing to do here, minus the boot. "Yes I'm ditching you," he said, "and the sooner the better."

He turned and reached out to grasp the handle of the saloon door when suddenly the door swung open and a **burly** man lurched out. The man grunted as he bumped hard into Twain, knocking him backward and off his feet. Before Twain knew what was happening he had landed on his buttocks in the soft layer of snow on the sidewalk and the drunken muscleman had staggered off down the street.

"Oh Mr. Clemens!" Isabel screeched. "Are you all right?"

"Yes, of course, and please stop calling me 'Mr. Clemens,'" he said, scrambling to his feet and brushing off the snow. He shook an angry fist at the departing figure of his intoxicated **assailant**. "You **lummox!**" he bellowed. "Come back and I'll buy you a drink—of strychnine!"

"Hey Mr. Clemens," said Isabel, looking at the snow where the writer had fallen, "I think you—"

"I'm sorry," Twain interrupted, opening the door of the bar, "but I have some urgent business to attend to, so if you'll excuse me."

Isabel pointed down at the snow. "But I think you—"

"Good-bye." He disappeared into the darkness and the door closed behind him.

Isabel bent down and retrieved the shiny object she had noticed in the snow. It was a key attached to a key chain featuring a miniature **bust** of a **brooding** Beethoven. She had seen her literary **idol** use it earlier that afternoon. It was the key to the room he had claimed was his daughter's, suite E-4 of Stormfield College.

Chapter 12

Renaissance Wolfman

Hank was amazed. The room was nothing like he had imagined. In fact, it defied his every **expectation**. It wasn't a gloomy and **sinister** lair. It wasn't a jumble of computers and a hopeless tangle of wires. It wasn't messy, or dirty, or even the slightest bit stuffy from the absence of windows. He kept blinking and gazing around with a **dumbfounded** expression because he just couldn't get over it. Geniuses weren't supposed to be neat.

Merle took one look at Hank and quickly disabused him of that **stereotype.** "What, you thought I was going to be some **slovenly,** absentminded, **maladroit** nerd with silicon chips for brains and the **aesthetic sensibility** of a June bug?" he said. "Forget about it, Clyde. I'm a Renaissance man, a person of **refinement** and taste."

He then further shocked Hank by metamorphosing from a surly **misanthrope** into an **amiable** and **hospitable** guy. He took Hank's coat and told him to make himself at home. "I know you're curious and you want to check out my place, and it's all right, go ahead," he said while he put on a blues CD and went to the refrigerator to fetch them both a beverage. And so Hank did.

As the **melancholy** voice of Howlin' Wolf began to ulu-late in the background, Hank surveyed the room. Merle's

subterranean residence was warm, **ample,** inviting, and, he had to admit despite his utter lack of interest in interior design, rather appealing to the eye. Sleek torchères **illuminated** the **commodious** space, which was about thirty feet wide and fifty feet long. The ceiling had no exposed pipes or ducts, as one might expect in a basement; instead it was finished in smooth white gypsum board like a normal apartment. The cement floor had been covered with a beige carpet and several Persian-style rugs.

At one end of the room there was a clean, modern kitchenette with a small round dining table and two metal chairs. A convertible futon couch—presumably Merle's bed, when he saw fit to stop working and use it—a cushiony armchair, an Eames chair, and a glass coffee table occupied the middle of the room. At the other end was Merle's workspace, a built-in desk that stretched the entire length of the wall and then turned the corner for about eight more feet. Four compact desktop computers were clustered in the corner with a black swivel chair facing them; on the rest of the desk sat all manner of other high-tech equipment, along with books, papers, and miscellaneous office supplies. Everything was **meticulously** organized. Not a single thing seemed out of place, not even the small wire cage on the desk containing a plump, white laboratory rat that was busy nibbling on a piece of lettuce.

The one **commonplace** household device Hank did not see anywhere, to his considerable surprise, was a television. Merle probably didn't have time for it, he **surmised.**

One long wall of the room was covered with open shelves containing **exotic** objets d'art and a **voluminous** and **eclectic** collection of books on everything from science to philosophy to literature. Hank saw the *Oxford English Dictionary,* the *Analects* of Confucius, the King James Bible, *The Yale Shakespeare,* the *I Ching, The Norton **Anthology** of Poetry,* John Milton's *Paradise Lost,* Miguel de Cervantes's *Don Quixote,* John Steinbeck's *Grapes of Wrath,* Gabriel García

Márquez's *One Hundred Years of Solitude,* Ralph Ellison's *Invisible Man,* and J. R. R. Tolkien's **epic** *Lord of the Rings.* Mark Twain's *Adventures of Huckleberry Finn* was there too, he noticed, beside a well-worn copy of *A Connecticut Yankee in King Arthur's Court.*

Over Merle's desk and along the other long wall were various framed prints of famous works of art. Thanks to the art history class he had taken sophomore year, Hank recognized a number of them, including Michelangelo's *Creation of Adam* from the Sistine Chapel, Vincent van Gogh's *Starry Night,* Pablo Picasso's *Guernica,* Joan Miró's *Inverted Personage,* and a strikingly lifelike self-portrait of Albrecht Dürer.

As Hank studied Dürer's image, it occurred to him that Merle looked a lot like the great printmaker of the Renaissance. He had the same **placid,** bearded **countenance,** the same thoughtful eyes and intelligent brow, the same **sinuous** locks of dark brown hair spilling over his shoulders. But Dürer had **portrayed** himself as a **solemn, idealized,** almost Christlike figure, gazing at the viewer with calm authority, and that's where the similarity **abruptly** ended. For there was one **salient** and alarming feature about Merle that wasn't even remotely **solemn** or **idealized** or Christlike. He was hairy. Seriously hairy. Way beyond hirsute hairy. This guy, thought Hank, was werewolf movie hairy— practically lycanthropic.

Except for the long, wiry locks on his head, Merle's hair was more like fur than hair. It descended from his face in a foot-long thicket. It sprouted in **luxuriant** tufts from the rolled-up sleeves of his flannel shirt. It blanketed his forearms and the backs of his hands and fingers. Hank inwardly shuddered at the thought of what the rest of Merle must look like, and he was relieved to see that his host wasn't barefoot.

"So I don't get it," he said as the **affable** wolfman handed him a can of Joka-Cola. "You look like a normal... well, pretty much like a normal guy. Why do people talk about you as if you're this weird, wild-eyed techno-dude who **skulks** around campus and **inhabits** some dark hole in the basement of Irving Lab?"

Merle let out a deep, rumbling laugh. "Because I want them to." He motioned for Hank to sit down in the Eames chair, which Hank found surprisingly comfortable despite its **spartan** design. Merle sat in the cushiony armchair and took a sip of Joke. "I've spent a lot of energy **cultivating** that **persona**," he said. "It's kind of like Robert Louis Stevenson's *Strange Case of Dr. Jekyll and Mr. Hyde*. Right now you're talking to Dr. Jekyll, the **virtuous** and **benevolent** man of science. But whenever I leave this place, which isn't often, I **purposefully** turn myself into the mysterious and **menacing** Mr. Hyde. I change my clothes and mess up my hair and play the part of a half-crazed computer geek on the loose. You see, I *want* to be **notorious.** I want people to be intimidated by me. I want them to believe I'm **eccentric** and **volatile** and possibly dangerous. And I want them to stand in awe of me and tell exaggerated stories about me and **mythologize** me. That way they'll be more likely to leave me the hell alone."

Hank took a swig of soda. "And why do you want to be left alone?" he asked.

The question **induced** another rumbling laugh from Merle. Then he fell silent and studied Hank from behind his dense **mass** of beard. Finally he spoke, quietly this time. "There is **profound, ineffable** power in the solitary man," he said, and suddenly Hank had the **eerie** sensation that those **enigmatic** words were lingering in the **static** atmosphere of the room, as if they were **loath** to depart until he could **infer** what they **implied.** Then, just as suddenly, the strange sensation **dissipated.** "All right, that's enough about me for now," Merle said, setting his drink down on the glass coffee table. "Tell me how you cracked the access code to TWAIN and why you need my help."

———

"So what do you think?" Hank asked. "Can you help me?"

He had just explained everything he could about his **quandary.** First he had given a **concise** summary of the situation. Then he had laid out all the **pertinent** facts concerning his infiltration of TWAIN—the months of experimentation and failure, the **exhilarating** breakthrough with the access code, his subsequent forays into the **labyrinth** of the machine, and his triumphant discovery last night of the sanctum sanctorum, which led to the **fortuitous encounter** with the fourth dimension.

Merle had listened attentively and **dispassionately,** with his brow wrinkled and his cheek on his fist, nodding or grunting occasionally to indicate that he understood. He did not **refute** or **repudiate** any of Hank's scientific **assumptions,** and he interrupted only to ask Hank to **clarify** something or **elaborate** on a **complex** and **intricate** technical detail. But when Hank got to the swapping of his laptop with the manuscript of *Huckleberry Finn* and the miraculous appearance of the famous writer in the stairway, Merle had seemed **skeptical** and rather amused.

"And how do you know this guy is really Mark Twain?" he had asked.

"Dude, we just know," Hank had replied, **citing** an **abundance** of other evidence to **substantiate** his **assertion.** "I mean, like, c'mon!" he had concluded, posing this **rhetorical question:** "Who in his right mind would go to such incredibly great lengths to impersonate Mark Twain in some strange entryway in the middle of the night?"

Merle had smiled, or at least he had appeared to smile beneath the heavy underbrush of whiskers. "My point exactly. But since you've established your **credibility** about my TWAIN, I guess I'll have to take your word for it about yours."

And so the **crucial** moment had arrived. Hank had spilled his guts. He had thrown himself at Merle's feet.

Would the legendary techno-wizard be willing to help? Would he even be able to?

Merle was stroking his beard and staring at the floor, **immersed** in thought. In a **tentative** voice, Hank repeated his question. "Merle, can you help me?"

The wizard stopped stroking his beard and slowly raised his head. He leaned back in the armchair, gripped the armrests, and sat there for a minute, **inscrutable** and sphinxlike with his mane of hair, furry forearms, and **impassive** eyes.

Finally Merle spoke, his voice deep but **subdued.** "I knew that you—or somebody, anyway—had hacked into TWAIN," he said. "I **detected** your footprints and fingerprints. I followed your trail until I was sure you were the intruder. Then I laid my traps and watched and waited for you like a **predator.** I wanted to catch you like the patient, **vigilant** spider catches the **unwary** fly. But you were lucky, or else incredibly smart, because you never took the bait or gave me enough of a chance to **ensnare** you in my web. When I finally concluded that you were a **benign** visitor, that you were just exploring and goofing around and you weren't in there to **wreak havoc,** I stopped trying so hard to **thwart** you. In retrospect, that was probably a mistake. I should have pinned you to the firewall and eaten your hard drive for breakfast."

There was a flash of teeth beneath the whiskers. A grin.

"I also knew that something **unprecedented** happened with TWAIN last night," he went on, "and I could tell right away that it was something **problematic.** I spent half the night and most of this morning trying to figure out what it was, but the answer kept **eluding** me." He paused and leaned forward in his chair. "Now I know. Now I know that it was my technology, my secret project, that you managed to invade."

Hank waved his hands in the air; it was an **ambiguous** gesture of both apology and denial. "Dude, I am totally sorry. I really am. I didn't mean to *invade* anything. I wasn't trying to mess you up. It's like you said—I was just exploring and goofing around." He shrugged. "I guess I got kind of carried away. TWAIN is so amazing and mysterious and **formidable**. The idea that I might be able to find a way to break in and **unravel** its mysteries was so **tantalizing**. After a while it became a challenge I just couldn't resist. And then it became like an obsession." He sighed and shook his head. "But you know, I have to confess it was the thrill of my life."

"I understand all that," Merle said. "But it doesn't alter the fact that hacking into TWAIN wasn't exactly **exemplary** behavior."

Hank lowered his head and looked at the floor. "I know."

"You could get expelled for it."

Hank nodded. "I know."

"You could have accidentally **encumbered** or even damaged TWAIN."

He nodded again. "I know."

"And something much worse than this could have happened."

Hank looked up. "Really? Like what?"

"With that technology—my technology—the possibilities are **infinite**," Merle said **gravely**. "Ignorance or **negligence** can quickly lead to **calamity**. You were guilty of both **offenses** but you got off fairly easy."

"You think so?"

"Yes, I do. And I think you should be very grateful for that."

"Oh, I am, dude," Hank said, nodding **vigorously**. "You bet I am."

Merle folded his arms and studied Hank. "On the other hand, I can't help admiring someone who has the gumption to try to do something he's not supposed to be able to do, even if it's something the rules say he's not allowed to do. I have great respect for people who have the confidence and the **initiative** to **transcend** their limitations, who **forge** ahead despite obstacles and **impediments,** all in the hope of accomplishing something that presumably can't be accomplished. That, to me, is the highest goal. That is life's **ideal.**" He paused and cleared his throat; the sound was like the distant rumble of thunder. "Hank, you've proved to me that you have that confidence and that drive, and you appear to have the **requisite** intelligence to go with it. So I'm going to forgive your **transgression.** And I'm going to help you."

Hank almost levitated off the Eames chair. "You are?"

Merle nodded slowly. "Or to put it more precisely, I'm going to let you help me. Together we'll find a way to **rectify** the situation, I promise you, or my name isn't Merlin Paige." He thumped the armrest with his fist, then pointed a hairy forefinger at Hank. "But **heed** my warning, wunderkind, and **heed** it well: There's no rest for the weary when you work for me. I'm going to work your butt off. And you'd better hope you're a quick study, because if you're not I'm going to grind your sad ass right into the ground. And that, my friend, is how you will **atone** for the sin of violating TWAIN."

Merle stood up. "But first we need sustenance," he said as he walked over to the kitchenette. Hank heard him open the refrigerator and a couple of cupboards. In a minute he returned and set a bowl, a plate, a spoon, and some napkins on the glass coffee table. "Comestibles for the brain," he said, returning to his chair. "Help yourself."

Hank looked at the lumpy, round flatbread on the plate and the pile of yellowish brown mush in the bowl, which was **garnished** with a slice of lemon and a sprig of parsley. "What is it?"

"You're kidding. You don't know what this is?"

"Nope."

"It's hummus and pita."

Hank studied the food and scratched his head. "Which is the hummus and which is the pita?"

Merle laughed. "I see you must **subscribe** to the humdrum school of gastronomy. Allow me to broaden your culinary horizons. Pita and hummus are **staples** of Middle Eastern cuisine. This is the pita," he said, pointing to the flatbread. He pointed to the mush. "And this is the hummus. It's made with chickpeas, a sesame-seed paste called tahini, olive oil, lemon juice, and garlic. Try it. I think you'll like it."

Hank picked up a slice of pita and tore off a huge hunk with his teeth. "Look, I can't help it if I'm not some dang gourmet food **connoisseur**," he said, chewing **ravenously**. "I grew up on a farm where we ate **unsophisticated**, all-American fare." He swallowed and tore off another sizable mouthful. "You know, hamburgers and hot dogs, macaroni and cheese, spaghetti and meatballs, pot roast with potatoes, ranch dressing on iceberg lettuce, pie with ice cream for dessert. It was just good, **unpretentious** cooking." He shoved the rest of the bread in his mouth, chewed briefly, then sucked it down. "Not bad," he said, reaching for another slice.

"By the way," said Merle, "you're supposed to put the hummus on the pita."

"Okay," Hank said. He took the spoon and slathered hummus on the entire slice.

Merle shook his head sadly. "No, man, not like that. You're supposed to tear off a bite-sized piece of the pita and put a little hummus on it. Like this, see?"

In the time it took for Merle to pick up a slice of pita and **adeptly** demonstrate the procedure, Hank devoured his whole hummus pizza. "Sure, whatever," he said as he wiped his mouth on his sleeve. "You know, that was pretty good. Almost as good as Squeeze Cheese on white bread. Hey, so when are you going to tell me about that new technology you're working on that's behind this whole thing?"

"Now," Merle said. He leaned forward and locked eyes with Hank. "But first you've got to swear that not a word of what I'm going to tell you ever leaves this room. Because if it does, your gonads are Squeeze Cheese."

Chapter 13

A Close Place

Isabel Lyon knocked on the door of suite E-4 of Stormfield College. She was there to return the key that she had found in the snow, but she also had an ulterior **motive.** She was hoping to meet the daughter that Twain had **alleged** he was visiting.

She had **initially** dismissed this claim as one of his **habitual fabrications,** but now she wasn't so sure. Could he possibly have come to the future accompanied by his darling Susy, and, if so, might there be some way to save her from her awful fate—to die of meningitis at only twenty-four? If Susy is indeed here, Isabel thought, I'll ply her for information. No doubt she'll be more **forthcoming** than her strangely **reticent** father.

But no one answered her knock. She rapped on the door again, louder this time. Still there was no answer. She tried one more time, just to make sure, but again the knock failed to summon anyone. Just my luck, she thought. Nobody's home.

This got Isabel to thinking. She considered her **alternatives.**

She could wait here in the stairway for one of the suite's residents to show up, but she had no idea how long that might be. Besides, it was chilly out here and as much as she was eager to interview Mark Twain or his daughter she had to admit that she was tired of **loitering** in odd and uncomfortable places waiting for a chance to talk to them. She could come back when it would be more likely for somebody to be home, but that was a hit-or-miss strategy and could wind up being a big waste of time. She could slip the key under the door, maybe with a little note with her phone number on it, but there was no guarantee that anyone would even **heed** the note, much less bother to call.

Then another, more venturesome option presented itself to her mind. Maybe there was something inside the suite, some **telling** piece of evidence, that would settle the question of this Mark Twain look-alike's true identity once and for all. Maybe there was something in there that would either **confirm** her **conviction** that he was the real Mark Twain or **verify** his **assertion** that he wasn't.

The suite was unoccupied and she had the key. She could enter and take a quick look around, then leave the key on the floor by the door so it would appear that she had slipped it underneath. The thought of doing something so **audacious** filled her with a **heady** mixture of excitement and **trepidation** that made her shiver.

The shiver was swiftly superseded by the twinge of a **scruple.** It would be **unethical,** snooping around somebody's place like that, she thought. How would she feel if someone nosed around her place looking for something **incriminating**? That's why the Founding Fathers wrote Article IV of the Bill of Rights, wasn't it? It said, "The right of the people to be secure in their persons, houses, papers, and effects, against unreasonable searches and seizures, shall not be violated."

But who's going to know, anyway? **countered** the **unscrupulous** voice in her head. No one will. And it's not as if she'd be going in there to steal something or **rummage** through somebody's drawers. She was just going to poke around for clues about this mysterious, Clemensian stranger. She would be **unobtrusive** and her search would be brief. Nothing would be disturbed and no one would be the wiser for it.

But searching the suite would be a **flagrant** invasion of privacy, said the first voice—her honest, **scrupulous** voice. It would also be a **gross** violation of campus regulations, an infraction that could result in disciplinary action, maybe even expulsion. It might even be a crime for which she could be prosecuted and sent to jail.

Oh, c'mon, said the **corrupt, cajoling** voice, which was **adept** at **rationalizing.** You might get a slap on the wrist or even some kind of formal **admonishment,** but you're not going to get expelled or **incarcerated** for such a minor **misdeed,** such a venial **transgression.** Police officers and attorneys do this kind of thing all the time, and they're supposed to **uphold** and enforce the law. Let's be honest here. This isn't a crime or a sin. It's just bending the rules. And besides, if someone walks in you can always say Mr. Clemens gave you the key and asked you to wait for him inside.

Don't *you* talk to *me* about honesty, replied the voice of **principle.** I can't believe you would even think of uttering that **shameless,** contemptible lie—which wouldn't fool anyone for one minute, anyway, and you know it. Opening this door is not bending the rules, it's breaking them. This door is closed and locked and if you didn't have that key you wouldn't even be debating whether to go in. You'd be on your merry way.

But it's not so cut-and-dried, argued the voice of **duplicity.** It's more complicated and **problematic.** There are **mitigating** circumstances.

And what might those be? asked the voice of **veracity.**

This is no ordinary case involving an **unwarranted** search or an invasion of privacy, answered the voice of **deceit**. It's an extraordinary case requiring **decisive** action. And in extraordinary circumstances sometimes it's necessary to engage in wrongdoing in the interest of the greater good.

And just what do you mean by that? said the honorable voice.

I mean that an **offense** can be **justified** if it serves a higher purpose, said the **dissembling** voice.

For example? said the high-minded voice.

For example, said the **fraudulent** voice, in World War II some people harbored **fugitives, falsified** information, and committed **forgery** to save other people from being sent to the Nazi concentration camps.

But those weren't crimes, the **guileless** voice objected. Those were selfless acts of humanity, courageous **deeds** in a noble struggle against evil and injustice. Those people were risking their own safety and their own lives to save others.

Precisely, replied the voice of sophistry. And entering this suite is a risk you must take in the service of a higher cause. Call it the cause of literary truth and justice, if you will. You're convinced this man you've just met is Mark Twain, who has somehow been transported to our time. Because of your **affinity** for Twain and his work, you have generously offered to take him under your wing and help him **navigate** the **hazardous** waters of the present until he can find his way back to the past. But out of confusion and **apprehension** he has **imprudently** refused your aid. Now he's alone and adrift and **vulnerable,** and he needs you more than ever.

What you have to do, the **fallacious** voice continued, is make him see that you can help him and that he can trust you. You have to make him believe that you'll protect him and **safeguard** his literary **legacy.** And the best way to do that is to stop waiting for him to confess that he's Mark Twain and find the evidence to prove it. That evidence may very well be inside this suite.

The **ethical** voice felt itself wavering. But it just isn't right to snoop around in there, it protested. You'd better slip that key under the door right now and get out of here before you do something you're going to regret.

The voice of **hypocrisy** shook its head. No, it said, what you'll regret is knowing you could have done something significant but you were too **timorous** to take the risk. The right thing to do is to help Mark Twain however you can. That's why you have to open that door.

But what if I get caught and punished? How is that going to help him?

What is wrong with you? You're so **tentative** and **timid**—and *so* **self-absorbed.** This isn't about you. You're not going in there for yourself. You're going in there for *him.* Stop being so **apprehensive** and just *do* it.

It was a close place, as Huckleberry Finn would have said, a real **dilemma.** Isabel took the key out of her coat pocket and held it in her hand. She looked at her hand and realized she was trembling. She had to decide, for better or for worse, between two unpleasant things.

She studied the key, **vacillating,** holding her breath. Then she said to herself, "All right, then, I'll *go* to jail"— and unlocked the door.

It was a little after six in the morning when George Griffin, the Clemens family butler, awoke in his spare and simply furnished room at the top of the house at 351 Farmington Avenue in Hartford. The crackling fire that had warmed the room when he went to bed had long since burned out. Now the hearth was dark and the room was cold. In the dim light of dawn filtering through the window he could see the **vapor** of his exhaled breath drifting in the **frigid** air.

As he **savored** a few delicious minutes of drowsy **tranquillity** under the blankets, George **envisioned** his pretty young wife and their infant daughter, just nine months old. How he loved that darling child and the mighty promise she **embodied**! What great hopes and **aspirations** he had for her! He imagined her peaceful, innocent face as she slept in her bassinet beside the half-empty bed where his wife lay sleeping, in the **modest** house he had bought for her as a wedding present. He longed to be with both of them, to kiss their soft cheeks and watch their delicate eyelids flutter as they woke up. But the conditions and **constraints** of his employment required that he spend most of his nights as well as days here, with another family.

To be sure, it was a fine, loving family that was fond of him and treated him with respect, a family he was more than proud to serve; but it was another family just the same, and not his own. Such was the life of a **domestic** servant: One set aside one's own needs to fulfill the needs of others. Yet George accepted this **subordinate** role with a **sanguine** heart, free of any **resentment** or regret. Having been born a slave, he knew only too well how much worse his lot could be.

And it wouldn't be long before he would see his own family again, he thought. Christmas was just around the corner and he had been given the holiday off. With this **consolation** in mind, George slipped one hand between his mattress and box spring to check on his sizable cache of greenbacks, then threw off the covers and jumped out of bed in his blazing red long johns, whistling softly. Not ten minutes later he was washed, shaved, and **impeccably attired** in the gray serge vest and trousers, starched white shirt, and silver bow tie that he preferred as his butler's uniform. When working in the kitchen or serving at table he protected this fine apparel with an **immaculate** linen apron.

George was a big man, strong and sturdy, **virile** and handsome. He was blessed with an **imperturbable equanimity** and a sunny **disposition,** and his **buoyant optimism** served as the perfect counterpoise to the **ingrained pessimism** of Mr. Clemens. Unlike the **irreverent** and **intemperate** writer, George was a **devout** Methodist who practiced **abstinence** from alcohol and tobacco. He never swore, while for Clemens swearing was almost as **cherished** a habit as smoking. And he was as **frugal** as Clemens was prodigal. But like his famous employer, George was a **gregarious** soul, and his **geniality** and **benevolent** good nature endeared him to the steady stream of **intimate** friends and neighbors who visited the house.

He doted on the three young Clemens girls, and they adored him. He would interrupt his work at any invitation to entertain them. He would play games with them and give them piggyback rides or astonish them with amazing tricks like putting a lighted candle in his mouth or magically summoning Abner the cat with four rings of the bell. For those mysterious powers the children **idolized** him. They regarded him with awe and **reverence** and showered him with **ebullient** affection.

He was **conscientious** and **scrupulously** honest in all his dealings and affairs, with but one **notable** exception— when circumstances required that he **embellish** the truth to protect the Clemens family's interests. He was a master of diplomacy who instinctively knew how to keep the peace among an **ethnically diverse** group of servants that included a German nurse, an Irish maid, and a black cook. And he was a respected **arbiter** who had the rare ability to **mediate** disagreements before they became **quarrels** and **mollify** wounded feelings before they went sour and **rancorous.**

George was also a **shrewd** and **astute entrepreneur,** and his chief business, in which he displayed exceptional

sagacity, was betting. In this **precarious enterprise** he was consistently and often hugely successful, for he never left anything to chance. He laid his bets only after the most **painstaking** legwork and **diligent, methodical** investigation. He figured—and figured correctly, as his **continual** success proved—that the more he knew about the circumstances and the participants involved, the more likely he was to win.

If it was a horse race he intended to lay his money on, he learned every detail about the horses and jockeys right down to the precise weight of each rider and whether the horse ate oats or corn for breakfast. If it was a boxing match, then he made sure he knew enough about the **pugilists** to write a **dissertation** on their strengths and **vulnerabilities.** And if it was the outcome of an election he was wagering on, then he would find out everything he could about the candidates, leaving no stone unturned. The **eminent** politicians and luminaries of public life with whom Mr. Clemens regularly socialized were some of his most reliable sources of inside information. Whenever they came for dinner George would subject them to a **jovial interrogation** in the front hall as he took their hats and coats, and the men were more than happy to **oblige,** for they all liked George and held him in high **esteem.**

George **extracted** a hundred dollars from the pile of cash **secreted** in his bed and slipped it in the watch pocket of his vest; he never went anywhere, even downstairs, without at least that **minimal** sum. He examined himself in the mirror resting on the mantel to make sure his tie was straight and his teeth were clean. Then he took a look outside to **ascertain** the **status** of the **fickle** New England weather. The view from his third-floor window was due east over the wide front lawn of the house. The ground was covered with a thick, **pristine** blanket of fresh snow punctured here and there by the trunks of young, bare trees. He could **discern** no other evidence of the night's ferocious storm. The **turbulent** wind had **subsided** and all was **serene**. The cloudless sky was **tinged** with blue and the sun was up and smiling. It was going to be one fine winter day.

George stepped out of his room holding his shoes in one hand so he wouldn't wake any of the family while going downstairs, especially Mr. Clemens, who didn't take kindly to being **roused** before nine o'clock. That's when he typically would **saunter** into the kitchen and ask for his **customary** breakfast—steak and coffee with cream— which George would cheerfully serve to him in the dining room along with the newspaper, the morning post, and a bit of friendly gossip or a joke.

With his free hand George closed and locked the door of his room and pocketed the key. As he headed for the stairs he saw a sliver of light coming from the crack beneath the door to the billiard room. Mr. Clemens was known to keep late hours and to retire to the billiard room after dinner for solitude, **solace**, or recreation. Had his employer stayed up all night working or **carousing**? George wondered.

He tiptoed across the hushed and darkened hall and paused, listening for any sounds coming from the room. There were none. He tapped gently with his knuckle on the door. "Mr. Clemens?" he whispered. "You in there? It's George." Maybe he fell asleep on the divan, he thought. I should check and see that he's properly covered up and that he didn't leave one of his cigars burning.

He opened the door halfway and peeked in. The writer was nowhere to be seen. Could he have gone to the bathroom? No. The bathroom was **adjacent** to George's room and he would have heard him enter. George noticed that the gaslights had been turned way up. If Mr. Clemens had already gone down to bed, why had he left the lights on? That would be **atypical** and **erratic** behavior, not to mention risky.

George shook his head. I shall have to talk to him about this, he thought. He extinguished the lights and was about to leave the room and head downstairs when something else peculiar caught his attention—something strange on the desk.

Still holding his shoes in one hand, George approached the desk and studied the **anomalous** object. He had no idea what it was. Could it be one of those **eccentric** inventions Mr. Clemens was always **squandering** his money on, hoping to strike it rich? He had never seen anything like it before, except maybe that noisy, newfangled writing machine that Mr. Clemens sometimes poked at with two fingers, swearing all the while. But this unusual contraption was divided into **perpendicular** halves and sat open on the desk like a valise. Stranger still, the upright half looked like a thick pane of glass behind which dozens of dots of light seemed to be rushing toward him out of the darkness and then disappearing, only to be instantly replaced by more and more darting dots of light.

He stared at the **fluent** image, **transfixed** by it. The **optical illusion** made him feel as if he were soaring into the sky and flying past the stars. It was a wonderful sensation, a thrilling sensation, at least until he began to grow dizzy. Then it became **unnerving.** Yet he couldn't manage to take his eyes off the **evanescent** stars hurtling by him on all sides. He was **mesmerized.**

Feeling queasy and slightly faint, George reached out a hand to steady himself. But instead of laying it on the top of the desk, as he had intended, he faltered and missed. His open hand landed squarely on the keyboard, depressing nearly half the keys.

Had he not been so dizzy and **disoriented,** perhaps he would have heard the queer machine crackle to life in response to his **indiscretion.** Perhaps he would have heard it **emit** a **perturbed** beep and seen the **cryptic** words *TEMPUS*

EDAX RERUM float **ominously** across the screen. But he didn't hear or see any of that because he was no longer there. He was soaring into the sky and flying past the stars.

"Omigod, omigod, omigod, omi*god*!" gasped the **effusive** Isabel Lyon. She was kneeling beside Aimee and Angela's coffee table, trembling with excitement. "I can't believe this. I really can't believe this. I mean like I *totally* can't believe this!"

Hey, will you shut up already, stupid? her inner voice scolded. This is serious business, girl, so zip it! She bit her tongue hard to enforce **compliance** with the **tacit** command. The last thing she needed right now was to attract somebody's attention. Yet it was all she could do to contain her surging emotions. She was dying to hop around the room squealing with **elation.**

The moment she laid eyes upon the large bundle of paper on the coffee table—which was about two-and-a-half seconds after she had unlocked the door and entered the suite—a shiver ran down her spine and she knew her instincts had been right. And when she untied the string and inspected the first few pages it was clear that she hadn't just found a **telling** piece of evidence to **verify** her **assumption** and **substantiate** her case. She had hit pay dirt. The question was, what to do now?

This bundle of paper was the manuscript of *The Adventures of Huckleberry Finn.* Of its **authenticity** she had no doubt. What she didn't know was how it had managed to make its way overnight from the library in Buffalo to this dormitory at Hadleyburg. Or had it? she wondered. The **notion** that a Mark Twain look-alike had stolen a Mark Twain manuscript was so **far-fetched** it was **farcical.** And why would he **abscond** with the stolen goods to the campus of a **prestigious** university, hole up in somebody's dormitory room, and then leave the **purloined** manuscript right out in the open on a coffee table? No, that **scenario** was beyond ridiculous. It was **absurd**. Almost any other explanation would be more **plausible**.

And there *was* another explanation, one no less **far-fetched** in its own way yet far more **cogent** and convincing, given the facts. It was the explanation she had settled on after spending only five minutes with the mysterious man she had met that afternoon: Samuel Clemens, better known as Mark Twain, had somehow traveled through time and arrived at Hadleyburg, and he had brought his priceless manuscript with him.

And now *she* had it.

Isabel ran a **reverent** finger over the first sentence of the novel, as if caressing the famous author's handwritten words: *You don't know about me, without you have read a book by the name of "The Adventures of Tom Sawyer," but that ain't no matter.* You don't know about me either, Mr. Clemens, she thought, but that ain't no matter. Because you will. Oh yes you will. I promise.

She put the **initial** pages back in their proper order and retied the string around the precious bundle. Then she gently placed it inside her backpack and slipped out the door.

Chapter 14

Someone's in the Kitchen
with *Dyna-*

"A physicist at Columbia, a guy by the name of Gerald Feinberg, once declared that 'everything possible will eventually be accomplished,'" Merle said. "What do you make of that prediction, Hank? Do you agree with it?"

Hank was **basking** in the glow of two agreeable sensations that **complemented** each other nicely: a belly full of food and a brain **stimulated** by conversation. Now he was listening to the **redoubtable** wizard **elucidate** the **complex** workings of his **erudite** and **supple** mind. "Yeah, I guess so," he replied. "I mean, it makes sense, doesn't it, that if it's possible to do something then people will eventually find a way to do it?"

"Sure," said Merle, "but that's kind of boring, isn't it? Where's the challenge in figuring out how to do something that you already know can be done? The way I see it, if you accept that everything possible can and will be accomplished, then it follows that you must reevaluate the meaning of *possible*."

Hank nodded. "Okay, I think I see where you're going."

"For example," Merle continued, "if something that is now **universally** believed to be impossible one day turns out to be possible, does that mean it was impossible until the moment it became possible or that it was possible all along?"

"I guess it was always possible," Hank said, "but we just didn't know it."

"Precisely," said Merle. "It's all a matter of **perception.** You can choose to believe that something is impossible simply because it's never been accomplished and does not appear capable of being accomplished. That's the **conventional** wisdom and the view of the **staid** scientific **orthodoxy.** Or you can be **irreverent** and **unorthodox** and boldly inquire whether some or even all of what is now considered impossible is in fact possible. And that's what's fascinating to me—the things we think we *can't* do that we probably *can*."

Merle put the tips of his fingers together and gazed up at the ceiling. "'Everything possible will eventually be accomplished,'" he repeated in a voice **imbued** with **reverence** and awe. "Hank, those words wake me up in the morning and keep me working all day—and sometimes all night. They're the source of all my **motivation** as a scientist. That statement **affirms** my existence."

He got up and began to pace the room as he spoke with increasing **animation.** "It's the **concept** of the impossible becoming possible, the ultimate challenge of it, that quickens me. That's the best **stimulus** a scientist can have. No scientist worth a dime wants to accept that something is impossible. That's an **affront** to your intelligence. Only an uninspired and **perfunctory** scientist is content to work within the **pedestrian** and **circumscribed domain** of the possible. Accomplishing the possible is about as exciting as adding up a column of numbers with a calculator. If it's possible, let somebody else do it. That's what I say. But tell me that something can't be done and right away I want to get to work figuring out how to prove you wrong."

As Merle held forth and **expounded** on his opinions

and his work, a fascinating portrait emerged of an **idealistic** and **visionary** man, a **quixotic** genius on a **quest** to save the world. He explained how he had always been a **zealous** environmentalist, deeply concerned about how we are **willfully** destroying our **fragile** planet and, by extension, ourselves. It made him sick to his stomach, he said, to think about the enormous amount of energy we waste every day just moving ourselves and our stuff back and forth and here and there by means of dirty and inefficient engines.

"We're choking ourselves on air that we've polluted and poisoning ourselves with pesticides and fertilizers and other baneful chemicals we've created and abused," he said. "We're **plundering** the earth's precious and **finite** resources and **obstinately** refusing to develop **alternative** sources of energy that are renewable and don't pollute."

Yes, Merle **conceded,** it was true that a growing number of **altruistic** people were working to address this **dire** situation through legislation and public education campaigns promoting recycling and **conservation.** But so far the effect had been, in his view, **negligible.** It's not that these efforts were **futile** or **misguided**; it's that they were too little too late. They might help to **ameliorate** the problem but they would never **eradicate** it. And that just wasn't good enough for Merle.

And so, several years ago, he **resolved** to tackle the impossible. He set out to reverse the greenhouse effect and halt global warming. To accomplish this **lofty objective** he knew he would have to create what computer scientists call a "killer app," an **innovative** program that **surpasses** the capabilities of its predecessors. But in this case the killer app couldn't just be something faster and smarter. It would have to be a hell of a lot more killer than that. It would have to do something that had never been done before, something almost laughably **absurd** in **concept** and vaulting in its **ambition.** It would have to connect the physical world to the virtual world and enable objects to move through cyberspace.

Inspired by the kinetic theory of matter—that all matter is composed of small particles in **random** motion—Merle began looking for a way to **exploit** the energy in that motion. He studied the groundbreaking theories and techniques of DNA computing, which uses biomolecular technology to interact with living things and communicate with cells. He studied nuclear magnetic resonance technology, which uses magnetic fields to visualize and influence **molecules.** And he began experimenting with **molecules,** trying to control, store, and recycle their reactive and motive power. Finally, he delved into philosophy, in particular Zen, in search of the **insight** and the **enlightenment** he needed to question the **traditional assumptions** of science and ultimately to **transcend** them.

"What I eventually discovered," Merle said, "was that, as Alan Watts teaches us in *The Way of Zen,* 'our world is a collection of processes rather than **entities.'** We see objects as **static** when they are in fact events. In other words, the **material** world is not just sitting there, fixed and **quiescent.** It's not just something that *is.* It's something that is *happening.*

"That was a liberating moment in my research. That was when I realized that what I was trying to do could not be accomplished merely through **abstract theoretical** calculations and computations. I saw that I needed to work at a more **fundamental** level, the level of raw creation. It wasn't enough to understand the nature of things. I needed to figure out how to make them happen."

Merle stopped pacing and turned to look at Hank. "And that's what led to my breakthrough. It took a long time to turn the corner, but I finally did, and that's when I discovered the **rudiments** of my new technology. Since then I've come a long way. I'm still not quite there yet, but I'm getting close. Really close. So close I can hear the **accolades** and taste the recognition. Hank, I'm on the verge of accomplishing something heretofore thought to be impossible. I'm creating something awesome, maybe the greatest killer app the world has ever seen. This is a whole new breed of computing that draws from a variety of **disciplines.** It combines **conventional** digital technology and advanced DNA technology with a **novel** technology of my own design. I call it DMI."

"What does that stand for?" Hank asked, sitting on the edge of his chair, his chin on his fist, **transfixed** by Merle's **discourse.**

"It stands for *dynamolecular intelligence.*"

"I get the *molecular* and the *intelligence* part, but what does *dyna-* mean?"

"It's Greek for 'power.' DMI is a biodigital **mechanism** for harnessing the **inherent** power of matter. It's capable of interacting with all forms of matter, living and inert, at the **molecular** level. I've already incorporated it into TWAIN, whose **prodigious** capabilities have helped me to further refine it."

"So how does DMI work?" Hank asked.

"In the usual way, with software and hardware," Merle explained as he began pacing the room again, "except that DMI is software and hardware like you've never seen before and like you've probably never imagined, because it unites the **concepts** and functions of hardware and software in a single processing **entity**—or perhaps I should say processing *event*—that I call the 'dynachip.'

"You know all about silicon chips and semiconductors. They can store a **vast** amount of binary data, but they consume a good deal of energy and they can **malfunction.** Then there are the biochips of DNA computing, which require **minimal** energy and can perform multiple parallel functions and calculations, but they still have many limitations. The dynachip **concept** I've been working on combines the power of the silicon chip and the **versatility** of the biochip to create a higher form of chip that can **simultaneously** control a task and perform it, and that can **infinitely** recycle its own energy. With the dynachip, we'll be able to produce energy and consume it without creating **deleterious** by-products and without ever **depleting** the energy source."

Hank could scarcely believe his ears. He felt his brain beginning to **swoon** as he **contemplated** the potential **ramifications** of DMI.

"This technology," Merle went on, "will have far-reaching **implications** for humankind and for the planet— revolutionary **implications**. Once perfected, DMI will enable us to transport objects 'through' a computer and over the Net the way we now send and receive email, or download or upload a file. And when I say 'objects' I mean people as well as things. This, of course, will change nearly every aspect of our lives.

"To begin with, DMI will **render** the internal **combustion** engine and the jet engine **obsolete,** so no more **toxic** emissions and particulates polluting the atmosphere. Planes, trains, and buses will become **outmoded** and **irrelevant** because people will be able to get where they want to go almost **instantaneously** via DMI. We won't need to truck or ship any **commodities,** either, and even the mail could be sorted and delivered using DMI."

Hank was so **dazzled** by these prognostications that he was having difficulty keeping his jaw from scraping the floor.

Merle stopped pacing and pointed at Hank. "Did you happen to notice that I did *not* include the automobile in my list of **antiquated modes** of transportation?"

Hank nodded obediently.

"And why didn't I, do you think? After all, the automobile is the worst polluter of them all, the **agent** most responsible for global warming. Wouldn't it be in humanity's best interest to use DMI as the excuse to **obliterate** this scourge from the earth?"

Hank nodded again, figuring it was a **rhetorical question.**

"I'm sorry, my dear, dimwitted **apprentice,** but the answer is no. I didn't include cars because even a numskull can see that people will be **loath** to give them up. And I mean *extremely* **loath.** Americans were willing to **abandon** the wagon, the stagecoach, and the steamboat to travel by train, and they were happy to let the railways **languish** in favor of the speedier airplane, but they are never, ever going to **relinquish** their cars—at least not without a very noisy, ugly, and **protracted** fight."

Merle began to pace again. "Now, I don't own a car nor do I drive, so I couldn't care less if one day all the cars in the world mysteriously wound up on Mars. But you don't need to be **clairvoyant** to see that people and cars are **inextricably** bound to each other, especially in America. The car is an **integral** part of American culture. It **enhances** personal freedom and gives people a sense of **uninhibited mobility** and power. Americans love their cars more than they love almost anything else, including their guns. Take away America's cars, my friend, and you eviscerate the American soul."

Merle returned to his armchair and addressed Hank across the glass coffee table. "So I would never try to use DMI to get rid of the automobile. That would be foolish and ultimately self-defeating, for it would surely **engender** a rebellion—and especially an adolescent rebellion, which is the last thing anybody needs. Instead, my strategy is to find a way to run cars with dynachips, which will have more power and potential than **alternative** energy sources like hydrogen fuel cells. They also won't need to be recharged or replaced because they will **continually** recycle their own energy.

"And when I've figured out how to do that," he said, "I want to use DMI to produce electricity. Then we'll be able to create energy that can be consumed without expending any energy to create it—and, of course, without polluting the atmosphere or having an **adverse** effect on the **ecology** of our lakes and rivers."

Suddenly something occurred to Hank that **sullied** the rosy picture Merle had been painting. There was no doubt that DMI would **radically** change society, but what assurance was there that things wouldn't get a whole lot worse before they got better? "This all sounds really great and really amazing," he said, "but won't DMI cause widespread economic instability?"

"How so?"

"Well," said Hank, scanning his brain for **remnants** of **jargon** from the **verbose** and **interminable** Economics 120 lectures he had dozed through sophomore year, "if you look at things from a macroeconomic perspective, it's clear that DMI will have a **profound** effect on **diverse** economic sectors. First, we've got these huge corporations that **exploit** fossil fuels, like the big oil companies, and we've got other huge corporations that make goods that consume their product, like auto and airplane manufacturers. Then we've got the airlines and the trucking industry buying the vehicles and using the fuel to move people and goods around. Then we've got a **vast** infrastructure to support all this commercial activity, like airports and highways and gas stations. And then we've got **myriad enterprises,** large and small, that in one way or another rely on everything I've just mentioned to do their business.

"So we're talking about practically the whole dang economy here, because everything's so interrelated and dependent on everything else. And we're talking about millions and millions of employees, across the entire **spectrum** of the economy. What's going to happen to all these companies and all these workers when we make the transition to DMI? Will the companies go belly-up before they can adapt? Will people lose their jobs in droves? Will the economy just break down and collapse?"

Merle stroked his beard. "I know, I know," he said. "Believe me, I've thought a lot about how such a major leap in technology can lead to social and economic **turmoil** that can sometimes become **cataclysmic.** And after much **reflection** and **rumination** I've concluded that it all boils down to how you decide to **resolve** a **moral dilemma,** which goes like this: You have invented something that can effect a **fundamental** change in society. You're convinced the change will ultimately be for the greater good, that it will significantly improve people's lives and make the world a better place. But you also know that it will **inevitably** cause some to suffer and allow others to advance themselves through **deceit** and **manipulation.** Should you **promulgate** your invention and effect the change, or should you **abandon** it because of the harm it will cause?"

"Wow, that's a tough one," Hank said. "I don't know."

Merle leaned forward, his eyes **scintillating** with brilliant energy. "Do you know the *Rubáiyát of Omar Khayyám*?"

Hank shook his head.

"Omar Khayyám was an eleventh-century Persian mathematician, the **preeminent** mathematician of his time and a pioneer of algebra. He was also an astronomer and a poet, and his significance as a scientist has been **eclipsed** by the **immense** popularity of his collection of **epigrammatic** quatrains called the *Rubáiyát,* which was translated into English by Edward FitzGerald and published in 1859. The *Rubáiyát* is a series of **succinct reflections** on life and death,

replete with wisdom and **suffused** with **melancholy.** There's a **stanza** in the poem, my favorite one, that perfectly expresses my **motivation** for developing DMI and my faith in what it'll do for us and for the earth. It goes like this:

> "Ah Love! could you and I with Fate **conspire**
> To grasp this sorry Scheme of Things entire,
> Would not we shatter it to bits—and then
> Remold it nearer to the Heart's Desire!"

"I see what you mean," said Hank. "That's really **profound.** And **plaintive,** too. The poet **yearns** to do something good and great that's beyond his power to do."

"And you know that if there were a chance that he *could* do it, he would—in a New York minute," Merle said. He stood up, went to the refrigerator, and returned with two more cans of Joke. "Hank, this isn't about jury-rigging things so they can keep on running the way they are," he said as he popped the top of his soda and sat down. "This is about shattering the whole sorry scheme of things to bits and remolding it nearer to the heart's desire. I didn't develop DMI because I want to *reform* society. I did it because I want to *transform* civilization as we know it."

He pointed an **admonishing** finger at Hank. "If the human race is going to survive it's going to need a healthy planet with a **temperate** climate. And that means we're going to have to make some painful sacrifices in the short run to get the major payoff in the long run." He took a sip of soda, then set the can on the coffee table. "*Novus ordo seclorum,*" he said. "That's the Latin motto on the Great Seal of the United States. Do you know what it means?"

"Sorry, my Latin's a little rusty," Hank said with a shrug. "I guess because I never took it."

"Here, let me show you," Merle said. He reached into

the back pocket of his jeans and pulled out a bulging, well-worn leather wallet. He flipped it open, removed a dollar bill, and held it up for Hank to see. On the back side, under that same mysterious pyramid with the **luminous** eye at the top, the words *novus ordo seclorum* appeared on an undulant banner.

"What does it mean?" asked Hank.

"'A new order of the ages is created.'" Merle put the dollar back in his wallet and his wallet back in his pocket. "That's what the people who founded this country were out to do when they rebelled against the English **monarchy** to gain their **autonomy** and establish democracy, and that's what I'm talking about here. But in this case it's not a violent, **turbulent** overthrow of an old order. It's a revolution in technology **provoking** a revolution in society. And this certainly won't be the first time that technological progress has revolutionized society. Nor will it be the last. In fact, one way of looking at history is to view it as a **continual** series of technological revolutions that overturn the old order of things and usher in a new **era**."

Merle got up and began pacing the room again like a restless, **incarcerated** tiger. "For example," he said, "the invention of the wheel and the plow transformed a rootless, peripatetic culture into a **domestic, agrarian** culture. Just like that, in the blink of an **archaeological** eye, we went from living as wandering tribes and **clans** to living in stable communities. We went from being cave-dwelling, hunting-and-gathering **nomads** struggling to **subsist** to being **thriving** farmers who **cultivated** crops, raised livestock, and crafted polished stone **implements**.

"Johannes Gutenberg was a **notable innovator** because his technology **initiated** an **intellectual** revolution. His invention of movable type in the fifteenth century opened a **benign** Pandora's box and released a **benevolent epidemic** of publishing, which, coupled with the **inexorable** spread of **literacy,** led to the **dissemination** of new and sometimes **subversive** ideas. This enabled people to **extricate** their **innate** power of ratiocination from the **dogmatic** stranglehold of the **medieval** Roman Catholic Church. And that, of course, paved the way for the **momentous theological** transformation of the Reformation and the even more **momentous** philosophical transformation of the Enlightenment. By the time all the dust from those movements finally settled, Europe had **jettisoned** the old **ecclesiastical** order and become a **secular** and **humanistic** society.

"Another **noteworthy** person who comes **readily** to mind is the twelfth-century Hindu mathematician and astronomer Bhaskara—called Acarya, which meant **'learned'** in Sanskrit. In Bhaskara's day it was **customary** to write academic **treatises** in verse, with supplementary **explanatory** material in **prose,** and the poetic chapters on arithmetic and algebra in his *Siddhāntaśiromani* **constitute** the earliest formal, **systematic** exposition of the decimal system. Thanks to Bhaskara and his **proponents,** by circa 1300 the decimal system was introduced into Europe. It employed so-called Arabic numerals, which Europeans had learned from Arabs but which scholars believe originated in India. Why was adopting the decimal system revolutionary? Because it liberated western civilization from those clunky and **cumbersome** Roman numerals, greatly simplified arithmetic, and laid the groundwork for all modern mathematics.

"And if you look at just the last three hundred years, it's like a great big blur of technological progress causing social and economic **upheaval.** The Industrial Revolution, which began about 1750, transformed England—then the rest of Europe, America, and the world—from a **rural, agrarian** society of farmers and **artisans** who relied on tools and used only wood for fuel into an **urban** society that toiled in factories, mills, and mines, relied on **complex** machinery for **mass** production, and used coal, steam, gas, and finally oil for fuel.

"The phenomenal inventions of the Industrial Revolution **profoundly** affected the economy and society. Whitney's cotton gin, Cartwright's power loom, and the Bessemer process for making steel revolutionized agriculture, manufacturing, and architecture; the railroad, the steamship, the automobile, and the airplane revolutionized travel and **commerce**; Morse's telegraph, the transatlantic cable of 1866, and Bell's telephone revolutionized communication; Mergenthaler's Linotype revolutionized printing and publishing; and the large-scale **exploitation** of electricity—which can be said to have begun with Edison's Pearl Street power plant in 1882—revolutionized just about everything. Were all these transitions that technology **imposed** on society smooth and easy? Hell no. They certainly weren't. Human beings are by nature conservative—and if you need any proof of that **assertion,** just look at your parents. Rarely are we eager to change, even when we know it's good for us. Technological progress had its **advocates,** of course, but most people were **skeptical** and **wary** of it. There was confusion, there was resistance, and there was opposition, some of it **vehement** and **hostile.** And occasionally there was outright rebellion, as in the case of the Luddites."

"Who were they?" Hank asked.

"The Luddites," Merle explained, "were the disciples of a **disgruntled** eighteenth-century English textile worker named Ned Ludd, who **advocated** technological **vandalism**—in other words, busting up mechanized looms—because they believed that machines were the cause of widespread unemployment and low wages. The **insatiable** English language has **ingested** the Luddites, and now *Luddite* is an eponymous word for someone **fanatically** opposed to technological **innovation,** especially to any machine or laborsaving device **perceived** to replace workers.

"Although philosophically I'm the exact opposite of a Luddite, I have to confess that those nutcases had a point. During the Industrial Revolution people *were* replaced by machines. Jobs *were* lost. And workers *were* **exploited:** Their wages were **manipulated** and kept cruelly low; their working conditions were **deplorable** and their hours were long. People were uprooted and displaced, often from communities where their families had lived for generations. The culture and **traditions** of **rural** life **languished** while the cities became overcrowded, unsanitary, and **perilous** places to live, especially for the **penurious masses.** An **elite** class of plutocrats, an **aristocracy** of wealth, rose to **prominence** and **wielded vast** and virtually unchecked power. And so grew the yawning **chasm** between the rich and the poor, which the poor were **deceived** into believing could be bridged by **embracing** technology and the drudgery of laboring in its service.

"Sociologically speaking, the Industrial Revolution made the individual **subordinate** to the machine, and the brute fact of this relationship has led to **grave consequences** both for the individual and for society. Because of its **preoccupation** with technology, society became **indifferent** to the individual and the individual became **alienated** from society. So, while the standard high school history textbooks tell us all about how technology was the **agent** of tremendous progress for society, they offer little **insight** into how the individual became technology's victim, its abuser, and its slave.

"And yet—because there's always another perspective wherever history and **morality** intersect—you have to ask whether technology itself was really the villain in the whole **scenario.** Was it the machines themselves that changed society, or did society use the machines to remake itself, for better or for worse?"

Hank started to answer, but Merle held up a forefinger

to show that this time the question was **rhetorical**. The **eclectic oration** continued.

"There's a Latin **axiom,** *abusus non tollit usum,*" Merle said, "which means 'abuse does not **nullify** good use.' In other words, the **intrinsic** value of a thing, its essential worth and usefulness, is not **rendered void** or **vitiated** by abuse. To put that **principle** more simply, the **beneficial** potential of something, its ability to do good, is not destroyed or compromised by putting it to bad use.

"A classic example of *abusus non tollit usum* is television. The legendary comedian Groucho Marx once quipped, 'I find TV very educational. The minute somebody turns it on, I go to the library and read a book.' Well, when they invented TV they didn't expect it would be used to broadcast mindless, **trivial, insipid** crap and turn succeeding generations of humanity into slack-jawed couch potatoes. They thought it would be a marvelous tool for education. They wanted to **edify** people and **enhance** communication. But we chose to use TV in less **wholesome** ways. We used it as a distraction and a **diversion** rather than for **edification.** We used it not as a stimulant for the mind but as a **soporific.** So it wasn't TV that made people stupid, slothful, and obese. It was how we abused it."

Merle paused and looked at Hank. "Yo, man, are you with me?"

Hank was sitting on the edge of his chair. His mouth was hanging open and his eyes were as wide as plates. He could almost feel his brain expanding like a balloon with all the knowledge and passionate **convictions** Merle had been pumping into him, and he was scrambling to keep up with the wizard's **erudite** train of thought.

Merle made a manual megaphone around his bewhiskered mouth. "Earth to Hank, come in please. Do you read me?"

Hank nodded slowly. "Ten-four," he mumbled.

"Good." Merle returned to the armchair and sat down. "So," he said, and Hank could tell from the wizard's **conclusive** tone that he was about to deliver his peroration, "we have seen how society has an **ambivalent** relationship with technology, and how technology can be both **beneficial** and **detrimental** to society. It can be **advantageous** to some but **odious** to others. It can be a **catalyst** for magnificent social reform and a source of misery and **alienation**. And which way the sword of progress cuts depends on the **inherent** nature of the technology and the specific manner in which it is used.

"We've also considered the **moral dilemma** of whether it is right or wrong to use technology to change society in a way that you know will ultimately be for the greater good but that will cause temporary suffering and **disruption**. History has revealed the answer to that **dilemma,** showing us time and time again that if you want to make an omelette you have to break some eggs. And if you want to fix 'this sorry scheme of things entire,' as the poem says, you may have to shatter it to bits.

"So that's why I undertook this **ostensibly futile quest** to redefine our understanding of the word *impossible*—to solve some of our **chronic** problems once and for all and significantly improve our quality of life. That's why I've made it my mission to bring about a **harmonious epoch** in society's relationship with technology and technology's relationship with the earth. I want to use the **unprecedented** power of DMI to lead humankind from the **stagnant** period it's stuck in now—a kind of postatomic, postdigital slump—into a new and **vital era** that I have **dubbed** the Trans-**Molecular** Age.

"I chose that name because the Latin combining form *trāns-* can mean beyond, across, or through. Thus, the Trans-**Molecular** Age will take us *beyond* our **expectations** of what is possible, lead us *across* the physical-digital divide, and enable us to transport and re-create matter *through* the **immaterial medium** of cyberspace."

Merle leaned back in his armchair, put the tips of his fingers together, and regarded Hank with sparkling, **exultant** eyes. "So, Mr. **Precocious** Undergraduate, hacker of TWAIN. What do you think of all this? Do you **discern** the method in my madness? Am I **credible,** or am I a crackpot?"

Hank took a deep breath. "Whew," he said, feeling the **salubrious** oxygen rush to his brain. "Dude, I think you're *in*credible."

"You mean *incredible* as in 'not believable'?"

"No, just the opposite. As in 'awesome,' 'excellent,' and 'tight.' You totally blow me away." Hank got down on one knee, like a **feudal** vassal genuflecting in **deference** to his lord. "O Great Techno-Wizard," he said, "I sit at your feet. I am your **humble** servant, a lowly **novice** ready to receive the gift of **insight** from your **exalted** mind. Teach me, O master of the mysteries of **Omniscience,** to **comprehend** the **esoteric** secrets of DMI."

Merle smiled. "All in good time, my **impetuous** young catechumen. All in good time. First you must learn the **rudiments.**"

"You know," Hank said, rising and returning to his chair, "I figured you were a genius, but I always assumed you were just a one-dimensional genius, a 'geek of nature.' How do you know all that **diverse** stuff?"

Merle laughed. "It's simple," he said. "I read. That's how. Didn't your pal Mark Twain tell you that the man who doesn't read good books has no advantage over the man who can't read them? Readers are leaders, Hank. You want to succeed? Read, read, read." It also didn't hurt, Merle added, to be on friendly terms with the director of Hadleyburg's main library. "I have a key to the staff entrance so I can sneak in after hours and read to my heart's content. She even trusts me to check out my own books. But I guess that's not really surprising because she's my mother."

Hank laughed. "You're kidding. Your *mother* is university librarian?"

"Now you know why my digs have that so-called woman's touch. She comes in a few times a week and tidies up, drops off some groceries, and picks up my laundry. She even remembers to feed Norman, my pet lab rat, when I get **preoccupied** and forget. It's great. I really appreciate it. She does it so I can just concentrate on my work and not have to worry about **mundane** distractions."

Wow, Hank thought, Merlin the Magician and Renaissance Wolfman is also Merle the Mama's Boy. This guy has more sides to him than Rubik's cube. "So Merle, what do you think happened to my laptop?" he asked. "And how in the hell did I manage to access the fourth dimension?"

Chapter 15

Anchor Barred

The first thing Mark Twain noticed as he entered the Anchor Bar, even before his eyes had adjusted to the dim light, was the music.

It wasn't like any music he knew; in fact, he was stretching the definition of the word by calling this **clamorous** jumble of sound music. There was nothing **harmonious** or euphonious about it. It was all thumps and twangs and howls so **strident** and **supernatural** as to **induce** horripilation. It was an outright assault upon the ears, and it seemed to be coming straight out of nowhere or out of the walls, for there wasn't a musician or a musical instrument in sight. In fact, the narrow saloon was empty except for a tall, trim figure behind the far end of the bar.

"Hey mister," a voice called through the **raucous** noise, a husky female voice. The bartender is a woman? How daringly **unconventional,** he thought. How risqué.

"Didn't you see the ashtray outside the door?" the bartender asked as he approached the bar. She was about forty, he guessed, with **filaments** of silver in her wavy brown hair, **amiable** brown eyes, and a face that radiated **empathy**— just the sort of friendly face a bartender should have. But this bartender wasn't exhibiting much **empathy** right now. "You can't come in here with that stogie," she said.

With a **bewildered** expression, Twain looked down at the cigar smoldering between his fingers, then back at the bartender. "Why not?" he asked.

"Smoking's not allowed in here. It's against the law. Didn't you know that?"

Twain's eyes widened in disbelief. "Against the law?" he croaked. "But..."

"I'm sorry," she said. "Now will you please take that cigar outside?" She looked at him as if to say, "Don't hold it against me. I'm just doing my job."

Twain was **flabbergasted,** stunned to the core. Smoking **banned** in a *bar,* for Pete's sake? What insane depths of **moralistic rigor** had society sunk to that it would see fit to **deprive** itself of such an elemental pleasure, such a **fundamental** need, as having a smoke with one's drink? Had everyone in the tobaccophobic twenty-first century gone roaring right off the deep end? It took every ounce of **fortitude** he could muster to refrain from firing off his **irreverent** mouth until he was plumb out of **profane** ammunition.

Incensed, he headed back to the entrance. **Tentatively** he opened the door and glanced around. There was no sign of Isabel Lyon. *Hooray! Huzzah!* The **sibilant, skulking** sea urchin was gone.

He heaved a sigh of thanks and stepped outside. Then he opened his mouth and unleashed a firestorm of **scurrilous invective** that would have scorched the ears and blistered the tongue of the most foul-mouthed, trash-talking rapper. It was an avalanche of **obscenity,** a **torrent** of billingsgate, a thunderous, **blasphemous tirade** against the damnable stupidity and **folly** of the twenty-first century, and especially its **fatuous** politicians. Fortunately, he had the good sense to address his **fervid** soliloquy to the **inanimate** brick wall so as not to attract **undue** notice. When every last **vestige** of **vituperative** bile had been spewed and his vessel was finally empty, he punched out his cigar in the ashtray by the door and smiled with satisfaction. Let us swear while we may, he thought as he reentered the bar, for in heaven it will not be allowed.

"Welcome back, mister," said the bartender as Twain settled on a stool. He noticed with relief that the **discordant cacophony** had **ceased.** "You know," she said, studying his face, "I've never seen you in here before. When you walked in with a lit cigar I figured you were probably from one of the last few states in the country that permit smoking in bars. Am I right?"

Twain gave a hesitant nod.

"Which one?"

The question caught him off guard. "I...uh...well, I'm originally from Missour*a*, but...but I've been living in Mexico for some time," he stuttered, trying to be as quick on his **prevaricating** feet as his ably mendacious character, Huckleberry Finn.

"Mexico, huh? It's nice and warm down there. So what brings you all the way up here to cold and snowy New England?"

That one the writer saw coming, and he was ready with his reply. "I've got a nephew here at Hadleyburg—a junior, engineering major. I decided I'd come visit and then take him traveling for the holidays."

"Sounds nice. Well, relax and have a drink on the house. I always buy a brand-new customer his first drink. It's my way of saying welcome to the Anchor Bar."

"Why, that's downright **beneficent** of you."

The bartender gave him a **cordial** smile. "My name's DeeDee. What's yours?"

"Mark." Twain cleared his throat. "Mark Morgan."

"So what'll it be, Mr. Morgan?"

"How about a hot Scotch?"

DeeDee could barely conceal her surprise at this **eccentric** request, and the writer could barely conceal his surprise when she poured the whiskey into a tumbler, placed the tumbler inside a rectangular box, pressed some numbers printed on the box, watched as a light went on inside and the tumbler slowly spun around for thirty seconds, then removed his drink and delivered it to him piping hot—so hot he had to wait a full minute before he could pick it up.

Then DeeDee asked him if he'd like to watch something called *teevee,* and Twain said he supposed that would be just fine. She picked up a small, dark object and pressed it with her thumb, and suddenly he was staring at a large square suspended over the end of the bar that **emanated** astonishingly **vivid** and lifelike moving pictures accompanied by realistic sound. He nearly fell off his barstool in amazement. Could this *teevee* be the realization of the "telectrophonoscope" he had often daydreamed of, a device that would enable one to see and hear a **simultaneous** event in a remote location?

"Sports or news?" DeeDee asked.

Twain explained that except for baseball he had never much cared for sports. But he did like to stay au courant, and his thirst for knowledge of the events of the day was not easily **sated.**

"The news it is, then," DeeDee said. She pressed another button on the mysterious object in her hand and instantly he saw a stylishly dressed young woman with short blond hair sitting at a desk. She was looking at him and talking about something called "the Israeli-Palestinian conflict." After a minute he still had no idea what on earth she was talking about, but he could tell from the **appalling** images he saw of violence, grief, and anger that it was a **grievous** conflict unlikely to be **resolved** soon.

As Twain watched the stories unfold on this magical *teevee* he found himself growing increasingly frustrated by his inability to **comprehend** what was going on. Everything happened so fast. Each **fleeting** report hastened breathlessly on to the next and the constantly shifting and changing images began to play **havoc** with his eyes. When two men came in and sat down nearby and asked DeeDee if she would put on the sports channel, the writer was only too happy to **accommodate** them. He had had enough of this hyperactive thing called *teevee* for now, and he was eager to turn his attention to a more sedate and familiar **medium** of communication—the printed word.

On the bar beside him lay a copy of something called the *National Enquirer.* Twain picked it up and skimmed it while he sipped his drink. He quickly realized that this was only **ostensibly** a newspaper, and that what it contained was not news but rather **sensationalism.** It was one **exposé** and **lurid scandal** after another, a cornucopia of gossip and **dubious speculation** about the private lives and **foibles** of famous people. He was **captivated** by the bold colors of the photographs, but he found the writing **hackneyed** and **incompetent.** As a former newspaper reporter who had been known to **fabricate** a story or two in his day, either as a practical joke or for revenge upon a **rival,** he was sorely disappointed by the **superficial** and **simplistic** tone of the articles, their **perfunctory** style, and the **abject** poverty of their vocabulary. If you're going to **promulgate** a canard, he thought, the least you can do is give it some panache.

His **intellectual** appetite **whetted** by this **bland** hors d'oeuvre, Twain looked around for something that might provide more **substantive** information. A few seats down the bar he spied another **abandoned** newspaper, which he presumed was now also **communal** property. He asked DeeDee if she would kindly fetch it for him and she did so with **alacrity,** delivering it with a smile and an inquiry whether he would like another drink. He said yes but make it a lager beer this time, and while she set about pouring his beer he set a double sawbuck on the bar to pay for it and then set about examining this more substantial periodical.

He was delighted to discover it was a **venerable** publication with which he was already **intimate:** the *Hartford Courant,* his very own local paper, which he **perused** every morning at breakfast.

The articles in this modern-day *Courant,* especially the editorials, were well-written, **sophisticated,** and **perspicacious.** From them he was able to **infer** many startling things about this strange world of the future: that there were **immense** flying machines that could **convey** people extraordinary distances in a matter of hours; that human beings had miraculously managed to explore outer space; that doctors could make a **diagnosis** by using machines that enabled them to see inside the human body; that there had been a puzzling, **enigmatic** change in the meaning of the word *gay*; that the world still had not seen the end of what was surely the most **grotesque swindle** ever **conceived** of by humankind—**monarchy**; that we had developed something called "weapons of **mass** destruction," which were capable of **annihilating** cities and destroying half the world; and that these were **perilous** times, with terrorism and **insurgency** and war **disrupting** life, liberty, and the pursuit of happiness all around the globe.

The articles also gave him deeper **insight** into the **profound** changes society had undergone since the 1880s. He saw that the **status** of women had changed dramatically, that they had achieved **suffrage,** that it was now **customary** for them to work in jobs formerly reserved for men, and that many now held positions of power—like the four female justices on the Supreme Court. He saw that the **status** of nonwhite citizens had greatly improved, as he had already **inferred** from his brief experience on campus; racial segregation was illegal and people were free to dwell where they wished and associate with whom they pleased. And he saw that the fledgling labor unions of his day had survived violence and **oppression** and succeeded in raising the standard of living for the working classes by securing a forty-hour workweek, a **mandatory** minimum wage, safety regulations for the workplace, and other significant **perquisites.**

Even the newspaper's numerous advertisements were **illuminating.** He saw that Christmas had been transformed from a hallowed holiday into a **vibrant** industry, that it was now a retail bonanza and an excuse for **enticing** the **gullible** public with every kind of sale and bargain imaginable. He saw that many advertisements—from clothing and cosmetics to household products and groceries—were **subtly** aimed at women, which **implied** that women now had their hands on the family purse strings. He also saw that images of attractive women were frequently used to **lure** the reader and **enhance** the desirability of an otherwise ordinary product. And he noted, grimly, that there were more advertisements for those annoying, **ubiquitous** cellphones than for anything else. It was a **fundamental principle** of **capitalism**, he thought. Supply will rise to meet demand. The more popular some damned thing becomes, the more the hawking of it will **proliferate.**

All of this **insight** into the modern **era** was eye-opening and **enlightening,** to say the least, and some of it Twain found fascinating and wondrous, beyond anything he could have imagined. But none of it, even the **bewildering** fact that Republicans now sounded like Democrats and Democrats sounded like Republicans, was **inconceivable** to him or even a great surprise. In the America of the 1880s things were being discovered and invented and manufactured at such a furious and **inexorable** rate that Twain reckoned if we kept it up at even half that pace, over the next century or two it was **inevitable** that we'd see all sorts of **monumental** scientific achievements and extraordinary social reforms. What he wasn't at all prepared for, and what took him utterly by storm, hitting him like a brick in the head, was the eye-popping discovery that it was now **morally** acceptable to publish **explicit** photographs of half-naked women.

Public nudity, and in a **reputable** newspaper of all places!

As a bawdy young buck, Twain had seen his share of forbidden flesh in the fleshpots of San Francisco, but never anything as **flagrantly** lewd and **licentious** as this. It was unbelievable, it was disgusting, and it was smack-dab in the middle of page A-5—two young and voluptuous women, one blond and one brunette, wearing only **apathetic** smiles and **scanty** scraps of **tenuous** fabric over their most private parts.

"SALE: $17.99, cleavage-**enhancing** push-up gel bra," the advertisement said. "SALE: $23.99, full-figure contour underwire bra." Despite his **profound** shock and **outrage** at such a **shameless** display, by the time he stopped staring at the picture and turned the page he had a pretty good **notion** of just what a *bra* was, along with a newfound respect for what it was designed to do.

As people gradually began to wander in and occupy the barstools, Twain sipped his beer and continued reading the newspaper. By the time he had **ingested** and digested every page the bar was humming with conversation and he had come to a conclusion. Or two conclusions, actually, one of **modest** significance and one of sweeping significance. The **modest** conclusion was that **contemporary** beer was watery and **vapid** and far inferior to the bold, **effervescent** lagers and ales of his own century. The sweeping conclusion was that the **species** *Homo ignoramus* was, sad to say, still *Homo ignoramus*.

It was incredible, but it was **incontrovertible.** After a hundred-odd years of "progress," those miserable, **benighted** creatures called human beings were still making the same stupid mistakes in their sorrowful march from cradle to grave. And, as if that weren't bad enough, they were doing it without the benefit and relief of smoking!

Yes, it was true that a great deal had changed and improved since the 1880s, Twain thought, but there were some things that hadn't changed at all. Not a whit. And unfortunately the things that hadn't changed were the very things that needed to change the most. He saw that humanity had solved a few severe problems, but only to create others that were even more **dire.** He saw that people still excelled at selfishness and greed and **indulged** in every **conceivable** kind of **chicanery** and foolishness. He saw that injustice was still **rife** and cruelty was still rampant. He saw that litigation had replaced baseball as the national **pastime,** that plutocrats still held America in **thrall,** that politicians were still liars and chameleons and clowns, that Congress was still an assembly of **confirmed** idiots, and that, as usual, there was a crook in the White House.

Given his **inherent skepticism** and **pessimism,** he wasn't the least bit surprised. For that was human nature, and it was impossible to **transcend** one's nature. You are what you are, and nothing can alter that—at least nothing short of **divine intervention,** which was highly **improbable.** You can straighten a worm, he thought, but the crook is in him and only waiting.

As he swallowed the last of his **insipid** beer, he thought of the words of the **jaded** Preacher of Ecclesiastes in the Old Testament:

> There is no new thing under the sun. . . . I have seen all the works that are done under the sun; and, behold, all is **vanity** and **vexation** of spirit. That which is crooked cannot be made straight: and that which is wanting cannot be numbered.

Twain had fallen into a **melancholy** mood, and he decided that another hot Scotch just might be the thing to cure him of it, or at least **alleviate** the symptoms. He **hailed** DeeDee and placed his order, and while she warmed his whiskey in that mysterious box he looked around the bar.

The place was long and narrow, perhaps only a little wider than a passenger train, and it was abuzz with customers. People of all stripes—male and female, old and young, fair-skinned and dark-skinned, **functionally** dressed and fashionably dressed—were sitting at the bar and the small tables along the wall, drinking and laughing and talking. As the loud crack of a fresh game of eight ball **commencing** came from the billiard table in the rear, Twain trained his ears on the **myriad** conversations around him, and for the next several minutes he was **privy** to a **multitude** of amusing **anecdotes** and adventures, **feeble** jokes and boasts, **withering** comebacks, empty promises, and even a **maudlin** confession of **unrequited** love. The bar, he thought, was a **microcosm** of humanity.

Then, for no particular reason, his attention was drawn to the two men who had come in earlier, when he had been the **sole** customer, and asked to watch sports on the *teevee*. They were probably in their mid-fifties, Twain figured, judging from their facial wrinkles and hairlines on the **wane**. Their style of dress was **dissimilar**—one wore a yellow necktie and a brown corduroy sports jacket that had seen better days, the other a rumpled plaid shirt he hadn't bothered to tuck into his weathered jeans—but their physical characteristics were identical, right down to the self-conscious way they had slicked their wispy hair over their bald spots and the **prominent** wart on the left side of their noses. Twins, Twain thought. Two unsightly peas in a pod.

Needless to say, it wasn't the appearance of these two

characters that had caught his attention. Rather, it was something about their less-than-**scintillating repartee,** which showed an **inordinate** fondness for the **vulgar** use of the word for the **dominion** over which Satan **presided,** and which at the moment happened to be **elucidating** how smoking had come to be prohibited in bars.

"It was all those joggers and health-food nuts in California that got everybody started on it," said the twin in the plaid shirt. "California was the first state to pass a law. And you know what I say? The hell with California. Buncha flakes. Who needs 'em?"

Twain was surprised. He could **envision** the **staid** citizens of puritanical New England leading the charge to **impose** such a **temperance** measure, but not **unfettered** and **freethinking** California.

"Yeah, the hell with California," agreed the twin in the corduroy jacket. "At least for a while we had a smoking section in here. You remember that?"

"You bet I do," answered Plaid Shirt, "and I miss the hell out of it, specially in the winter."

"Yeah, so do I," said Corduroy Jacket. "It was a good idea, which is probably why the damn fools got rid of it. Some wiseass politician—hell, I can't remember her name right now—said that having a smoking section in a bar is like having a peeing section in a swimming pool. So they passed another damned law and everything went to hell in a handbasket."

"Hell no, brother, you got that wrong," objected Plaid Shirt. "It wasn't no wiseass politican who said that. It was George Carlin."

"Who in the hell is George Carlin?" said Corduroy Jacket.

"Some wiseass," said Plaid Shirt. "How the hell should I know?"

"You just said he was the guy who said that."

"Said what?"

"Said that about swimming pools. Hell, you know."

"Know what? I don't know what the hell you're talking about."

"Aw, go to hell why don't ya."

"Hey, what the hell are ya chewin' *my* butt for?" Plaid Shirt protested.

Corduroy Jacket took a swig of beer and sighed. "The hell with it, ya dimwit."

At that, the twins seemed to **lapse** into a **reverie.** But by and by they were up and at it again like a house afire, confabulating and arguing and speechifying **incoherently** about everything under the sun, and it was about the most ridiculous, **inane,** foolishly **meandering** and **desultory** conversation that Twain had ever heard.

First they got talking about dogs, and their different kinds of habits, and which ones were the most loyal. Next about the **capriciousness** and **vanity** of women, and their damnable desire to reform a man, and how an ornery dog was a better companion than a dame with a high opinion of herself. Next about the best way to get an **obstinate** creditor off your back; and next what ought to be done about those good-for-nothing sponges on something called "welfare"; and next about what that "nerdy" billionaire Bill Gates did all day, and how they'd heard that if the **monarch** of Microsoft dropped ten thousand dollars on the ground he'd be wasting his time picking it up because that's how much money he made *every fifteen seconds.*

And that was just the beginning. Then they got off about doughnuts, and which kind tasted better, glazed buttermilk or coconut cream; and next about the best remedy for a hangover; and next about why the hell they ever came up with a dumb idea like daylight saving time; and next about when the hell the Boston Red Sox were going to win the World Series; and next about something called "high cholesterol," and how the whole damn **concept** was a **hoax** and a **conspiracy** among those greedy doctors who are in **collusion** with those **avaricious** drug companies, and who the hell did those idiots think they were, anyway, trying to tell us what not to eat?

"And don't even get me started, brother, about those lawyers," said Plaid Shirt.

Twain motioned to DeeDee and she approached with her **luminous** smile. "Ready for another?" she asked.

"Not yet, thank you," said the writer. "I'm just curious about something." He leaned forward and cocked his head in the direction of the twins. "Who are those guys?" he asked in a stage whisper. As soon as the question was out of his mouth it struck him that he had used the word *guys* quite naturally and without any forethought. The word *guy*, meaning a man or fellow, was a slang term that had only recently come into vogue in his time. But it appeared to enjoy **universal** acceptance now, and it was certainly the preference of his Hadleyburg friends. He had often heard them use it **indiscriminately,** of women as well as men.

"Why do you ask?" said DeeDee.

"Because I've been eavesdropping on their conversation and I've never heard anything so funny in all my life," Twain said. "They seem to be **endowed** with a stupidity you could stretch four times around the globe and tie into a bow."

DeeDee laughed. "Yeah, those two aren't the sharpest tools in the shed. They like to think they're the bar's resident **pundits** and philosophers, but there's not a whole lot upstairs. But they're regulars, they behave themselves most of the time, and they're decent tippers, so I've got a soft spot for 'em. I don't know their real names, but they call themselves the Prince and the Pauper."

"Which one is which?" Twain asked.

A booming voice interrupted before DeeDee could respond.

"I, sir, am the Prince," announced the twin in the corduroy jacket, straightening his tie. He pointed to his brother in the rumpled plaid shirt. "And he is the Pauper."

The Pauper looked at Twain. "He knows all there is to know," he said with a doltish grin. "And I know the rest."

Yesterday This Day's Madness
Did Prepare

"With DMI, intersecting the space-time continuum is entirely **conceivable**," Merle **postulated** as he **simultaneously manipulated** three of his four computers. The fourth he had **delegated** to Hank. "In fact, I'd say it's entirely possible."

Once again Hank felt his jaw growing slack in the presence of the amazing Techno-Wizard. He had never seen anyone use a computer—or three—with such **dexterity** and speed, not to mention **ingenuity.** Merle was nine times faster and more **competent** than even the geekiest of geeks in the computer science department. Watching him perform was like watching a **virtuoso** play prestissimo on three pianos at once while delivering a lecture. It was more than spellbinding. It was preternatural.

"DMI is an extraordinarily powerful and **subtle** instrument, capable of effecting a **multiplicity** of **permutations**," Merle explained, his hands flying from keyboard to keyboard and mouse to mouse. "As I said before, with this technology the possibilities are **infinite.** And once you can move things through space, it's not much more of a leap to move them through time. It's just a matter of opening up a wormhole in cyberspace."

"Do you think that's what I **unwittingly** did last night?" Hank asked.

"That was my **assumption** going in, but now I'm not so sure." Merle scratched his head. "I'm having a hard time believing that you were the **sole instigating agent** in this **improbable escapade**." He looked at Hank. "No **offense**, man, but you're just not technically **savvy** enough. You're smart, but not *that* smart."

"Dude, that's for sure," said Hank, watching Merle **adeptly** execute the computer programming equivalent of a **dazzling** triple Lutz.

"I can believe TWAIN was **vulnerable** enough for you to hack into," Merle continued. "You're certainly **sophisticated** enough to do that. But with all the internal layers of security I've got in place, with all those **formidable** firewalls I built and traps I laid, it's highly **dubious** that you could have accessed the fourth dimension alone."

"So you don't think it was just a stupid accident I caused?"

"No, I don't," Merle said. He stopped typing and looked up at the ceiling. "There was definitely a **random** element involved, which I suspect was you," he said after a **contemplative** pause. "But there was something else going on, something intentional and **purposeful**, and I just don't know yet what it was."

Merle turned his attention back to his computers, and there was a **hiatus** in the conversation.

"So are you saying DMI could be used for time travel?" Hank asked after a while.

In one fluid motion, Merle checked all three monitors and nodded. "Definitely," he said. "But I would never do it. Not for a million bucks and not in a million years."

Hank was surprised. This from the man who had pledged his life to making the impossible possible? "Why not? Scientists and philosophers have **speculated** and theorized about time travel for eons. Isn't it in some ways the ultimate challenge?"

Merle snorted. "It's the ultimate **folly,** if you ask me. And it's **unethical.**"

Folly? Unethical? Now Hank was confused. "But why?"

"Because it has no **advantageous** purpose, no useful benefit, and science, I seem to recall, is about accomplishing **beneficial** things. Whenever I think about time travel, I'm reminded of a line from *King Lear:* 'That way madness lies.'"

Hank shook his head. "Dude, I'm sorry, but I just don't get it."

"The **reference** to Shakespeare or the mad foolishness of time travel?"

"The **latter.** I get the Shakespeare part."

"Okay," said Merle, tapping out a cadenza on the keys, "I see my poor **neophyte** is an **unwitting** victim of all the usual **misconceptions** about time travel. I suppose you believe that if we could somehow master the space-time continuum then we could **manipulate** it to **avert calamities, alleviate** suffering, and **intervene** to rescue people just in the nick of time, so to speak. You think that's what it's good for, am I right?"

"Uh, yeah," said Hank, "In general, I guess."

"Well, that's the general **stereotype.** Time travel is probably the most ridiculously **romanticized** and misunderstood scientific **concept** in the popular imagination. Nobody seems to **comprehend** just how **pernicious** it is.

"When you have the power to travel through time you possess the **concomitant** power to alter events—sometimes **inadvertently,** as you learned last night to your **chagrin.** And if you alter events, even in what you think is only a **minuscule** and **innocuous** way, then you alter history. And when you alter history, even with the most **altruistic** intentions, you set the stage for all sorts of other unintended, **unforeseen,** and **ineluctable consequences.**

"People don't seem to realize that any **chronological in-trusion** will **inevitably** have **innumerable ramifications,** all of them **random** and **unpredictable.** That's why time travel is **unethical.**"

"So you don't think there's *any* way time travel can be used to do good?"

Merle swiveled around in his chair and locked eyes with Hank. "Look, my friend, going back in time to save the *Titanic* or assassinate Hitler or **thwart** the 9/11 terrorists sounds noble and brave and makes a good plot for a book or a movie, but that's fiction, and what works in fiction doesn't necessarily work in reality.

"It's **simplistic** and **naive** to think that we can use time travel to prevent **mishaps,** correct mistakes, or avoid mak-ing them in the first place. We want to believe that, but it's as **fallacious** as the **notion** that having nuclear weapons makes the world a safer place. You want to know the truth? The truth is that time travel will only **induce** us to flirt with the devil or play God."

Merle raised a furry forefinger and pointed it at Hank. "And one other thing. You may think that by agreeing to help you get out of this **predicament** I'm making an excep-tion to my vow never to use DMI for time travel. Not so at all. I'm not going to **initiate** or change anything. I'm simply going to reverse the process and undo the damage that's been done. My job is to try to find that open worm-hole, get things back in their proper places, and then close it before there's any more **havoc.** I'll give you a **metaphor** for the problem we're facing. Think of it as a puncture wound in time, and we're the surgeons who have to clean the wound and sew it up."

With that pronouncement, Merle swiveled back and was about to resume his computer concerto when there was a rhythmic knock on the door—two slow taps followed by three quick ones.

"Who could that be?" said Hank, startled by the unexpected interruption. Who else could have come to visit the **reclusive** hermit of Science Hill?

"Oh, it's just my mom," said Merle. He began typing and clicking again.

"Aren't you going to go let her in?"

"I don't need to. She's got a key. After she knocks she always waits for exactly one minute before she opens the door. That's so I can get my pants on if I need to. She knows I like to work in my underwear."

"Allow me to propose a toast," drawled Mark Twain, raising his glass.

For the past half hour he had been drinking and **bantering** with the **pompous** and dimwitted Prince and the even more dimwitted Pauper, making **spontaneous** toasts and engaging in tall talk about this, that, and the other— although with these two **specimens** of *Homo ignoramus* it was mostly the other. The twins had turned out to be even greater **paragons** of mental **vacuity** and **egregious obtuseness** than he could have imagined. Their capacity for **blatant** stupidity seemed **boundless,** and Twain found it **vastly** entertaining.

"Did you know," the Prince had said, "that Lincoln wrote the Gettysburg Address while traveling from Washington to Gettysburg on the back of an envelope?"

"That's fascinating," Twain replied. "I didn't know that envelopes were capable of **autonomous locomotion.**"

"You know," the Pauper remarked, "I always liked the way that speech began: 'Four score and seven beers ago...'" Then he grinned his doltish grin and said, "Hell, I'll bet Honest Abe could really put 'em away!"

When the twins had inquired where he was from and what he did, Twain explained that he was a former correspondent for the *Hartford Courant* who had published nine bestselling novels and was currently living in a **secluded** village in Mexico. Mr. Twain, it should be observed, never told an outright lie if he could help it. But he rarely missed an opportunity to **embellish** the truth.

"So what's your line, mainly?" Twain asked them.

"Hell, most anything that'll pay the rent and buy me a few beers," said the Pauper, "long as it ain't real work. Y'know, the kind that uses these." He tapped an index finger on his forehead. "But I don't much like work even when somebody else does it."

"My brother's the handy one," explained the Prince. "I'm the one with the brains."

"I see," said Twain, **suppressing** a chuckle. "And what do you do, sir?"

"Hell, you might be better off asking what *don't* I do," said the Prince. "I'm an advertising man by trade, but I've done consider'ble work in sales and marketing—door to door, telephones, spamming, you name it—and I've got some 'sperience in retail too—in the discount resale industry, mainly—and my degree's in accounting."

"Yeah," mumbled the Pauper, "*creative* accounting."

"Financial management is my latest venture," the Prince continued. "I'm an independent market **analyst** specializing in asset accumulation and short-term growth through high-risk **speculation**—futures, **commodities,** junk bonds, insider trading, that sort of thing."

"I'll bet that keeps you busy," Twain said.

"Busy staying out of trouble," mumbled the Pauper.

Twain just listened and sipped his whiskey and silently laughed, and didn't let on for a minute that he knew these two simpletons were a couple of **frauds** just like the king and the duke, the low-down humbugs in his novel *The Adventures of Huckleberry Finn.* And now their **desultory** talk had turned to the subject of potation, and Twain was raising his glass to propose a toast.

"Let us drink to the **inestimable merits** and **venerable** history of whiskey," he said. He looked up at the ceiling and spoke in a **sonorous** voice filled with **reverence**. "How **solemn** and beautiful is the thought that the earliest pioneer of civilization, the **vanguard** of civilization, is never the steamboat, never the railroad, never the newspaper, never the **humanitarian**, never the missionary—but always whiskey!"

"What in the hell does whiskey have to do with civilization?" said the Pauper. "And who the hell rides a steamboat, 'cept maybe at Disneyland?"

"Shut the hell up, brother, and let the man speak," **chastised** the Prince. "He's published nine books. I 'spect he knows somethin' about somethin', 'specially whiskey."

"Look history over; you will see," said Twain. "The missionary comes after the whiskey—I mean he arrives after the whisky has arrived; next comes the poor immigrant, with ax and hoe and rifle; next, the trader; next the gambler, the desperado, the highwayman, and all their kindred in sin of both sexes; and next, the **sagacious** fellow who's bought up an old grant that covers all the land; this brings the lawyer tribe; the **vigilance** committee brings the undertaker. All these interests bring the newspaper; the newspaper starts up politics and a railroad; all hands turn to and build a church and a jail—and behold! civilization is established forever in the land. But whiskey, you see, was at the **vanguard** in this **beneficent** work. It always is."

"Well now, ain't that somethin'," said the Pauper. "That gives me a whole new way of looking at things, a whole new perspective."

"You mean a whole new prospectus," corrected the Prince.

"Hell, whatever. Now I know that when I have myself a drink I can feel proud to be a prisoner of civilization."

"Yes, we're mighty proud to be part of the rank file of

progress," said the Prince, "and if that means having another drink, hell, bring it on. Gentlemen, whaddaya say we have another round? And what the hell, let's have it on my brother."

"Hey, the hell you will!" cried the Pauper.

"Cheapskate," grumbled the Prince. "All right, I'll pay."

"Why, that's downright **magnanimous** of you, Mr. Prince," Twain said, noticing that the double sawbuck he had placed on the bar had swiftly **dwindled** to a mere five dollars and change.

The Prince summoned DeeDee and placed his order, and when the fresh drinks arrived Twain raised his glass to toast again. This time he recited one of his favorites, a toast he often turned to when entertaining guests or **intimate** friends in his billiard room late into the night:

YESTERDAY *This* Day's Madness did prepare;
TOMORROW's Silence, Triumph, or Despair:
Drink! for you know not whence you came, nor
     why:
Drink! for you know not why you go, nor where.

"Hell, that's poetry, ain't it?" said the Pauper.

"That wasn't just poetry, brother," said the Prince, "that was damned good poetry! I didn't know there were poems about drinking. Did you make that up, Morgan?"

Twain was sorely tempted to take credit for the verse, but to his own credit the wagging, **censuring** finger of conscience stopped his **unethical** sense of humor at the door. "No, I didn't make it up, though I wish I had," he said. "It's one of the quatrains from that glorious celebration of life and **meditation** on death, the *Rubáiyát of Omar Khayyám*."

"Hey, whaddaya say we all step outside for a friendly smoke?" said the Pauper, his brief enthusiasm for poetry evidently **exhausted.**

Twain, needless to say, was only too eager to **endorse** the proposal.

George Griffin, his shoes still clutched in his hand, wasn't sure whether he was alive or dead. The terrible ringing in his ears had stopped, the strange feeling of weightlessness was gone, and he seemed to be standing on something firm. But he was **reluctant** to open his eyes—no, more than **reluctant**, he was afraid—because Lord knows *what* he would see. It might be the familiar and comforting surroundings of Mr. Clemens's billiard room or the Four Horsemen of the Apocalypse and the fires of hell.

He extended his free hand and cautiously explored the space around him. His **probing** fingers **discerned** what appeared to be walls on all sides, a ceiling above, and a floor below—**tangible** evidence that led him to wonder if he were inside some sort of large box. What if I'm trapped? he thought. What if I've been buried alive?

That terrifying **prospect** threw him into such a state of **perturbation** that he didn't know what to do next. For an **interminable**, agonizing moment he was frozen, **immobilized**, unable to think or act. Now he was certain that death was **imminent** or that he had made the transition to the world beyond.

Then somehow, miraculously, he regained self-control. And he knew that he must open his eyes and confront his fate. Far better to face it like a man, he thought, than to have it thrust upon you like a dagger while you **cower** in darkness.

Slowly he parted his eyelids into the **minutest** sliver of a squint, and his heart leapt with joy and relief when he **perceived** a **modicum** of pale light. Surely if there was light, he couldn't be entombed. Had he crossed the River Jordan and entered the Promised Land?

He opened his eyes a little bit more, and then a little bit

more—and then, when his vision began to clear, he opened them wide with surprise.

This is the Promised Land? he thought.

He was standing on a tiled floor, surrounded by three gray walls, staring down at a white bowl half filled with **murky** brown water. On the floor beside the bowl was the strange, **mesmerizing** contraption from Mr. Clemens's desk.

"Hey look, the pool table's free now, brother," said the Pauper as he, the Prince, and Twain reentered the Anchor Bar. They had just spent ten shivering minutes in the bitter cold **indulging** their **mutual** craving for tobacco.

"Hell, it's about time those clumsy hogs gave it a rest," said the Prince. He looked at Twain. "Do you shoot pool, Morgan?"

The writer nodded. "Billiards is my game, but I can hold my own at pool."

"Billiards, eh?" said the Prince, cocking an eyebrow. "Not many people play that anymore, at least around here." He straightened his tie and tried in **vain** to smooth the stubborn wrinkles in his corduroy jacket. "Well, let's see what you can do with a cue and a cue ball, then."

"It would be my pleasure, Mr. Prince," said Twain, "but first, my friends, I've got to see a man about a dog."

"Huh? What's with the dog?" said the Pauper. "Are ya coming right back?"

"Hell, you don't know a damn thing, do you?" said the Prince in a **condescending** voice. "Goin' to see a man about a dog is *euthanasia*."

Twain almost exploded with laughter at the Prince's **absurd** malapropism, a confusion of *euthanasia* with *euphemism*.

The Pauper looked doltishly **bewildered**. "'Youth in Asia?' I don't get it."

"Brother, I swear you are an idiot. Morgan here, being a polite sort of guy, doesn't want to come right out and say he's going to check the plumbing. So he practiced *euthanasia*."

"But I still don't get it," the Pauper protested. "What in the hell do Asian kids have to do with going to the can?"

It was all Twain could do to get himself inside the men's room before unleashing a hearty and thunderous **guffaw**.

Chapter 17

Tempus Fugit

"Merlin, it's so nice to see you have a friend visiting today," said the Techno-Wizard's mother as she swept into the room carrying two bulging bags of groceries. "I worry about you sometimes, dear. You spend so much time alone."

Her voice was mellifluous and full of **mirth,** Hank thought, almost like a little girl's. He took a **furtive** glance over his shoulder and caught a glimpse of a woman in a long red coat with lustrous gray hair spilling out from under a red pillbox hat.

"Mom, you know I'm too busy to entertain company," Merle replied without taking his hands or eyes off the three computers he was **navigating** through cyberspace. "How many times have I told you that?"

"Oh, many times, dear," she trilled. "Too many times."

Hank **surreptitiously** watched the tall and graceful woman as she crossed the room and set the groceries on the dining table, then took off her hat and coat and spotless white gloves and laid them on a chair along with her compact sequined purse. He was struck by the stylish **sophistication** of her outfit. She was wearing black leather boots, black slacks, and a white form-fitting, funnel-neck sweater that he couldn't help noticing nicely flattered her appealing hourglass figure. She reminded him of a **Sensual** Secret supermodel, only fully dressed and with a head of **incongruous** gray hair. Even to Hank's youth-hungry eyes, this fiftysomething fashion plate was a total knockout.

This is the university librarian? he thought. This is Merle's *mother*?

"So who's your friend, dear?" she said, fixing her hair with a brisk toss of her head and a couple of quick pats. "Aren't you going to introduce me?"

"Oh yeah, sure," Merle said, still not bothering to look up. "Mom, this is Hank Morgan. Hank, this is my mom, Blanche Paige."

"How do you do, Hank?" she said with a friendly wave and a sparkling smile.

Hank smiled back self-consciously. "Uh, I'm doing great, Mrs. Paige." He cleared his throat. "I mean, it's nice to meet you." How in the world, he wondered, could a woman so attractive produce **offspring** so...well, so dang *hairy*!

"It's *Ms.* Paige, if you don't mind," she said in her pleasant voice.

"Oh. Right. Sorry," Hank said.

"My mother likes to disguise the fact that she never married," Merle said.

"Merlin, dear, please try to be more **tactful**," said Ms. Paige. Her voice was as **melodious** and soothing as a songbird in a blooming garden. "And what are you two boys up to today?"

"Not much," said Merle over his shoulder.

"Yeah, we're just chillin'," Hank chimed in.

"Hank's an undergraduate intern," Merle **clarified**. "I've hired him to help me with my project."

"That's nice, dear," said Ms. Paige. "It's about time you had some normal interaction with Hadleyburg students."

"Sure, Mom, whatever you say."

"May I get you boys a snack or something to drink?"

"No thanks, Mom. We're fine. Really."

"Well then," she said, adjusting her **resplendent** hair, "I'll just put these groceries away and go about my business and let you get back to work."

"Dadblame this cottonpickin' thing," Twain muttered as he struggled with his mutinous zipper. When all was safely **ensconced,** he went to the sink and began washing his hands—or, to be more precise, he began wrestling with the soap dispenser on the wall, swearing at it as he tried to figure out how to make it **dispense.**

"Damn this dadgummed, ding-busted device!" he cried, manhandling the **intractable** object. "By criminy, I don't know why they make things so damned *complicated* when a simple bar of soap would do." He managed to pull something that moved and a puddle of pink oleaginous liquid squirted into his palm. He stared at it with **repugnance** and **contempt.** "And what in the Sam Hill kind of soap is *this,* anyway? It looks like something expectorated by a consumptive."

Perhaps that **distasteful** thought made him wash his hands more thoroughly and swear more furiously than usual. He turned off the water and was about to look for a towel when he heard a sound behind him. A voice.

"Lord have mercy," it whispered.

Twain glanced up into the mirror over the sink and saw the top half of a black face peering wide-eyed over one of the toilet stall doors.

"Mr. Clemens, is that you?"

"What the devil!" cried the writer, turning around. "Who in the dickens—"

"Mr. Clemens, it's me, George Griffin," said the butler, stepping out of the stall. He spread his arms. "See?"

"George?"

"Sure as you born."

"Why, it *is* you!"

"Yessir!"

"Holy cats, you scared the bejabbers out of me." Twain slapped his forehead and then wished he hadn't. His hand was still dripping wet. "But boy am I delighted to see you, Mr. Griffin." He smiled warmly. "Just delighted."

"And I'm sure glad to see you, Mr. Clemens," said George, returning the smile.

The writer tossed all **etiquette, decorum,** and **punctiliousness** straight out the window and dried his face on his sleeve and his hands on his pants. Then the two men shook hands.

"How did you figure out who I was?" asked Twain.

"Well," George replied, "first I heard that **robust** laugh of yours when you came in. There's no mistaking that. And then I heard you cussin' and carryin' on the way you're wont to when you know the ladyfolk ain't around. And finally I peeked out and saw your face in the mirror and then I knew it was really you."

"So what on earth are you doing here?"

George shook his head. "I rightly don't know, sir. What are *you* doing here?"

Twain shrugged. "I rightly don't know, either. But I'm hoping that you've come to rescue me from this awful limbo I'm in."

In the blink of an eye, George's expression went from cheerful and **optimistic** to fearful and **apprehensive.** "Limbo? We're in limbo?" he cried, wringing his big hands. "Oh Lord, I knew it, Mr. Clemens, I just knew it. The two of us have passed! We've left our poor families **bereft** and all alone in the cold, cold world."

"Wait a minute, that's—"

"Oh, Mr. Clemens, what are they going to do without us?"

"But that's not what I—"

"And all that money between my mattresses," George moaned. "Land sakes alive, I had fifteen hundred dollars that I won in the last election!"

Twain gripped the butler's shoulders and gave him a shake. "George, you can stop your worrying about that right now. You took me all wrong. We're not in limbo."

George stopped wringing his hands, but he still looked **skeptical**. "Then where are we, besides in somebody's bathroom?"

Twain stroked his chin. "Well, now this is going to sound like a stretcher, but it ain't. It's God's honest truth." He looked at his friend with a **sober** expression—or as **sober** an expression as he could manage after **indulging** in several drinks. "George, I don't know how else to say this, so I'll say it straight. We've traveled through time. We're in the future."

George's look of **skepticism** became several degrees more **skeptical**. "Aw, come on now, Mr. Clemens. You expect me to believe that? You're putting me on."

Twain shook his head **emphatically**. "No I'm not. I swear by my good name. As sure as we're both standing here, this is the twenty-first century."

George still wasn't buying it. "Golly, Mr. Clemens," he said, **feigning** a disappointed tone of voice, "if this is the twenty-first century, then don't you think that after all that time they'd have figured out how to make a better-looking bathroom?"

Twain stamped his foot. "Dagnabit, that's not funny!"

George shrugged. "It's about as funny as the **notion** that the two of us are confabulatin' in a lavatory when we've been dead for over a hundred years."

Twain ran an impatient hand through his hair. "All right, look. If you insist on doubting my **veracity** then I suggest you **verify** my claim on your own. Go take a peek through that door over there and *then* tell me that I'm wrong."

George eagerly took him up on the suggestion. But a

moment later he returned, **astounded** and **chagrined.** "I'm sorry I doubted you, sir," he said, the **jauntiness** in his voice replaced by **humility.** "I surely do believe you now."

"What did you see, George?"

The butler looked down at the floor. "Mr. Clemens," the big man said in a voice so hesitant it was almost **timid,** "I saw white folks and black folks—and what looked like other colors, too—all sitting together around those tables and at that bar like it was the most natural thing in the world for them to be socializing like that." He looked up at his employer. "Was that some kind of **illusion,** or is that really what it's like in the future?"

Twain's heart filled with **empathy.** "That's really what it's like, my friend," he said. "Things are different now. People are on a much more equal footing." The writer explained how black people no longer felt **compelled** to be **deferential** to white people, how they no longer were a **servile** underclass, **relegated** to a lower **stratum** of society and denied equal opportunity. "And it's certainly not a spectacle anymore for a white person and a black person to be seen together. Companionship between the races is quite acceptable and proper."

"Goodness!" George cried after a long pause.

That was the only word he uttered, but it was enough. From the look of wondrous **rapture** on his face Twain could **infer** the rest.

"Hank," said Merle quietly, "what did you say was the Latin phrase that appeared on the screen when you accessed TWAIN last night?" For several minutes they had not exchanged a word as Merle **probed** deeper and deeper into **uncharted** virtual territory and Hank did his best to keep up.

"I didn't," Hank said. "It was *tempus* something or other."

Merle's fingers paused and hovered over a keyboard. *"Tempus?"*

"Yeah, wait a sec..." Hank scratched his head and stared at the ceiling. "Okay, now I remember. It was *tempus edax rerum.* Angela said it means—"

"'Time, devourer of all things.'"

"Yeah, that's right. How did you know?"

"I studied Latin, how else? And you know what?"

"What?"

"Learning some Latin was the best thing I ever did for my English vocabulary. *Verbum sat sapienti,* pal. 'A word to the wise.'"

Merle issued a few technical instructions to Hank and then turned his attention back to his bank of computers. Hank did what he was told and a minute later, to his **acute** surprise, everything on his panel display vanished. Then the unit burped and crackled and flickered and the **lugubrious** Latin **adage** began scrolling across an otherwise black screen: TEMPUS EDAX RERUM ... TEMPUS EDAX RERUM ...

"Merle, what's happening?"

Merle leaned back in his chair and crossed his arms. "I knew it," he said, shaking his head. "I just had a gut feeling the trail would lead us here—and my **visceral** instincts are usually right."

"Lead us where?" asked Hank. "Where are we? What did you find out?"

Before Merle could answer, a euphonious voice interrupted.

"Merlin," Ms. Paige sang out from the kitchenette, "do you want me to put these chunks of *Parmigiano-Reggiano* and *Pecorino Romano* in the refrigerator or leave them out the way they do at the store?"

Hank saw Merle roll his eyes. "Just put them in the fridge, Mom," he said. "They'll be fine."

"You were all out of basmati rice, so I got you some more."

"Thanks. I hope it was the organic brand."

"Yes it was, dear. And I made you a plate of my special

Rice Crusty cookies, which I know you just love. Where shall I put them?"

Hank thought he saw Merle wince. "On the counter," he mumbled.

"What was that, dear?"

Merle practically shouted. "I said leave them on the counter!"

"Please, Merlin dear, you don't have to yell. I'm not hard of hearing, you know. I'm still in my prime, or at least I'd like to think so."

"Oh you are, Ms. Paige, you definitely are." The **telltale** words were out of Hank's mouth before he realized what they **implied.**

She smiled and looked at him the way the sultry, middle-aged Mrs. Robinson looked at Benjamin in the movie *The Graduate*—at least that's how it seemed to Hank. "Thank you, Hank," she said in that **celestial** voice. "You're very sweet to say so."

Hank felt himself blush to the roots of his hair. What a gaffe! That dorky **blunder** was tailor-made for the next round of "**Mortifying** Moments."

"Will it bother you boys if I do some vacuuming?" asked Ms. Paige.

"No, not at all, Mom," said Merle. "You go right ahead."

While Ms. Paige vacuumed, Merle picked up where they had left off. He told Hank that *Tempus* was the code name of a **classified** research project led by Professor Gideon Reisenzeit, a brilliant physicist and computer scientist and Merle's arch **rival** since his earliest days at Hadleyburg. The goal of *Tempus* was as breathtakingly **ambitious** as Merle's **aspirations** for DMI—to use the power of TWAIN to penetrate the space-time continuum, explicate the mysteries of the fourth dimension, and develop technology that would enable human beings and objects to travel through time.

"Everything that you believe is **unethical** and unconscionable," said Hank. "Flirting with the devil and playing God."

"Precisely," said Merle.

Unlike his own solitary and **idealistic** DMI research, Merle explained, *Tempus* was a **massive** project funded by huge grants from the Department of Defense, the Department of Homeland Security, and the Irving Foundation—as in Miles "Cosmo" Irving, the computer chip **magnate** and Hadleyburg **benefactor** after whom Irving Laboratory had been named. Should Professor Reisenzeit manage to succeed in his **quest** to **exploit** the fourth dimension and master time travel, Irving's multinational corporation, CosmoLogicon, would win a **lucrative** contract to assist the government in using *Tempus* in a variety of **covert** military and security operations.

"Wow, that *is* pretty scary," said Hank.

"You bet it is," said Merle. "There's a pile of money behind *Tempus* and an even bigger pile that may come out of it, and it's **axiomatic** that whenever **vast** wealth and science come together the wealth will **corrupt** the science for its **mercenary** ends. **Valid, ethical** science has no more chance against the vitiating power of money than an old man **brandishing** a cane has against an advancing army."

"How do you know all this top-secret stuff, anyway?"

Merle stopped tapping the keyboards and looked at Hank. His eyes were like two coruscating opals. "If it has to do with TWAIN, I make it my business to know. And if it has to do with that **venal, deceitful,** vicious bastard Reisenzeit, I especially make it my business to know."

Whoa, there must be some serious bad blood between these dudes, Hank thought. He looked at the Latin phrase scrolling across his screen and a **hypothesis** gradually began to **crystallize** in his brain. "You said there was something intentional and **purposeful** behind what happened last night. Could it have been *Tempus*?"

Merle nodded. "You're reading my mind."

"And you said my hacking into TWAIN was a **random** element in the exchange. What did you mean by that?"

"That you were the **proverbial** wrench in the works."

"You mean *Tempus* was up to something and somehow I got in the way?"

"Yup."

"So, if I'm getting this right, my laptop got tangled up with *Tempus*—"

"Yup."

"Which sucked it through a wormhole and exchanged it with the manuscript of *Huckleberry Finn*."

"Yup, that's exactly what I'm thinking." Merle paused and stroked his beard. "But why *Huckleberry Finn*?"

"Good question," said Hank.

"And how did Mark Twain happen to tag along?"

"He told us he banged his head and lost consciousness, and when he woke up the manuscript was gone and my laptop was in its place. He said he fiddled around with it a bit, and the next thing he knew he was standing outside the door to my friends' suite."

"So he messes with your laptop, which is still connected to *Tempus* and TWAIN, and transports himself by accident."

"Yeah, that makes sense."

"Or maybe the **sinister** Reisenzeit was after the manuscript *and* Mark Twain, and you foiled him twice." Merle grinned beneath his dense beard. "I like that idea."

"Yeah, that's **plausible**, too," said Hank. "So now that you've accessed *Tempus,* can you recover my laptop?"

"Merlin?" Ms. Paige chirped from the dining area where she was putting on her elegant red wool coat. "I'm going now, dear."

"Okay," Merle called back over his shoulder.

"I put two bottles of Joke in the fridge and a pint of Bud

and Georgie's in the freezer, and I'm taking your laundry and the trash."

"Thanks, Mom, that's great."

Hank couldn't resist watching Ms. Paige out of the corner of his eye as she pulled on her white gloves and adjusted her dainty pillbox hat.

"And I fed Norman, but don't forget to give him some fresh water tomorrow."

Who's Norman? thought Hank. Oh yeah, Merle's pet rat.

"I won't," said Merle.

"Are you going to participate in the Winter Bacchanal?" Ms. Paige asked as she picked up the bag of laundry in one hand and the bag of trash in the other.

Dang, Hank thought, I totally forgot that was tonight.

"I don't think so," said Merle. "I've got a lot of stuff to do."

"It's a shame you don't get out more," she said with a shake of her head. "Well then, dear, you should at least try to get a little extra sleep tonight. You look tired."

"Sure, Mom, whatever. Thanks for coming."

For once, Hank remembered his manners. Noticing how **encumbered** Ms. Paige was with the two **bulky** bags, he stood up. "May I get the door for you, ma'am?"

"Why yes, if you don't mind," she said. "How thoughtful of you."

"It was nice meeting you, Ms. Paige," Hank said as he pulled open the door.

"It was a pleasure meeting you, too, Hank," she replied with that sparkling smile. "And thank you for playing with—I mean spending time with Merlin." She giggled at her **maternal** faux pas, then called out to her son. "Be a good host now and share those Rice Crusties with Hank. I'm sure he'll love them as much as you do."

"Okay, Mom, I will. Good-bye."

"Good-bye," she replied melodically. She looked at Hank—that Mrs. Robinson look again. "Good-bye now," she said in a surprisingly lower, almost breathy voice.

Hank felt himself blushing again. "Good-bye," he mumbled.

Ms. Paige stepped out into the hallway, leaving a trace of perfume in Hank's nostrils. The door closed behind her with an **ominous,** metallic clang. Whew, what a lady, he thought as he crossed the room and sat down again beside Merle.

Hank looked at the wizard. He was strangely **immobile,** gripping the armrests of his chair. And there was something odd about his face. It was pink.

"Merle, are you okay?" asked Hank.

"I hate Rice Crusties!" the wizard exploded. "I hate them, hate them, *hate them!*" He slammed a fist on the desk. "She's always bringing me some kind of **insipid** garbage that she calls food. She thinks I love it, but I **loathe** it. It's sickening, **abominable,** and **vile.** Every time she brings something she's **concocted** I chuck it down the disposal. Then I have to tell her how delicious it was. And then she brings me *more!* It's a vicious circle." He rubbed his forehead like a desperate man caught in a hopeless **quandary.** "What can I say? The woman just can't cook. She never could. It's such a pity."

Hank glanced over at the tray Ms. Paige had left on the kitchenette counter and felt his stomach gurgle. "Hey, I'll eat those babies if you don't want to."

"I *definitely* don't want to," Merle said. "Go ahead. Good riddance."

"Thanks, dude!" Hank popped out of his chair and headed for the counter with **alacrity.**

"But I'll have to ask you not to eat them in here," Merle said. "I can't even stand the smell of those things. Makes me want to puke."

"No problem."

Hank sat down outside in the hallway and chowed down on Ms. Paige's Rice Crusties under the buzzing fluorescent lights. They were delicious, sticky and sweet and still slightly warm. He ate and ate until he was **surfeited** and had to admit that, much as he wanted to, he couldn't finish them all.

"Guess what?" Merle said as Hank came inside and shut the door. He was standing with his hands on his hips, staring down at one of the monitors.

"What?" said Hank, licking the crumbs off his lips.

"Your laptop isn't where you think it is."

"Really?"

Merle turned around. "It's not in the past. It's in the present."

Hank was stunned. "You're kidding. How did that happen—and where is it?"

"I don't know yet," Merle said, crossing his arms, "but we're gonna find out."

Chapter 18

The Mighty Massé

George Griffin was cleaning up, not as a nineteenth-century butler but as a twenty-first-century gambler, and he was loving every minute of it.

The wad of nineteenth-century money he had stashed in his pocket was useless now, and Mr. Clemens had only five modern dollars to bet with, but that was no **impediment** to George. He quickly and handsomely magnified that **meager** sum thanks to the overconfident, **reckless** wagering of the **arrogant** and prodigal Prince, who was **continually goaded** to raise the stakes by his loudmouth twin, the Pauper.

George had spent many hours on the sidelines watching his boss display his **artful** command of the billiard table, and from the Prince's **initial** break, which did a poor job of scattering the balls and failed to sink one, he could tell which man would be **dominant** in this contest. But he had also learned from the **affable** and **forthcoming** bartender, DeeDee, that the twins considered themselves **shrewd** customers when it came to pool, and that he and "Mr. Morgan" should be **wary** and on the lookout for a **ruse**.

"What the hell's wrong with me today?" the Prince complained as he missed another shot and his **dexterous** opponent proceeded to run the table again.

"Hell, brother, you're just havin' a string of bad luck," the Pauper commiserated. "I bet you'll bounce back this next round. My money's on you."

"Oh yeah?" said the Prince. "Well, then howzabout puttin' up some of it yourself, ya cheapskate? Put your moola where your mouth is."

"All right, all right, shut your piehole," said the Pauper, **reluctantly** producing a ten-dollar bill from a **shabby** wallet.

"Aw c'mon, you cheeseparing skinflint," said the Prince, **scoffing** at his brother's stingy offering. "Can't you do better than that? Hell, I've lost ten times that much already."

"Uh, nine actually," said the Pauper, "but who's counting?"

"C'mon, brother, make it worth it," **coaxed** the Prince. "Hell, I think you're right. I *am* gonna win this next game. I can sure as hell feel it."

"Right on, brother, get pumped," said the Pauper, grinning his **fatuous** grin. "That's the 'tude."

Twain frowned and looked at George. "'Right on, get pumped'? What the heck does that mean?" he whispered, chalking his cue. "And what's a 'tood'?"

"Beats me," George whispered back. "Maybe they're talking in code. We'd better be **vigilant** in case they're up to something."

The Pauper pulled a twenty from his wallet and combined it with the ten. Then he laid the money on the long rail of the pool table and looked at George. "Thirty bucks says my man beats your man this time around."

"You're on, Mr. Pauper." George peeled off three tens from his wad of bills and laid them on the rail.

"But we want the break," the Pauper added. "It's only fair considering your guy's won every game so far."

"All right," George said, "but you'll have to put up another twenty dollars."

"Hell, that's highway robbery," the Pauper objected.

"Otherwise known as contortion," said the Prince with a **supercilious** air.

Twain sputtered with laughter that he quickly disguised as a cough. Another outrageous malapropism! This time it was *contortion* for **extortion**.

"Not if you believe your man's going to win," said George. "You can't get something for nothing, gentlemen. That's what my momma always told me. If you want the advantage of the break, you've got to risk something for it."

The twins looked at each other and the Prince gave **tacit** approval with a nod.

"Hell, I ain't got but twenty bucks left," the Pauper whined.

"And I ain't got but ten," said the Prince. He lifted his chin and stared down his nose at his parsimonious twin. "Fork it over, brother," he commanded in a **domineering** voice, "because I aim to win this one."

The Pauper did as he was told and emptied his wallet. Five quick minutes later it was all over, with Mark Twain once again triumphant and the **haughty** and hapless Prince **writhing** in the ignominious ashes of defeat.

"Morgan," said the **disheartened** Prince, flopping into a chair, "either you're the best player I've ever seen or today I just suck."

"I think you suck eggs, you drunken bum," said the Pauper. "Gimme that." He unceremoniously relieved the Prince of his cue. "I'll take over from here."

While the Prince stumbled off to the men's room, the Pauper **fastidiously** chalked his cue. Then he collected all the balls from the six tasseled pockets and carefully racked them up in a neat triangle. Finally he approached George and stood before him with a **defiant** look in his eye. "If my brother can't beat your man, then I sure as hell will," he said. "I'm challenging you to double or nothing—on everything we've staked so far."

In the Pauper's clumsy and cocksure attempt to intimidate him George **detected** the unmistakable odor of **subterfuge**—or was it just the smell of **audacious** stupidity? Were these two characters merely bumbling **boors** who thought they were **shrewd** customers, or were they a couple of **scheming swindlers** fixing to sting him? George wasn't sure, and not being sure about a bet made him nervous, especially when the bet was with a white person.

He smiled at the Pauper. It was a cautious smile, the kind of **detached** and defensive smile he had long ago learned to wear when confronted by **inscrutable** and **unpredictable** white folks. Then he remembered where he was, and how things had changed, and he let the smile fade and segue into an expression of calm determination. "Mr. Pauper," he said, "I just saw you bet your last dollar, and I heard your brother say he has only ten left. What are you two going to pay me with if you lose?"

The little man glared up at the big one. "Nothin', because I ain't gonna lose."

Twain came to George's side. "I'm afraid we'll need some kind of assurance that you can honor your debt in the event that you don't **prevail**."

"Otherwise no bet," George added **tersely**.

The Pauper snickered. "What, are you guys afraid? You think I got my mojo workin' or something?" He looked at Twain. "Don't you want to find out who's the better man, or are you scared you'll get beat?"

"I'd be delighted to test my **mettle** against yours," said Twain, maintaining his **equanimity**, "but I must insist on fair and **equitable** terms."

Just then the Prince stumbled back from the bathroom. "Look what I found, brother," he said. "Some damned fool left it on the floor next to the toilet." He held up his discovery so all could see. It was a gray, slightly battered laptop computer.

George bent down and whispered in Twain's ear. "Mr.

Clemens, that contraption was on your desk in the billiard room. I touched it and the next thing I knew I was standing in that lavatory with it, and then you walked in."

Leapin' lizards, thought Twain, that's the danged dingus Hank used to get me and my manuscript here—and that he said he needs to send us all *back*. "Mr. Prince," he said, thinking fast, "that, uh...that there 'computer' you just found. I imagine it would have considerable value on the resale market, is that right?"

"That's for damn sure," replied the Prince. "Hell, I bet I could get a coupla hundred rutabagas for it, maybe more."

"Well then," said Twain, turning to address the Pauper, "how about we make that your pledge? If I win I get the computer. If you win you get back all your spondulicks times two. What do you say?"

An asinine smile spread across the Pauper's face. "I say bring it on, baby, 'cause it's eight-ball butt-kickin' time!"

Hank chugged a glass of milk to wash away the sticky **residue** of Rice Crusties in his mouth. "How did you manage to find my laptop?" he asked as he put the glass in the sink and returned to his station beside Merle.

"You see that?" Merle said. He pointed to one of the displays where string after string of **arcane** symbols and characters trailed across the screen from left to right and then from right to left like an **indecipherable** rebus being composed in boustrophedon. "Your hard drive's still connected with TWAIN. That's the interface right there."

Hank leaned forward and **scrutinized** the scrolling code. He was able to **interpret** only bits and pieces of it. The rest was **incomprehensible** to him.

"You probably find that **jargon esoteric**," said Merle.

Hank nodded. "I've never seen anything like it before."

"That's because some of it's coming from *Tempus*,"

Merle said. He crossed his arms and scowled. "And the rest of it is DMI."

"*Tempus* is **exploiting** your DMI?"

"That's putting it mildly, my friend. It's outright **plagiarizing** it. Reisenzeit has ripped me off **verbatim.**" Merle pounded the armrest of his chair with his fist. "And I can't for the life of me **fathom** how that thieving **opportunist** got his filthy hands on my technology. That's what kills me. I thought DMI was more secure than Fort Knox."

"Dang, that sucks," said Hank. "What are you going to do about it?"

"Do about it? I'll tell you what I'm going to do about it." Merle stomped to the far end of his built-in desk and plucked his portable Pictafone from its cradle. "I'm going to confront the weasel-faced little creep, that's what I'm going to do about it." He flipped open the phone and furiously punched several keys. Then he returned to his chair and laid the device on the desk so they both could view the compact display.

After a series of **persistent** beeps a young man's face appeared. "Professor Reisenzeit's office. May I help you?" he said.

"One of his many **sycophants,**" Merle whispered behind his hand.

"Excuse me?" said the young man. His face, Hank thought, registered the kind of mild shock that you might expect from a person seeing Merle's **redoubtable** visage for the first time.

"Is Professor Reisenzeit available?" asked Merle.

"May I ask who's calling?" Hank knew this question was unnecessary, a **vestigial** formality left over from the days before phones automatically **verified** the identity of the caller.

"Tell him it's his **nemesis,** Merle Paige."

"And what is this regarding?"

Merle grinned slyly at Hank, then addressed the Pictafone. "**Retribution.**"

The young man's expression remained humorless and
indifferent. "Thank you, please hold," he said **blandly.**

The image of his face vanished from the display, replaced
by a picture of Mark Twain—older, and in profile. With his
tousled white hair, spectacular eyebrows, **resolute** jaw, and
immaculate white suit, the writer looked **stately, regal,** very
much the **venerable monarch** of American literature. Of
course, as a **zealous** foe of **monarchy,** Twain would have
found such a description of himself **appalling.**

Hank and Merle exchanged a look of surprise. Could
there be some mysterious connection between Gideon
Reisenzeit and Mark Twain?

The word *TWAIN* appeared in glowing gold letters next
to the writer's head. There was a brief musical **embellishment** and then a **resonant** male voice announced, "TWAIN:
Technology Willing to **Aspire,** Inspire, and **Nurture**; a project dedicated to our common future, founded by Dr.
Gideon Reisenzeit."

"What the hell kind of slogan is that?" said Merle.

"A freakin' stupid one," said Hank.

"No kidding," said Merle. "It's gibberish. Can you believe the chutzpah of this guy? First he steals my work and
then he **usurps** my acronym. Gimme a break!"

A moment later the **august** head of Mark Twain disin-
tegrated into pixels that reintegrated themselves into the
face of a mousy, bald, bespectacled man of about fifty.
"Hello, Merlin," the man said in a pinched, nasal voice.
"You're looking magnificently hirsute, as always. And
rather angry, I might add. Is something wrong? Have you
finally come to the realization that DMI is a **colossal** waste
of time?"

Hank had seen Professor Reisenzeit a few times before,
hurrying down the hallways of Irving Lab with a clipboard

in hand and his **fawning** assistants at his side, but he had never seen him up close and personal like this. Merle wasn't being **hyperbolic,** he thought. The professor really did look like a weasel-faced little creep.

Merle leaned forward and roared at the Pictafone. "Reisenzeit, you bootlicking, **obsequious** reprobate! You **remorseless intellectual** cholera! Where the hell do you get off stealing my work and using it for that unspeakable **atrocity** you call *Tempus*? Did you think I wouldn't find out? Did you think I would just sit there **passively** and let you do it? I doubt you've forgotten that I exposed your lying, **plundering, plagiarizing** ass once before, and believe me, professor, I won't hesitate to do it again. It would be a **distinct** pleasure to pull down your **pathetic intellectual** pants and show the world just what a **pompous, despicable fraud** you are."

The professor started to respond but Merle roared on. "And another thing, you **perambulating** sack of rotten potatoes for brains! What fit of **egotistical** insanity **induced** you to take credit for the acronym TWAIN? That was my invention, and you damn well know it. And I can't believe what you came up with: 'Technology Willing to **Aspire,** Inspire, and **Nurture'**? For crying out loud, any idiot could compose something better than that crap. With his hands tied behind his back. Dead drunk.

"Let me tell you something, Professor Ripoffzit. You're no scientist. You're an insult to science. When you're gone you won't even **merit** a footnote in the annals of science. You know what you are? You're just a dirty scientific joke scribbled on a bathroom wall." Merle sat back and heaved a sigh of disgust.

There was a pause. Then Professor Reisenzeit licked his thin lips. "Are you finished with your **diatribe,** Mr. Paige?"

The wizard laughed. "You want some more **invective**? Just say the word."

"No, I think that will suffice," said the professor, "for the Committee on Academic **Ethics.** I've recorded your little outburst, and the committee will be **duly** informed. Would you like a copy of your performance? It was quite impressive."

Merle leaned forward again, an **incensed** bundle of bearded fury. "I'll tell you what, Ripoffzit. How about I send you a copy of my next performance on the toilet and you can submit *that* to the committee? Because that's exactly what you're going to look like when I prove to them that you stole my work!"

Touché! thought Hank. Go Merle!

The professor licked his saurian lips again. "Your **paranoid delusions** are well **documented,** Mr. Paige, and, quite **frankly,** they're becoming rather tiresome. So let me make this perfectly clear, once and for all. Your **allegation** that I have **plagiarized** you is **flagrant** nonsense. It is **spurious** and **erroneous.** I have not stolen any of your work. I have not *tried* to steal any of your work. And I have no *intention* of stealing any of your work. In fact, I have no interest in your work at all. And, I would venture to say, neither does anyone else. Good afternoon."

The professor punched a button and the display on the Pictafone went blank. *Ouch,* thought Hank as Merle spewed several choice **obscenities** at the empty screen.

It was just as George had feared. The two dopes had **deceived** them. The Pauper was a far better player than the Prince, or at least than the Prince had pretended to be, and right from the break he had taken control of the game. Now he was on the verge of winning it.

There were three balls left on the table. One was what pool **connoisseurs** call an "insurance ball"—an easy shot intentionally left unmade for later—which sat a couple of inches in front of a corner pocket. This ball belonged to Mr.

Clemens. The second was the eight ball, which sat a few inches in front of the side pocket along the same rail as the insurance ball. The third was the cue ball, which sat roughly halfway between the eight ball and the insurance ball about a foot off the rail. The next shot belonged to the Pauper, and with it he stood to win the game.

"Eight ball in the side pocket," he announced, confidently twirling chalk on the tip of his cue. "Then this baby's history, and we keep the laptop *and* get the bucks." Behind him the **smirking, complacent** Prince rubbed his hands together and chortled in anticipation.

It was not a particularly difficult shot to make, especially compared with some of the challenging shots he had executed so far. The Pauper lined up his stick behind the cue ball and sighted down the shaft. He wiggled the stick back and forth over the bridge of his fingers, determining precisely where to strike the cue ball so that it would hit the eight ball at just the right angle to send it sideways into the pocket. Then he slowly drew back the cue and let it hover for a second, **poised** to strike.

Behind him, the Prince suddenly sucked in his breath like a man whose head had been forcibly held underwater and then released. As the tip of the Pauper's stick descended on the cue ball, the Prince let fly with a spectacular, rafter-rattling sneeze.

"*Gaah-aahh-ssshhooooo!*" he thundered.

The stick struck the cue ball, which took off with far more speed than the Pauper had intended. It nicked the eight ball, sending it rolling toward the side pocket—defeat for Twain and George. But instead of falling into the pocket the ball struck the far side of the opening, rebounded to the near side of the opening, bounced back to the far side again, and then rolled slowly away from the pocket, stopping at almost the same spot it had occupied before the shot. Meanwhile, the cue ball rolled to the end of the table, bounced off the cushion, and rolled most of the way back, coming to rest about six inches from the eight ball.

"Why, I oughtta murder you, ya dumb galoot!" cried the Pauper, turning on the Prince. "What the hell is wrong with you, brother? You made me jaw the ball."*

The Prince shrugged. "How the hell am I gonna stop a sneeze?" he said with a **sheepish** look. "I'm sorry, but it's **inviolable.**"

Twain struggled to convert another **spontaneous** laugh into a cough. This time the Prince had **pompously** used *inviolable* when he meant *inevitable.*

"For cryin' out loud!" yelled the Pauper. "Your stupid 'vile-bull' just cost us the game."

"Hold on there, brother, take it easy now," said the Prince, attempting to **assuage** the Pauper's anger and **mitigate** his disappointment. "Look at where you left the cue ball. It's deadly. There's no way Morgan's gonna make his shot."

The Pauper turned around and **assessed** the situation on the table. What his brother had said was true, he realized. Morgan had to shoot for his ball down by the corner pocket, and the eight ball was squarely in the way. A kick shot—bouncing the cue ball off a cushion into the object ball—wasn't **practicable** because the required angle would send the cue ball dangerously close to the center pocket on the other side. Nor could his opponent hit the eight ball into his ball, for if he struck the eight ball with the cue ball before first pocketing all of his balls he would violate the rules of the table and **forfeit** the game. His only option was to position the cue ball defensively and hope the Pauper would miss again.

Meanwhile, the **intrepid** Mark Twain, granted a mirac-

---

*In the **jargon** of pool, "jawing" a ball means that the ball you're trying to sink bounces back and forth at the opening of the pocket without falling in.

ulous **reprieve** by the Prince's propitious sneeze, had examined the layout on the table and arrived at a different **assessment** of the situation. What he saw before him was not a **predicament** requiring him to **resort** to a **stratagem** born of desperation but a perfect opportunity for a rare and unusual shot that he had once worked hard to master but that he had not attempted for a long time. It was a stunning trick shot he had first seen performed in Paris in 1867, and it was called a massé.

"This doesn't look good, sir," whispered George. "What are you going to do?"

"Don't worry," Twain whispered back, reaching for the chalk. Then he winked. "I'm going to put a little English on the ball."

Twain slowly chalked his cue and **contemplated** his shot. It was certainly risky, as were all shots involving so much spin, and the cue ball would have to travel farther than he had ever sent it in a massé before. But it was hardly impossible, he thought. Though the odds were against him, they weren't **insurmountable.** He would just have to take extra care to keep both arms steady and hit the cue ball as hard as he could.

"Well, are ya gonna shoot the ball already or are ya just gonna look at it?" the Pauper **taunted.**

"Yeah, Morgan," **sneered** the Prince, "some of us need to get to the bank to make a deposit before it closes."

"Will you two please shut up and let the man shoot?" George scolded. He crossed his arms and looked at the Prince and the Pauper with a **menacing** scowl, and the twins quickly **ceased harassing** Twain.

George had never spoken to a white person like that before; in his own time such **insolence** would be unthinkable. But here, in the liberating air of the twenty-first century, he sensed he could **assert** himself and speak his mind without fear of **reprisal.** This realization gave him such an **ineffable** feeling of joy that he wanted to laugh and holler and grab Mr.

Clemens and dance. Unfortunately, there was the serious matter of winning a bet to attend to first.

"One ball in the corner pocket," Twain announced.

The Prince and the Pauper responded to the call with
inarticulate exclamations of **disdain** and disbelief, which
George quickly silenced with another stern look.

Twain set the chalk down on the short rail, then proceeded to sit up on the long rail beside the cue ball with
one foot dangling and one foot on the floor. He raised his
cue until it was nearly **perpendicular** to the table, with the
tip directly over the cue ball. Then he placed the inside of
his forearm against his hip to brace his hand and arm and
create a steady bridge.

Now George realized what his boss was about to do. He
had seen him attempt this shot once before, several years
ago, in one of his frequent late-night games in the billiard
room. That night Mr. Clemens was entertaining a certain
Mr. Bret Harte, who was a frequent visitor to the house in
those days. Mr. Harte was constantly in debt, George remembered, and he was always borrowing money from Mr.
Clemens and not paying him back; why Mr. Clemens kept
indulging the man in this atrocious and **predatory** habit
was beyond George. At any rate, he had been summoned to
deliver more whiskey and cigars to the billiard room, and he
arrived just in time to watch as Mr. Clemens impossibly
spun the cue ball around an **intervening** ball and into another ball—to the considerable **chagrin** of Mr. Harte.

"Easy now," Twain thought, trying to control his
breathing and steady the hand gripping the thick end of
the cue above his head. "Take it nice and slow and easy."

He moved the tip of the cue a whisker to the right so it
was positioned above the half of the cue ball closer to the
rail. He wanted to strike the ball not in the center but low
along the right side; that would create the most spin. As he
drew up the cue through the stabilizing loop of his thumb

and forefinger he thought of all the time he had spent practicing this shot years ago, and he recalled with **distinct** pleasure the occasion when he had used it to **vanquish** that **arrogant** snob and **despicable** sponge, his erstwhile literary **colleague** and **collaborator** Bret Harte.

Now, he told himself, exhaling slowly, imagine that you're going to drive this stick straight through the table into the floor.

The cue descended swiftly and struck the cue ball hard. Twain grunted as the stick thudded on the surface of the table and then **recoiled.**

With a silent prayer on his lips, George watched in **mute** suspense as the cue ball spun wildly to the left, out and around the eight ball in a wide arc. It was spinning so fast that by the time it reached the middle of the table it looked like a miniature meteor tearing across a deep-green sky. It seemed **improbable,** if not impossible, that this twirling, **wayward** ball would ever reach the **zenith** of its arc in time to find its way to the ball in the corner. But at what seemed the last possible moment, as if it had suddenly glimpsed the remote ball out of the corner of its eye, the cue ball paused at its **apex, veered** hard to the right, and headed for the corner pocket. A moment later it clicked smartly against the one ball, which dropped obediently into the pocket. Then it ricocheted off the cushion and rolled to the center of the table, stopping in an **ideal** position for the writer to pocket the eight ball and win the game.

"Damn, damn, double damn!" yelled the furious and **indignant** Pauper, pounding his thighs with his fists in time with his execration.

The Prince slapped his forehead—way too hard for comfort. "Ouch!" he cried. "What the hell kind of crazy shot was that?"

"It's called a massé," Twain said **nonchalantly** as he

chalked up again. "It means 'hammered' in French, much like what you just did to your forehead." He leaned over the table and sighted down his cue. "Eight ball in the side pocket," he said, and then calmly sank the game-winning ball.

Cheers erupted from the dozen or so **patrons** of the bar who had been hanging around the pool table following the progress of the game. They had just watched a player pluck himself from the jaws of defeat with an astonishing shot, the likes of which had never been seen in the Anchor Bar before. They were overcome with amazement and—especially those who had wagered on Twain—**jubilation.**

In a **spontaneous breach** of **etiquette** that doubtless would have earned him a **reprimand** from his boss in their proper century, George threw his **brawny** arms around Twain and gave him an **ecstatic** hug. "You did it, Mr. Clem—I mean Mr. Morgan!" he cried, swinging the surprised writer from side to side like a child hugging a rag doll. "Lord have mercy, I just knew you would. My oh my, but that was *some* shot!"

"Gee, thanks," croaked Twain, not knowing what to make of this unbridled show of affection, but knowing full well that if the big man didn't let up soon he was **liable** to have some seriously bruised ribs tomorrow morning.

By the time George freed his boss, the **exultant** spectators had crowded around the pool table and surrounded the two victorious men. As they cheered and danced they raised their hands in the air and repeatedly exchanged **vigorous** slaps of the palm.

"What are they doing?" asked George, a puzzled look on his face.

Twain shook his head. "I don't know. Maybe it's a victory **ritual.**" He looked at George and raised his hand. "Well, my friend, when in Rome..."

George laughed and raised his hand, and the two men

engaged in that **universal** modern **convention** of greeting, congratulation, and triumph, which they would sadly never know was called a high-five.

Meanwhile, ignored by the **boisterous** crowd, the Prince and the Pauper had finally managed to stop swearing at each other long enough to realize, with identical idiotic grins, that the **chaotic revelry** of the moment provided the perfect distraction for them to slip away unnoticed by Twain and George.

"C'mon, brother," said the Pauper, "let's cut our losses and get the hell out of here while we still can."

"Hell yeah, but not without this," said the Prince, picking up the laptop from a chair. "I can pawn it tomorrow at Lendoland and we'll be back in business."

They were making their **surreptitious** way toward the exit when George, ever **vigilant** when it came to collecting on his bets, spotted them **absconding**. "Look," he said, grabbing his boss's arm, "those flimflammers are trying to give us the slip."

Twain spun around and saw, to his horror, that the twins were making off with Hank's computer. "Stop, you **perfidious rascals**!" he hollered as the **devious** pair **scurried** out the door. "C'mon," he said to George, "let's get those bastards."

"Okay, so you've shown me how DMI works in **concept**," said Hank, "but have you ever actually succeeded in transporting anything with it?"

Merle shrugged. "Yeah, kind of. I've moved some pencils around my desk and I've taken a book off the shelf and put it back. And once I managed to get my lab rat Norman out of his cage, which was a big deal because it proved that obstructions in meatspace wouldn't **impede** the matter I was transporting through cyberspace. But I had trouble getting him back in the cage because as soon as he was out he wasn't stationary. He started running around and I couldn't get a lock on him."

"So I take it you don't have any experience retrieving runaway laptops."

"Uh, that would be no. But have no fear—the wizard is here!" He gave Hank a hearty slap on the back. "C'mon, pal. Let's get to work."

For the next half hour they patiently and **diligently** tracked Hank's laptop, trying to **ascertain** its precise whereabouts in the present. Hank **laboriously** followed in Merle's footsteps, marveling at the speed and **complexity** of his movements as the wizard marched, waded, and hacked through a **forbidding** jungle of virtual territory like a seasoned hunter on safari.

Hank spotted it a split second before Merle. "That's it, isn't it?" he said, pointing to a **minuscule** icon, a mere green blip, pulsating amid the **chaotic turmoil** of techno-clutter on the screen. "That's my laptop!"

Merle zoomed in. "Yup, that's our baby," he **affirmed.** "Way to go, Hank. Good eye. I'm impressed. You're getting better at this stuff every minute."

Hank felt his chest swell at Merle's **plaudits.** For the wizard, he thought, such praise was practically **effusive.**

"Okay, buddy, this is it," said Merle. "Let's line up this sucker in the crosshairs and lock it in."

That was easier said than done, it turned out. As Merle maneuvered into position the pulsating icon disappeared, then reappeared in a remote corner, then vanished again.

"There it is!" cried Hank as it surfaced on another display.

Merle grunted and gave chase, but the **elusive** green blip kept disappearing and reappearing, moving **erratically** around the screen and jumping from display to display.

This is like a real-life video game, Hank thought, with my precious laptop as the **fugitive prey.** "Merle, what's going on?"

"Somebody must be carrying the damn thing or something."

Or playing catch with it, Hank thought as he anxiously watched the icon bounce from one display to the other and back again.

"Hank, you'd better grab your mouse and hang on!" Merle shouted, his hands a blur on the controls. "It looks like we're in for a **turbulent** ride."

Chapter 19

The Men That **Disrupted** Hadleyburg

Mark Twain and George Griffin burst out of the Anchor Bar in hot pursuit of the twins.

"Wait, hold on a second," said Twain, skidding to a halt. He pulled a cigarillo from the pocket of his baggy sweatshirt and stuck it in his mouth. Then he lit a match and cupped it in his hands.

"Aw, for pity's sake, Mr. Clemens," said George, shaking his head, "you can't stop to smoke now. Those two bunco brothers are going to get away."

"No they won't," Twain said through his teeth as he puffed hard to ignite the tip. "I can run just as fast with a cigar in my mouth as I can without one. And when we catch those thieving buggers, I can brand 'em."

He emerged from an **acrid** cloud of smoke and they hustled down the street.

"Don't look back, brother," said the Pauper as the middle-aged twins **scurried** down Anchor Street toward Village Road, their potbellies jiggling and their chests heaving. "Somebody might be gaining on us."

"That's *exactly* what they're doing," said the Prince, glancing over his shoulder, "Hell, they already got almost every cent we had. Why the hell do they want to chase us for a secondamnhand laptop?"

"Hell if I know, brother," said the Pauper. "Just keep working those legs."

As they turned the corner onto Village Road, the Prince slipped on an ice patch concealed by the snow on the sidewalk. He waved one arm wildly to right himself. "Brother, I think you'd better carry this damn thing," he said as he regained **equilibrium.** He tossed Hank's laptop to the Pauper, who caught it **reluctantly.**

"Hell, what'd you do that for?" said the Pauper.

"Because I almost fell and broke my butt, ya moron. Didn't ya see me slip?"

"Yeah, I saw. But you didn't fall—so here." The Pauper tossed the laptop back.

"It's safer with you, brother, believe me." The Prince tossed it to the Pauper.

"The hell it is," said the Pauper, lateraling it back again.

This time the Prince almost dropped it. "You stupid bozo! You see what I mean? You take it." He threw the laptop at the Pauper.

The Pauper caught it and threw it back. "Why the hell should I carry it?"

"Because you can run faster," said the Prince, unloading it on his brother.

"But I didn't steal it," said the Pauper. "I didn't even find it." He tossed it to the Prince, who almost dropped it again.

"Hotdammit, brother, you're gonna make me break the damn thing," said the Prince. "Just take it, will ya?" He shoved it into the Pauper's chest.

The Pauper took it and thrust it back. "I don't want it!" he yelled.

"Yes you do!" the Prince yelled back, warding off the thrust with his forearm.

"No I don't," yelled the Pauper, banging the laptop against his brother's elbow. "(*bang*) I don't (*bang*) know why (*bang*) the hell (*bang*) you took it (*bang*) anyway!"

"Cut it out, for cryin' out loud!" the Prince hollered. He wrenched the laptop from the Pauper's grasp and whacked him with it on the side of the head.

"Hey, that hurts!" cried the Pauper, snatching it back and thumping the Prince on the shoulder.

By this time the twins had reached Charter Road. They both stopped running—or enthusiastic jogging would be a more accurate way of characterizing it—and began wrestling for possession of Hank's computer.

"Hell, brother, gimme that thing," said the Prince, pulling it toward him. "I'm gonna whup you good."

"The hell you will, you maniac," said the Pauper, pulling it back.

And back and forth they went, grunting and swearing and looking like a couple of laughably **inept** lumberjacks trying to saw the air.

Angela McGuinn was walking down Charter Road on her way back from her job at the **bursar**'s office when she saw the strangest thing—two middle-aged men standing on the corner, violently **contending** for possession of a laptop computer. As she got closer she **discerned** that these **vying** men were identical twins, and they were shouting at each other as they yanked the laptop back and forth.

"Let go, you moron!"

"No, *you* let go, you freak!"

Like the other Hadleyburg students and professors hurrying by in the **transient** winter twilight, Angela cautiously **averted** her eyes and pretended not to notice this **bizarre altercation**. The police would **intervene** if necessary, she figured. But as she reached the corner and began to cross the street she was startled by a familiar voice.

"**Cease** and **desist,** you **despicable scoundrels!**" it fulminated.

Hey, that's Mr. Twain, she thought as she turned around and looked up Village Road. And sure enough there he was, with a cigar clenched in his teeth and an **indignant** fist in the air, rushing toward the **quarreling** twins. He was accompanied by a handsome and **imposing** black man wearing no coat over his white shirt, vest, and silver bow tie.

At the sound of Twain's voice, both twins froze. Then one twin pulled on the laptop so hard that he tore it from the other's grasp. The force of this violent seizure sent the first twin tumbling backward onto his rear end. It also sent the laptop sailing six feet into the air—and straight toward Angela.

Up it soared like a flat football. Angela raised one arm like a punt returner calling for a fair catch. "I've got it!" she cried, and a moment later the laptop **plummeted** safely into her hands. But it didn't remain there for long.

"Hey you, gimme that!" the other twin growled, wrenching it away. Before she knew what was happening, he had taken off down Charter Road followed by the twin who had fallen to the ground.

"Why, if it isn't my good friend Angela," said Twain as he and George reached the corner. "Impressive catch, my dear. A pity you couldn't hang on."

Angela caught a whiff of Twain's **pungent** cigar and coughed. "Mr. T, what's going on?" She looked at George. "And who is this guy?"

"This is George, my uh...my friend," Twain replied, **prudently** sensing that it would sound **archaic** and **incongruous** for him to call George his butler. "He came from my house to...to visit, so to speak, and brought along Hank's computer." He pointed down the street at the

fleeing twins. "Now those two con men have **purloined** it, and it's **imperative** that we 'get a move on,' as they say."

In room 111 of Stoddard Hall, the **dignified** brick building on Charter Road that housed Hadleyburg's English department, the anxiety was almost as **palpable** as the **frenetic** clicking of keys on NoteMasters was **audible.**

A hundred and fifty-odd students were scattered around the **capacious** lecture hall, hunched over the compact terminals built into the swiveling armrests of their seats. On a normal day during the semester these students would have been listening to their professor lecture while **diligently** or **somnolently** typing in notes, which they would afterward store in their online university account. But today these **innocuous** and helpful NoteMasters had metamorphosed into evil taskmasters, for they were now the electronic **purveyors** of a cruel and unusual final exam on nineteenth-century American literature.

Orlando Ortiz scratched his head, rubbed his brow, then typed in a few more words. He was struggling to conclude his essay on Melville's *Moby-Dick,* which would **constitute** 50 percent of his grade on the test. He glanced at the **merciless, inexorably** advancing clock on the wall. Only ten minutes left!

He looked at the sentence he had just written:

> Thus, Melville **conceived** his magnum opus both as thinly veiled autobiography in which he could couch his social and philosophical **reflections,** and as an **epic** tale of the **primordial** struggle between humankind and nature, played out upon the stage of the "howling **infinite**"—the **amoral, irrational,** and **unpredictable** sea.

Not bad, he thought, but could he end it there? He nibbled his lip and stared at the screen. He squeezed his earlobe and stared at the ceiling. He flexed the muscles in his jaw and stared at the screen again. And then something really weird happened.

One of the double doors to the hall burst open and two men rushed in, panting and swearing. They paused and looked around with vacant and **bewildered** expressions, as if they had never seen a lecture hall full of desperate students before. A hundred and fifty-odd students looked desperately back.

The men were dressed differently but their features were identical, Orlando noticed. One clutched a laptop under his arm.

"Excuse me, but what are you doing?" said the graduate student proctor, who had had nothing to do until now and was hoping to keep it that way for another ten minutes. "We're administering an exam in here."

"The hell with that," said the twin with the laptop. "We're tryin' to get the hell *outta* here." They **scampered** around the proctor and across the hall, and made their noisy way out the double doors on the other side.

Then the door through which the twins had entered burst open again and three more people ran **headlong** into the room—a big man in a vest and bow tie, a young woman with bouncing corkscrew hair, and a man with a mustache and a fuming cigar in his mouth, wearing a maroon sweatshirt emblazoned with the **salutation** SAPPNIN BRO?

Hot dang! It's Angela and Mr. Twain, thought Orlando. But who's that other guy?

"Hey, what do you think you're doing?" said the proctor, wrinkling her nose at the sour smell of cigar smoke. "You can't smoke in here."

"Thank you for informing me, I'll make a note of that," Twain called out as the threesome raced across the room toward the doors on the opposite side.

"You're **disrupting** this exam and violating state law,"

said the proctor, reaching for the white phone on the wall. "I'm calling campus security right now."

And I'm going to find out what the heck is going on, thought Orlando. He punched the "Submit" key on his NoteMaster. Then he grabbed his coat, clambered down from his perch at the top of the hall, and hurried to catch up with the chase.

Aimee Lee sat at the **sonorous** grand piano in the Phyllis Dean Auditorium of Henley Hall, her slender, **agile** fingers flying over the keys. Three stone-faced, **dispassionate** professors sat in the front row, listening **intently** and occasionally taking notes.

She was playing the concluding piece in her winter recital program, Chopin's Ballade no. 1 in G Minor, an **ardent** composition that **ebbs** and flows dramatically between **humble entreaty** and **adamant** rejection, between tender **supplication** and **withering scorn**, **evoking** the pain, longing, and despair of **unrequited** love. She had reached the stormy, keyboard-sweeping **finale** and, like a long-distance runner entering the last lap of a race, she was stepping up the intensity and giving it everything she had.

Until she was rudely interrupted.

As a **rigorously** trained and **disciplined** musician, Aimee knew how to focus on her performance to the exclusion of all else—to "enter the envelope," as her musician parents liked to say. All the **commonplace**, run-of-the-mill interruptions, like **persistent** coughing and sneezing, beeping watches, and even the obnoxious tootling of a cellphone, were old hat to her by now. They didn't **disconcert** her in the least. This particular interruption, however, was not of the **commonplace** variety. It wasn't even of the **atypical** variety, like the time when an old man in the third row nodded off and began to snore with remarkable **virtuosity**. This was a red-alert, all-hands-on-deck **disruption** that threatened to transform her recital from a tour de force into a **debacle.**

It began with the auditorium doors clattering open and smacking against the wall, as if someone had burst through them at full tilt. This was followed by footsteps clomping down the aisle and **sibilant** shushing from the three professors. Then the footsteps halted and a pair of loud, **contentious** voices with a **penchant** for using the word *hell* competed with Aimee's raging scales and crashing minor chords. There was more **vehement** shushing and **chastisement** from the professors, and then the doors clattered open and smacked the wall again, and twice as many footsteps clomped down the aisle accompanied by shouts of **outrage** and **indignation.**

All right, that's it, enough is enough, Aimee thought as she skipped the coda and went straight to the closing chords. She lifted her foot off the pedal and looked up.

Her hand went to her mouth. Then she jumped up from the piano bench and did a jeté from the dais to the floor. "Hey, you guys, I'm coming!" she cried, and ran past the **flabbergasted** professors to join the **fracas.**

Isabel Lyon sat in a stiff-backed captain's chair in the cluttered office of her **thesis** adviser, Professor Justin Shelley, the head of the American Studies department and a **distinguished** Twain scholar. Her backpack, with its **invaluable** literary cargo, lay on the floor between her feet.

Isabel's emotions were in **turmoil.** She was both **apprehensive** and **euphoric,** afraid that she might get into trouble for what she had done but riding a wave of **elation** that she had been the one to recover the manuscript of *Huckleberry Finn.* Would the professor find her story **plausible** and her **motives** beyond **reproach**? Would he believe the **improbable** claim that Mark Twain was alive and well and visiting Hadleyburg, and was last seen entering a neighborhood bar on Anchor Street?

She gripped the arms of the wooden chair and tried to focus on the **benevolent countenance** of Professor Shelley, who was sitting calmly behind his desk. But his face seemed **indistinct** and **surreal,** like something out of a dream. The only thing she was fully **cognizant** of was her rapid, shallow breathing and the wild thumping of her heart.

The professor **scrutinized** her, **pensively** rubbing his chin with his thumb and forefinger like someone engaged in deep **contemplation.** "Why did you want to see me so urgently, Ms. Lyon? Is something the matter?" His tone was sympathetic and **solicitous.** "I must say, you seem quite agitated, even more so than usual."

Isabel swallowed and looked at the professor blankly for a moment. Then a **turbulent maelstrom** of words rose to her lips and poured forth in a **tumultuous** stream. "Omigod, Professor, wait'll you hear what just happened to me, like you are *so* not going to believe it because it's like *so* incredible, I mean it's like *so* unbelievable, like, so *totally* unreal—no wait, that's not what I mean—I don't mean it's not real because it really did happen, I'm not kidding, it's just like *so* hard to believe—no wait, what I'm trying to say is that it's not unbelievable because you can't believe it, you know?—it's just like amazing, like unbelievable in an incredible way, you know?—like it freaks you out and you can't believe it but you really do believe it because it's so amazingly cool it just has to be true? Like you just want to pinch yourself because what happened couldn't possibly have happened but you're really really absolutely convinced that it did—you know what I mean?"

The professor frowned. "No, I'm afraid I don't know what you mean, Ms. Lyon. Did you discover something **unforeseen** in your research? Did you have some sort of **revelation**?"

"Yes, yes I did, Professor, that's exactly it, that's exactly what happened, and I'm so glad you understand, I really really am. It was a totally unexpected **encounter,** I mean like 100 percent **fortuitous,** but it was also like complete and utter **serendipity,** and I'm like *so* freaked out because I know it's going to lead to some really special and **profound insights** into the mind of Mark Twain. Can I tell you about it, Professor?"

Professor Shelley nodded. "I'm listening. Please **elucidate.**"

And **elucidate** she did, at half the speed of light and with hardly a pause for breath. "Well I was having lunch today in the Rotunda and reading the *Herald-Tribune* and talking on the phone and I saw the article on how the manuscript of *Huckleberry Finn* disappeared from the library in Buffalo last night, and I was like so upset because I thought who on earth could do such an awful thing, and then I was like even more upset because I remembered I was planning to go up there during winter vacation and hang out in the library studying some sections of the manuscript that are **relevant** to my **thesis,** and then I happened to look over at one of the nearby tables and like my eyes almost popped out of my head because lo and behold there he was, just sitting there like he'd been at Hadleyburg all his life, and he was like disguised in some **contemporary** clothing that made him look kind of like a **buffoon,** but that didn't fool me at all no not in the slightest because it was just **uncanny** what a perfect match he was what a dead ringer for the man himself right down to the broad mustache and the hooked nose and those intense intelligent eyes and that amazing wavy reddish brown hair—"

"Ms. Lyon?" **interjected** Professor Shelley. "You're speaking **incoherently,** even more so than usual."

"—and so I asked him was he like some kind of impersonator or **obscure** relative or something or was he the real

deal and he ignored me but that was okay because I knew
the truth anyway, and so I asked him if he would give me
his autograph and he said my 'dadblamed blimblammin'
would make a preacher swear,' and I was like yeah that's totally tight—"

"Ms. Lyon, you're becoming **inarticulate** and **irrational**."

"—and then I waited for him while he hid in the bathroom until he came raging out again with those pink spots
on his face, and I followed him out of the Rotunda and saw
that he like totally walked the same way and I was like yeah
again, and then he said 'I daresay' which was like so **blatantly archaic,** and then I followed him to this bar on Anchor Street while he like blew smoke rings in my face
which was like so cool yeah—"

"Ms. Lyon, are you all right?"

"—and he asked me how old I was yeah and I told him
yeah and then I asked him was he going to ditch me and
he said yeah he was and I thought well you might as well
get ditched by him than by another and then somebody
burst out of the bar and knocked him down into the snow
and I just wanted to put my arms around him yeah and
draw him to my breast so he could smell my perfume yeah
and feel my heart going like mad and tell him yeah would
I like yeah say yeah I will yeah—"

"Ms. Lyon, snap out of it!" said Professor Shelley in his
most **authoritative** lecturing voice. "You're hysterical!
Please get ahold of yourself."

Isabel paused and gasped. "Omigod, I'm…I'm so
sorry." She paused and gasped again. "I don't know what
came over me. I guess I kind of lost it for a minute."

"Yes," said the professor as Isabel struggled to stop **hy-
perventilating,** "you apparently got caught in your own
stream of consciousness and **lapsed** into a Joycean interior
monologue. Are you all right now?"

"Yes, I'm…I'm okay…I think."

"Are you sure you haven't been working too hard on your **thesis**? Have you had to stay up late studying for your final exams? Perhaps you're sleep-**deprived**."

"No, I'm okay, really I am."

"Are you sure?"

"Yeah, I'm sure. But I'm a little freaked out because... well, I like found something, something significant, and I don't know what to... what I should..."

"What exactly are you trying to tell me?"

"I'm... I'm trying to tell you I found something I think you should see."

"What is it?"

"The missing manuscript of *Huckleberry Finn*."

"Ms. Lyon, I am not in any mood for **levity**."

"I know, I know, and I'm sorry but I'm not kidding and I need your help. I really did find the manuscript and I don't know what to do about it and I thought you would."

Professor Shelley studied her for a long moment, attempting to **discern** whether all of this was poppycock or truth. "Where is the manuscript?" he said finally.

"It's right here, Professor," said Isabel. "I've got it right here safe and **sound,** don't worry, let me get it for you." She leaned over and unzipped her backpack.

Then she screamed.

Professor Shelley jumped up from his chair, his hands over his ears. "Ms. Lyon, what's wrong?"

"Omigod," Isabel moaned. "I swear it was in my backpack when I came in, and now it's... it's disappeared."

"Hey, watch where you're going, you stupid jerks!"

The Prince and the Pauper didn't stop to apologize to the **irate** group of Hadleyburg students they had just crashed through like a pair of bowling balls scattering a rack of pins. They were too busy sucking air and running for dear life. Their two **initial** pursuers had somehow been

augmented into a small posse, and it was clear this posse wanted blood.

"Why the hell don't we just dump the damn thing?" wheezed the Prince as they dashed past the broad front steps of the Hadleyburg University library. "Maybe then they'll stop chasing us."

"Y'know, brother," the Pauper wheezed back, "for once I think you may be right." He glanced over his shoulder and saw the **menacing** posse closing in fast. "Quick, down here," he said, grabbing the Prince's sleeve with his free hand.

They **veered** left into a narrow cobblestone street that ran alongside the library and skidded and scrambled over the icy stones.

Suddenly the Prince slipped and fell flat on his butt. "Aw hell, that's it," he gasped. "I'm all in."

"The hell you are," said the Pauper, pulling his brother up. "Let's go."

"But I'm pooped," the Prince gasped. "I can't...run... another foot."

The Pauper looked behind them. The posse hadn't yet turned the corner. He quickly **assessed** their options and concluded they had three: run, hide, or get pounded. He didn't care much for the last one, and the first looked out of the question, what with the Prince now beginning to retch from exhaustion.

Frantically, he searched the street for a place to hide. A few yards away there was an opening in the wall that appeared to be a sheltered side entrance to the building. There were several blue recycling bins on one side of the alcove and an **imposing** metal Chuckster on the other.

"You're not gonna like this, brother," the Pauper muttered, "but it's the only chance we've got." He dragged the Prince over to the Chuckster and the two of them, with the **requisite** shoving and swearing, managed to climb in and close the lid just as the **relentless** posse, led by Orlando and George, careered around the corner.

The luckless twins crouched in darkness on top of a **putrid** layer of garbage and listened as the shouts and footsteps approached and paused beside the Chuckster.

"Where in tarnation did those dastardly varmints go?" a male voice drawled.

"I'll check this alcove," said another male voice. "Nobody there," it announced a moment later.

"They must have gotten around the corner faster than we thought," said a female voice. "C'mon guys, let's go."

The posse took off again down the street. When the sound of footsteps had **subsided,** the Pauper raised the lid of the Chuckster a couple of inches and peeked out. The street was empty.

"C'mon brother," he whispered as he pushed the lid open all the way. "Now's our chance to beat it before they figure out we've doubled back."

They struggled to **extricate** themselves from the **malodorous confines** of the Chuckster. The Pauper climbed out first, took Hank's laptop from the Prince and set it on the ground, then helped the Prince get out.

"Where the hell?" said the Pauper as he bent over to retrieve the laptop.

"Where the hell what?" said the Prince.

"Where the hell's the damn laptop?" the Pauper **clarified, futilely** searching all around and inside the Chuckster.

"Hell if I know," said the Prince. "Where'd you put it?"

"Right there, where that is." The Pauper pointed to a spot beside the Chuckster where there was a large bundle of paper neatly tied with string.

"And what the hell is that?" said the Prince, giving the bundle a kick.

"The hell if I know," said the Pauper, scratching his head. "Aw, what the hell."

"Yeah, what the hell," agreed the Prince, giving his twin a **fraternal** pat on the back. "C'mon, brother, let's just get the hell outta here."

They hurried back down the darkening street the way they had come, leaving the priceless bundle of paper behind them in the snow.

Hank clutched his mouse and followed the **random** and **frenetic** movements of the green blip that represented his laptop as it moved **erratically** around Merle's four displays. Beside him, Merle silently worked his software magic at breakneck speed, **continually** making **minute** adjustments and **refinements** to make sure he'd be ready to lock in the moment Hank could position his cursor and pounce.

It was like trying to swat a pesky fly inside a giant kaleidoscope, Hank thought. He would trail the **fickle** blip one way and then back, this way and then that, until he felt his eyes were rolling in his head and his vision began to blur. Then all of a sudden the **devious, audacious** little bugger would buzz right past him in plain sight, as if daring him to strike. But the second he moved his mouse it would zip around a corner and blend into the **complex** and **continuously** shifting colors and patterns in the background. And there was no clue where it might turn up next.

They had been chasing it now for over fifteen **fruitless** minutes, and Hank was starting to feel dizzy and tired. Where was his usual **stamina**? he wondered. On any given day he could easily **endure** a three-hour session of ultra-high-speed video games, and he had once played Bodacious Blasticon II for a five-hour stretch. But this blip-hunt wasn't an innocent **pastime**; it was real life with real stakes, and it was *hard*. It definitely wasn't **stimulating** like a video game. It was **enervating.**

"Hang in there, pal, I know you can do it," Merle said, as if sensing Hank's **waning** level of intensity. "I have a feeling we're getting close."

Hank blinked hard and commanded himself to focus as the pulsating blip darted into view again. It zigged and zagged and then lazily wandered to the middle of the display, where it hovered for a **precarious** instant, as if uncertain where to go next.

Hank quickly tightened his grip on the mouse. It was now or never.

"Go for it!" Merle called out as Hank made his move. Like a hawk or an eagle swooping out of the sky to snatch an unsuspecting rodent on the ground, Hank made a swift and silent **descent** and **deftly** wrapped his digital talons around his **prey**.

The laptop was finally in their grasp.

"Way to go!" Merle cried, giving Hank a high-five. Then he typed in a string of commands and checked the displays. "Okay, buddy, we're locked in. This is it. Forget the books and pencils and the **recalcitrant** lab rat. Now we're going to find out whether DMI can really bring home the bacon."

Merle typed and clicked madly like a man composing his last will and testament with a gun at his head. Then he stopped **abruptly** and looked at Hank. "Okay, the DMI Master Macro is enabled and ready to go. Cross your fingers," he advised, and Hank did.

Merle pressed a key and all four screens crackled and went blank. After a few seconds they became **illuminated** again and each displayed a **vivid** moving image of Hank's laptop passing through a different stage of dematerialization. Or was it rematerialization? There was no way to be sure.

Witnessing this attempted miracle of science and waiting to observe its outcome, Hank was emotionally **ambivalent**—both **exhilarated** and horrified. What if this risky, experimental DMI transport failed? What if his laptop was damaged? What if it was irretrievably and **irrevocably** lost?

But just as that **unsettling** thought gripped him, the displays went blank again and Hank felt a tingling sensation in his thighs. He looked down and saw a gray, **amorphous** cloud in his lap. He watched in breathless wonder as it gradually densified and became his lost computer.

"Hot damn!" he yelped.

An exultant smile appeared under Merle's thick tangle of whiskers. "How's that for a perfect landing?"

"It was beautiful," said Hank, hugging the **itinerant** machine like a missing child that had been miraculously found.

Merle touched Hank's laptop to assure himself it was real. Then he took a deep breath and exhaled slowly. "Well, now that we've done that, all we have to do is find the *Tempus* wormhole and get the rest of this time warp straightened out."

As Blanche Paige pushed open the staff door of the university library and crossed the alcove leading into the cobblestone-covered lane, she noticed something **anomalous**—a large stack of paper beside the Chuckster. Now why would someone just leave all that paper on the ground, she thought, when the recycling bins were right on the other side of the entrance?

Ms. Paige, the **meticulous** university librarian, was also a **conscientious** recycler. She knew that a pile of paper left on the ground next to a Chuckster would either be heedlessly thrown out by some irresponsible person or eventually get too wet to recycle and then have to be thrown out. She stooped over and looked at the stack. It was bound neatly with string, and it still looked dry. It probably hadn't been there long.

She bent down and lifted the bundle in her white-gloved hands. As she carried it to the recycling bin, she noticed that it did not consist of regular printer paper. The pages were smaller and slightly rumpled. And the words on the topmost page were not printed but handwritten in a bold cursive that was **vaguely** familiar. She lifted the lid of the recycling bin and was about to drop the bundle inside when the realization struck her.

"Oh dear me, it's *Huckleberry Finn!*" she cried in her **lucid, melodious** voice, then clapped her hand over her mouth as if she had said something **unbecoming** or **incriminating.**

What luck, what astonishing **serendipity,** she thought, that she of all people should be the one to recover the missing manuscript of this **celebrated** book. Had some **anonymous** good Samaritan left it by the staff door so that a librarian would find it?

She closed the lid of the recycling bin and clutched the manuscript to her chest. She felt herself beginning to tremble with excitement. What should she do now? she wondered. Should she take it back in the library and lock it up in her office for the night? Or should she keep it with her until she figured out what to do next?

Leaving it in the library wasn't sufficiently secure, she thought. Too many people—campus security officers, various library **colleagues,** and even her son Merle—had master passcards to the building. What a **catastrophe** it would be should the manuscript disappear yet again because of her **indiscretion.** No, she decided, the **prudent** thing to do was not to let this remarkable **windfall** out of her sight.

She squeezed the treasured bundle in her arms, cast a **circumspect** glance over her shoulder, and took off at a brisk pace down the darkling lane.

The last dim **remnants** of daylight were fading from the sky when a **rueful** Isabel Lyon trudged by the Hadleyburg Library with her heart in her boots.

She looked across the frozen university common and

saw an expectant, **exuberant** crowd gathering in the courtyard of the Rotunda, where President Addams would soon
ring the bell to signal that the Winter Bacchanal had officially **commenced.** In past years Isabel had always looked
forward to participating in the near-riotous **abandon** of
this **ritual** celebration, but tonight she was not in any
mood to be **boisterous.** Somehow—inexplicably, and in
defiance of all reason—the manuscript of *Huckleberry Finn*
had vanished from her backpack, and she had made a complete, babbling fool of herself in front of Professor Shelley.
The last thing in the world she wanted to do right now was
party.

   Mortified and **despondent,** she sat down on one of the
cold stone library steps and put her chin in her hands.
What could possibly have happened to that manuscript,
and where was it now? she wondered. She began to doubt
her own **perception** of reality, even her own sanity. Was it
all just a stress-**induced** hallucination, as Professor Shelley
had **tactfully implied** when he recommended that she avail
herself of the free counseling at the university's mental
health clinic? Was the man she met in the Rotunda this afternoon—the man she was so firmly convinced was the
real Mark Twain transported through time—only a **phantasm,** a figment of her hyperactive imagination?

   The crowd in front of the Rotunda cheered **vociferously.** She looked up and saw four students—the Bacchanal
Bellsters—rolling a **massive** bell suspended from a sturdy
wooden frame into the center of the courtyard. It wouldn't
be long now before the festivities began. As President Addams appeared in front of the bell and started to address
the crowd, Isabel stood up. She couldn't bear to watch any
longer. The entire campus was about to disport itself and
wallow in wild fun while she was left to **fret** and **wallow** in
misery and confusion.

   She walked past the library steps to the end of the block

and turned left into a narrow cobblestone street. The street was empty and, except for a lone light fixture above a side entrance to the library, almost completely dark. The enveloping darkness perfectly suited Isabel's **melancholy** mood. She wanted to dissolve into it and disappear.

As she drifted in the deep shadow of the library's towering brick wall, she heard the sound of a heavy door opening and closing, and a moment later she saw a tall gray-haired woman in a long red coat and pillbox hat emerge from the alcove into the light. The woman paused next to the Chuckster beside the entrance and stooped to look at something on the ground. Then she bent down and lifted it up.

Isabel couldn't believe her eyes when she saw what it was: a large, neatly tied stack of paper strikingly similar to the one that had so unaccountably disappeared from her backpack. She stopped walking and pressed herself against the wall. Then she watched, **shrouded** in darkness and holding her breath, as the woman carried the bundle to a recycling bin on the other side of the entrance. The woman lifted the lid and was about to drop it in when Isabel heard her cry out softly in a clear, musical voice.

"Oh dear me, it's *Huckleberry Finn!*" the woman blurted. Then, as if she had said something **immodest,** she covered her mouth with her hand.

Isabel's heart leapt into her throat. Could it really be the manuscript, or was she hallucinating this scene too?

The woman stepped back from the recycling bin, cast a **furtive** glance over her shoulder, and took off down the street, the heels of her shiny black boots rapping against the cobblestones.

Isabel sucked in her breath and bit her lip. If I'm totally imagining this, then I am *definitely* the biggest nutcase at Hadleyburg, she thought. But if I'm not imagining it—and it's pretty hard to imagine that I am—then I'd better do something fast. If that lady in the red coat really does have Mark Twain's manuscript, I'd better not let her out of my sight until I find out who she is and what she intends to do with it.

As Isabel slipped quietly along the wall she heard more **obstreperous** cheering coming from the Rotunda court-yard, then the **ominous** and **deliberate** tolling of the bac-chanal bell. Night had officially descended and the madness had begun.

Chapter 20

Bacchanal to the Future

It was Hadleyburg's hibernal version of Mardi Gras, a madcap carnival amid the snow and ice. The Winter Bacchanal had barely begun, but by all appearances it was already shaping up to be one of the biggest and most outrageous blowouts ever.

Upon the tolling of the bell, the rollicking crowd in the Rotunda courtyard did not **disperse** in an orderly fashion, heading off in different directions to the various banquets and parties around campus. Instead it continued to cheer and dance and ring the bell for several minutes, working itself up to a **frenzied** pitch until it could no longer contain its **ebullience** and it erupted into an **impromptu** parade.

Led by the Spiffenspoofs, an a cappella singing group famous for its stylish **renditions** of bawdy limericks and dirty jokes, the **spontaneous** and colorful procession **meandered** across the university common in a long, **sinuous, serpentine** line. A **disinterested** observer could not have failed to be impressed by the simian verisimilitude of the grunting and snorting Gadfly Gorillas, uncouth creatures **notorious** for their **disruptive** antics, such as scratching people in unusual places and pelting professors with banana peels. Another zoological standout was the **farcically** fishy Gumbo Quintet, which featured a tuna on trumpet, a squid on alto sax, a codfish on clarinet, a guppy on guitar, and a bongo-slapping octopus.

There were gods and goddesses, Roman gladiators, juggling court jesters, prancing harlequins, two friendly ogres, a cyclops, a bevy of veiled and bare-waisted odalisques, and all manner of knights in shining armor and princesses in distress. There was a small tribe of prehistoric cave dwellers dancing with various creatures from outer space. There were two women dressed up as Sherlock Holmes and Dr. Watson and two men dressed up as Desi Arnaz and Lucille Ball. There was even a refrigerator labeled EAT ME strolling contentedly beside an inflatable toilet labeled FEED ME.

Michelangelo was there, with his paintbrush and mallet and chiseled looks; Cleopatra was there, barging down the Nile in all her dark, **aloof** beauty; Diogenes, the ancient Greek **cynical** philosopher, was there with his lantern, searching for an honest man; Marilyn Monroe was there, with an oversized bottle of antidepressants and a **sycophantic** retinue; and Wild Will Shakespeare was there in his doublet and ruff, wearing a large button that said, KISS ME, M'LADY, AND I'LL GO FROM **BARD** TO VERSE.

Mark Twain and Orlando stood on the library steps, watching the rambunctious parade turn onto Charter Road. "When we remember that we are all mad," Twain observed, "the mysteries disappear and life stands explained."

"I'll second that," drawled a nearby voice in a passable imitation of the writer. "My **sentiments** exactly. In fact, those are my *words* exactly."

They turned in the direction of the voice and saw a slender man in a white suit and a comically ill-fitting Mark Twain mask and wig. He was **flourishing** an unlit cigar.

Twain laughed at the sight of this wiggly, rubberized version of himself. "Why, if it ain't my old friend Mark Twain," he said, pumping the **impostor's** hand. "It's a pleasure to see you. They told me you were dead."

"The reports of my death are greatly exaggerated," drawled the imitation Twain.

"Are you sure about that?" the real Twain drawled back. He pointed to the rubber mask. "You're not looking so well."

"I'm not? What do you mean?"

"You're rather **wan.** Have you been eating properly?"

"Of course not," said the **spurious** Twain, "I have been **persistently** strict in sticking to the things which didn't agree with me until one or the other of us got the best of it."

"A **sound regimen,** I daresay," said the real Twain. "Are you taking regular exercise?"

"Of course not," said the **counterfeit** Twain. "I have never taken any exercise, except sleeping and resting, and I never intend to take any. Exercise is **loathsome.** And it cannot be any benefit when you are tired; and I am always tired."

"Well," said the real Twain, pointing to his doppelgänger's unlit cigar, "perhaps you're not smoking as much as you ought to. Would you like a light?"

This seemed to throw the faux Twain off. "Uh, actually I'm allergic to smoke."

"I see, my friend," said the real Twain, stroking his chin. "Well, now that we've found what's ailing you, I suppose you won't be needing this." He **deftly** plucked the stogie from his impersonator's fingers and popped it between his teeth.

"Hey, mister, that's my cigar," the fake Twain protested **feebly.**

"Not anymore," said the genuine article, striking a match and lighting up.

Aimee, Angela, and George walked down Charter Road toward the library alongside the **clamorous** parade. Fifteen minutes earlier they had split up with Orlando and Twain in a two-pronged search for the twins, with all agreeing to

reconvene in front of the library if their efforts failed, which they had.

"Mr. Griffin, aren't you freezing?" said Aimee. "All you have on is that skimpy vest."

George laughed and shook his head. "Believe it or not, Miss Aimee, I've never felt so warm in my entire life. You've got some crazy things going on in this here future, and just watching it all is so exciting I don't have any time to feel cold."

As if to **corroborate** his **assertion,** a giant frankfurter covered with mustard ran by chasing a princess in distress.

"Don't be silly," said Angela. "As soon as we find Orlando and Mr. Twain we'll take you back to our suite and get you something warm to wear."

"Yo, Aimee, Angela! How ya doin'?" cried a voice from behind them. They stopped and turned around. It was the giant frankfurter, and the face leering out at them from it belonged to none other than Hadleyburg's number-one hound dog, Marty Rocheblatt. "Hey, it's me, your man Marty—rhymes with *party,* remember?"

"Oh, no," Aimee groaned. "Not him again. That's twice in twenty-four hours."

Marty approached them and grinned his hideous, tooth-deformed grin. "How would you two luscious hot-cakes like a bite of this dog? You wanna lick my mustard? It's real Dijon, you know."

"Marty," said Angela, "I would rather lick a toilet seat in a bus station than let one iota of my skin touch you or your ridiculous costume."

George didn't know what a bus station was, nor was he familiar with the words *frankfurter* and *hot dog,* which wouldn't come into the language until the 1890s. But he certainly knew enough about people and the way they ought to behave to be shocked by Marty's crudely **vivid proposition** and Angela's **outspoken retort.** "Ladies," he said to Aimee and Angela, "is this...this sausage bothering you?"

"You mean this loser?" said Aimee, making the sign of the L with her thumb and forefinger and jerking her thumb to indicate Marty.

"Yes," said George. "Would you like me to **dispatch** him for you?"

"Hey, will you get a load of this guy?" said Marty. "'Would you like me to **dispatch** him for you?'" he **mimicked.** "What is he, your butler?"

"Is there something wrong with being a butler?" said George, drawing himself up and glaring at the mustard-drenched dog. "It's an honorable position. I wouldn't **mock** it if you know what's good for you."

Marty poked his plump chest with his finger. "Are you threatening me?" he snarled. "You want a piece of me, Mr. Butler, come and get it."

Angela quickly stepped between the two men. "That's enough," she commanded. "Step back, both of you, and put your hands down." George **complied** but Marty Dog stood his ground. "Marty," Angela said, "step back and put your hands down now or Aimee and I will have the campus police here faster than you can say *hold the kraut*—but not before Mr. Griffin makes ketchup outta yo' face."

With a **sullen** look, Marty stepped back. Angela gave him her coldest, most **condescending** stare, her prosecutor-about-to-grill-the-guilty-defendant look.

"Why is it, Mr. Rocheblatt," she said, "that the only thing you know how to do with a woman is come on to her?" Marty started to answer but Angela cut him off. "Zip it, dogface, and listen up. Aimee and I have had enough of these **altercations** with you. So get this through your thick, dumb linebacker skull once and for all: You are gross. You make us sick. And if you ever come on to either of us again I'll file a sexual **harassment grievance** with the **Ethics** Committee and tear your sorry loser ass to shreds."

"Oh yeah?" Marty **sneered.** "Well, you ugly dogs make me sick, too. You're just a coupla stuck-up chicks." The

spurned wiener stomped off angrily into the frolicking crowd.

George chuckled. "Look who's calling who an ugly dog," he said, not fully appreciating his **inadvertent** pun.

He could smell her **cloying** perfume before he heard her voice at his ear. "Hey Orlando," she crooned.

Orlando turned around and gazed down upon the dangerous curves of Brenda Kinkaid. She was wearing a French maid's costume under her skunky fur coat. Her eyes were bleary and bloodshot and her mascara was smudged. She sounded quite drunk.

"How come you didn't call me? You said you would," Brenda said, slurring half the words. "I wanted to see you before winter vacation."

"I'm sorry. I had an Am lit final. But here I am now. What's up?"

"Femme fatale," Twain **admonished** in a low voice. "Watch yourself."

Orlando wasn't sure which was more **offensive,** Brenda's excessive perfume or the reek of Twain's cigar.

"I just wanted to..." Brenda started to speak, but her voiced trailed off. Then she lost her balance and staggered to the side.

Orlando reached out and grabbed her arm to keep her from falling. "Brenda, what's going on? Are you okay?"

"Ah, so we meet again, Señor Ortiz, *eh-heh, eh-heh,*" said Preston Atwater Doolittle III, suddenly appearing from behind them and stepping up to Brenda's side.

"Well, if it isn't the **distinguished** Mr. Bilgewater Doohickey the Dadblamed Third," Twain announced, sending a blast of cigar smoke toward Preston's head.

Preston wrinkled his nose and waved away the fumes. "Same to you, Morgan. I hope your shoulder still hurts." He looked at Orlando. "Ah, I see you're still having trouble keeping your filthy paws off my date." Orlando let go of Brenda's arm. "I can't really blame you, though. She's looking exceptionally lovely tonight, isn't she?"

"Actually, she's looking exceptionally wasted," said Orlando. He checked out Preston. His erstwhile roommate was wearing evening dress—tuxedo pants and cutaway tails with a frilly shirt, bow tie, scarf, and silk top hat. "And what are you supposed to be tonight, Doolittle? Fred Astaire's evil, underachieving twin?"

Preston smiled **complacently.** "I am simply myself, as always, *eh-heh, eh-heh.*"

Yeah, thought Orlando, a **haughty, pretentious, ostentatious, affected** jerk.

Brenda swayed and staggered again—this time straight into Orlando's arms. "Y'know, sweetie, I don't feel too good," she moaned, her face pressed against his chest. "I think I wanna lie down."

Orlando held up Brenda and glared at Preston. "Dude, what's wrong with her? She's not just drunk, I can tell."

"Don't worry, *mon ami.* She'll be fine. I'll take good care of her."

"I don't believe you. You did something to her, didn't you?"

Preston **smirked** and patted his chest where the inside pocket of his coat would be. "Two little white ones in the beer and she's all yours for the evening," he said. "And maybe somebody else's later," he added with a wink.

The muscles in Orlando's jaw twitched. "Y'know, Doolittle," he said as he shifted Brenda to his left side and held her up with one arm, "there's something I've been wanting to ask you ever since freshman year."

"Ah, and what's that, *Seen-your* Or—"

The boot reached its target before Preston could pronounce the second syllable of Orlando's last name. With an agonized howl, Preston doubled over and fell to the ground. He lay there on his side, groaning in pain, his knees drawn up and his hands between his thighs.

"How does *that* feel?" Orlando said. "That's what I've been wanting to ask, you selfish, **condescending** creep."

Twain cupped a hand around his ear and leaned over Preston, as if pretending to **interpret** a message in the groans. "Why of course, Doohickey," he said. "I'd be glad to give your regards to Bret Harte when I return."

Isabel Lyon watched from the shadow of a parked car across the street as the gray-haired lady in the red coat and pillbox hat unlocked the glass front door of a three-story **antebellum** house and entered the vestibule. With the big bundle of paper still wedged under her arm, the lady checked her mailbox on the wall, then unlocked the inner door and disappeared inside.

Isabel knew that the **capacious** building was owned by the university, and that long ago it had been converted into six luxury apartments for faculty members who wanted to live in style near the campus. She knew this because one of her professors sophomore year had invited the class to have tea and finger sandwiches at her apartment here, and Isabel had marveled at all the elegant and **subtle** architectural touches—smooth-grained maple floors, **intricate** stenciled wallpaper, **burnished** wainscoting, cloisonné enamel lighting fixtures, silver-plated hardware on the doors, translucent marble in the bathroom and kitchen, and handmade tiles set in polished brass around the fireplace in the living room.

Right now the windows of two of the apartments were **illuminated** and four were dark. Isabel watched and waited and a minute later a light on the right side of the third floor came on. So she's up there, Isabel thought. Then it looks like I'll have to **resort** to the fire escape.

She crossed the street and crept down the darkened

alley along the side of the building. She was in luck. The bottom rung of the fire escape was just within her grasp. She set down her backpack and unzipped one of the compartments, removed her compact CamFone, and slipped it in the pocket of her jacket. Then, using every ounce of upper-body strength she had and trying desperately not to grunt, she pulled herself up and managed to attain the second-floor platform. Then she tiptoed up to the third floor, slipped silently to the window, and peeked in.

It was the living room of the apartment, and it was **lavishly** furnished with gilt-framed paintings, costly antique furniture, and ornamental Persian rugs. Scores of curios and objets d'art were littered around the room and took the place of books in the spacious built-in bookcases on either side of the fireplace. Isabel scanned the room and spotted the bundle of paper on top of an **ornate** credenza by the door.

The gray-haired lady had taken off her red coat and pillbox hat, and her shiny black boots as well. She was crouched on both knees by the fireplace, rolling up pages of newspaper into slender sticks and placing them underneath a pile of kindling on the grate. Eventually she stood up and retrieved a box of matches from the top of the mantel. She knelt down again, struck a match, and lit the fire. When the kindling had ignited sufficiently she placed two small logs on the grate. Then she got up and left the room, returning a minute later with a glass of white wine, which she carefully set on a crystal coaster on the Chippendale coffee table.

As the logs caught fire, the lady took the bundle from the credenza and set it on the coffee table. She sat down on the sofa with her stocking feet tucked underneath her and stared at the pile of paper for a long time, occasionally sipping her wine. Every so often she would nod or shake her head or smile at something she was thinking, and several times Isabel saw her lips move as if she were muttering to herself. At one point she threw her head back and laughed **uproariously,** then slapped the stack of paper as if she expected it to share in the **mirth** of some private joke.

Now that the bundle was only about ten feet away from the window, Isabel had a much better view of it, and the more she **scrutinized** it from her **frigid** perch on the fire escape the more she was convinced that she was right. The bundle was the same size and shape as the one she had stumbled upon in suite E-4 of Stormfield College. It was tied in the same way, with the same sort of string. And if she strained her eyes and looked hard enough she could see several bold splashes of Twain's **distinctive** handwriting on the topmost page. As if that weren't enough, there were the gray-haired lady's **telling** words as she was about to drop the bundle into the recycling bin.

No, she was not imagining things. She was not a nutcase. This was the real deal.

And it was real, too, when the handsome gray-haired lady finished her wine and set down her glass. It was quite real when she picked up the bundled manuscript and set it down on the hearth next to the crackling fire. It was extremely real when she sat down on the hearth and untied the string around the manuscript. And it was **excruciatingly** real when she picked up the first page and whispered three horrifying words that Isabel could have read on anybody's lips: *Good-bye, Huckleberry Finn.*

Isabel's heart began to pound wildly. Omigod, she thought, she's going to burn the book!

She quickly checked the window. Could she break it and get into the apartment in time to stop this maniac from destroying an **invaluable** literary masterpiece? No, there was no way. The window was locked and secure.

She was frantic. What could she do? Nothing. There was nothing she could do. She was helpless, **impotent,** utterly powerless to prevent the **imminent catastrophe.**

Then she remembered her CamFone. If she couldn't stop this **heinous** crime, at least she would **document** it.

Isabel pulled the CamFone out of her pocket, flipped it open, and got it positioned at the window just in time to get a shot of the gray-haired lady dropping the pieces of string in the fire. She snapped another one as the lady picked up at least a hundred pages from the stack, and another as she held them out over the fire. Then, with tears of rage and disbelief clouding her eyes, and no longer **comprehending** the **magnitude** of what she was recording, only aware that she must at all costs record it, she snapped another picture as the lady let go of the pages, another as they hovered for an instant above the flames, and another as they vanished. She snapped one final picture as the lady turned from the fire with a look of fury on her face and stared at the empty spot on the hearth where, only moments before, the rest of the manuscript had been.

Orlando and Aimee left the sterile, **antiseptic confines** of the emergency clinic at Hadleyburg Health Services in a **somber** mood.

It's never a happy day, Aimee thought, when you have to take some poor person to HHS to have her stomach pumped, especially when she's the ex-girlfriend of the boy you've had a crush on for ages. Orlando was **entertaining** the same depressing thought, except he was thinking that it's even more depressing when the person you're taking in is your ex-girlfriend and the person who's helping you do it is the girl you think you love.

Aimee rubbed her gloved hands together and took a deep breath of the clear night air. It had grown strangely warmer. Was it because of all the passionate, pent-up **fervor** released into the atmosphere by the **carousing** and **reveling** of the bacchanal? Such a **whimsical notion** made Aimee smile in spite of herself.

Orlando shoved his hands into the pockets of his parka

and gazed up at the falciform moon. If I only had a poem for every time I looked at you, old man, said his **melancholy** inner voice. Yeah, but you know what you'd be then? quipped his **flippant** inner voice. A freakin' lunatic, that's what.

They walked in silence for a while, enveloped in their own thoughts and the swiftly **dissipating vapor** of their exhaled breath. Their footsteps crunched the light layer of snow on the sidewalk. In the distance they could hear the **chaotic uproar** of the bacchanal.

"Aims," Orlando said finally, "thanks for coming with me down to HHS tonight. It was beyond the call of duty."

"Well, I'm always happy to help out when one of your old flames gets herself in trouble."

"No, I'm serious. That was really big of you."

"No it wasn't." Aimee looked up at Orlando. He was still staring at the moon. "You know I'd do almost anything for you," she said.

"Thanks, Aims. You're such a good friend."

Good friend? Aimee thought. I wish I were more than just a good friend—and maybe it's time to tell him that. She swallowed quickly and spoke before she could change her mind. "Orlando?"

"Yeah?"

"Can I tell you something?"

"Sure."

"I've always liked you—I mean like really liked you, you know? Ever since freshman year."

Orlando stopped looking at the moon and focused on Aimee. "Are you kidding?" he asked in an **incredulous** voice.

Aimee swallowed again. "No, I'm not. I always hoped we'd go out together."

"Wow, that's amazing," Orlando said, "because I've always liked you too, and maybe that was the problem."

"What do you mean?"

"I mean you're such a good friend that it was kind of weird to think of you as a girlfriend. And you were always kind of hard to read. I was never sure if you were interested or **indifferent.** You have a kind of...I don't know...a **mystique,** I guess."

"Omigod, that's incredible," said Aimee, "because that's exactly how I've always felt about you—that you were there for me, and you cared and everything, but when it came to being more than just friends you were kind of **aloof** and unapproachable."

They stopped walking and looked at each other. Orlando reached out and took Aimee's hands. Her silky black hair glistened in the moonlight.

"Well, Aims," he said, "if you like me and I like you, then what are we waiting around for?"

Aimee laughed and looked up into Orlando's glittering blue eyes. "Nothing, I guess. Nothing at all."

She reached up as he reached down and their warm lips met. Then the tender kiss and the quiet night were rudely rent asunder by the **strident, supernatural** warbling of a cellphone.

"Ah, crap, that's me," Orlando said. "Sorry."

It figures, Aimee thought. Of course the stupid phone rings just when things are starting to get interesting. It's like a **meddling** chaperone or something.

Orlando pulled out his phone. "Hey, this is Big O. Huh? No. This is Orlando, who's this?" There was a pause and Aimee heard an excited voice jabbering through the phone. "Dude, I think you've got the wrong number," Orlando said. More jabbering. "Correction. I *know* you've got the wrong number."

He hung up and looked at Aimee. "Sorry about that," he said **sheepishly.** Then he smiled. "So where were we?"

Despite her **exasperation** over the annoying interruption, Aimee smiled back. "Making up for lost time, I think."

They reached for each other and kissed again, long and hungrily.

Finally Aimee broke away. "This is going to sound stupid, but I have to ask you. It doesn't bother you that I'm so short and you're so tall?"

Orlando laughed. "I think we've both just proved that particular **disparity** is **irrelevant**. But if you need further **substantiation** . . ." He pulled her close and leaned down for another kiss, but the romantic moment was once again **obliterated** by the **shrill intrusion** of a cellphone—this time Aimee's.

She apologized **profusely** and retrieved her phone. "Hello?"

"Aims, it's Angela. Is everything okay?"

"Yeah, everything's fine. Are you okay? You sound a little freaked."

"Yeah, I am. After you guys left for HHS, Mr. Twain and Mr. Griffin and I hung out at the bacchanal for a while. We just got back to the suite right now, and guess what? You're not gonna believe this."

"What?" said Aimee, feeling her heart beginning to race.

"We can't find the manuscript of *Huck Finn*. It was right on the coffee table when we left the room this morning, and now it's gone. I think somebody stole it."

"Omigod," said Aimee, "we'll be right there. We're on our way." She hung up and looked at Orlando. "Angela said Twain's manuscript disappeared from our suite. She thinks it was stolen."

"Whoa, you're kidding!"

"C'mon, let's go." As she grabbed Orlando's hand his cellphone rang again.

"Dang, this is getting ridiculous," he said. "But it might be important."

"What, like they're calling to say you just won the Nobel Prize?"

Orlando **judiciously** chose to answer his phone instead of Aimee's **ironic rhetorical question.** "This is Big O."

"Yo, dude, it's Hank."

"Hey, what's up? I've been wondering about you. Did you manage to find Merlin the Magician?"

"Did I ever. And the guy's incredible—nothing like his **eccentric** reputation."

"So did he do anything?"

"Dude, he found my laptop and brought it back."

"He did? Wow. And I thought those two clowns got away with it."

"What two clowns?"

"These townie scam artists we were chasing."

"Oh, so that's why it was bouncing all over the place."

"What do you mean?"

"I'll explain later."

"Hank, what about the manuscript of *Huck Finn*? Angela just called Aimee and said somebody stole it from their suite."

"Chill out, dude. The manuscript's right here. Merle just recovered it a couple of minutes ago. Now he's trying to find the wormhole that got opened up to the fourth dimension so he can send Mr. Twain and his book back. Wait, hang on a sec."

Orlando heard a **muffled** exchange in the background. Then Hank came on again. "Merle says he wants you guys to bring Mr. Twain up here. It'll be easier that way. He won't have to deal with something in a remote location."

"Does Merle know there's another guy who has to go back too?" Orlando asked.

"There is?"

"Yeah. He's a friend of Mr. Twain's—George Griffin. They said he messed with your laptop at Twain's house and then he and the laptop wound up here."

"That's wild. I didn't know that. Hang on."

There was another **indistinct** exchange and Hank came

on again. "Merle says the more the merrier. Just get your butts up here as soon as you can. It's in the basement of Irving Lab. Room B-9."

"Dude, we're there." Orlando hung up and looked at Aimee. "Aims, call Angela and tell her everything's cool. C'mon, I'll explain the rest as we go."

Up on Science Hill, in room B-9 of Irving Lab, Hank hung up the phone and turned to Merle. "They're on their way."

"Good," said Merle. "Okay, now do me a big favor. Call Firenze's and order three Monster Works with extra cheese, to go. I'll give you some cash and you can go pick them up while I **unravel** the rest of this **conundrum.** I should have it figured out by the time you get back."

Hank never asked questions when free food was in the offing, especially pizza. "Right away, chief," he said, picking up the phone again.

"We're gonna need something to celebrate with when this is over, you know what I mean?" Merle said. "Besides, we can't let Mark Twain and his friend go back to the nineteenth century without ever tasting pizza. That would be a tragedy of **inestimable proportions!**"

Isabel Lyon easily followed the lady in the red coat and pillbox hat as she wended her way through the crowds and pandemonium in the center of the Hadleyburg campus. There was plenty of cover and she hardly needed to hide. But as the lady headed up High Street, which was practically empty, toward the **periphery** of the campus on Science Hill, it became more challenging to **evade detection.**

It was also a challenge for Isabel to keep up. The lady was striding like a cross-country skier, and Isabel, whose legs were not particularly long, had to hustle so as not to lose ground. By the time they reached Irving Lab at the top of the hill she was grateful for a chance to catch her breath.

She leaned against the trunk of a large tree, out of range of the nearest streetlight, and watched as the lady swiped her passcard and entered the **dreary** building. Then she counted to ten and followed suit. She didn't see the lady anywhere in the lobby, so she approached the **phlegmatic** security guard at his desk, pretending to be **scatterbrained** and flustered and in a rush. For Isabel, this didn't require any special **histrionic** ability.

"Oh sir, I'm sorry, excuse me," she said, "but that gray-haired woman in the red coat and hat who just came in?"

The guard nodded.

Isabel pulled her own key chain out of her pocket and held it so the guard could see. "I, like, just saw her drop her keys in the snow out there, so I picked them up and rushed in here to return them. But I, like, don't see her. Do you know where she went?"

The guard yawned. "You can leave the keys with me and I'll make sure she gets them on her way out."

"Oh that's like really nice of you and everything, but I'd really like to return them myself—you know, for the satisfaction of, like...like doing a good **deed**. You know?"

"All right, whatever."

"So, like, can you tell me where I can find her?"

"She usually goes to visit her son in the basement. Room B-9."

Isabel was **perplexed.** Visit her son? In the basement of Irving Lab? During the Winter Bacchanal? Then all of a sudden she connected the dots. Omigod, she thought, the lady's son must be that **misanthropic** computer genius she'd heard weird stories about, the Hermit of Science Hill.

"Helluo librorum, hoc quaere, hoc titulo, hoc tempore."

This was the **conundrum** Merle was trying to **unravel.** He knew from long experience grappling with many such **cryptic** computer **mechanisms** that they were usually doorkeepers. The proper answer in this case, he felt certain, would lead him right to the wormhole that had been opened in time.

It was Latin, of course, and he had figured out what it meant—*Devourer of books, seek this, by this title, at this time.* But he had yet to **decipher** its significance. He sat there staring at the display, jiggling his leg and stroking his beard, **pondering** a **myriad** of possible answers to the mystery.

He knew that TWAIN could be of little help in this **endeavor.** Computers, and even herculean supercomputers, were hopelessly clumsy at untangling **conundrums**; their **unswerving rationality** made them ill-suited to the task. Because of the fanciful and often illogical nature of **conundrums,** they were best solved by something equally fanciful and illogical, something that could make **spontaneous** and **arbitrary** associations. In other words, they were best solved by the human brain.

A **conundrum,** Merle kept reminding himself, was a riddle in which there is often some odd resemblance between **dissimilar** things, and the answer involves a play on words—a pun. But where was the buried **dissimilarity** in this **enigmatic** sentence? Where was the pun?

He read it over again and **ruminated.** "*Helluo librorum, hoc quaere, hoc titulo, hoc tempore.* 'Devourer of books, seek this, by this title, at this time.'" What could it be?

He was **roused** from his **reverie** by a rhythmic knock at the door. Could that be Hank returning from Firenze's so soon? He heard two slow taps followed by three quick ones. His mother. What was *she* coming back for?

It was a lucky thing Merle had his pants on because this time his mother didn't wait the **requisite** minute before opening the door. Instead she barged right in without saying a word, practically threw down her coat, gloves, and hat on the dining room table, then stood with her hands on her hips in the middle of the room. "All right, dear," she said, pronouncing *dear* as if it were synonymous with *you little worm.* "I know what you're up to, and I know what you just did, and I'm not about to let you get away with any of it. You'd better fess up right now."

Up to what? Did what? Get away with what? Merle thought. He had never seen his mother so furious. With her statuesque and Amazonian physique, he had to admit she struck a rather **formidable** pose.

"I'm sorry, Mom, but I don't understand. Fess up to what?"

"You know what I'm talking about, dear." *You little worm.*

"Mom, I really don't."

"Come on, you **deceitful, scheming** boy, where is it? Give it to me right now." She was beginning to raise her voice.

Merle couldn't help raising his voice too. "Give you *what,* Mom?"

"The manuscript of *Huckleberry Finn!*"

Merle was speechless. "I . . . uh . . . I don't . . . it's . . ."

Blanche Paige snorted with **disdain.** "Oh, don't even bother trying."

"Trying what?"

"Trying to lie. You always stutter and stammer when you're about to lie. It's so transparent."

Merle rubbed his forehead and sat down in the chair by his desk. "How in the world did you find out about the manuscript?"

Blanche remained standing. She crossed her arms. "I found it tonight outside the staff door of the library. Somebody had left it there, perhaps a good Samaritan, someone who knew that a librarian would be likely to find it and **safeguard** it and ensure that it was returned to its caretakers in Buffalo."

"And what did you do with it?"

"There was no place in the library secure enough to leave it overnight, so I took it home with me. I put it on my coffee table and went to fetch a glass of wine, and the next thing I knew it was vanishing before my very eyes. That's when I knew you were the **culprit**—you, with your dangerous and demented dynamolecular intelligence."

Now Merle was stunned. "You know about my work? About DMI?"

"Of course I do, dear." That **contemptuous** *dear* again.

"But how?"

"Oh, Merlin, I'm your damned mother, for Pete's sake."

"What's that supposed to mean?"

Blanche issued another **disdainful** snort. "You think I'm just here to serve you and pick up after you and tolerate you while you ignore me and do whatever you like, don't you, dear?"

Merle was silent.

Blanche went on. "You don't think we mothers know our children's secrets? You don't think we **ferret** them out when you're not looking? You don't think we take a **clandestine** peek in your drawers and under your beds?"

And maybe in my computers, it occurred to Merle.

"Merlin, did you use DMI to take the manuscript of *Huckleberry Finn* from the library in Buffalo?"

Merle shook his head. "No, I didn't, and that's the truth."

"I don't believe you," said Blanche, sitting down in the Eames chair and crossing her long legs. "You know, I'm worried about you, Merlin. What are you trying to do with this crazy technology? Make millions? Alter history? I'm warning you, it won't work. It's going to backfire someday and you'll be sorry."

"Mom," Merle said quietly, "I'm trying to change the world—for the better."

Blanche shook her head sadly. "Oh, Merlin, when are you going to grow up?"

"Look, Mom, you don't understand," Merle said in a **placating** tone of voice. "There's been some peculiar time-traveling going on involving that manuscript, and all I'm trying to do is set things right. That may sound strange to you, but I swear it's true. The manuscript of *Huck Finn* that you found and that I transported from your apartment didn't come from the library in Buffalo. It came straight from Mark Twain's house in Hartford in 1883. I didn't bring it here, and I'm not sure yet who did."

Blanche looked at Merle. Then she tossed her head back and **emitted** a hearty, almost cackling laugh. "Time travel? Do you really expect me to believe that? Oh my goodness, dear, I think all this time you've been spending alone down in this awful basement has sent you right around the bend."

Merle listened to his mother laughing and **deriding** him and suddenly something clicked into place in his brain. He swiveled around in his chair and read the **conundrum** on the display again: "*Helluo librorum, hoc quaere, hoc titulo, hoc tempore.* 'Devourer of books, seek this, by this title, at this time.'" Could *hoc* stand for *Huck*? he wondered. Yes, that must be the play on words. The riddle was a command to open the door to the wormhole, seek out the manuscript titled *Huckleberry Finn,* and transport it through time. But what, or who, was this "devourer of books"?

He swiveled around and looked at his mother again. She was no longer laughing or even smiling. She was staring at him with cool, **impassive** eyes.

"Are you going to give me that manuscript now, Merlin dear?" she said in her **deceptively** sweet and **melodious** voice. "You can trust me with it, you know. After all, I'm a librarian."

Helluo librorum. Devourer of books. How strange. It looked and sounded almost like... *Hello librarian.* Oh my god, Merle thought. No, it can't be.

There was a fierce pounding on the door.

"Who on earth could that be, dear?" said Blanche.

"Actually, Mom, believe it or not I'm having company over."

"Oh really? How delightful. I'm looking forward to meeting your friends."

Merle opened the door expecting to see Hank and the others, not a young woman in a leather jacket with spiky bleached hair and a silver stud in her lower lip.

"Why, Merlin," Blanche exclaimed, "I didn't realize you had a date for the Winter Bacchanal."

Neither did I, Merle thought as the young woman barged into the room. Before he could protest or even open his mouth she began talking in a rapid, squeaky voice that Merle found strangely enchanting. And as she spoke she **punctuated** her speech and **emphasized** certain words by poking the air with her finger.

"Excuse me, sir, but my name's Isabel Lyon, and I already know who you are, you're Merlin the Magician, the Techno-Wizard and Hermit of Science Hill, and I know you're like some kind of genius who's been like moving stuff around with computers because I've seen you do it like twice now, but I'll get to that in a minute because there's something I've got to get off my chest right now, and it isn't going to be easy—for anybody in this room. It's something really urgent I need to tell you, I mean show you, or show *and* tell you—whatever, anyway—"

"Isabel, what is this about?" Merle managed to **interject.**

"Hey, I'm sorry, I know you're busy so I'll cut to the chase." She jabbed an accusing finger in the direction of Blanche Paige. "It's about Mark Twain's manuscript of

Huckleberry Finn and that woman sitting over there. Your mother, right?"

"Yes," Merle **confirmed.**

"The book burner," Isabel said.

The librarian stood bolt upright. "What was that you said, young lady?"

"I said the book burner, *old* lady."

Blanche paled for a moment, then regained her ruddy color. "What on earth are you talking about?"

Isabel looked at Blanche and her words poured out in an **unadulterated** stream of righteous **indignation.** "I'll tell you what I'm talking about. I'm talking about how you found the manuscript in the alley by the side entrance to the library and you were about to drop it in the recycling bin when you suddenly realized what it was, and then you took it home and made a cozy little fire in your fireplace and got yourself a glass of wine and put the manuscript on your coffee table and looked at it for a while, and then you picked it up and took it over to the fire and untied the string and proceeded to try to *burn* it. You were going to destroy the only **extant** manuscript of Mark Twain's masterpiece! But you were just about to drop that irreplaceable literary treasure in the flames when something happened—I don't know exactly what but I suspect it had something to do with Merlin—and the manuscript just disappeared into thin air, the same way it disappeared from my backpack earlier this afternoon in Professor Shelley's office."

"That's the most ridiculous rubbish I have ever heard," Blanche **scoffed.** "You're lying—no, I'm not even going to dignify that **preposterous** and **inarticulate** charge by calling it a lie. Young lady, you're insane."

"Hey, I'm sorry, but you're the crazy one around here," Isabel shot back, **undeterred.** "You just cooked your goose and cooked it good because you're lying and I have *proof.*" She set down her backpack on the floor, removed her

CamFone, and turned it on. "Look at this," she said, showing the first photo to Merle. "And this, and this," she continued, showing him the **incriminating** photos in **chronological** order.

"You took pictures of me?" Blanche cried, striding across the room. "You were spying on me? How dare you." She lunged for Isabel's camera, but Merle gripped her arms and held her back. "Let me see those! I demand to see them!" Blanche shouted.

"Don't give her the manuscript, Merlin, whatever you do," Isabel implored, "because that's what she's going to do with it. I hate to say it, but your mom's totally psycho!"

There was a **vigorous** knock at the door. "Hey Merle, open up! It's me, Hank. I've got the pizza and the gang's all here."

Without thinking about the potential **consequences,** Merle let go of his mother and went to answer the door. And the moment he released her, Blanche fell upon Isabel with a **vengeance.** As the door swung open and the **jovial** group poured in, Blanche pummeled her about the head, tore at her hair, and kicked her viciously in the shins. Isabel tucked her camera into the pit of her chest, then curled up like a **timid** snail retreating into its shell.

"Give me that camera, you spiky-haired little bitch," Blanche seethed through clenched teeth, but Isabel silently vowed to protect it with her life.

As soon as they saw what was happening, everyone came running to Isabel's aid. They pried off the raging Blanche and dragged her kicking and screaming to the futon couch, where they pinned her on her back. Orlando and George each held down a leg, Twain and Hank each held down an arm, and Angela worked to **immobilize** her thrashing head. Aimee, mindful of the victim in this one-sided **altercation,** went to comfort Isabel and tend to her wounds.

Meanwhile, Merle stood over his mother, his chest heaving. He looked down at her with **ineffable contempt, outrage,** and humiliation. "For God's sake, Mom, you're a librarian," he said, "How could you destroy a book? What could make you want to?"

Blanche Paige suddenly stopped struggling and began to sob. Through her tears, the university librarian confessed that she had never felt at home in her ill-chosen profession, where books are **revered** and the protection of free speech is **paramount.** Although she sometimes had to read books because of the requirements of her job, she had never liked them, and over the years her distaste for the printed word grew into an **aversion** and finally a **phobia.** Long ago she had tossed out the books at home, and she had not read a newspaper or magazine for years. She was, in effect, purposely aliterate. And as she **languished** in a career she felt stuck in and that she **loathed,** she began to **cultivate** a consuming interest in computer science.

And that's how she **aspired** to become *helluo librorum,* the librarian devourer of books, thought Merle. He directed the others to let his mother sit up on the couch while they talked, but to stay close by. Then he continued the **interrogation.** "But I don't get it. How did you get so good that you could access a wormhole?"

"Oh, come on now, Merlin. Are you dismissing me because I'm a woman? I'm *your* mother, aren't I? Where do you think you got your inflated IQ, anyway? From that **avaricious** clod Miles Irving?"

Merle did a double take. "Are you saying Cosmo Irving is my father?"

"Yes, I made you with that **pontificating** windbag. Where do you think all your atrocious hair comes from?"

"For crying out loud, Mom, why didn't you ever tell me?"

"It would only have been an unnecessary distraction.

Miles was **irrelevant** to me, so why shouldn't he be **irrelevant** to you?"

Merle was speechless. This **cynical**, hardhearted woman was not his mother. Neither was that doting woman with the tinkling voice who did his laundry.

"At any rate," Blanche went on, "I'm quite capable of downloading your programs when I'm here tidying up and you're in the bathroom or on one of your silly 'visitations.'"

"You downloaded my stuff? My DMI? That's how you did it?"

"And Professor Reisenzeit's *Tempus* fumblings, too. That **pompous,** lecherous fool couldn't wait to show off to me when I **feigned** interest in him and his project."

"But how did you put it all together? It took me years to figure that stuff out."

"I know. And I appreciate your laying all that groundwork for me, dear. It made my task much easier."

"May I ask a question?" said Mark Twain.

Merle nodded.

Twain looked at Blanche. "Of all the possible manuscripts you could have retrieved from the past, you chose *Huckleberry Finn.* Why did you want to destroy it?"

"It was an **arbitrary** choice," Blanche said. "I wanted to go after something famous and **controversial.** *Huck Finn* is probably the most famous novel in all of American literature and practically every high school student reads it, but every year some school board somewhere tries to **ban** it. I thought I'd save everybody all the trouble and just take it out of circulation."

Merle looked down at this woman he had thought was his mother but who was now a stranger. Could she really be so **misguided**? Could she ever be reformed?

Then an idea came to him. "Get up," he said to her. She stood up and he took her arm. He led her to his bank of computers and put her in a chair. "All right," he said, taking his own seat, "now you're going to make *my* task much easier."

"What do you mean?" said Blanche.

"I'm going to give you a chance to **redeem** yourself by undoing the damage you've done. First, you're going to guide me through your **conundrum** and we're going to open up that wormhole together. Then we're going to send everybody back where they belong and sew up that hole for good. Then you're going to make me a promise."

"What sort of promise?"

"You're going to promise me three things: that you'll immediately resign your post at the library, that you'll get psychological counseling for your **antipathy** to books and reading, and that you'll work with me as a partner and help me perfect DMI. If you do all that, I'll forgive you—both for what you've done and the **heinous** thing you almost did." He held out his furry hand. "What do you say...partner?"

Blanche Paige pulled a tissue from a cardboard box on the desk and wiped her eyes. Then she took her son's proffered hand. "All right," she said. "I promise."

She placed her fingers on the keyboard in front of her and **adroitly** typed in a string of commands, as fast or maybe even faster than Merle. A small smile spread across her lips and she looked up. "You know, I think I'm going to like this new arrangement. What are you waiting for, partner? Let's get to work."

Lighting Out

"Please, please take me with you," pleaded Isabel Lyon. She was sitting between Mark Twain and George at Merle's dining table. The two visitors from the nineteenth century, dressed in their nineteenth-century duds, had just finished eating a farewell feast of Firenze's Monster Works pizza. George had pronounced it "almost better than fresh hot biscuits and butter," and Twain had pronounced it "delectable in the mouth but a dadblamed nuisance in the hand."

"I'm such an admirer of yours, you know," Isabel said.

"I know, and it's a pity," said Twain.

"I want to be part of your life. I'll do anything to be near you."

"And I'll do anything *not* to be near *you*."

As usual, Isabel was **undaunted** by the writer's **disdainful** rejections. "I'll take dictation, I'll tutor your children, I'll scrub the floors, empty the trash, clean the stable, whatever you guys need done in the nineteenth century," she said. "Just please oh please oh please take me with you, okay, will you please?"

"Woman," said Twain, "I do declare, you cause more trouble and **consternation** than the German language!

When you get a **notion** in your head you work it and squeeze it and knead it and pound it until it's gasping for breath and on its knees begging for mercy."

Isabel cracked up. "Mr. Twain, I'm just kidding. I can't help it. You're so much fun to **provoke**. I get such a kick out of seeing you get **riled**. But I'm not really serious about going back with you."

Twain's face lit up. "Really? Well, now that's a relief. No, not simply a relief—a **panacea**."

Soon Merle and Blanche announced that they had successfully opened the wormhole and were ready to proceed with the transport. It was time to say farewell.

"But Mr. Clemens got to visit the future longer than I did," George complained. "Can't you send me back later after I've had a better taste of it?"

"Sorry, Mr. Griffin, this is a one-shot deal," said Merle. "We close the wormhole for good after this."

"That's just as well, I suppose," said George. "I've got bets riding at home that I need to attend to, and I'm dying to see my wife and darling baby girl for Christmas. I miss them something awful." Then he had an afterthought. "Can we at least take back some souvenirs?"

Merle shook his head. "To every thing there is a season," he recited. "A time to keep, and a time to cast away. As ye came, so shall ye go."

"That's from Ecclesiastes," said George. "I always like to read a chapter or two from it before I go to bed."

"I daresay it's a good tonic for keeping one's **vanity** in check," said Twain. "Judging by your admirably **modest endowment** in that regard, George, I'm thinking maybe I should try it too—but no more than once a week."

Merle went to his bookshelf and pulled out his copies of *The Adventures of Huckleberry Finn* and *A Connecticut Yankee in King Arthur's Court.* "I know you haven't published *Huck* yet, and you haven't even written *Connecticut Yankee*," he said to Twain, "but I'm not going to have another chance like this. These are first editions. Would you please sign them for me?"

"With pleasure," Twain said. "I always enjoy taking credit for writing I haven't published, or even written." He winked. "Yet."

Then Orlando, Aimee, Hank, and Angela stepped up and shook hands with both men, and said their good-byes.

"Mr. Twain, it's been *so* cool having you at Hadley-burg," said Angela. "I'll never forget our conversation at dawn about **grandiloquent** words, and about *Huck Finn.*"

"Neither will I, my dear," Twain said, feeling a bit of a lump rise in his throat.

"Please don't forget about my great-great-great-grandpa, Warner T. McGuinn. You'll be meeting him at Yale Law School soon enough."

"You can rest assured I'll do my best for the lad."

"And you won't forget your promise not to use *resistentialism,* will you?"

Twain smiled. "I'll be a good boy. Even when I see a rake."

Angela gave him a hug, and those **idiosyncratic** pink spots appeared on the writer's cheeks.

"Good-bye, Mr. Griffin, good-bye, Mr. Twain," Aimee said. "Hanging out with you guys was *such* a blast. I'll always remember when you barged into my recital, and how I banged out the last chord, jumped off the platform, and joined the chase."

"I must say you do a fine jeté, my dear," said Twain, giving his mustache a rakish tweak. "Maybe you should figure out how to dance and accompany yourself on the piano at the same time. Oh, by the way, thank you for mending my trousers."

"You know, that's something else I'll always remember," Aimee said with a grin. "Wait'll I tell my mom I sewed up Mark Twain's pants."

The writer laughed and turned to Orlando and Hank. "And what do you two rapscallions have to say for yourselves?"

The boys looked at each other and shrugged.

"Well, we learned in a hurry not to call you 'dude,'" Orlando said.

"And you owe us each twenty bucks," Hank deadpanned.

Twain chuckled. "Well, gentlemen, I ask your forgiveness for **imposing** my **archaic, petty** vices on your **virtuous, pristine epoch.** I am guilty of immoderate smoking, the barefaced theft of a cigar—which the **impostor** wasn't going to smoke anyway, so that serves to **mitigate** the **offense**—and of course borrowing money from the two of you that I cannot possibly pay back."

"Hey, I've got an idea," said Hank. "We could send you back with a laptop connected to the Internet and you could email us a postdated check."

"Yo, Hank," rumbled Merle, "let's not go down *that* road again, okay?"

"Boys," Twain said to Orlando and Hank, "I have enjoyed being your uncle pro tempore during my brief **sojourn** at Hadleyburg, and I should like to leave you with a final piece of avuncular advice." He looked at them with a **benevolent** smile that faded into a disapproving frown. "Get a new couch! That thing damn near murdered me."

Everybody laughed and then it was Isabel's turn to say good-bye. She shook hands with George. "I **envy** you, Mr. Griffin, for all the time you get to spend by this amazing man's side. I wish I could be there for the **banter** and the jokes."

"Young lady," Twain cautioned, "you're starting to speak German again."

Isabel laughed and then surprised the writer by giving him a quick peck on the cheek. The **vivid** pink spots exploded like fireworks all over his face.

Now Blanche Paige approached Twain. "I want you to know that I'm sorry," she said. "I'm terribly ashamed of how I've behaved and what I did." The writer could tell from the tone of her voice that she was **sincerely contrite.**

"No hard feelings, ma'am," he replied, swaying slowly from side to side as was his wont when faced with an awkward social situation. He had always found apologies embarrassing for both parties.

She smiled. "Thank you, sir. Maybe someday I'll have the courage to read *Huckleberry Finn*."

"Ma'am, I don't think you need any special courage to read that book," Twain said. "Just an open mind."

Merle tied fresh string around the manuscript of *Huckleberry Finn* and placed the heavy bundle in Twain's hands. "Take good care of that, my friend," he said. "There are a lot of people looking forward to reading it."

"Thank you. I certainly will."

Merle positioned Twain and George side by side in the center of the room. "How's that, Mom—I mean partner?"

Blanche laughed. "Perfect. An easy lock." Her **blithe,** trilling voice was back.

Merle sat down next to her in his chair and made some quick adjustments. He looked at Blanche and she flashed him a thumbs-up. "Okay, gentlemen," he said, "are you ready?"

"Yessir!" said George. He looked at Twain. "My man, let's rock and roll!"

Twain raised his eyebrows in alarm. "By criminy, George, where did you pick up that **outlandish idiom**?"

George laughed his booming laugh. "Last night at the party. In fact, I learned a lot more **contemporary** expressions: *get down, go for it, shake your booty, just chillin', that's tight.* And at one point somebody came up and said those strange words on the pullover you were wearing: *Sappnin Bro*? I must confess I didn't know how to respond."

Twain chuckled. "Please, let us return innocent to the past and leave the gibberish of the future **intact.**" The writer raised one arm in a **valedictory** salute. "My friends," he said in his platform drawl, "I have seen the future and I'm not so sure it works." He paused and stroked his chin. "But it was worth the price of admission."

Everyone laughed and applauded and waved good-bye. Then Merle motioned for quiet. "Try to remain still," he told the two men. "This may take a minute or so."

A hush fell over the room. Mother and son worked their keyboards in wordless tandem. Then she stopped typing and pointed at something on his display. He nodded and his hand went to the mouse. He looked at his mother. "Go ahead, son," she said.

Merle moved the mouse and clicked.

At first nothing happened. Then the room gradually grew lighter, as if someone were turning up an adjustable light switch. Then it got uncomfortably bright, as if someone had turned the light switch up too far on a lamp that was way too **luminous** for its own good. Then it got so bright, so **keenly radiant,** that it was like staring at white-hot sand or a refulgent snowdrift or directly at the midday sun. It was painful, **intolerable,** and everyone wanted to turn away but there was nowhere to turn that wasn't just as intensely and **excruciatingly** bright.

And then, just like that, it was over. The light returned to normal and people were left blinking and rubbing their eyes. When they could manage to see again they gazed in awe at the empty space in the middle of the room.

There was a **collective, contemplative** silence. "It's done," Merle said finally. He sighed and leaned back in his chair. "They're home."

"Way to go," said Isabel, squeezing Merle's shoulder.

At the sound of her charmingly squeaky voice, he swiveled around in his chair and smiled up at her.

She smiled back and bent down and whispered in his ear. "Did I tell you I've really got a thing for hairy guys?"

Beside them, Blanche Paige **tactfully** cleared her throat. "Now don't get distracted. We still have to close that wormhole."

A moment later, mother and son were busy composing an impassioned duet.

The next thing Mark Twain was aware of, after the blinding light had finally passed, was pain. Crushing pain. A **massive** weight was pressing down on him, squeezing the life out of him. "What the devil!" he grunted. "George, are you there?"

From somewhere above came a **muffled** reply. "Mr. Clemens? Where are you?"

"Underneath *you*, I think. Will you please get up? Your elbow's in my ear."

"I'm sorry, Mr. Clemens. I can't seem to budge."

"You can't? Why not?"

"There are walls all around. We're in some kind of small chamber."

"Dagnabit, George, I don't care if we're in a chamber *pot*! Get off me!"

"But I'm stuck."

"You may be stuck, but I can't breathe!"

"All right, I'll do my best. But don't hold me responsible for the **consequences**."

George pushed down and Twain pushed up, and the wrestling match was on. The next minute consisted of a **tumultuous** flurry of flailing elbows and jabbing knees, of limbs unnaturally twisted around other limbs, of shoving and straining, bruised ribs, bumped heads, gouged eyes, and squashed toes—all accompanied by **profuse** grunting and groaning from both parties and by **prodigious** swearing from Twain.

Suddenly there was a loud and **prolonged** rip, like the sound of a door being torn off its hinges. Then the two men spilled **headlong** out of the booth and tumbled onto the cold marble floor of the grand entrance hall at 351 Farmington Avenue in Hartford.

George looked up with a grin. "Mr. Clemens, we're home."

"I reckon so, George," Twain said with a painful sigh. "I reckon so."

Just then the maid, Katy, bustled into the hall from the dining room. "Mercy me!" she cried when she saw the two men **prostrate** on the floor. "Why, Mr. Clemens! George! What on earth happened? I heard a commotion and I thought it was a burglar."

"It's all right, Katy," said Twain, scraping himself off the floor and feeling not unlike a badly fried egg. "It was just a minor **mishap** involving a refractory telephone and a **recalcitrant** doorknob. Isn't that right, George?"

"That's right, Mr. Clemens," George said, getting up and brushing himself off. "I told you you'd get stuck in that booth someday if you didn't fix that door." He picked up the broken door and made a **futile** attempt to reattach it.

"Katy?" said Twain.

"Yes, Mr. Clemens?"

"No need to bother Mrs. Clemens about this misadventure. I wouldn't want to needlessly upset her."

"I understand, sir."

"By the way, where is Mrs. Clemens?"

"Why, she's still upstairs in bed, sir, asleep. And so are the children. It's only six thirty in the morning, or didn't you know that?"

"Er, well, no I didn't. I'm afraid I've quite lost track of time."

"Ay, you've been up in your billiard room working all night again, have you?"

"Yes, that's right, Katy. That's exactly right."

"Would you like some coffee then, sir? I just brewed a strong pot of it."

"Why yes I would. That would be swell." Twain looked at George. "Would you kindly bring it up to me in the billiard room in a few minutes? I'm going to look in on Mrs. Clemens and the children."

"I'd be happy to, sir," said George, and he and Katy went off to the kitchen.

Suddenly Twain remembered his book. Where was it? He looked inside the telephone booth, then all around the entrance hall. It was nowhere in sight.

Panicking, he ran up the stairs two steps at a time, crossed the third-floor landing, and opened the door to the billiard room. The room was dark and cold. He groped his way to the mantel and lit a candle. There was his beloved billiard table. There was his desk. And there, sitting on top of the desk as if he had left it there just a moment ago, was the **itinerant,** peripatetic manuscript of *Huckleberry Finn.*

Fifteen minutes later the writer was lounging at his desk, sipping hot coffee and puffing on his favorite brand of cigar. The gaslights were on low and a crackling fire was **flourishing** in the fireplace. He had peeked in on his wife and children and found them all secure in their beds, and he had dismissed George for the Christmas holiday, sending him home to his wife and daughter a day early with an extra forty dollars in his pocket—more than a month's wages.

He was trying to recall what precisely had happened before he opened his eyes to find George's **formidable bulk** pressing down upon his head and chest. There had been a brilliant **effusion** of light, and before that a **diversity** of young, intelligent faces—one of them surrounded by some very strange hair and another one completely covered with it—and all these faces were smiling at him and saying good-bye. And there was one face in particular, a face surrounded by beautiful black corkscrews of hair, that belonged to a woman whose name kept **eluding** him, a woman who had taught him something extraordinary, an unusual word both amusing and **profound.**

What was that word? he thought. Something about resisting arrest? Civil disobedience, maybe? He tried hard to summon it from the tenebrous and **benighted** cavern of his mind but it was no use. The word, the faces, and any significance he might attach to them had all become a **vague** and **transient** blur, fading into the recesses of his memory and the interstices of time.

While Twain was absorbed in these **ruminations, oblivious** of any hazards that might be **lurking** nearby, the drooping ash on the tip of his cigar decided it was time to **flee** the nest. It took off silently and landed in a gray, powdery pile in the writer's lap.

"Dadfetchit!" he cried, brushing away the hot ash and making an unsightly mess of his trousers.

He leaned back in his chair again and looked at the towering stack of pages on his desk, not with pride but with a strange sort of **detached** amusement. What a dadblamed, infernal nuisance it is to write a book, he thought, and he smiled as he remembered what Huck Finn had to say about the whole **endeavor:** "If I'd a knowed what a trouble it was to make a book I wouldn't a tackled it and ain't agoing to no more."

He almost laughed out loud at the tempting **notion** of never writing another book again. But then his **fastidious vanity** came tugging at his sleeve, followed by the loud, **goading** voice of his **ambition** and the quiet, **judicious** voice of his conscience. He let them all have their say, and in the end it was his conscience that won out.

Why else do you write, his conscience had asked him, but with the **fragile** hope that the fruits of your great labor will touch the hearts and minds of others and stand the test of time?

Exercises

Group One: True or False?

Consider the following statements and decide whether each one is true or false.

1. If you are **adept** at something, you do it skillfully and well.
2. A **gullible** person is hard to fool.
3. An **aloof** person is emotionally cool or unwilling to associate with others.
4. Something **lethal** can kill you.
5. A shy and retiring look is **withering.**
6. A **concise** explanation is **protracted.**
7. A **blatant** attempt is quiet and inconspicuous.
8. A **benign** expression is gentle and good-natured.
9. If you take the lead in doing something, you are in the **vanguard.**
10. When two people **concur,** they argue or disagree.
11. Seeing a UFO land on your street would be **eerie** and **uncanny.**
12. The **capricious** person's life is governed by routine.
13. It's illegal to **admonish** a child.
14. If you have a **penchant** for something, you have a strong liking for it.
15. A **terse** speaker is long-winded and boring.
16. When you have a **plethora** of food, you don't have enough.
17. An **ingratiating** person would use flattery to win approval.
18. An **erudite** person lacks knowledge.
19. The squeak of a mouse or the squeal of a pig is a **sonorous** noise.

20. A **reticent** person is **loquacious.**
21. **Effusive** speech or writing is restrained and **concise.**
22. Something **prodigious** is very bad or wicked.
23. A **contentious** person tends to engage in arguments or debates.
24. A **sycophantic** person is **obsequious.**
25. Something **incessant** is **continual.**

Group Two: Synonyms or Antonyms?

Decide whether the pairs of words below are synonyms—words with the same or almost the same meaning—or antonyms, words opposite in meaning.

1. **Wholesome** and **noxious** are...synonyms or antonyms?
2. **Conceive** and **concoct** are...
3. **Resolute** and **indecisive** are...
4. **Dreary** and **somber** are...
5. **Ambiguous** and **explicit** are...
6. **Prudent** and **discreet** are...
7. **Altruism** and **egoism** are...
8. **Scrutinize** and **peruse** are...
9. **Extinct** and **extant** are...
10. **Flamboyant** and **ostentatious** are...
11. **Zealous** and **ardent** are...
12. **Quandary** and **predicament** are...
13. **Naive** and **guileless** are...
14. **Fervent** and **impassive** are...
15. **Disingenuous** and **candid** are...
16. **Fleeting** and **evanescent** are...
17. **Disconcerted** and **perturbed** are...
18. **Secular** and **ecclesiastical** are...
19. **Impudent** and **insolent** are...

20. **Garrulous** and **voluble** are...
21. **Opulent** and **sumptuous** are...
22. **Paramount** and **negligible** are...
23. **Mercurial** and **volatile** are...
24. **Pragmatic** and **quixotic** are...
25. **Transient** and **ephemeral** are...

Group Three: Which Word Is NOT a Synonym?

In each statement below, a word is followed by three apparent synonyms. Two of the three words or phrases are true synonyms; one is unrelated in meaning. Which of the three synonym choices does *not* fit the word?

1. **Ambivalent** means uncertain, **indecisive,** inconsistent.
2. A **calamity** is a disaster, **controversy, catastrophe.**
3. A **gregarious** person is **amiable, affable, affluent.**
4. A **pompous** statement is **plaintive, pretentious,** puffed-up.
5. To **goad** means to order, urge, prod.
6. **Pensive** means concerned, thoughtful, **contemplative.**
7. To **acquiesce** means to agree, make do, give in.
8. **Deleterious** means **detrimental,** injurious, **incongruous.**
9. **Impeccably** means perfectly, flawlessly, fantastically.
10. Something **loathsome** is **treacherous, vile, despicable.**
11. **Surreptitious** means **furtive,** wicked, stealthy.
12. **Impetuous** means **foolhardy, reckless, histrionic.**
13. **Exemplary** means **memorable,** praiseworthy, **commendable.**
14. A **surmise** is a plan, a guess, a **conjecture.**

15. **Lugubrious** means **mournful,** gloomy, **grotesque.**
16. **Impromptu** means improvised, **spontaneous,
    unpredictable.**
17. **Unscrupulous** means **corrupt, indignant, deceitful.**
18. A **respite** is a **lull, hiatus, impasse.**
19. **Insatiable** means **vociferous, ravenous, voracious.**
20. Something **malodorous** is **fetid, penurious, putrid.**
21. **Transitory** means **ephemeral, transient, ebullient.**
22. Something **heinous** is **inexorable, abominable,
    egregious.**
23. A **phlegmatic** person is **listless, licentious, lethargic.**
24. A **magnanimous** gesture is **benevolent,
    conciliatory, altruistic.**
25. **Perfunctory** means inflexible, routine, mechanical.

Group Four: Finding the Meaning

In each question below, the test word is followed by three
words or phrases. Decide which of those three answer
choices comes nearest the meaning of the test word.

1. Is a **convivial** person excitable, **sociable,** or silly?
2. Is a **formidable** task very difficult, dull and boring,
   or **enlightening?**
3. Is something **overt** hidden, honest, or easily seen?
4. When you **infer** something, do you make a
   suggestion, come to a conclusion, or make it clear?
5. When people are **indifferent,** are they **apathetic,**
   identical, or **distinctive?**
6. Is something **forbidding** disturbing, grim and
   threatening, or very strict or severe?
7. When something is expressed in **colloquial** terms,
   is it **incomprehensible, ironic,** or informal?
8. Is something **irrelevant** not **straightforward,** not
   pertinent, or not **reputable?**

9. If something is **inherent,** is it **innate, indispensable,** or **fundamental**?
10. If you **disparage** something, does that mean you evaluate it, regret it, or belittle it?
11. Is a **fastidious** person thoughtful and patient, pushy and obnoxious, or fussy and demanding?
12. Would something **jocular** be **contemptuous, appalling,** or characterized by **levity**?
13. Does an **itinerant** person get **irate, meander,** or refuse to **comply**?
14. Would something **inscrutable** be hard to use, hard to repair, or hard to understand?
15. Does an **enervated** person feel weak, nervous, or **stimulated**?
16. Is a **belligerent** person **insistent, hostile,** or **strident**?
17. Is **cacophony** a bad habit, a harsh sound, or a pleasing similarity?
18. When you **substantiate,** do you **embellish, clarify,** or **verify**?
19. Would something **eccentric** be **anomalous, relentless,** or **abundant**?
20. Is an **idiosyncrasy** an unlikable **trait,** a peculiar **trait,** or an obvious **trait**?
21. Would something **spurious** be **ludicrous, counterfeit,** or **unwarranted**?
22. When you engage in **speculation,** do you make **allegations, arbitrary** decisions, or **assumptions**?
23. If something is **practicable,** is it doable, sensible, or **conceivable**?
24. If you are **disdainful,** are you **obstinate, haughty,** or **impertinent**?
25. Is a **cynical** person **devious, dogmatic,** or **skeptical**?

ANSWERS

Group One: True or False?

1. True	15. False
2. False	16. False
3. True	17. True
4. True	18. False
5. False	19. False
6. False	20. False
7. False	21. False
8. True	22. False
9. True	23. True
10. False	24. True
11. True	25. False—This was an intentionally
12. False	**deceptive** question; if you got it
13. False	wrong, see **continual** and
14. True	**continuous** in the glossary.

Group Two: Synonyms or Antonyms?

1. Antonyms	10. Synonyms	19. Synonyms
2. Synonyms	11. Synonyms	20. Synonyms
3. Antonyms	12. Synonyms	21. Synonyms
4. Synonyms	13. Synonyms	22. Antonyms
5. Antonyms	14. Antonyms	23. Synonyms
6. Synonyms	15. Antonyms	24. Antonyms
7. Antonyms	16. Synonyms	25. Synonyms
8. Synonyms	17. Synonyms	
9. Antonyms	18. Antonyms	

Group Three: Which Word Is NOT a Synonym?

1. inconsistent	5. order	9. fantastically
2. **controversy**	6. concerned	10. **treacherous**
3. **affluent**	7. make do	11. wicked
4. **plaintive**	8. **incongruous**	12. **histrionic**

13. **memorable**   18. **impasse**   23. **licentious**
14. plan   19. **vociferous**   24. **conciliatory**
15. **grotesque**   20. **penurious**   25. inflexible
16. **unpredictable** 21. **ebullient**
17. **indignant**   22. **inexorable**

Group Four: Finding the Meaning

1. **sociable**
2. very difficult
3. easily seen
4. come to a conclusion
5. **apathetic**
6. grim and threatening
7. informal
8. not **pertinent**
9. **innate**
10. belittle
11. fussy and demanding
12. characterized by **levity**
13. **meander**
14. hard to understand
15. weak
16. **hostile**
17. a harsh sound
18. **verify**
19. **anomalous**
20. a peculiar **trait**
21. **counterfeit**
22. **assumptions**
23. doable
24. **haughty**
25. **skeptical**

Glossary

Key to Abbreviations

adj.	adjective
adv.	adverb
cf.	compare
e.g.	for example (Latin *exempli gratia*)
esp.	especially
etc.	et cetera, and so forth
i.e.	that is, namely (Latin *id est*)
n.	noun
n.b.	nota bene (Latin for note well, take note)
pert.	pertaining
pl.	plural
sing.	singular
spec.	specifically
usu.	usually
v.	verb

Note: This glossary includes only selected definitions—those that apply to the ways in which the test words are used in this book. For additional definitions, as well as for guidance on pronunciation, consult your dictionary. The symbol ★ beside a word means that it appears frequently on the SAT and ACT. A superscript number after a cross-referenced synonym refers to the definition of that number for that word (e.g. **lofty**^{2} = definition 2 for **lofty**). The numbers in brackets refer to the pages in this book on which you will find the test words used.

A

★ **abandon,** *v.* to leave or give up (synonyms: **forsake, relinquish**). [15, 16, 71, 90, 124, 200, 202, 216]

abandon, *n.* a giving in to one's nature without concern for what others think: to dance with *abandon.* [95, 286]

abate, *v.* to reduce or become less in value, amount, or intensity: The storm *abated.* [82]

aberration, *n.* a deviation or departure from what is usual, normal, or expected. [125]

abet, *v.* to assist or encourage, esp. in wrongdoing. [109]

abhor, *v.* to regard with hatred or disgust, detest (synonym: **loathe**). **abhorrent,** *adj.* (synonym: **loathsome**) [xiii, 44, 96]

abject, *adj.* miserable, wretched. [216]

★ **abolition,** *n.* the act of doing away with or getting rid of. [57]

abominable, *adj.* causing or worthy of hatred or disgust; detestable (synonym: **heinous**). [248]

abruptly, *adv.* 1. suddenly, unexpectedly. 2. surprisingly blunt or direct in speech or manner (synonym: **brusquely**). [76, 129, 158, 174, 283]

abscond, *v.* to depart in a sudden and secret way, esp. to avoid arrest or capture. [192, 265]

abstinence, *n.* voluntarily refraining from using or doing something. [188]

abstract, *adj.* not thought of as an object or real thing or in connection with any specific example: *Honesty* and *love* are *abstract* words. 2. not dealing with or representing anything concrete or particular: *abstract* ideas; *abstract* art. [xiv, 58, 153, 197]

abstraction, *n.* something **abstract,** such as an idea, picture, or word. [169]

abstruse, *adj.* very hard to understand, deep, complicated. [159]

absurd, *adj.* ridiculous, nonsensical, unreasonable, foolish, stupid (synonyms: **farcical, ludicrous, preposterous**). [193, 196, 235]

★ **abundance,** *n.* a large amount, great supply, more than enough (synonyms: **plethora, profusion**). [xii, 89, 176]

★ **abundant,** *adj.* in great supply, present in great quantity (synonyms: **ample, plentiful**). **abundantly,** *adv.* [1]

★ **accessible,** *adj.* capable of being approached or reached; allowing access. [25, 155]

accessory, *n.* in law, a person who helps or encourages another to commit a crime but is not present when the crime is committed (*accessory* before the fact); or a person who helps or conceals a person who has committed a crime (*accessory* after the fact). [143]

accolade, *n.* 1. special acknowledgment or praise. 2. an award. [40, 198]

★ **accommodate,** *v.* 1. to hold or provide room for comfortably. 2. do a favor, kindness, or service for (synonym: **oblige**). [22, 216]

accost, *v.* to approach and speak to, often in an **aggressive** manner: *accosted* by a stranger. [62]

acquiesce, *v.* to give in or agree without protest or complaint but also without interest or excitement. [105]

acquisition, *n.* the act of obtaining, coming into possession of. [141]

acrid, *adj.* harsh, burning, or biting to the taste or smell: *acrid* chili peppers. [268]

acute, *adj.* sharp, intense (synonym: **keen**). [243]

adage, *n.* an expression of popular wisdom, an old saying, proverb (synonyms: **aphorism, axiom, maxim**). [112, 243]

adamant, *adj.* stubborn, unyielding, inflexible (synonyms: **intractable, obstinate**). [274]

★ **adept,** *adj.* very skillful, expert (synonyms: **dexterous, proficient**). **adeptly,** *adv.* (synonym: **adroitly**). [26, 180, 184, 227]

adjacent, *adj.* close, lying near but not necessarily in contact with. [8, 138, 166, 190]

admonish, *v.* to warn, caution, scold, or criticize gently, esp. against doing something wrong or bad. **admonishment,** *n.* [6, 123, 184, 203, 294]

admonition, *n.* a mild criticism or reprimand, a gentle warning: an *admonition* not to lie. [xvi, 109]

adorn, *v.* to decorate or make beautiful. [73]

adroitly, *adv.* skillfully; smoothly and efficiently (synonym: **deftly**). [8, 104, 315]

★ **advantageous,** *adj.* favorable, useful, profitable, providing a benefit or gain (synonym: **beneficial**[2]). [209, 228]

adversary, *n.* a person one fights against, enemy, opponent. [106]

adverse, *adj.* unfavorable, damaging to one's interests: *adverse* criticism. [201]

★ **advocate,** *n.* a person who speaks or writes in support of another person or of a cause or issue; defender (synonyms: **champion, proponent**). [162, 206]

advocate, *v.* to support, argue in favor of. [206]

★ **aesthetic,** *adj.* of or pert. to beauty, showing appreciation of or sensitivity to beauty in art or nature, tasteful, artistic. [21, 172]

affable, *adj.* easy to talk to, pleasant, courteous (synonyms: **congenial, cordial, gracious, jovial,** and see note at **amiable**). [174, 250]

affectation, *n.* artificial speech or action; a habit or behavior that is fake and unnatural and adopted for show or to attract attention. [96]

affected, *adj.* 1. fake, unnatural, pretended, assumed only for effect or show. 2. marked by or full of **affectation** (synonyms: **grandiose, ostentatious, pompous, pretentious**). [96, 295]

affinity, *n.* a natural attraction, close relationship, or intense liking. [185]

★ **affirm,** *v.* 1. to support, uphold the importance of, establish as **valid**. 2. to state positively, maintain as true. [xiv, 195, 266]

affirmation, *n.* a formal expression of support, **solemn** declaration of truth. [7, 132]

affix, *v.* to attach, fasten, or join. [59, 170]

affluent, *adj.* wealthy (synonym: **prosperous**). [1, 39, 52]

affront, *n.* an intentional **offense**[1] or insult. [51, 76, 88, 195]

agent, *n.* an active cause, something that produces an effect or a means by which something gets done. [xix, 200, 207, 227]

aggression, *n.* 1. the practice of attacking or assaulting, esp. to rule or control an **adversary**. 2. an attack or assault, esp. when un**provoked**. [38, 53]

★ **aggressive,** *adj.* 1. forceful, bold, strong and energetic (synonyms: **emphatic, vigorous**). 2. pushy and overly forward. 3. showing **aggression**. **aggressively,** *adv.* **aggressiveness,** *n.* [28, 62, 157]

agile, *adj.* moving quickly, gracefully, and with skillful ease; nimble. [10, 274]

agrarian, *adj.* having to do with farmers and farming; of or pert. to land and its ownership and cultivation. [204, 205]

ailment, *n.* an illness or physical disorder, esp. a mild one. [89]

alacrity, *n.* eager willingness and promptness, speed, quickness: She performed the task with *alacrity.* [216, 248, 420]

alien, *adj.* strange, foreign, extremely unusual or different in nature or character (synonym: **exotic**). [11, 64, 104]

alienated, *adj.* emotionally distant or cut off, disconnected (synonym: **estranged**). [207]

alienation, *n.* emotional isolation or disconnection, a sense of not belonging or fitting in. [209]

allegation, *n.* claim, charge, accusation without proof. [93, 111, 258]

allege, *v.* to state as true without proof. [182]

alleged, *adj.* declared or assumed to be true but not proved; supposed. **allegedly,** *adv.* [58, 130]

allegorical, *adj.* consisting of or pert. to an *allegory,* a story or play with a symbolic meaning usu. intended to teach a **moral** or lesson. [56]

★ **alleviate,** *v.* to make easier to bear, lessen the severity or intensity of (synonyms: **assuage, mitigate, mollify**). [221, 228]

alliteration, *n.* the repetition of the same letter or sound at the beginning of two or more neighboring words or stressed syllables: e.g. *And still the wind wailed and the* **incessant** *snow swirled and fell.* [84]

alluring, *adj.* highly attractive, tempting, charming (synonym: **tantalizing**). [59]

allusion, *n.* an indirect reference, by casual mention or quotation, to something generally familiar, esp. to something literary or cultural: "That's the rub," she said, making an *allusion* to Shakespeare's *Hamlet.* [95]

Usage note: Take care not to use *allusion* when you mean **reference**. In an *allusion* the source is **implied**; it is not stated directly. In a *reference* the source is identified, mentioned specifically. " 'We have miles to go before we sleep,' said John" is an *allusion* to the poem "Stopping by Woods on a Snowy Evening" by Robert Frost. "As Mark Twain observed, 'It is better to support schools than jails' " is a *reference.*

aloof, *adj.* distant or removed in manner or action, cool, reserved: She remained *aloof* during the crisis (synonyms: **detached, indifferent**). [2, 290, 301]

altercation, *n.* an angry, loud dispute; **vehement quarrel.** [44, 79, 93, 270, 293, 312]

alternative, *n.* one of two or more possible choices. [145, 182]

★ **alternative,** *adj.* 1. providing a choice between two or more things, available in place of another. 2. not like the usual, accepted, or **conventional:** *alternative* lifestyles; *alternative* newspaper. [168, 196, 200]

altruism, *n.* devotion to the needs and welfare of others rather than to oneself; unselfish concern for others (antonym: **egoism**). [126]

altruistic, *adj.* unselfishly concerned with or interested in the welfare of others. [196, 228]

alumnus, *n.* a male graduate of a school, college, or university. [153]

Usage note: A female graduate is an *alumna* (pl. *alumnae*). Male graduates collectively or male and female graduates collectively are *alumni*. Do not use *alumni* as a singular: *She's an alumni of Yale* is a **gross** error.

ambiguous, *adj.* having more than one possible meaning or **interpretation,** unclear, indefinite, uncertain, **vague.** [77, 177]

★ **ambitious,** *adj.* 1. eager to succeed or achieve something. 2. requiring great ability or effort, challenging. **ambition,** *n.* [16, 151, 197, 244, 325]

★ **ambivalent,** *adj.* uncertain, **indecisive; simultaneously** drawn in opposite directions; having conflicting feelings or desires. [21, 54, 209, 283]

ameliorate, *v.* to make better or more satisfactory, improve the state or condition of: *ameliorate* the neighborhood. **amelioration,** *n.* [54, 145, 196]

amiable, *adj.* friendly, good-natured, agreeable (synonyms: **affable, congenial, cordial, gracious, jovial**). **amiably,** *adv.* [ix, 4, 22, 102, 147, 172, 212, 420] —*Amiable* and *affable* both mean friendly and likable. *Amiable* suggests someone with a pleasant personality; *affable* suggests someone easy to approach and talk to.

amoral, *adj.* neither **moral** nor **immoral,** in any of these ways: (a) not concerned with right and wrong; (b) not knowing right from wrong, as an animal or infant; (c) existing outside the moral order or the sphere in which moral judgments apply: the human world is moral; the natural world is *amoral.* [272]

amorphous, *adj.* lacking definite form or shape; formless, shapeless. [153, 284]

ample, *adj.* 1. fully sufficient, more than enough to meet the need or purpose (synonyms: **abundant, plentiful**). 2. of considerable size, extent, amount, or capacity (synonyms: **capacious, commodious**). [xix, 108, 173]

amplify, *v.* to make larger or greater; make more **ample.** [136]

anachronistic, *adj.* misplaced in time, not in proper **chronological** place or order. An *anachronism* is something out of its proper historical place. [113]

★ **analysis,** *n.* a close examination; spec., the process of separating a whole into its parts to study or **interpret** them. **analyze,** *v.* **analyst,** *n.* [xi, xv, 26, 154, 162, 231]

★ **anecdote,** *n.* a short, entertaining, often humorous story. [151, 221, 420]

★ **animated,** *adj.* lively, active, full of spirit (synonyms: **robust, vibrant, vigorous, vivacious**). **animation,** *n.* [20, 195]

annihilate, *v.* to wipe out, destroy completely, reduce to nothing (synonyms: **eradicate, obliterate**). [18, 217]

anomalous, *adj.* deviating from what is usual, common, normal, or expected; irregular (synonyms: **eccentric, idiosyncratic**). **anomaly,** *n.* [80, 191, 284]

★ **anonymous,** *adj.* unnamed; by or from a person who is not named or is not identified. **anonymously,** *adv.* [113, 168, 285]

antebellum, *adj.* existing or belonging to the time before the Civil War (1861–1865). [11, 31, 130, 296]

anthology, *n.* a collection of selected writings. [173]

antipathy, *n.* a deep-seated dislike or distaste; hatred or ill will (synonyms: **aversion, enmity, hostility, repugnance**). [xii, 315]

antiquated, *adj.* old-fashioned, out-of-date (synonyms: see **obsolete**). [199]

antiseptic, *adj.* 1. clean and orderly, esp. in a way that lacks warmth, feeling, or interest. 2. extremely clean, spec. free from germs and micro**organisms**. [153, 299]

antisocial, *adj.* not caring to associate with other people, shunning society. [144]

apathetic, *adj.* 1. having or showing little or no interest or concern (synonyms: **indifferent, perfunctory**). 2. having or showing little or no emotion, unresponsive (synonym: **impassive,** and see **phlegmatic**). [51, 91, 219]

apex, *n.* the highest point; tip, point, or peak: the *apex* of her career (synonyms: **summit, zenith**). [154, 263]

aphorism, *n.* a briefly expressed truth, opinion, **principle,** or rule of conduct (synonyms: **adage, axiom, maxim**). [145]

appalling, *adj.* causing dismay, horror, or disgust; frightful (synonyms: **distasteful, loathsome, odious, offensive, repugnant, repulsive**). [215, 256]

applicable, *adj.* able to be applied, appropriate, suitable (synonyms: **pertinent, relevant**). [xiv]

apprehension, *n.* fear or worry of what may happen (synonyms: **dread, trepidation**). [185]

★ **apprehensive,** *adj.* fearful, anxious about something in the future (synonym: **timorous**). [186, 240, 275]

apprentice, *n.* a learner, beginner; esp. a person learning a trade or profession from an expert or master (synonyms: **neophyte, novice**). [200]

apt, *adj.* to the point, suitable: an *apt* proposal. Also, having a natural tendency, likely: *apt* to agree. [164]

arbiter, *n.* a person who settles disputes; umpire; judge. [188]

arbitrary, *adj.* based only on one's own will or feelings, not based on reason or law: an *arbitrary* decision. [x, 130, 306, 314]

arcane, *adj.* understood or known only by a few, mysterious (synonym: **esoteric**). [58, 254]

archaeological, *adj.* pert. to the science of archaeology, the recovery and study of **material** evidence of ancient human life and culture. [204]

archaic, *adj.* of an earlier period, of a time long past, old-fashioned, no longer in ordinary use: Words such as *methinks* and *forsooth* are *archaic* (synonyms: see **obsolete**). [77, 110, 167, 271, 278, 319]

ardent, *adj.* 1. burning, fiery, glowing, shining (synonyms: **fervid, torrid**). 2. filled with enthusiasm and eagerness: an *ardent* supporter (synonyms: **avid, fervent, zealous**). [12, 109, 162, 274]

★ **arid,** *adj.* extremely dry or dull. [169]

★ **aristocracy,** *n.* a ruling class, esp. a hereditary one; a group considered superior to others. [207]

★ **aristocratic,** *adj.* belonging to or characteristic of the **aristocracy**. [2, 96]

aromatic, *adj.* having a pleasant smell, fragrant. [22, 117]

★ **arouse,** *v.* to awaken, stir into action or motion, excite (synonyms: **rouse, stimulate**) [87]

★ **arrogant,** *adj.* acting superior or self-important, **aggressively** proud, making false claims to greatness (synonyms: **haughty, pretentious, supercilious**). **arrogance,** *n.* [45, 47, 73, 105, 157, 250, 263]

artful, *adj.* showing art or skill, skillful, expert; also, skillful in a crafty, cunning way. [250]

articulated, *adj.* expressed, esp. in a clear or forceful manner. [154]

★ **artifact,** *n.* an object produced by human work or art, esp. something of historical or **archaeological** interest. [140, 143]

artisan, *n.* a worker trained or skilled in some trade, craftsperson. [205]

ascend, *v.* to go or move up, climb or rise. [24, 152]

ascertain, *v.* to find out, make certain of. [xiv, 189, 266]

★ **aspiration,** *n.* a strong wish or desire, esp. to attain a goal or to achieve something (synonym: **ambition**). [5, 17, 121, 141, 187, 244]

aspire, *v.* to strive to attain a goal, to eagerly desire to achieve something. **aspiring,** *adj.* [xii, 121, 126, 256, 257, 313]

assailant, *n.* an attacker. [171]

assent, *n.* agreement, acceptance, consent. [38]

★ **assert,** *v.* to state confidently or declare firmly. ★ **assertion,** *n.* [xiii, 1, 65, 88, 93, 103, 122, 176, 183, 206, 261, 292]

assess, *v.* to determine the value, importance, or extent of; to evaluate, estimate, weigh. **assessment,** *n.* [xiii, 72, 93, 260, 261, 280]

★ **assiduous,** *adj.* showing careful, constant attention (synonyms: **diligent, industrious, sedulous**). [xi, 150, 161]

assuage, *v.* to make less severe or intense (synonyms: **alleviate, mitigate, mollify**). [260]

★ **assumption,** *n.* something taken for granted or supposed to be true without proof. [133, 176, 192, 197, 227]

astounded, *adj.* greatly astonished or amazed (synonyms: see **flabbergasted**). [242]

astute, *adj.* very smart, intelligent, clever, cunning (synonyms: **keen, penetrating, perceptive, perspicacious, sagacious, shrewd**). **astutely,** *adv.* [xvii, 22, 188]

asylum, *n.* an **institution**[2] devoted to caring for people with mental or physical disabilities. [167]

atone, *v.* to make amends, pay for something one has done wrong. [179]

atrocity, *n.* something extremely evil, wicked, or bad. [257]

attire, *n.* clothes, dress, apparel, esp. if fancy or **elaborate. attired,** *adj.* [70, 94, 187]

attribute, *n.* a quality or characteristic (synonym: **trait**). [64]

★ **attribute,** *v.* to put forward as the source, origin, or author of; assign, ascribe. [72]

atypical, *adj.* unusual, out of the ordinary, not regular or typical. [190, 274]

audacious, *adj.* daring, bold, adventurous. [183, 253, 282]

audible, *adj.* able to be heard. **audibly,** *adv.* [4, 18, 57, 137, 272]

augmented, *adj.* made greater in size, number, or amount. [280]

august, *adj.* inspiring awe and admiration, magnificent; also, inspiring respect and **reverence** because of age, rank, or popularity (synonyms: **majestic, stately**). [256]

auspicious, *adj.* showing signs of future success, indicating a happy or fortunate outcome, favorable. [71, 152]

austere, *adj.* severely simple and plain, without ornament or luxury (synonym: **spartan**). [153]

authenticity, *n.* the condition or quality of being genuine or true. [142, 192]

authoritative, *adj.* commanding, giving orders, showing authority. [79, 278]

automaton, *n.* a robot, or a person who acts in a mechanical, robotic way. [36]

autonomous, *adj.* independent, self-directed. [84, 230]

autonomy, *n.* independence, self-reliance, self-government. [204]

avant-garde, *adj.* experimental, new and different (synonyms: **innovative, unorthodox**). [21]

avaricious, *adj.* greedy for wealth or possessions, miserly, **mercenary. avarice,** *n.* [84, 131, 224, 313]

★ **aversion,** *n.* an intense, extreme dislike or disgust (synonyms: **antipathy, repugnance**). [163, 313]

avert, *v.* 1. to prevent, ward off: *avert* a disaster. 2. to turn away: *avert* one's eyes. [228, 270]

avid, *adj.* enthusiastic, having a **keen** interest in or intense desire for something (synonyms: **ardent, fervent, zealous**). **avidly,** *adv.* [87, 120]

awry, *adj.* off course, in the wrong or an unintended direction, amiss. [153]

axiom, *n.* a self-evident and accepted truth, **principle,** or rule (synonyms: **adage, aphorism, maxim**). [xviii, 208]

axiomatic, *adj.* self-evident, plain; obvious and **inevitable.** [245]

B

baffle, *v.* to confuse, puzzle, frustrate by presenting obstacles or difficulties (synonym: **thwart**). **baffled,** *adj.* [55, 139]

ban, *v.* to prohibit, esp. by law or official decree. [130, 131, 213, 314]

banish, *v.* to send into exile, expel, send or drive away. [33]

banter, *v.* to speak to in a witty, teasing, and playful manner. **banter,** *n.* good-humored, playful teasing or joking conversation (synonym: **repartee**). [230, 319]

bard, *n.* a poet, esp. Shakespeare (called the *bard* of Avon). [290]

barrage, *n.* a rapid and overwhelming outpouring: a *barrage* of questions. [93]

★ **barren,** *adj.* bare, without vegetation, unproductive, not **fruitful,** desolate. [1]

bask, *v.* to lie in or be exposed to a pleasant warmth; to take pleasure in, **derive** satisfaction or enjoyment from. [40, 87, 194]

belligerent, *adj.* ready and eager to fight, **quarrel,** or make war (synonyms: **contentious, hostile**). [18]

bemused, *adj.* 1. lost in thought (synonyms: **engrossed, immersed, preoccupied**). 2. puzzled, confused (synonyms: **bewildered, perplexed**). [2]

benefactor, *n.* 1. one who confers a benefit, a kindly helper. 2. one who gives a gift, esp. of money. [67, 126, 153, 245]

beneficent, *adj.* marked by good will and charity, serving a kind and worthy purpose. [214, 232]

★ **beneficial,** *adj.* 1. contributing to health and well-being (synonyms: see **wholesome**). 2. providing a benefit, having a favorable or useful result (synonym: **advantageous**). [xvi, 17, 54, 208, 209, 228]

benevolence, *n.* a desire or **inclination** to do good, kindliness. [111]

★ **benevolent,** *adj.* showing good will, marked by a desire to do good, kind, charitable. [21, 73, 175, 188, 204, 276, 319]

benighted, *adj.* in a state of mental or **moral** ignorance. [219, 325]

benign, *adj.* kind, good-natured, arising from or indicative of goodness or happiness, not **malevolent** or **malicious**. [156, 177, 204]

bereft, *adj.* 1. **deprived** of or lacking something needed, wanted, or expected. 2. **deprived** of a loved one, bereaved. [68, 240]

beseech, *v.* to beg, plead with, request earnestly, implore. [9]

bewilder, *v.* to confuse, puzzle, perplex, befuddle, disorient, discombobulate. **bewildered** *adj.* (synonyms: **bemused**[2], **perplexed**). **bewilderment,** *n.* [54, 69, 107, 213, 218, 235, 273]

★ **bizarre,** *adj.* extremely unusual in style or manner (synonym: **outlandish**). [11, 17, 136, 166, 270]

bland, *adj.* 1. lacking flavor or interest, dull (synonym: **insipid**). 2. smooth and pleasant in manner, esp. while showing no personal interest or concern. **blandly,** *adv.* [216, 256]

blasphemous, *adj.* pert. to language that shows disrespect or **contempt** for what is sacred (synonym: **profane**). [213]

blatant, *adj.* totally obvious or **conspicuous**, esp. standing out in an unpleasant or offensive way. **blatantly,** *adv.* (synonym: **patently**). [230, 278]
Usage note: Blatant and *flagrant* both refer to the extremely obvious, esp. when it's **offensive**. With *blatant* there is no attempt to disguise or conceal the obvious; something *blatant* stands out in a glaring or **repugnant** way: *blatant* lies. *Flagrant* implies serious wrongdoing. Something *flagrant* stands out in a shocking way; it is **deplorable,** worthy of outrage: a *flagrant* **breach**[2] of trust. Avoid the phrase *blatantly obvious,* which is redundant.

blithe, *adj.* carefree, lighthearted. [320]

blunder, *n.* a stupid, careless, or ignorant mistake. [244]

blunder, *v.* 1. to move in a clumsy, blind, or confused way. 2. to make a stupid, careless, or ignorant mistake. [66]

boisterous, *adj.* noisy and wild, lacking restraint (synonyms: see **vociferous**). [11, 146, 265, 286]

bombastic, *adj.* using or pert. to speech or writing that sounds grand or impressive but has little meaning or substance (synonym: **grandiloquent**). [169]

bona fide, *adj.* genuine, authentic, not fake. [88, 143]

boor, *n.* a crude, coarse, clumsy, insensitive person; one who lacks **refinement**[2]. [253]

boorish, *adj.* like a **boor**; coarse, clumsy, and rude in speech and behavior (synonyms: **unrefined, vulgar**). [53, 92]

boundless, *adj.* without limits or boundaries (synonyms: **infinite, vast**). [230]

brandish, *v.* to wave, display, or shake, esp. in a threatening manner: *brandish* a fist. [245]

brawny, *adj.* strong and muscular (synonym: **burly**). [264]

breach, *n.* 1. a tear, rupture, opening, gap. 2. a violation or infraction, as of a rule, a legal obligation, or a promise. [10, 264]

breadth, *n.* width, the measure of something from side to side; **figuratively,** range, scope, **comprehensiveness.** [121]

brood, *v.* to think about long and anxiously, dwell on a subject, meditate intensely (synonym: **fret**). **brooding,** *adj.* [86, 145, 171]

brusque, *adj.* surprisingly blunt and direct in speech, often in a rude way. **brusquely,** *adv.* (synonym: **abruptly**). **brusqueness,** *n.* [29, 76, 103, 170]

buffoon, *n.* a silly, bumbling fool; a clown or jester. **buffoonery,** *n.* clowning or joking around; silly, foolish behavior. [38, 71, 166, 277]

bulk, *n.* a large, heavy **mass** or body. **bulky,** *adj.* large and heavy; also, unwieldy (synonyms: **cumbersome, massive**[1], **ponderous**[1]). [158, 247, 324]

buoyant, *adj.* cheerful, lighthearted, upbeat. [188]

burly, *adj.* big, heavy, and muscular; husky (synonym: **brawny**). [29, 171]

burnished, *adj.* polished; having a smooth, glossy finish. [2, 296]

bursar, *n.* a treasurer, esp. at a college or university. [147, 270]

bust, *n.* a sculpture of a person's head, shoulders, and usu. part of the chest. [171]

C

cacophony, *n.* a harsh or unpleasant blending of sounds. [135, 214]

cajole, *v.* to persuade (a **reluctant** or unresponsive person) with gentle and repeated urging, flattery, or teasing. **cajolery,** *n.* the act or an instance of cajoling. **cajoling,** *adj.* [161, 184]

calamity, *n.* any great misfortune or cause of misery; a terrible disaster (see **catastrophe**). [41, 178, 228]

candid, *adj.* open and direct (synonyms: **forthcoming**[1], **frank, sincere, straightforward**). [79, 159]

cantankerous, *adj.* quick to dispute or **quarrel,** argumentative. [26, 138]

capacious, *adj.* able to contain a large quantity, roomy, large (synonyms: **ample, commodious**). [24, 108, 133, 272, 296]

capitalism, *n.* an economic system characterized by private investment and private or corporate control of business and industry, in which production, distribution, wages, and prices are determined chiefly by free-market competition. [218]

capricious, *adj.* changing suddenly for no apparent reason, inconstant (synonyms: **erratic, fickle, unpredictable, volatile, wayward**). **capriciously,** *adv.* **capriciousness,** *n.* [26, 86, 112, 150, 223]

captivate, *v.* to attract, fascinate, charm, capture the attention of (synonym: **enthrall**). **captivating,** *adj.* (synonym: **enticing**). [9, 48, 216]

carouse, *v.* to drink and celebrate in a **boisterous** fashion, engage in drunken revelry. [190, 299]

cataclysmic, *adj.* causing great upheaval, violent destruction, or **fundamental** change. [202]

catalyst, *n.* that which causes or speeds up an important change, esp. without being affected by or involved in the result. [209]

★ **catastrophe,** *n.* a great misfortune, terrible disaster, or complete failure. [161, 285, 298]

—A *catastrophe* and a *calamity* are both disasters. *Catastrophe* puts the emphasis on the tragedy of the event; *calamity* puts the emphasis on the toll of the event, on the grief, suffering, and misery it causes.

categorical, *adj.* absolute, without any question or condition: The company issued a *categorical* denial of all the charges against it. [122]

cease, *v.* to stop, come to an end (synonym: **desist**). [82, 133, 143, 156, 214, 261, 271]

celebrated, *adj.* famous, widely known and praised (synonyms: see **distinguished**). [15, 119, 285]

celestial, *adj.* heavenly, lovely, sublime (**literally,** pert. to the sky or the heavens). [244]

censuring, *adj.* strongly disapproving, criticizing, or finding fault with. [233]

certainty, *n.* the state of knowing or being sure of something beyond any doubt (synonym: **conviction;** cf. **uncertainty**). [63]

chagrin, *n.* embarrassment or annoyance resulting from failure, humiliation, or disappointment. **chagrined,** *adj.* [228, 242, 262]

champion, *n.* a defender or supporter (synonyms: **advocate, proponent**). [xxi, 12]

★ **chaos,** *n.* an unformed state or condition. [15, 58]

chaotic, *adj.* completely disordered and confused. [265, 266, 300]

chasm, *n.* a pronounced gap, division, or separation. [207]

chastise, *v.* to criticize or scold harshly. **chastisement,** *n.* [232, 275]

★ **cherish,** *v.* to hold and treat as dear, shelter fondly in the mind (synonym: **nurture**). **cherished,** *adj.* held dear, fondly regarded, beloved. [132, 188]

chic, *adj.* stylish, fashionable (synonyms: **sophisticated, suave, urbane**). [68]

chicanery, *n.* clever, cunning trickery (synonyms: **deception, hoax, ruse, subterfuge**). [31, 220]

chide, *v.* to scold gently or criticize mildly, usu. in a helpful or constructive way. [6, 40, 117]

chronic, *adj.* lasting for a long time, continuing, not going away (cf. **confirmed,** *adj.*). [209]

★ **chronological,** *adj.* pert. to or arranged in the order of time. [125, 229, 312]

circumscribe, *v.* to narrowly confine, as if by drawing a circle around, limit, restrict. [151]

circumscribed, *adj.* narrowly limited, restricted, confined. [195]

circumspect, *adj.* cautious, careful, considering all conditions before acting (synonyms: **discreet, prudent, tactful, vigilant, wary**). **circumspection,** *n.* [145, 285]

★ **cite,** *v.* to quote, esp. as an authority, example, or proof. [22, 176]

civic, *adj.* pert. to a citizen, citizenship, or a city. [141, 142]

clairvoyant, *adj.* able to see beyond the physical and the present; possessing
   extrasensory **perception.** [61, 200]

clamor, *n.* loud, continued noise (synonyms: **din, uproar**). [145]

clamorous, *adj.* marked by loud, continued noise (synonyms: see **vociferous**).
   [212, 291]

clan, *n.* an extended family, group of people descended from a common
   ancestor. [204]

clandestine, *adj.* done in secret, kept hidden, esp. to conceal something that
   is illegal or **immoral** (synonyms: **covert, devious, furtive, surreptitious**).
   [36, 71, 106, 308]

★ **clarify,** *v.* to make clear or easier to understand (synonyms: **elucidate,
   illuminate**). **clarification,** *n.* [xiv, 67, 73, 102, 176, 238, 281]

classified, *adj.* secret, confidential, restricted to authorized people. [244]

classify, *v.* to arrange or sort by class or kind. [80]

cliché, *n.* an overused expression that has become stale and has almost lost its
   meaning: "Smart as a whip" is a *cliché.* [80, 143]

climactic, *adj.* being or pert. to a climax, the **decisive**[1] moment or point of
   greatest dramatic intensity in a work of art. [56]

cloying, *adj.* excessive to the point of being **distasteful** or disgusting (cf.
   surfeited). [294]

coax, *v.* to try to persuade or influence by gentle urging, pleading, or
   flattery. [161, 251]

coercion, *n.* forcing or driving another by pressure, threats, intimidation, or
   violence. [161]

cogent, *adj.* believable, persuasive, convincing, strongly appealing to the
   mind. [xii, 193]

cognizant, *adj.* aware, conscious. [276]

★ **coherent,** *adj.* expressed or constructed in an orderly, consistent, logical
   manner. [64]

collaborator, *n.* a partner in work, esp. **intellectual** or creative work.
   [100, 263]

colleague, *n.* a fellow worker, associate, fellow member of a profession.
   [152, 263, 285]

★ **collective,** *adj.* pert. to or done by a number of persons acting as a group.
   [58, 131, 321]

colloquial, *adj.* characteristic of or suitable to ordinary, everyday speech or to
   writing that tries to imitate speech; conversational, informal. [32, 166]

collusion, *n.* secret cooperation between persons for an illegal or wrongful
   purpose. [224]

★ **colonial,** *adj.* of or pert. to the historical period of the thirteen British colonies
   (settlements) that in 1776 became the thirteen original states of the
   United States. [153]

colossal, *adj.* very great in size or extent, gigantic, enormous (synonyms:
   gargantuan, immense, massive[2], **monumental**[1], **prodigious**[2]). [49, 256]

combustion, *n.* the act or process of burning. [83, 199]

commence, *v.* to begin, start. [221, 286]

commend, *v.* to praise, mention as worthy of approval or favorable attention. [99]

commendable, *adj.* praiseworthy, admirable, worthy of approval: Building your vocabulary is a *commendable* **endeavor** (synonym: **exemplary**). [167]

★ **commentary,** *n.* an expression of opinion, series of observations or remarks (cf. **interpretation**). [131]

commerce, *n.* the buying and selling of goods, esp. on a large scale; the interchange of **commodities**; trade. [206]

commodious, *adj.* having plenty of room, spacious (synonyms: **ample, capacious**). [62, 140, 173]

★ **commodity,** *n.* 1. an economic product, something bought and sold, article of **commerce**. 2. something useful or valuable: Time is a precious *commodity.* [129, 199, 231]

★ **commonplace,** *adj.* ordinary, dull, unremarkable (synonyms: **hackneyed, mundane, pedestrian**). [89, 164, 173, 274]

★ **communal,** *adj.* shared or done in common; of or relating to a community; public. [20, 133, 216]

★ **compel,** *v.* to force, drive, urge, exert pressure on, bring about by force. [92, 102, 169, 242]

compelling, *adj.* forceful, commanding attention, having a powerful effect. [129]

compensate, *v.* to pay or make up for; reimburse. [19]

competent, *adj.* sufficiently skilled, qualified, or knowledgeable; able, capable. [140, 226]

complacency, *n.* self-satisfaction or contentment, esp. accompanied by a lack of awareness or concern in the face of trouble, problems, or danger. [84]

★ **complacent,** *adj.* uncritically pleased with oneself or one's circumstances, esp. in a narrow-minded or annoying way; self-satisfied (synonym: **smug**). **complacently,** *adv.* [38, 73, 259, 295]

★ **complement,** *v.* to combine with so as to complete, make whole, or bring to perfection. [2, 94, 194]

★ **complex,** *adj.* not simple, complicated, involved, hard to understand (synonyms: **convoluted, intricate**). **complexity,** *n.* [37, 75, 142, 159, 176, 194, 205, 266, 282]

compliance, *n.* the act of **complying**, giving in or going along; obeying, yielding, conforming, or **acquiescing**. [192]

comply, *v.* to give in, yield, obey; to submit to another's request, wish, rule, or command. [106, 118, 293]

★ **comprehend,** *v.* to understand, grasp, see the meaning or nature of (synonym: **perceive**; cf. **detect, discern**). [xiv, 31, 130, 131, 169, 210, 215, 228, 299]

comprehensible, *adj.* understandable, able to be **comprehended**. [104]

★ **comprehensive,** *adj.* including or covering much, of large scope, inclusive. [121]

concave, *adj.* curving in, hollowed inward like the inside of a bowl. [55]

concede, *v.* to acknowledge, often in a grudging or **reluctant** way, that something is true, reasonable, or proper. [15, 196]

conceited, *adj.* having an overly high opinion of oneself (synonyms: **egotistical, vain**[1]). [44, 155]

conceivable, *adj.* imaginable; capable of being **conceived**. [92, 220, 226]

★ **conceive**, *v.* to imagine, think up, form in the mind, develop as a **concept** (synonyms: see **fabricate**). [163, 217, 272]

★ **concept**, *n.* a general idea, broad mental image (synonym: **notion**). [37, 88, 123, 141, 195, 196, 198, 199, 224, 228, 265]

conciliatory, *adj.* trying to overcome distrust and regain friendship and goodwill. [20]

★ **concise**, *adj.* short and to the point, brief and clear (synonyms: **succinct**, **terse**). [xiv, 176]

conclusive, *adj.* 1. being an ending or conclusion. 2. serving to settle a question and putting an end to doubt or debate (cf. **crucial**, **decisive**[1]). [209]

concoct, *v.* 1. to invent, think or make up: *concoct* a plan (synonyms: see **fabricate**). 2. to cook up, prepare from ingredients. [126, 248]

concomitant, *adj.* existing with or alongside, accompanying, attendant. [228]

concur, *v.* to agree. [111, 137]

condemn, *v.* to judge or pronounce as bad, wrong, or evil; express strong disapproval of. [31]

condescend, *v.* to lower oneself in rank or standing to the level of another. [101]

★ **condescending**, *adj.* behaving in a proud, snobbish way and treating others as if they are inferior (synonyms: **haughty**, **disdainful**). [44, 132, 235, 293, 296]

confidentiality, *n.* secrecy, privacy. [38]

★ **confine**, *v.* to restrict, limit, hold within bounds. [119]

confines, *n.* the limits or borders of a space or area. [112, 281, 299]

★ **confirm**, *v.* to establish as true or certain, make firm or binding, strengthen, support (synonyms: **corroborate**, **substantiate**, **verify**). [54, 71, 183, 311]

confirmed, *adj.* firmly established or settled, fixed and unlikely to change (cf. **chronic**). [220]

confrontation, *n.* a face-to-face meeting, esp. one that is **hostile** or **defiant**; a conflict, clash. **confrontational**, *adj.* [62, 123, 165]

congenial, *adj.* pleasant, friendly, sociable (synonyms: **affable**, **cordial**, **gracious**, **jovial**, and see note at **amiable**). [30]

congregate, *v.* to gather, assemble, come together in a group or crowd. [74]

conjecture, *n.* an opinion or conclusion based on insufficient evidence, a guess (synonyms: **speculation**, **surmise**, and see **surmise**, *v.*). [xv, 66]

connoisseur, *n.* an expert, esp. a person with special training in a field or an informed taste for something. [180, 258]

conscientious, *adj.* 1. guided by conscience, following an inner urge to prefer right over wrong and good over evil (synonyms: **ethical**, **scrupulous**[1], **upright**, **virtuous**). 2. showing thought and care: *conscientious* work (synonyms: **fastidious**, **meticulous**, **painstaking**). **conscientiously**, *adv.* [xi, 188, 284]

★ **consequence**, *n.* a logical or natural result, outcome, or effect. [46, 113, 125, 145, 207, 228, 312, 322]

conservation, *n.* the act of protecting from loss or harm, preservation. [196]

consolation, *n.* something that comforts or gives **solace.** [187]

conspicuous, *adj.* easy to see, obvious, noticeable (synonyms: **prominent**^{2}, **salient**). **conspicuously,** *adv.* [11, 68, 80, 87, 97, 102, 112]

conspiracy, *n.* a secret plot to commit an evil or illegal act. [138, 224]

conspiratorial, *adj.* pert. to or characteristic of a **conspiracy** or of the persons involved in it. [8, 102]

conspire, *v.* to work together toward a common goal, act in harmony. (n.b. This is the less common meaning; the usual meaning is to join in a secret agreement to do something wrong or illegal.) [203]

consternation, *n.* utter confusion, shock, amazement, or dismay that **renders** one helpless or unable to act (synonym: **trepidation**). [168, 316]

constitute, *v.* to make up, form, compose. [xii, 75, 205, 272]

constraint, *n.* a restriction or limitation. [187]

consummate, *adj.* of the highest degree, utmost. [26]

★ **contemplate,** *v.* to think seriously about, consider carefully, reflect or meditate on (synonyms: **ponder, ruminate**). [ix, 18, 23, 25, 29, 77, 80, 93, 98, 199, 261]

contemplation, *n.* serious thought, **meditation, reflection.** [276]

contemplative, *adj.* thoughtful, devoted to **reflection** or **meditation** (synonym: **pensive**). [227, 321]

★ **contemporary,** *adj.* current, modern, of the present time. [11, 21, 68, 89, 99, 136, 161, 166, 219, 277, 320]

★ **contempt,** *n.* the feeling that someone or something is low, undesirable, or disgusting; a display of this feeling (synonyms: **disdain, scorn**). [163, 239, 313]

★ **contemptuous,** *adj.* full of **contempt,** thinking of or treating as inferior or worthless (synonyms: **disdainful, supercilious**). **contemptuously,** *adv.* [44, 104, 138, 308]

contend, *v.* to compete, struggle, strive in opposition. [270]

contentious, *adj.* tending to dispute, strive against, or **quarrel** (synonyms: **belligerent, hostile**). [275]

★ **context,** *n.* 1. the part of something written or spoken that comes before or after a word or passage and affects or casts light upon its meaning; surrounding material. 2. setting, situation, environment. [xiv, xv, xvi, 11, 44, 130, 131]

continual, *adj.* happening frequently or at regular intervals, repeated often; **recurring,** intermittent (see **continuous**). **continually,** *adv.* [96, 151, 189, 201, 204, 250, 282]

continuous, *adj.* happening without interruption (synonyms: **incessant, unremitting**). **continuously,** *adv.* [82, 156, 282]

—*Usage note:* Take care to distinguish between *continuous* and *continual,* for they are properly *not* synonyms. Something *continuous* is unbroken; it goes on without any pauses or interruptions, like the flow of a river: *continuous* noise. Something *continual* happens again and again; it occurs repeatedly and frequently, like the tapping of a woodpecker on a tree: a *continual* desire to smoke.

contrite, *adj.* filled with regret, sorrow, or guilt (synonyms: **penitent, remorseful**). [19, 109, 320]

contrive, *v.* to plan or manage cleverly, invent with ingenuity (synonyms: see **fabricate**). [168]

★ **controversial,** *adj.* characterized by or **arousing controversy**. [130, 314]

★ **controversy,** *n.* a heated public dispute or difference of opinion. [130]

conundrum, *n.* a riddle whose answer involves a play on words; also, any difficult and **perplexing** problem. [304, 305, 306, 309, 315]

★ **convention,** *n.* custom; a practice or rule of conduct established by long usage. [31, 265]

★ **conventional,** *adj.* established by widely accepted custom or practice, according to generally accepted standards and rules (synonym: **traditional**) [2, 39, 195, 198]

★ **convey,** *v.* to transport, take or carry from one place to another. [77, 217]

★ **conviction,** *n.* a strong or firm belief (synonym: **certainty**). [99, 183, 208]

convivial, *adj.* festive, merry; pert. to or fond of eating, drinking, and good company (synonyms: **gregarious, sociable**). [169]

convoluted, *adj.* complicated, very involved, hard to **unravel** (synonyms: **complex, intricate**). [141, 154]

coquette, *n.* a woman who flirts with and teases men only to gain their attention and admiration, without having any **sincere** affection for them. [17]

cordial, *adj.* warm, friendly, and courteous: a *cordial* reception (synonyms: **affable, congenial, gracious, jovial**, and see note at **amiable**). [214]

corpulent, *adj.* having a large, **bulky** body; fat, stout, portly, obese. [135]

corrective, *adj.* serving to correct or set right. [109]

corroborate, *v.* to support with more evidence, make more certain or believable, provide further proof (synonyms: **confirm, substantiate, verify**). [164, 292]

★ **corrupt,** *v.* to make dishonest, evil, wicked, or impure (synonyms: **debase, undermine, vitiate**). **corrupt,** *adj.* (synonym: **unethical**). [54, 184, 245]

counsel, *n.* advice, guidance, instruction. [99]

countenance, *n.* the appearance or expression of the face, visage. [2, 108, 174, 276]

counter, *v.* to offer in response, meet or return, oppose. [99, 183]

counterfeit, *adj.* not real or genuine, fake, made in imitation to **deceive** (synonyms: **fraudulent, spurious**). [291]

covert, *adj.* secret, concealed, hidden, sheltered; not done in an open, visible manner; not **overt** (synonyms: **clandestine, devious, furtive, surreptitious**). [245]

covet, *v.* to desire greatly and usu. excessively and wrongfully. [123, 152]

coveted, *adj.* greatly desired, esp. possessing so much value as to inspire greed or envy. [23]

cower, *v.* to crouch, cringe, or shrink away, as in fear or dismay. [234]

crass, *adj.* crude, coarse, showing an utter lack of sensitivity and **refinement**[2]. [167]

credible, *adj.* believable, **trustworthy,** reliable: a *credible* witness. **credibility,** *n.* [78, 164, 176, 210]

credulous, *adj.* overly willing or eager to believe or trust (synonym: **gullible**). [2]

creed, *n.* a belief or system of belief (synonym: **doctrine**). [155]

crevice, *n.* a crack, split, narrow opening. [104]

★ **critic,** *n.* 1. a person, esp. one with expert knowledge, who judges or evaluates the strengths and weaknesses of something. 2. a person who finds fault or makes harsh judgments. [153, 168]

★ **crucial,** *adj.* of great importance, essential to resolving an issue or crisis (cf. **conclusive, decisive**[1]). [158, 176]

cryptic, *adj.* mysterious, having a hidden meaning, **baffling** (synonyms: **enigmatic, inscrutable, perplexing**). **cryptically,** *adv.* [56, 57, 86, 159, 191, 305]

crystallize, *v.* to give or take on definite or precise form. [245]

culpable, *adj.* deserving blame, guilty. **culpability,** *n.* [73, 139, 140]

culprit, *n.* a person guilty of or charged with a crime. [308]

cultivate, *v.* to promote the growth or development of, improve by care and training, foster (synonym: **nurture**). [21, 152, 175, 204, 313]

cultivated, *adj.* marked by skill and taste, refined by study and training. [165]

cumbersome, *adj.* 1. heavy and difficult to handle, burdensome, unwieldy (synonyms: **bulky, massive**[1], **ponderous**[1]). 2. causing trouble or difficulty, clumsy, awkward. [35, 74, 205]

★ **curator,** *n.* a manager or overseer, esp. a person in charge of a collection or an **institution**[2] (e.g. a museum or library). [140, 141]

★ **cursory,** *adj.* done quickly with little attention to detail (synonyms: **perfunctory, superficial**). [140]

curtail, *v.* to cut short, reduce, restrict. [92]

customary, *adj.* usual, normal, commonly occurring or practiced. [120, 139, 190, 205, 217]

★ **cynical,** *adj.* 1. expressing disbelief in or distrust of others out of a sense that everyone's **motives** and actions are selfish. 2. pert. to the philosophy of the ancient Greek Cynics, who believed that virtue is the only good, that the essence of virtue is self-control, and that pleasure is an evil if sought for its own sake. [290, 314]

D

daunting, *adj.* discouraging, disheartening, intimidating. [116]

★ **dazzle,** *v.* to amaze, impress deeply, or overwhelm, esp. with brilliance. **dazzling,** *adj.* [26, 199, 227]

debacle, *n.* a total failure or defeat. [275]

debase, *v.* to make lower in value, quality, character, or dignity (synonyms: **corrupt, undermine, vitiate**). [47]

debilitate, *v.* to make weak, make **feeble, deprive** of strength or energy (synonym: **enervate**). **debilitating,** *adj.* [151]

debunk, *v.* to expose as false, exaggerated, or **counterfeit.** [151]

debut, *n.* a first formal appearance or performance. [38]

decadent, *adj.* showing **moral** decline or decay (synonym: **self-indulgent**). [118]

★ **deceit,** *n.* the act of lying, tricking, or misleading (synonym: **duplicity**). [185, 202]

★ **deceitful,** *adj.* dishonest, given to lying and trickery (synonyms: **deceptive, disingenuous, fallacious**). **deceitfulness,** *n.* [45, 111, 159, 245, 307]

★ **deceive,** *v.* to lie, trick, intentionally mislead (synonym: **dupe**). [108, 163, 207, 258]

★ **deception,** *n.* something that **deceives,** a lie or trick (synonyms: **chicanery, hoax, ruse, subterfuge**). [165]

deceptive, *adj.* 1. misleading, intended to **deceive** (synonyms: **deceitful, disingenuous, fallacious**). 2. misleading to the senses, having a false appearance of. **deceptively,** *adv.* [26, 124, 159, 309]

decidedly, *adv.* without doubt, definitely. [76, 170]

decipher, *v.* to figure out the meaning of (something hard to understand); change from code into ordinary language. [58, 61, 159, 306]

decisive, *adj.* 1. settling an issue or question (cf. **conclusive, crucial**). 2. showing firmness and determination. [105, 185]

decorum, *n.* formal, proper, or suitable behavior, dress, speech, etc.; conduct suitable to a situation. [240]

deduction, *n.* a conclusion reached by reasoning or by **inferring.** [99]

deed, *n.* an act, something done. [185, 305]

deem, *v.* to think of as, consider, regard. [141]

defer, *v.* to show **deference,** give in to the wishes or opinion of another out of respect. [146]

deference, *n.* showing courteous respect by yielding to the will, wishes, or judgment of another, esp. one considered superior. [210]

deferential, *adj.* showing **deference,** yielding to the will or wishes of another (synonym: **humble**[3]). [242]

★ **defiance,** *n.* a bold refusal to obey or submit. [105, 286]

★ **defiant,** *adj.* boldly refusing to obey or submit. [252]

defile, *v.* to make filthy, foul, or impure (cf. **corrupt,** *v.*). [112]

deftly, *adv.* in a quick, smooth, and skillful way. [12, 26, 108, 283, 291]

degradation, *n.* a lowering in dignity or honor, disgrace, the act of **debasing.** [37, 53]

delegate, *v.* to entrust or assign to another. [226]

deleterious, *adj.* harmful in general or harmful to health (synonyms: **detrimental, noxious, pernicious**). [xv, 199]

★ **deliberate,** *adj.* unhurried, slow and steady. [288]

deliverance, *n.* freedom or rescue from trouble or danger; salvation. [169]

delusion, *n.* a false and firmly held belief or opinion; spec. in psychiatry, a false and firmly held belief that contradicts reality or reason. [258]

demeanor, *n.* behavior, conduct, bearing, manner of treating others. [2]

demise, *n.* death, end of existence. [136]

★ **depict,** *v.* to represent in a picture, drawing sculpture, etc. (synonym: **portray**). [59, 88]

★ **deplete,** *v.* to seriously decrease the supply of, use up, drain, empty. [199]

　deplorable, *adj.* 1. worthy of strong disapproval or **contempt**. 2. miserable, wretched, extremely bad. [12, 207]

★ **deprive,** *v.* to take away or refuse to give. **deprived,** *adj.* without, at a loss for. [213, 279]

★ **deride,** *v.* to show **contempt** for esp. by making fun of; to **taunt, mock, sneer** at. [152, 309]

★ **derision,** *n.* **contemptuous** or **sneering** laughter, **taunting, mockery.** [99]

　derivative, *adj.* originating, received, or traced from (a source). [151]

★ **derive,** *v.* to get or gain, receive or obtain from a particular source. [xii, 37, 170]

　derogatory, *adj.* insulting, esp. diminishing the character or reputation of (synonym: **disparaging**). [93]

　descent, *n.* the act of going down, movement from a higher place or level to a lower one. [106, 283]

　desist, *v.* to stop, esp. to restrain oneself from continuing (synonym: **cease**). [85, 271]

　despicable, *adj.* lowdown and worthless, deserving **scorn** and **contempt** (synonym: **vile**). [53, 92, 257, 263, 271]

　despondent, *adj.* feeling hopeless and extremely discouraged; despairing. [18, 113, 286]

　desultory, *adj.* moving or passing from one thing to another, not proceeding in an orderly or organized way, aimless, disconnected (synonyms: see **random**). [223, 231]

★ **detached,** *adj.* not emotionally involved, not influenced by personal feelings or opinions, objective (synonyms: **aloof, indifferent**). [253, 325]

★ **detect,** *v.* to discover the existence of, notice the presence of (synonym: **discern;** cf. **comprehend, perceive**). [72, 101, 177, 253]

　detection, *n.* discovery, notice, the act of **detecting**. [304]

　deter, *v.* to discourage, prevent from acting or going ahead, turn aside. [157, 162]

　detrimental, *adj.* damaging, harmful, injurious (synonyms: **deleterious, noxious, pernicious**). [209]

★ **devastate,** *v.* to destroy, lay waste, bring to ruin. [54]

　devastating, *adj.* completely overwhelming, utterly shocking or ruinous (synonym: **withering**). [29, 41]

　devious, *adj.* not honest, not **straightforward**, sly, shifty, tricky (synonyms: **clandestine, covert, furtive, surreptitious**). [36, 49, 110, 265, 282]

★ **devise,** *v.* to design, invent, form, or plan in the mind (synonyms: see **fabricate**). [ix, 54, 145]

★ **devoid,** *adj.* completely without, totally lacking. [86]

　devotee, *n.* a fan, enthusiast; an **ardent** follower, admirer, or practitioner. [112, 168]

　devout, *adj.* religious, showing devotion to religious practice (synonym: **pious**). [188]

dexterous, *adj.* skillful with the hands or body (synonyms: **adept, proficient**). **dexterity,** *n.* [226, 250]

diabolical, *adj.* of or like the devil, devilish; fiendishly cruel or wicked. [164, 165]

diagnose, *v.* to identify a medical or psychological condition by close examination. [167]

diagnosis, *n.* a careful examination of the facts or nature of something or a decision based on such an examination, esp. one made by a physician. [217]

dialect, *n.* a form of a language spoken in a particular region or by a certain class that differs somewhat in vocabulary, **idioms,** and pronunciation from the standard language. [30, 31, 122, 127]

diatribe, *n.* a bitter and abusive speech or piece of writing that denounces or **condemns** (synonyms: **harangue, tirade**). [257]

diction, *n.* manner of expression, choice and arrangement of words. [30, 84, 165]

didactic, *adj.* designed to instruct or guide behavior; also, teaching or lecturing excessively. [x]

★ **dignified,** *adj.* 1. honorable, worthy, of a high rank (cf. **distinguished, venerable**). 2. having or showing formality and seriousness (synonym: **stately**). [99, 272]

★ **digress,** *v.* to depart from the main subject in writing or speaking, stray, ramble. [41, 50, 74]

★ **dilemma,** *n.* a situation in which one must choose between equally unpleasant or unfavorable options or **alternatives** (synonyms: see **quandary**). [133, 145, 186, 202, 209]

diligence, *n.* steady and careful attention, esp. to work or duties. [150]

★ **diligent,** *adj.* 1. hardworking: a *diligent* student (synonyms: **assiduous, industrious, sedulous**). 2. characterized by or done with steady and careful effort: a *diligent* search (synonym: **painstaking**). **diligently,** *adv.* [xi, 17, 30, 54, 119, 140, 189, 266, 272]

diminutive, *adj.* very small, tiny. [65, 134]

din, *n.* a **continuous,** loud, annoying noise (synonyms: **clamor, uproar**). [135]

dire, *adj.* causing great fear, trouble, or distress; disastrous, terrible: a *dire* situation. [18, 196, 220]

★ **discern,** *v.* to **detect** with the eyes or other senses, recognize mentally (cf. **comprehend, perceive**). **discernible,** *adj.* [xiv, 22, 33, 55, 107, 190, 210, 234, 270, 279]

discipline, *n.* a field of knowledge, branch of learning or instruction. **disciplined,** *adj.* [198, 274]

disclosure, *n.* the act of revealing or uncovering (something secret or unknown). [144]

disconcert, *v.* to upset, embarrass, disturb the self-control of. **disconcerted,** *adj.* (synonym: **perturbed**; antonym: **unruffled**). [96, 166, 274]

discordant, *adj.* disagreeing, conflicting, clashing, not in harmony (synonym: **dissonant**). [214]

★ **discourse,** *n.* 1. oral communication; talk. 2. formal discussion or communication. 3. an orderly speech or writing on a subject. [119, 156, 198]

★ **discourse,** *v.* to talk, converse; also, to lecture, discuss a subject formally in speech or writing. [119]

discreet, *adj.* showing caution and self-restraint in one's speech or actions, esp. by keeping silent about a delicate or difficult matter (synonyms: **circumspect, prudent, tactful, vigilant, wary**). **discreetly,** *adv.* [12, 21, 71]

★ **disdain,** *n.* a feeling or show of dislike or disregard for something or someone considered inferior (synonyms: **contempt, scorn**). **disdain,** *v.* **disdainful,** *adj.* (synonyms: **condescending, contemptuous, haughty, supercilious**). [xii, 96, 152, 262, 307, 308, 316]

disgruntled, *adj.* dissatisfied, discontented, angrily unhappy (synonym: **resentful**). [206]

disheartened, *adj.* discouraged, depressed, lacking hope or courage. [252]

disheveled, *adj.* untidy, disarranged, out of proper place or order (synonym: **unkempt**). [15, 116]

disingenuous, *adj.* dishonest, false and misleading (synonyms: **deceitful, deceptive, fallacious, insincere**; antonyms: **candid, forthcoming**[1]**, frank, sincere, straightforward**). [132]

disinterested, *adj.* not biased, not influenced by self-interest, having nothing to gain from taking a position one way or the other (synonym: **dispassionate**). [289]

disorderly, *adj.* out of control, unruly, disturbing the peace. [123]

disoriented, *adj.* having a confused sense of time, place, or one's identity. [191]

★ **disparage,** *v.* to speak of, treat, or regard as inferior or unimportant. [96, 110]

disparaging, *adj.* belittling, speaking of or treating as inferior (synonym: **derogatory**). [17]

disparity, *n.* difference, inequality, lack of similarity: the *disparity* in their ages. [74, 302]

dispassionate, *adj.* having no strong emotion or prejudice (synonym: **disinterested,** and see **phlegmatic**). **dispassionately,** *adv.* [176, 274]

dispatch, *v.* to send on specific business or dispose of promptly. [293]

dispense, *v.* to deal out in portions, distribute, administer. [239]

disperse, *v.* to move or scatter in different directions (synonym: **disseminate**; cf. **dissipate**). [74, 147, 289]

★ **disposition,** *n.* one's typical attitude or mood (synonym: **temperament**). [96, 188]

disreputable, *adj.* not respectable or honorable; not of good quality or character. [4]

★ **disrupt,** *v.* 1. to throw into confusion or disorder. 2. to interrupt the normal progress of. **disruption,** *n.* **disruptive,** *adj.* [43, 209, 217, 268, 273, 275, 289]

dissemble, *v.* to put on a false appearance in order to hide or disguise one's true purpose, **motives,** thoughts, or feelings; to speak or act in a **hypocritical** manner. [185]

★ **disseminate,** *v.* to spread widely, scatter as if sowing seed (synonym: **disperse;** cf. **dissipate**). **dissemination,** *n.* [151, 205]

dissertation, *n.* a lengthy, formal piece of writing, spec. a **thesis** prepared for a doctoral degree. [189]

dissimilar, *adj.* different, not alike. **dissimilarity,** *n.* (synonym: **diversity**). [221, 306]

dissipate, *v.* to vanish as if by scattering (cf. **disperse, disseminate**). [82, 175, 300]

dissociate, *v.* separate or withdraw from, disconnect. [156]

dissonant, *adj.* harsh and disagreeable in sound, jarring to the ear (synonym: **discordant**). [134]

distasteful, *adj.* unpleasant, disgusting, causing intense dislike (synonyms: **appalling, loathsome, odious, offensive, repugnant, repulsive**). [239]

★ **distinct,** *adj.* 1. different from others, separate, not the same. 2. clear, unmistakable, plain to the mind or the senses (synonym: **lucid**[1]). [30, 99, 158, 169, 257, 263]

★ **distinctive,** *adj.* serving to set apart as different or characterize as special. [298]

★ **distinguished,** *adj.* characterized by excellence; made **conspicuous** by superior abilities, achievements, character, or reputation: a *distinguished* writer (cf. **dignified, venerable**). [24, 126, 155, 275, 294]

—*Distinguished, prominent, notable, eminent, celebrated, renowned,* and *illustrious* all are used of persons or things that are well known and respected. *Distinguished,* the most general of these words, may be used of anyone who is better known than others in the same class or profession. *Prominent* and *notable* stress the relative importance or rank of a person, suggesting that he or she stands out in comparison with others. *Eminent, celebrated,* and *renowned* stress the person's fame, suggesting that he or she is widely known. *Illustrious* suggests an outstanding reputation, esp. one based on brilliant achievement.

★ **diverse,** *adj.* varied, not alike, different (synonym: see **eclectic**). [21, 95, 153, 188, 201, 210]

diversity, *n.* variety, difference, range, array (synonym: **dissimilarity**). [324]

★ **diversion,** *n.* something that turns or draws the mind away from care, business, or study, and thus relaxes or entertains; amusement, sport, play (synonym: **pastime**). [31, 37, 92, 147, 208]

★ **divine,** *adj.* of, pert. to, or coming from God or a god. [40, 220]

divisive, *adj.* creating or characterized by disagreement, disunity, tension, and **strife.** [21]

★ **doctrine,** *n.* a rule, theory, **principle,** or set of **principles** actively taught and promoted by those who believe it (synonym: **creed**). [78, 154]

★ **document,** *v.* to provide evidence of the truth of something. [258, 299]

★ **document,** *n.* something written or printed. [143]

dogged, *adj.* refusing to give up despite difficulties: *dogged* determination (synonyms: **persistent, tenacious, undaunted**). [165]

dogmatic, *adj.* 1. stating opinions in an overbearing manner, opinionated, dictatorial. 2. of or pert. to *dogma,* a system of beliefs and rules, esp.

of a church, set forth to be accepted and followed without question. [122, 205]

domain, *n.* an area over which control is exercised, sphere of activity, field of interest or knowledge (synonyms: **dominion, realm**). [15, 143, 195]

★ **domestic,** *adj.* of or pert. to the home; relating to family life and household affairs. [22, 25, 187, 204]

★ **dominant,** *adj.* having the most influence or power, exerting authority or control. [100, 250]

★ **dominate,** *v.* to occupy a commanding or **conspicuous** position. [25]

domineering, *adj.* dictatorial, tyrannical, overbearing in exercising authority. [252]

dominion, *n.* a territory subject to supreme authority or rule (synonyms: **domain, realm**). [222]

dour, *adj.* severe, stern, gloomy, ill-humored. [12]

dread, *n.* great fear, esp. of what may happen; fearful **expectation** (synonyms: **apprehension, trepidation**). [152]

dreary, *adj.* 1. gloomy, dismal, bleak; causing sadness. 2. boring, dull (synonyms: **tedious, tiresome**). **dreariness,** *n.* [1, 69, 305]

dub, *v.* to give a name or title to. [209]

dubious, *adj.* 1. **arousing** doubt, uncertain, unlikely to be true: a *dubious* tale. 2. of a questionable character or nature: *dubious* business practices. 3. doubtful, hesitating or wavering in opinion: *dubious* about what she had heard (synonyms: **incredulous, skeptical**). [88, 107, 170, 216, 227]

duly, *adv.* in a proper or prompt manner. [258]

dumbfounded, *adj.* astonished and confused, esp. to the point of speechlessness (synonyms: see **flabbergasted**). [11, 172]

dupe, *v.* to fool, trick, cheat (synonym: **deceive**). [165]

duplicity, *n.* dishonesty, double-dealing, acting contrary to one's real feelings and beliefs in order to fool, mislead, or cheat (synonym: **deceit**). [184]

dwindle, *v.* to decrease steadily, shrink, diminish. [233]

E

ebb, *v.* to flow or fall back or away, recede. [274]

ebullient, *adj.* overflowing with high spirits, enthusiasm, or excitement. **ebullience,** *n.* [6, 188, 289]

★ **eccentric,** *adj.* deviating from what is considered normal or accepted, out of the ordinary, peculiar, odd (synonyms: **anomalous, idiosyncratic**). [xii, 2, 11, 55, 144, 153, 175, 191, 214, 303]

ecclesiastical, *adj.* of or pert. to a church, the clergy, or organized religion (antonym: **secular**). [205]

eclectic, *adj.* selecting, or consisting of selections, from a variety of sources, esp. the best of those sources; varied in an interesting way. [xiii, 2, 173, 208]

—*Diverse* and *eclectic* both suggest variety. A *diverse* collection contains strikingly different elements; *diverse* stresses difference. *Eclectic* stresses

both diversity and quality; an *eclectic* collection contains the best
material selected with care from a wide variety of sources.

eclipse, *v.* to diminish the importance of, make less outstanding, overshadow,
outshine (synonym: **surpass**). [202]

ecology, *n.* the relationship between **organisms** and their environment. [201]

ecstatic, *adj.* overcome by powerful emotion, esp. delight or bliss (synonym:
rapturous). [264]

edification, *n.* **moral,** spiritual, or **intellectual** improvement or instruction
(synonyms: **enlightenment, insight**). [xvii, 141, 208]

edifice, *n.* a building, often one that is **imposing** or **elaborate.** [88, 153]

edify, *v.* to instruct, esp. so as to uplift **morally,** spiritually, or **intellectually.** [208]

eerie, *adj.* strange and mysterious, often in a frightening way (synonyms: see
uncanny). [62, 175]

effervescent, *adj.* bubbling, full of small bubbles of gas. [219]

effusion, *n.* an unrestrained pouring out or forth. [135, 324]

effusive, *adj.* emotionally excessive or unrestrained, gushy. [192, 266]

★ **ego,** *n.* the "I"; that which feels, thinks, and acts; one's conscious being; any
person's self apart from other selves. [71, 154, 155]

egoism, *n.* self-centeredness, spec. the **doctrine** that self-interest is the proper
goal of the individual (antonym: **altruism;** see **egotism**). [154]

egotism, *n.* exaggerated and boastful self-importance. [102]

   —*Egotism* and *egoism* are similar but not synonymous. *Egotism* is
   extreme self-involvement, excessive reference to oneself in speech or
   writing; the *egotist* cannot stop talking about himself. *Egoism* implies self-
   centeredness, concern for oneself; the *egoist* cares only about his own
   needs and desires. *Egoism* is unpleasant but less intense and disagreeable
   than *egotism.*

egotistical, *adj.* full of self-importance, overly self-involved, selfish and
boastful (synonyms: **conceited, vain**[1]). [132, 257]

egregious, *adj.* very bad, **offensive,** or wrong in an obvious way (synonyms:
flagrant, gross). [53, 230]

egress, *n.* a way out, exit. [161]

elaborate, *v.* to give details or additional information, discuss at greater
length. [176]

elaborate, *adj.* 1. made or done with great labor, skill, and attention to detail.
2. rich in detail, **intricate** or **ornate. elaborately,** *adv.* [24, 29, 116, 153]

elation, *n.* great joy or happiness, bliss. [192, 275]

elevate, *v.* 1. to raise to a higher cultural, **intellectual,** or **moral** level. 2. to
raise to a higher place, position, or rank (cf. **embellish, enhance**).
elevation, *n.* [31, 154, 155]

elicit, *v.* to draw out, bring forth (synonym: **evoke**). [10]

★ **elite,** *adj.* of the first rank or highest class; belonging to or characteristic of
people considered the best, brightest, most powerful, etc. **elite,** *n.* the
best or highest-ranked members of a group or class. [57, 155, 207]

eloquent, *adj.* expressed in a strong, clear, graceful, and persuasive way;
moving, forceful. **eloquence,** *n.* [23, 93, 120]

elucidate, *v.* to make clear, explain (synonyms: **clarify, illuminate**; cf. **lucid**). [194, 222, 277]

elude, *v.* 1. to escape, avoid, esp. in a skillful, clever, or daring way (synonym: **evade**). 2. to escape the awareness or understanding of. [97, 124, 177, 324]

★ **elusive,** *adj.* hard to get hold of or capture. [143, 161, 266]

emanate, *v.* to flow out or send forth, issue (synonym: **emit**). [215]

emancipation, *n.* the act of freeing from bondage or slavery. [57]

embellish, *v.* to decorate, **adorn,** make more beautiful or attractive (cf. **elevate, enhance**). [188, 231]

★ **embellishment,** *n.* an ornament, decoration; an **elaborate**[2] feature or addition intended to beautify (synonym: **flourish,** *n.*). [10, 153, 256]

★ **embody,** *v.* to give bodily or concrete form to: to *embody* thought in words. [187]

★ **embrace,** *v.* to welcome, accept or take up willingly and eagerly. [152, 207]

emend, *v.* to edit (a text), revise, correct. [33, 65]

eminent, *adj.* well-known because of one's position or accomplishments; standing out from others in importance (synonyms: see **distinguished**). [80, 141, 189]

emit, *v.* to give or send out, utter, express, discharge (synonym: **emanate**). [57, 138, 191, 309]

★ **empathy,** *n.* understanding of the thoughts, feelings, or experiences of another as if they were one's own. [212, 242]

★ **emphasize,** *v.* to stress, give special forcefulness or importance to. [4, 310]

★ **emphatic,** *adj.* expressed or done with special force, effort, or intensity. **emphatically,** *adv.* [136, 168, 241, 419]

emulate, *v.* to try to do as well as or better than, esp. by imitating; compete with, rival. [23, 24, 126]

★ **encounter,** *v.* to meet or come into contact, esp. in a sudden, accidental, or unexpected way. **encounter,** *n.* [xiii, 110, 176, 277]

encumber, *v.* 1. to hinder, hamper, slow down or stop the functioning or performance of (synonym: **impede**). 2. to burden, weigh down, place a heavy load upon. [178, 247]

endeavor, *n.* an earnest attempt or effort (synonym: **enterprise**). [306, 325]

endeavor, *v.* to try hard, make an earnest effort. [85]

endorse, *v.* to support, give one's approval to. [155, 234]

endow, *v.* to provide or supply with something, such as a quality or ability. [138, 224]

endowment, *n.* a natural quality, characteristic, or ability of body or mind. [317]

★ **endure,** *v.* 1. to carry on in spite of trouble, difficulty, or suffering; to undergo or bear patiently. 2. to last, continue to exist in the same state or condition. [27, 47, 124, 131, 164, 282]

enduring, *adj.* lasting, durable, permanent. [69, 113]

enervated, *adj.* weakened, drained of strength or energy. **enervate,** *v.* (synonym: **debilitate**). [xv, 115, 282]

engender, *v.* to cause, give rise to, bring into being. [200]

engrossed, *adj.* completely absorbed or involved (synonyms: **bemused**[1], **immersed, preoccupied**). **engrossing,** *adj.* [57, 87, 420]

★ **enhance,** *v.* to make greater, better, or more attractive; improve the quality or increase the desirability of (cf. **elevate, embellish**). [xiv, 39, 200, 208, 218, 219]

enigmatic, *adj.* mysterious, puzzling, **baffling,** hard to understand or explain (synonyms: **cryptic, inscrutable, perplexing**). [2, 58, 98, 175, 217, 306]

enlightening, *adj.* instructive, serving to make the truth or nature of something clear. [131, 218]

enlightenment, *n.* knowledge, understanding, instruction, education (synonyms: **edification, insight**). [xvii, 141, 197]

enmity, *n.* a deep-seated hatred or mistrust (synonyms: **antipathy, hostility**). [xii, 151]

ensconced, *adj.* settled securely or snugly. [xvi, 85, 239]

ensnare, *v.* to trap, catch, capture. [177]

ensue, *v.* to follow as a result, occur next. **ensuing,** *adj.* [107]

★ **enterprise,** *n.* 1. a project or undertaking, esp. a difficult, complicated, or risky one (synonym: **endeavor**). 2. a business organization, company, firm. [30, 81, 189, 201]

entertain, *v.* to hold in the mind, consider, think about (synonym: **contemplate**). [31, 54, 299]

enthrall, *v.* to hold spellbound, charm (synonym: **captivate**). [54, 74]

★ **entice,** *v.* to tempt, lead on or attract by exciting hope or desire (synonym: **lure**). **enticing,** *adj.* (synonym: **captivating**) [101, 123, 218]

entity, *n.* something that exists, a thing. [197, 198]

entourage, *n.* a group of attendants or associates accompanying an important person. [45]

entreaty, *n.* an earnest request, plea. [274]

entrenched, *adj.* firmly or deeply established, securely in place. [31]

entrepreneur, *n.* someone who starts, manages, and takes on the risks of a business or **enterprise**. [188]

environs, *n.* surroundings or surrounding area; environment. [xiv, 114]

★ **envision,** *v.* to imagine, see in the mind. [187, 222]

envy, *v.* to feel discontented longing for another person's advantages or possessions. [319]

ephemeral, *adj.* passing swiftly, lasting for only a short time (synonyms: see **transient**). [92]

epic, *n.* a long poem, novel, or play, usu. written in a **dignified** or **elevated** style, celebrating heroes and heroic **deeds. epic,** *adj.* [37, 174, 272]

epidemic, *n.* a rapid spread or sudden increase of something, esp. a disease. [135, 204]

epigrammatic, *adj.* like or expressing an *epigram,* a **concise** and pointed statement or observation that is esp. **ingenious,** witty, or wise. [202]

epoch, *n.* a particular period of time known for its **distinctive** developments, remarkable characteristics, or **noteworthy** events. **epochal,** *adj.* [88, 209, 319]

equanimity, *n.* the quality or state of being calm, composed, and even-tempered. [105, 188, 253]

equilibrium, *n.* balance, stability. [269]

equitable, *adj.* fair, reasonable, and just. [253]

era, *n.* a period of time reckoned from a particular date, person, historical event, or significant change in the order of things: the pre-Columbian *era,* the Internet *era.* [73, 94, 141, 204, 209, 218]

★ **eradicate,** *v.* to get rid of, remove, wipe out (synonyms: **annihilate, obliterate**). [196]

erratic, *adj.* 1. not regular or consistent: *erratic* performance (synonyms: **capricious, fickle, unpredictable, volatile, wayward**). 2. wandering, having no fixed or definite course. 3. odd or peculiar, deviating from what is usual: *erratic* conduct (cf. **eccentric**). **erratically,** *adv.* [4, 161, 190, 266, 282]

★ **erroneous,** *adj.* wrong, mistaken, in error. [xii, 258]

erudite, *adj.* having or exhibiting deep and extensive learning (synonym: **learned**). [194, 208]

escapade, *n.* an adventure or adventurous act, esp. a foolish, wild, **reckless** one. [108, 227]

esoteric, *adj.* intended for or understood only by a select group (synonym: **arcane**). [26, 57, 210, 254]

establishment, *n.* a place of business. [29, 169]

esteem, *v.* to respect deeply, hold in high regard (cf. **glorify**). **esteemed,** *adj.* (synonym: **prestigious**). [24, 113, 151]

esteem, *n.* high regard, great respect. [162, 189]

estranged, *adj.* made unfriendly, **indifferent,** or **hostile** (synonym: **alienated**). [100]

eternal, *adj.* existing or continuing forever, without beginning or end (antonyms: see **transient**). [113, 158, 164]

★ **ethical,** *adj.* of or pert. to ethics; conforming to the standards or rules for proper conduct (synonyms: **conscientious**[1], **upright, virtuous**). [125, 152, 186, 245]

ethics, *n.* the standards or rules governing proper conduct; also, the study of the general nature of **morals** and **moral** choices. [258, 293]

ethnic, *adj.* of or pert. to large groups of people that share a common and **distinctive** background or **heritage,** as of race, religion, language, nationality, or culture. **ethnically,** *adv.* [30, 188]

ethos, *n.* the basic character or cast of mind of a people or culture; guiding spirit or belief. [86]

etiquette, *n.* proper and well-bred social behavior, as required by custom or authority. [137, 240, 264]

etymology, *n.* the history of a word or the study of the origin and development of words. [121]

euphemism, *n.* the substitution of a milder, nicer, more agreeable word or expression for one considered unpleasant, blunt, or **offensive.** [235]

euphoric, *adj.* filled with a feeling of great happiness and well-being. [275]

evade, *v.* to escape or avoid, esp. through trickery or cleverness: to *evade* responsibility (synonym: **elude**). [304]

evanescent, *adj.* fading or passing swiftly away, vanishing as if into thin air (synonyms: see **transient**). [191]

evasive, *adj.* meaning to **evade**, not direct or **straightforward**, intentionally **vague. evasively,** *adv.* [123, 164]

★ **evoke,** *v.* to call forth, call to mind, create or produce in the mind (synonym: **elicit**). [70, 274]

exacerbate, *v.* to make worse, increase the severity of, aggravate: the remark *exacerbated* the tension between them. [64, 159]

exact, *v.* to demand and get by force or authority. [152]

exalted, *adj.* of high rank or character, raised above others, **glorified, elevated** (synonym: **lofty**²). [78, 210]

exasperate, *v.* to irritate extremely, try the patience of. **exasperating,** *adj.* **exasperation,** *n.* [69, 133, 170, 301]

exclamation, *n.* a loud, sudden, forceful utterance. [262]

excruciating, *adj.* causing intense pain or suffering, agonizing. **excruciatingly,** *adj.* [166, 298, 321]

★ **exemplary,** *adj.* worthy to serve as a model (synonym: **commendable**). [178]

exertion, *n.* strenuous, **vigorous** effort or action. **exert,** *v.* [xiv, 70, 167]

exhausted, *v.* used up, drained, emptied, **depleted.** [233]

exhilarate, *v.* to cause to feel excited, energetic, and cheerful. **exhilarating,** *adj.* (synonym: **heady**). [114, 176, 283]

exhort, *v.* to urge strongly, advise or appeal to earnestly. [157]

exodus, *n.* a departure of many people at once. [12]

exonerate, *v.* to declare blameless, find innocent: *exonerated* by the jury. [139]

★ **exotic,** *adj.* strikingly different or strange; from far away, foreign (synonym: **alien**). [114, 173]

★ **expectation,** *n.* the act of expecting or something expected. [85, 111, 172, 209]

expedient, *adj.* serving as an appropriate means to an end, immediately **advantageous.** [84]

explanatory, *adj.* helping to make clear, serving to explain. [205]

★ **explicit,** *adj.* 1. fully and clearly expressed, not **vague,** unreserved in expression. 2. openly **depicting** nudity or sexual activity. [xiv, 96, 219]

★ **exploit,** *n.* a daring, brilliant, or heroic action; a **notable deed** (synonym: **feat**). [26, 151]

★ **exploit,** *v.* 1. to use productively or to greatest advantage: to *exploit* an idea. 2. to use in a selfish way: to *exploit* others' labor. **exploitation,** *n.* [197, 201, 206, 207, 245, 255]

exposé, *n.* a public exposure of something damaging to a person's reputation. [216]

expound, *v.* to make a detailed statement, give a thorough explanation. [154, 195]

expressive, *adj.* clearly communicating meaning or feeling, full of expression. [56]

exquisitely, *adv.* in a beautiful and excellent way. [87, 169]

extant, *adj.* still existing, not destroyed or lost: the *extant* sculpture of ancient Greece (antonym: **extinct**). [311]

★ **extinct,** *adj.* no longer existing, completely gone or lost (antonym: **extant**). [152]

extortion, *n.* the crime of getting money or something of value from someone by force, intimidation, or abuse of one's power. [252]

★ **extract,** *v.* to pull out, draw out, often with effort or despite resistance. [70, 102, 108, 189]

extraterrestrial, *adj.* not of the earth, otherworldly, from outer space. [152]

extravagance, *n.* something excessive, an immoderate action or thing. [118]

★ **extravagant,** *adj.* lacking moderation or restraint; excessively showy or elaborate (**opulent, sumptuous;** cf. **lavishly**). [94]

extricate, *v.* to free or remove from entanglement or difficulty, disengage. [61, 205, 281]

exuberant, *adj.* filled with unrestrained enthusiasm and excitement. [86, 286]

exultant, *adj.* filled with great joy, expressing triumph. [210, 264]

F

fabricate, *v.* to make up, invent, esp. to fool or **deceive. fabrication,** *n.* [182, 216, 420]

—*Conceive, devise, contrive, concoct,* and *fabricate* all mean to think or make up. *Conceive* is the most general of these terms, and may be used of anything formed or developed in the mind: *conceive* an idea; *conceive* a plan; *conceive* a work of art. *Devise* suggests creativity or novelty in the design: *devised* a new way to do it. *Contrive* suggests cleverness or ingenuity in the planning or execution: they *contrived* to meet secretly. *Concoct* means to cook up, either **literally** or **figuratively**; it often suggests invention marked by skill and intelligence: he *concocted* a brilliant strategy. *Fabricate* may be used neutrally to mean to make, create, or invent, but more often it means to create something fake, invent in order to trick or mislead: *fabricate* an excuse.

facade, *n.* in architecture, the front or face of a building. [153]

facetious, *adj.* meant to be funny or playfully disrespectful. [151]

fallacious, *adj.* misleading, tending to **deceive**; logically wrong, reasoning falsely (synonyms: **deceitful, deceptive, disingenuous**). [185, 229]

falsify, *v.* to make false or misrepresent, esp. by altering in order to **deceive**. [185]

fanatic, *n.* a person motivated by extreme, unreasoning enthusiasm. **fanatically,** *adv.* [168, 206]

farcical, *adj.* laughable, comical, ridiculous (synonyms: **absurd, ludicrous, preposterous**). **farcically,** *adv.* [ix, 192, 289]

far-fetched, *adj.* not likely to be true or to happen: a *far-fetched* story; a *far-fetched* plan. [192, 193]

fashion, *v.* to make, give form or shape to. [26]

fastidious, *adj.* 1. overly particular, hard to please. 2. excessively sensitive in matters of taste. 3. extremely careful about details (synonyms: **conscientious², meticulous, painstaking**). **fastidiously,** *adv.* [15, 76, 77, 107, 167, 252, 325]

fatal, *adj.* deadly; causing or capable of causing death, destruction, or ruinous misfortune (synonym: **lethal**). [119]

fathom, *v.* to figure out or get to the bottom of. [55, 255]

fatuous, *adj.* silly or stupid in a **complacent** way (synonym: **inane**). [213, 251]

fawning, *adj.* seeking attention or favor by being overly affectionate, flattering, or submissive (synonyms: **obsequious, servile, sycophantic**). [96, 257]

feat, *n.* a remarkable or extraordinary act or accomplishment (synonym: **exploit,** *n.*). [10, 151]

feeble, *adj.* 1. weak, lacking strength or force. 2. inadequate or ineffective. **feebly,** *adv.* [12, 154, 221, 291]

feign, *v.* to make believe, pretend. [241, 314]

feigned, *adj.* pretended, faked. [97, 137]

ferret, *v.* to search for and uncover, bring to light. [308]

fervent, *adj.* full of intense feeling or spirit: a *fervent* plea (synonyms: **ardent, avid, zealous**). [95]

fervid, *adj.* full of passionate feeling, impassioned, fiery, burning: a *fervid* desire (synonyms: **torrid, vehement**). [213]

fervor, *n.* great passion, intensity of feeling. [299]

fetid, *adj.* stinking; having a foul smell, as of decay (synonyms: **malodorous, putrid, rancid**). [117]

feud, *v.* to quarrel, argue, or fight bitterly, esp. over a long period of time. **feuding,** *adj.* [79]

feudal, *adj.* of or pert. to *feudalism,* the social, political, and economic system in Europe in the Middle Ages in which lords granted vassals the right to hold land in return for their loyalty and protection. [210]

fickle, *adj.* not constant, unstable, given to casual change (synonyms: **capricious, erratic, unpredictable, wayward**). [189, 282]

figuratively, *adv.* not actually, in a symbolic or **metaphorical** way (cf. **literally**). [104]

filament, *n.* a thin, fine thread or fiber. [212]

finale, *n.* the conclusion, esp. of a musical composition or performance. [39, 274]

finite, *adj.* having limits, not **boundless** or permanent. [196]

flabbergasted, *adj.* overcome with astonishment, thoroughly confused and dismayed. [11, 91, 93, 213, 275]

—*Flabbergasted, dumbfounded,* and *astounded* all describe a state of astonishment or confusion caused by something unexpected or highly unusual. *Astounded* suggests shock: *astounded* to learn the truth. *Dumbfounded* suggests being speechless from surprise or **bewilderment**: Her refusal left him *dumbfounded. Flabbergasted,* a colorful and sometimes **jocular** word, may also suggest speechlessness and often **implies** dismay: *flabbergasted* by the enormous bill.

★ **flagrant,** *adj.* shockingly and shamelessly bad, **offensive,** or **immoral** (synonyms: **egregious, gross;** *usage note*: see **blatant**). **flagrantly,** *adv.* [59, 184, 219, 258]

★ **flamboyant,** *adj.* flashy, colorful, or showy in style (synonym: **ostentatious**). [8, 95]

flee, *v.* to run away, esp. from a pursuer or from danger; fly away from. **fleeing,** *adj.* [161, 272, 325]

fleeting, *adj.* passing swiftly, happening quickly (synonyms: see **transient**). [105, 216]

flippant, *adj.* lacking proper seriousness or respect; inappropriately foolish or funny. [300]

flog, *v.* to whip, beat severely, thrash. [93, 136]

★ **flourish,** *n.* a showy or stylish ornament, decoration (synonym: **embellishment**). [5]

★ **flourish,** *v.* 1. to **thrive,** be **vigorous** or successful, grow or do well. 2. to gesture with, wave around, **wield** dramatically. [290, 324]

fluent, *adj.* flowing, moving smoothly and effortlessly, fluid. [32, 191]

foible, *n.* a minor weakness or character flaw, small failing or shortcoming. [216]

folly, *n.* 1. foolishness, lack of good sense or judgment. 2. a foolish, costly, and ruinous undertaking. [31, 213, 228]

foolhardy, *adj.* bold in a thoughtless, foolish manner (synonyms: **impetuous, reckless**). [141]

forbidding, *adj.* 1. unpleasant, uninviting, grim. 2. threatening (synonyms: **menacing, ominous, sinister**) 3. obstructing or hindering progress. [153, 163, 266]

foresight, *n.* the ability to anticipate and provide for the future. [54]

forfeit, *v.* to give up or lose the right to because of an error, crime, or **breach**[2]. [260]

★ **forge,** *v.* to move or proceed steadily or with increased speed and power. [9, 165, 179]

★ **forgery,** *n.* 1. an imitation (as of a signature, **document,** or work of art) meant to be passed off as the real thing; a fake, counterfeit. 2. the act of making a forgery. [143, 185]

★ **formidable,** *adj.* 1. inspiring admiration, **arousing** awe or wonder. 2. of awesome or intimidating size. 3. difficult to defeat or overcome. 4. **arousing apprehension** or **dread.** [2, 60, 73, 95, 178, 227, 307, 324]

forsake, *v.* to give up, quit (synonyms: **abandon, relinquish**). [166]

forthcoming, *adj.* 1. willing to talk freely and openly, cooperative and responsive (synonyms: **candid, frank, sincere, straightforward**). 2. friendly and outgoing (synonyms: **affable, amiable**). [182, 250]

fortitude, *n.* strength of mind in the face of trouble or temptation. [213]

fortuitous, *adj.* occurring by chance, accidental, not planned or intentional (synonyms: see **random**). [99, 176, 277]
Usage note: Be careful not to confuse *fortuitous* with *fortunate,* which means "lucky." Something *fortuitous* is accidental, unexpected, and may or may not be *fortunate*: The *fortuitous* **encounter** was the cause of his death.

fracas, *n.* a noisy and disorderly disturbance or **quarrel.** [275]

★ **fragile,** *adj.* easily damaged or destroyed, delicate. [xii, 196, 325]

frank, *adj.* open and direct in expression, expressed without reserve or restraint (synonyms: **candid, forthcoming**[1], **sincere, straightforward**). **frankly,** *adv.* [25, 64, 69, 121, 258]

fraternal, *adj.* brotherly, of or like a brother. [282]

fraud, *n.* 1. a person who pretends to be something he or she is not (synonym: **impostor**). 2. someone who lies and cheats, a **deceitful** person. [231, 257]

fraudulent, *adj.* dishonest, lying, cheating (synonyms: **counterfeit, deceitful, spurious**). [185]

fray, *n.* a fight, scuffle, disorderly struggle or **quarrel.** [106]

freethinking, *adj.* rejecting authority, **tradition**, and dogma (see **dogmatic**) and forming an opinion based on independent reasoning. [222]

frenetic, *adj.* wildly active or excited (synonym: **frenzied**). [15, 163, 272, 282]

frenzied, *adj.* wildly excited or enthusiastic (synonym: **frenetic**). [163, 289]

fret, *v.* to worry, become troubled or **vexed** (synonym: **brood**). [145, 286]

frigid, *adj.* very cold, freezing. [59, 186, 298]

★ **frugal,** *adj.* careful in spending, thrifty, sparing, economical. [xii, 188]

fruitful, *adj.* yielding good or rich results, productive: a *fruitful* discussion. [119]

fruitless, *adj.* producing nothing, not successful, useless (synonyms: **futile, vain**[2]). [159, 282]

fugitive, *adj.* **fleeing,** escaping. [16, 266]

fugitive, *n.* a person who **flees.** [185]

functional, *adj.* having a particular practical purpose; designed simply to be used rather than admired for beauty or style. **functionally,** *adv.* [153, 221]

★ **fundamental,** *adj.* basic, elementary, essential, of or pert. to the foundation. [xii, 78, 197, 202, 213, 218]

furtive, *adj.* done secretly or so as not to be seen, sly, shifty, stealthy (synonyms: **clandestine, covert, devious, surreptitious**). **furtively,** *adv.* [51, 71, 89, 124, 237, 287]

★ **futile,** *adj.* unsuccessful, ineffective, pointless, of no use (synonyms: **fruitless, vain**[2]). **futilely,** *adv.* [xii, 112, 196, 209, 281, 323]

G

gait, *n.* a particular manner of walking or moving on foot. [167]

gargantuan, *adj.* of great size or capacity, huge, enormous (synonyms: **colossal, immense, massive**[2], **monumental**[1], **prodigious**[2]). [9, 75, 84]

★ **garish,** *adj.* excessively showy or bright, loud and flashy (synonyms: **gaudy, tawdry**). [87]

garnish, *v.* to decorate, spec. to decorate food with something that adds color or flavor (cf. **embellish**). [179]

garrulous, *adj.* overly talkative, esp. about unimportant things (synonyms: **loquacious, voluble**). [98, 136, 170]

gaudy, *adj.* showy in a cheap and tasteless way (synonyms: **garish, tawdry**). [85]

geniality, *n.* a pleasant and cheerful manner, warm and friendly **disposition.** [188]

genteel, *adj.* of or pert. to polite society, elegant and stylish, refined (synonyms: **sophisticated, urbane**). [11, 94]

gingerly, *adv.* cautiously, with great care. [18, 54]

glorify, *v.* to praise highly, honor (cf. **esteem,** *v.*). [155]

glutton, *n.* someone who eats and drinks excessively and greedily. [35]

goad, *v.* to prod, urge, or drive as if with a *goad,* a pointed stick or rod (synonyms: **incite, instigate, provoke**). **goading,** *adj.* [250, 325]

gobbledygook, *n.* wordy, dense, **abstract,** and circumlocutory language that has intentionally been made hard to understand (synonym: **jargon**). [56]

gracious, *adj.* kind and courteous (synonyms: **affable, congenial, cordial, jovial,** and see note at **amiable**). [64, 121]

grandiloquent, *adj.* of or pert. to grand, elegant, **lofty**[2] language; speech or writing that is **elevated** in tone but often highfalutin and overblown (synonym: **bombastic**). [318]

grandiose, *adj.* showy and grand in an exaggerated, artificial way (synonyms: **affected, ostentatious, pompous, pretentious**). [78]

gratify, *v.* to please, satisfy, delight. **gratification,** *n.* **gratifying,** *adj.* [27, 69, 92, 168]

gratuitously, *adv.* without cause, reason, or justification. [92]

grave, *adj.* 1. serious (synonym: **solemn**[1]). 2. important, significant, weighty. **gravely,** *adv.* [30, 170, 178, 207]

gravity, *n.* seriousness, importance, weight. [77]

gregarious, *adj.* liking the companionship of others (synonyms: **convivial, sociable**). [188]

grievance, *n.* a complaint, esp. a formal one. [293]

grievous, *adj.* characterized by pain, suffering, and grief. [215]
Pronunciation: Grievous properly has two syllables, not three. Take care to say *grieve-us,* not *gree-vee-us.*

gross, *adj.* extremely obvious, esp. because inexcusably bad or wrong (synonyms: **egregious, flagrant**). [184]

grotesque, *adj.* odd, misshapen, or horrible in appearance or manner; fantastically **absurd** or **bizarre. grotesquely,** *adv.* [49, 136, 168, 217]

guffaw, *v.* to laugh in a loud, hearty way. [19]

guffaw, *n.* a loud, hearty burst of laughter. [236]

guileless, *adj.* innocent, without cunning or **deceitfulness** (synonym: **naive**). [185]

★ **gullible,** *adj.* easily fooled, cheated, or **deceived** (synonym: **credulous**). [50, 218]

H

★ **habitat,** *n.* the place where someone or something is usu. found; dwelling place. [xiv, 22]

habitual, *adj.* resulting from habit, **customary,** usual. [182]

hackneyed, *adj.* made ordinary and dull by overuse (synonym: **commonplace**): a *hackneyed* style, a *hackneyed* plot. [216]

hail, *v.* 1. to come (from), have as one's birthplace or place of residence: he *hails* from Missouri. 2. to call out to, catch the attention of: *hail* a cab. [22, 221]

hamlet, *n.* a very small village. [1]

haphazard, *adj.* without order, plan, or direction; accidental (synonyms: see **random**). [31]

harangue, *n.* a long, passionate, **vehement** speech; a **prolonged** verbal attack or complaint (synonyms: **diatribe, tirade**). [133]

harass, *v.* to annoy or irritate, disturb **persistently,** pester, badger (synonyms: **torment, vex**). **harassment,** *n.* (synonym: **persecution**). [147, 161, 261, 293]

harmonious, *adj.* 1. orderly and pleasing in sound or arrangement. 2. being in harmony, characterized by agreement in feeling, opinion, action, etc. [87, 169, 209, 212]

harried, *adj.* disturbed or distressed by constant trouble or attack; **harassed, vexed.** [165]

haughty, *adj.* excessively proud and scornful of others (synonyms: **arrogant, condescending, contemptuous, pretentious, supercilious**). [96, 152, 252, 295]

haven, *n.* a place of shelter and safety; sanctuary (synonym: **refuge**). [18, 25]

havoc, *n.* great disorder, confusion, or destruction. [177, 216, 229]

hazardous, *adj.* dangerous, risky (synonyms: **perilous, treacherous**). [81, 185]

headlong, *adj.* **literally,** headfirst; **figuratively,** rash or **reckless.** [18, 113, 273, 323]

heady, *adj.* greatly exciting or intoxicating (synonym: **exhilarating**). [183]

heed, *v.* to pay attention to, listen to, notice. [179, 183]

heinous, *adj.* thoroughly evil, shockingly wicked (synonym: **abominable**). [31, 139, 299, 315]
Pronunciation: Heinous is properly pronounced in two syllables, with the first one like *hay* (HAY-nuhs).

★ **heritage,** *n.* 1. that which belongs or comes to one by birth; one's family and cultural background (cf. **legacy**). 2. something passed down from previous generations. [96, 140]

hermetic, *adj.* airtight, completely sealed. [140]

hewn, *adj.* shaped as if with an ax or a sharp, heavy tool. [153]

hiatus, *n.* a gap or break in the flow of something, pause, interruption (cf. **lull, respite**). [149, 227]

hindrance, *n.* someone or something that delays or blocks progress; an obstruction (synonym: **impediment**). [162]

histrionic, *adj.* 1. overly dramatic, exaggerated for emotional effect. 2. of or pert. to actors or acting. [62, 91, 305]

hoax, *n.* an act meant to trick, fool, or cheat; a **fraudulent** act (synonyms: **chicanery, deception, ruse, subterfuge**). [ix, 159, 224]

hodgepodge, *n.* a mixture of all kinds, jumble. [152]

hospitable, *adj.* giving guests warm, friendly, generous treatment. [172]

★ **hostile,** *adj.* exhibiting opposition, open distrust, dislike, ill will, or hatred: a *hostile* attitude (synonyms: **belligerent, contentious**). **hostility,** *n.* (synonyms: **antipathy, enmity**). [xii, 21, 52, 96, 104, 123, 206]

humanistic, *adj.* of or pert. to *humanism,* a cultural and **intellectual** movement inspired by the classical civilization of ancient Greece and Rome that arose in the Renaissance; it sparked a revival of scholarly interest in literature and the liberal arts and later evolved into a **doctrine** that stressed concern for the interests, welfare, and dignity of human beings. [205]

humanitarian, *n.* a person who works to promote human welfare and social reform. [232]

humble, *adj.* 1. common, ordinary, low in importance, rank, or condition: *humble* work; *humble* food, a *humble* apartment. 2. not proud or self-important; gentle and meek; courteous and respectful (synonym: **modest**[1]) 3. inferior, submissive (synonym: **deferential**). [72, 92, 96, 155, 210, 274]

★ **humility,** *n.* the quality or state of being **humble**[2]. [242]

hyperbole, *n.* intentional and obvious exaggeration for emphasis or effect. **hyperbolic,** *adj.* **hyperbolically,** *adv.* [40, 120, 257]

hyperventilate, *v.* to breathe abnormally fast because of overexcitement. [278]

hypocrisy, *n.* the act of pretending to believe, feel, or be something; putting on a false show, esp. claiming that one is **ethical** or **virtuous** when one is not. [186]

★ **hypocrite,** *n.* a person who says one thing and does another. [31]

★ **hypocritical,** *adj.* characterized by **hypocrisy** (synonyms: **disingenuous, insincere**; antonyms: **candid, forthcoming**[1]**, frank, straightforward**). [131]

★ **hypothesis,** *n.* (pl. **hypotheses**) an **assumption** made for the sake of argument, consideration, or further study. [77, 143, 245]

I

★ **ideal,** *n.* ultimate goal, highest aim. [179]

ideal, *adj.* perfect, excellent. [155, 263]

idealistic, *adj.* pursuing noble goals regardless of whether they are practical or achievable (synonyms: **quixotic, visionary**). [196, 245]

★ **idealize,** *adj.* represented as excellent or perfect, regarded or rendered as **ideal**. **idealized,** *adj.* [174]

idiom, *n.* an expression whose meaning cannot be understood **literally** or by putting together the usual meanings of each separate word: "to put your nose to the grindstone" is an *idiom* meaning "to be **diligent** or **assiduous**, to stick to a job and work hard." [136, 164, 320]

idiosyncrasy, *n.* a characteristic or quality peculiar to a particular person; a quirk (synonym: **mannerism**). **idiosyncratic,** *adj.* (synonyms: **anomalous, eccentric**). [64, 318]

idol, *n.* a person or thing that is worshiped or adored. [154, 171]

idolize, *v.* to look upon with great admiration and devotion. [188]

illicit, *adj.* not lawful or permitted, illegal. [107]

illiterate, *adj.* unable to read or write. [165]

★ **illuminate,** *v.* 1. to light up, brighten. 2. to make clear, provide understanding (synonyms: **clarify, elucidate**). **illuminating,** *adj.* [xix, 55, 59, 78, 85, 89, 122, 155, 173, 218, 283, 296]

★ **illusion,** *n.* a misleading image, false impression of reality. [191, 242]

illustrious, *adj.* very well known and respected (synonyms: see **distinguished**). [135]

★ **imagery,** *n.* pictures or images created in the mind. [129]

imbue, *v.* to saturate or spread through, permeate (synonym: **suffuse**). [195]

immaculate, *adj.* spotlessly clean. [2, 15, 112, 187, 256]

immaterial, *adj.* having no definite form, not consisting of physical matter. [210]

★ **immense,** *adj.* very large, enormous, huge, **vast** (synonyms: **colossal, gargantuan, massive**[2]**, monumental**[1]**, prodigious**[2]**).** [8, 49, 85, 91, 202, 217]

immersed, *adj.* absorbed, caught up, deeply involved (synonyms: **bemused**[1]**, engrossed, preoccupied**). [21, 51, 56, 177]

imminent, *adj.* about to happen at any moment (synonym: **impending**). [15, 134, 234, 298]

immobile, *adj.* motionless or unable to move. [248]

immobilize, *v.* to hold or fix in place, make **immobile. immobilized,** *adj.* [234, 312]

immodest, *adj.* not **modest. immodestly,** *adv.* [9, 287]

immoral, *adj.* not **moral. immorality,** *n.* [31, 44]

impasse, *n.* a dead end or deadlock, a situation from which there is no escape. [145]

impassive, *adj.* unaffected by emotion, giving no sign of feeling (synonyms: see **phlegmatic**). [78, 101, 108, 177, 309]

impeccably, *adv.* flawlessly, perfectly, without fault or blemish. [187]

impede, *v.* get in the way of, obstruct, retard or hinder the progess of. **impediment,** *n.* (synonym: **hindrance**). [116, 179, 250, 265]

impending, *adj.* threatening to happen or about to take place (synonym: **imminent**). [1]

impenetrable, *adj.* 1. impossible to see or get through. 2. impossible to understand (synonyms: **inarticulate**[1]**, incomprehensible, indecipherable**). [1, 78, 159]

imperative, *adj.* absolutely necessary, urgent. [272]

imperceptible, *adj.* very slight or **subtle,** difficult or impossible to **perceive.** [155]

impertinent, *adj.* overly forward or bold; rude or inappropriate. **impertinence,** *n.* [47, 68, 77, 93, 170]

imperturbable, *adj.* not able to be upset or disturbed, calm and cool. [188]

impervious, *adj.* immune, unaffected by or unreceptive to. [41]

★ **impetuous,** *adj.* acting with great energy, eagerness, or impatience; acting with much emotion and little thought (synonyms: **foolhardy, reckless**). **impetuously,** *adv.* [6, 109, 210]

★ **implement,** *n.* a tool or device used in doing work or accomplishing a task. [25, 123, 204]

implementation, *n.* the act or process of putting something into effect. [169]

★ **implications,** *n.* pl. involvement with or effect upon other things (synonym: **ramifications**). [199]

★ **imply,** *v.* to suggest, express or indicate without directly stating (see *usage note* at **infer**). [xii, xiv, 92, 175, 218, 244, 286]

impose, *v.* to establish or bring about by or as if by authority; thrust or force upon (someone or something). [206, 222, 319]

imposing, *adj.* impressive in appearance, manner, or size. [16, 82, 89, 153, 271, 280]

impostor, *n.* a person who pretends to be someone else in order to **deceive.** [290, 319]

impotent, *adj.* [IM-puh-tint] helpless, powerless, lacking force or ability. [298]

★ **improbable,** *adj.* unlikely to be true or to occur. [220, 227, 263, 275]

impromptu, *adj.* not planned or prepared, produced on the spur of the moment (synonym: **spontaneous**). [289]

impropriety, *n.* 1. the state or fact of being improper, esp. of being socially unacceptable or in bad taste. 2. an improper, unseemly, socially unacceptable act. [32, 169]

imprudently, *adv.* not in a **prudent** manner, unwisely, rashly. [185]

impudent, *adj.* disrespectful, often in a bold and cocky way (synonym: **insolent**). [7]

impugn, *v.* to challenge as false or questionable, attack by argument. [135]

★ **impulse,** *n.* a sudden, involuntary urge or wish to do something. [89, 118, 156]

inaccessible, *adj.* not **accessible.** [87]

inadvertent, *adj.* not intentional. **inadvertently,** *adv.* [18, 109, 139, 158, 228, 294]

inane, *adj.* without sense or substance, silly, foolish, pointless: an *inane* comment (synonym: **fatuous**). [19, 38, 223]

inanimate, *adj.* not living, not alive or **animated.** [123, 213]

inarticulate, *adj.* 1. not clearly understandable, garbled, unintelligible (synonyms: **impenetrable**[2], **incomprehensible, indecipherable**). 2. unable to express oneself clearly and effectively. [262, 278, 311]

incarcerated, *adj.* put in jail or in a cage, locked up. [145, 184, 204]

incarnate, *adj.* given bodily, and esp. human, form; **embodied,** made flesh, personified (cf. **personification**). [161]

incensed, *adj.* furious, enraged. [213, 258]

incessant, *adj.* not stopping or **ceasing,** continuing without interruption (synonyms: **continuous, unremitting**). [1, 21, 115, 135]

incipient, *adj.* coming into being, beginning to exist or appear: an *incipient* headache. [152]

incite, *v.* to urge to action, inspire, stir up (synonyms: **goad, instigate, provoke**). [117, 169]

inclination, *n.* a leaning or tendency toward, desire to do or prefer something. [118]

incoherently, *adv.* not in a **coherent** manner. [85, 223, 277]

incomparable, *adj.* so great or outstanding as to be beyond comparison, having no equal, matchless (synonym: **unparalleled**). [v, 127]

incompetent, *adj.* without ability or skill, not **competent** (synonyms: **inept, maladroit**). [96, 216]

incomprehensible, *adj.* impossible to understand, not **comprehensible** (synonyms: **impenetrable**[2], **inarticulate**[1], **indecipherable**). [57, 254]

inconceivable, *adj.* unimaginable, not **conceivable**. [218]

incongruous, *adj.* inappropriate, not suitable, incompatible, out of place. [153, 238, 271]

inconsequential, *adj.* of no importance or significance (synonym: **trivial**). [162]

incontrovertible, *adj.* not possible to argue, unquestionable (synonym: **indisputable**). [219]

incredulous, *adj.* unwilling to believe, unable to accept as true, doubting (synonyms: **dubious**[3], **skeptical**). [75, 105, 134, 300]

incriminating, *adj.* showing evidence of guilt or fault. [183, 285, 312]

indecipherable, *adj.* not capable of being **deciphered** (synonyms: **impenetrable**[2], **inarticulate**[1], **incomprehensible**). [254]

indecisive, *adj.* unable to decide, not able to make up one's mind (antonym: **resolute**). [92]

indecorous, *adj.* socially inappropriate, unseemly, violating standards of good conduct or good taste (synonym: **unbecoming**). [4, 166]

indefatigably, *adv.* in an *indefatigable* manner, tirelessly, never running out of steam. [170]

indictment, *n.* a formal accusation of wrongdoing, a serious criticism of or charge against. [31]

★ **indifferent,** *adj.* having no interest or concern, not caring (synonyms: **aloof, apathetic, detached,** and see **phlegmatic**). ★ **indifference,** *n.* [xii, 36, 51, 135, 136, 162, 207, 256, 301]

indigenous, *adj.* native, homegrown, belonging to or originating in a particular place. [21]

★ **indignant,** *adj.* filled with or expressing **indignation**. [263, 271]

indignation, *n.* anger **aroused** by something unjust or unfair (synonyms: **outrage, resentment**). [163, 275, 311]

indiscretion, *n.* a failure to be **discreet**; a lack of proper caution, control, and **sound** judgment. [191, 285]

indiscriminately, *adv.* in an *indiscriminate* manner, without making any distinctions or judgments, unselectively. [224]

indispensable, *adj.* essential, absolutely necessary (synonyms: **mandatory, requisite**). [64, 81, 124, 152, 420]

indisputable, *adj.* undeniable, impossible to doubt or dispute (synonym: **incontrovertible**). [69]

★ **indistinct,** *adj.* not clear to the mind or the senses, hard to recognize, blurred, hazy, dim, faint, **vague,** not **distinct**[2]. [156, 276, 303]

indolent, *adj.* lazy, avoiding **exertion** (synonyms: **listless, lethargic**). [92]

★ **induce,** *v.* 1. to cause, bring about. 2. to influence or persuade to do something. [175, 212, 229, 257, 286]

★ **indulge,** *v.* 1. to do, enjoy, or partake of, esp. immoderately; take unrestrained pleasure in. 2. to yield to or **gratify** the wishes or desires of another, humor, tolerate, be permissive with. **indulgence,** *n.* [17, 85, 92, 118, 220, 235, 241, 262]

industrious, *adj.* hardworking (synonyms: **assiduous, diligent, sedulous**). [xi, 17]

ineffable, *adj.* indescribable, inexpressible, unutterable. **ineffably,** *adv.* [112, 175, 261, 313]

ineluctable, *adj.* unavoidable, incapable of being **evaded** (synonyms: **inescapable, inevitable**). [228]

inept, *adj.* having no skill or ability for a task, clumsy, bungling, awkward (synonyms: **incompetent, maladroit**). [270]

inescapable, *adj.* impossible to escape, ignore, or avoid (synonyms: **ineluctable, inevitable**). [88, 113]

inestimable, *adj.* impossible to estimate, calculate, or **assess.** [232, 304]

★ **inevitable,** *adj.* certain to happen, impossible to prevent, unavoidable (synonyms: **ineluctable, inescapable**). **inevitably,** *adv.* [51, 106, 142, 202, 218, 229, 260]

inexorable, *adj.* not able to be stopped, changed, or moved by pleading or persuasion (synonym: **relentless**). **inexorably,** *adv.* [204, 218, 272]

inextricably, *adv.* in a way that cannot be undone, disentangled, or **extricated.** [200]

infamous, *adj.* having a very bad reputation (synonym: **notorious**). [144]

infantile, *adj.* childish, babyish. [53]

★ **infer,** *v.* to reason or conclude from evidence, figure out a meaning. **inference,** *n.* [xii, 42, 121, 170, 175, 217, 242]
Usage note: Be careful not to confuse the verbs *imply* and *infer.* To *imply* is to hint or suggest rather than say something outright: Her statement *implies* support for his proposal. To *infer* is to use one's power of reasoning to come to a conclusion based on evidence: He *inferred* from her statement that she supported his proposal. You may *infer* (come to a conclusion, **derive** a meaning) from something *implied* (hinted at, suggested, stated indirectly). But don't use *infer* when you mean *imply*: "She declined to comment on his proposal, *inferring* that she did not support it" is **erroneous.**

infiltrate, *v.* to penetrate, enter **surreptitiously** or by stealth. [57, 61]

infinite, *adj.* 1. immeasurably great, unlimited. 2. without beginning or end, endless (synonyms: **boundless, vast**). **infinitely,** *adv.* [84, 178, 199, 226]

infinite, *n.* something **infinite**: She gazed up into the sky, into space, into the *infinite.* [272]

inflammation, *n.* redness and swelling in an area of the body in response to irritation or infection. [107]

★ **inflation,** *n.* the steady increase over time in how much things cost, accompanied by a decline in the purchasing power of money. [111]

inflict, *v.* to give or **impose** something unpleasant and unwelcome that must be **endured.** [151]

ingenious, *adj.* very clever, creative, and imaginative: an *ingenious* plan. [78]

ingenuity, *n.* cleverness, skill, and imagination. [226]

ingest, *v.* to eat, take into the body for nourishment; **figuratively,** to absorb, take in to nourish the mind: *ingesting* many new ideas from her recent reading. [206, 219]

ingrained, *adj.* firmly fixed or established, worked deeply into, deep-seated (cf. **institutionalized**). [64, 188]

ingratiate, *v.* to try to gain the favor of; try to get in someone's good graces; work deliberately to make oneself acceptable or likable to another. [110]

★ **inhabit,** *v.* to live in, dwell or reside in. [175]

★ **inhabitant,** *n.* a person who lives in a certain place. [15, 86, 116]

★ **inherent,** *adj.* essential, existing within someone or something as a natural, permanent element or condition (synonyms: **innate, intrinsic**). **inherently,** *adv.* [xii, 141, 198, 209, 220]

★ **initial,** *adj.* of or coming at the beginning, earliest, first. **initially,** *adv.* [140, 182, 193, 250, 279]

★ **initiate,** *v.* to start, begin, get going, set in motion. [92, 146, 204, 229]

initiative, *n.* the power, ability, and readiness to accomplish something; determination. [179]

innate, *adj.* 1. inborn, possessed at birth, natural as opposed to acquired. 2. having as an essential quality or characteristic (synonyms: **inherent, intrinsic**). [132, 205]

innocuous, *adj.* harmless, not causing injury or ill will: an *innocuous* remark. [17, 68, 228, 272]

★ **innovation,** *n.* 1. the introduction of new things, e.g. devices, ideas, methods, etc.; invention. 2. something new, different, or improved that is introduced; an invention. [54, 86, 88, 206]

★ **innovative,** *adj.* characterized by **innovation,** introducing something new (synonym: **novel**). [x, 31, 196]

innovator, *n.* someone who introduces new devices, methods, or ideas; an inventor or reformer. [204]

innumerable, *adj.* countless, numberless, incalculable, too numerous to be counted (synonym: **myriad**). [83, 229]

inordinate, *adj.* excessive, immoderate, going beyond reasonable or acceptable limits. [167, 222]

★ **inquisitive,** *adj.* inclined to ask questions, extremely curious: an *inquisitive* child. [10, 62]

inquisitor, *n.* a questioner, a person who conducts an **interrogation**, esp. a harsh one. [167]

insatiable, *adj.* never satisfied, never getting enough (synonyms: **ravenous, voracious**). **insatiably,** *adv.* [66, 206]

inscrutable, *adj.* mysterious, difficult to **interpret** or understand (synonyms: **cryptic, enigmatic, perplexing**). [1, 177, 253]

insidious, *adj.* evil or **treacherous** in a sly, underhanded manner; working or spreading ill or harm in a hidden, dangerous way. [123, 131]

★ **insight,** *n.* 1. the power or ability to understand something by **discerning** its true nature or meaning (synonyms: **edification, enlightenment**). 2. **keen** or **penetrating** understanding, knowledge of the true nature or meaning of something (synonym: **enlightenment**). 3. an instance of seeing deeply into something or someone. [197, 207, 210, 217, 218, 277, 420]

insincere, *adj.* not **sincere** (synonyms: **disingenuous, hypocritical**; antonyms: **candid, forthcoming**[1]**, frank, straightforward**). [121]

insinuate, *v.* to suggest in a sly way, make a nasty hint. [93]

insipid, *adj.* 1. not having enough flavor, not tasty, lacking **zest**. 2. not interesting, dull, boring (synonyms: **bland, vapid**). [xiii, 82, 91, 208, 220, 248]

insistent, *adj.* demanding attention or notice in an **emphatic** manner. [6, 147]

insolence, *n.* bold disrespect; **presumptuous** rudeness. [44, 261]

insolent, *adj.* boldly insulting and disrespectful; rudely **presumptuous** (synonym: **impudent**). [68, 110, 124]

insomniac, *n.* a person who consistently has trouble falling and remaining asleep. [117]

instantaneously, *adv.* happening in an instant, without any apparent delay. [199]

instigate, *v.* to cause to happen by stirring up (synonyms: **goad, incite, provoke**). **instigating,** *adj.* [227]

★ **institution,** *n.* 1. a well-established custom or practice accepted as basic to a society or culture: the *institution* of marriage. 2. an organization dedicated to education, the arts, public service, or charity. [31, 154]

institutionalized, *adj.* made into an **institution**[1], firmly established (cf. **ingrained**). [131]

insufferable, *adj.* impossible to **endure** (synonym: **intolerable**). [28, 136, 161, 170]

insurgency, *n.* rebellion, armed opposition or resistance. [217]

insurmountable, *adj.* impossible to overcome. [261]

intact, *adj.* entire, whole, with no part removed or damaged. [143, 321]

intangible, *adj.* indefinite, hard to grasp with the mind or senses; not **tangible**, not **palpable** (synonyms: **elusive, vague**). [74, 143]

integral, *adj.* essential as a part of the whole, necessary for completeness. [200]

★ **intellect,** *n.* the ability to think and learn; capacity for acquiring **complex** knowledge. [155]

★ **intellectual,** *adj.* of or pert. to the **intellect**. [79, 131, 151, 204, 216, 257]

intemperate, *adj.* excessive, immoderate, esp. in drinking alcoholic beverages. [188]

intent, *adj.* 1. determined, firmly fixed or focused on something. 2. concentrated, sharply attentive. **intently,** *adv.* [45, 121, 138, 143, 156, 274]

interject, *v.* to insert or introduce between other elements, often quickly or **abruptly**; toss or throw in, interrupt, interpose. [43, 79, 104, 135, 277, 310]

interminable, *adj.* never-ending or seeming never to end, painfully **protracted.** [95, 158, 161, 170, 201, 234]

★ **interpret,** *v.* to figure out the meaning of, make sense of, understand, construe. [xii, xiv, 254, 296]

★ **interpretation,** *n.* a way of understanding or regarding something, an explanation or **inference** (cf. **commentary**). [119]

interrogation, *n.* an examination by questioning. [66, 170, 189, 313]

intervene, *v.* to come between, interfere, esp. to change a situation. **intervening,** *adj.* **intervention,** *n.* [111, 220, 228, 262, 270]

★ **intimate,** *adj.* 1. physically close, amorous or sexual. 2. cozy and familiar. 3. very dear, emotionally close. 4. closely acquainted, thoroughly familiar. [28, 133, 188, 217, 233]

intolerable, *adj.* unbearable, agonizing (synonym: **insufferable**). [117, 135, 321]

intolerance, *n.* unwillingness to accept or respect others' beliefs or practices. [102]

intractable, *adj.* stubbornly uncooperative, difficult to manage or control, unruly (synonyms: **adamant, obstinate, recalcitrant**). [2, 3, 239]

intrepid, *adj.* brave, courageous, daring, unafraid. [114, 260]

intricate, *adj.* highly detailed, **elaborate,** complicated, or **complex.** [176, 296]

intrigued, *adj.* fascinated, excited, **captivated.** [65]

intrinsic, *adj.* belonging to the essential nature of a thing (synonyms: **inherent, innate**). [208]

intrusion, *n.* an unwelcome interruption, unexpected and uninvited interference. [229, 302]

★ **intuition,** *n.* the ability to know or understand immediately, without conscious reasoning. **intuitively,** *adv.* [31, 156]

inundate, *v.* to overwhelm, swamp, flood. [149]

invaluable, *adj.* worth more than can be estimated, priceless. [129, 139, 275, 298, 419]

invective, *n.* **vehement,** scathing language that accuses or denounces: the radio talk show host issued a stream of *invective.* [93, 134, 213, 257]

★ **invigorate,** *v.* to give strength and energy to, make **vigorous** or **animated. invigorating,** *adj.* [30, 120]

inviolable, *adj.* not able to be violated, secure, safe from harm or assault. [57, 260]

irascibility, *n.* sudden anger or extreme annoyance, angry outburst, irritable fit. [150]

irate, *adj.* filled with *ire,* extreme anger often openly displayed. [279]

★ **irony,** *n.* a manner of expression that **implies** the opposite of what the words **literally** mean, as when one says "Thanks for sharing" after hearing something unpleasant (see **sarcasm**). ★ **ironic,** *adj.* (synonym: **satirical,** cf. **irreverent**). ★ **ironically,** *adv.* [2, 33, 37, 44, 88, 103, 303]

★ **irrational,** *adj.* 1. not **rational,** not governed by reason. 2. not logical or sensible. [272, 278]

★ **irrelevant,** *adj.* not **relevant,** unrelated or unimportant, having no bearing on the matter at hand. [58, 151, 199, 302, 314]

irreverent, *adj.* criticizing or challenging what is generally accepted or respected, esp. by making fun of it in an **ironic** way (cf. **satirical**). **irreverence,** *n.* [xxi, 188, 195, 213]

irrevocable, *adj.* impossible to bring back, undo, or alter: an *irrevocable* decision. **irrevocably,** *adj.* [283]

★ **isolate,** *v.* to set apart or separate from others. [156]

itinerant, *adj.* traveling from place to place. [284, 324]

J

jaded, *adj.* worn out, tired, esp. from experiencing too much of something. [53, 220]

jargon, *n.* the technical language used by members of a particular profession; a specialized, **abstruse** vocabulary, often one unnecesarily hard to understand (synonym: **gobbledygook**). [57, 201, 254, 260]

jaunty, *adj.* lively, brisk, and self-confident in manner. **jauntiness,** *n.* [94, 105, 242]

jeopardize, *v.* to put at risk, expose to loss or damage, imperil. [141]

jettison, *v.* to discard, throw away, cast overboard. [205]

jocular, *adj.* given to or characterized by joking or jesting, playful, witty. [2]

jovial, *adj.* jolly, good-natured, full of good cheer (synonyms: **affable, congenial, cordial, gracious,** and see note at **amiable**). [2, 189, 312]

jubilation, *n.* great satisfaction and joy, esp. triumphant joy. [264]

judicious, *adj.* characterized by good judgment, sensible, wise (synonym: **prudent**). **judiciously,** *adv.* [98, 118, 303, 325]

justified, *adj.* warranted, having sufficient reason or grounds for. [170]

★ **justify,** *v.* to show or prove to be right and reasonable. [21, 118, 185]

juvenile, *adj.* 1. childish, immature. 2. youthful, typical of young people. [44, 94, 128]

K

keen, *adj.* 1. **intellectually** sharp or sensitive (synonyms: **astute, penetrating, perceptive, perspicacious, sagacious, shrewd**). 2. intense, strong (synonyms: **acute, vivid**). **keenly,** *adv.* [xvi, 25, 86, 131, 321]

L

laborious, *adj.* requiring hard work and **diligence. laboriously,** *adv.* [58, 122, 266]

labyrinth, *n.* a maze; a **bewildering** place in which it is hard to find one's way around or get out. [77, 176]

laconic, *adj.* inclined to use few words, speaking briefly and often bluntly (synonym: **reticent**). [xi, xii, 98]

languid, *adj.* having no energy or interest, weak, spiritless (see **phlegmatic**). [16]

languish, *v.* 1. to lose strength or health, become weak or **feeble,** suffer hardship or neglect. 2. to exist in a continued state of distress, misery, or depression. [200, 207, 313]

lapse, *v.* to fall, slip, or sink gradually and smoothly. [112, 223, 278]

latter, *adj.* the second of two things mentioned. [54, 119, 228]

lavishly, *adv.* in an overly rich and fancy manner (cf. **extravagant, sumptuous**). [297]

learned, *adj.* [LUR-nid] having extensive knowledge, scholarly (synonym: **erudite**). [205]

leery, *adj.* suspicious, distrustful, **wary.** [110]

★ **legacy,** *n.* something handed down from an ancestor or from the past (cf. **heritage**[2]). [24, 69, 185, 420]

leniency, *n.* mercy, forgiveness. [109]

lethal, *adj.* deadly, **fatal.** [117]

lethargic, *adj.* having little or no energy, drowsy and dull (synonyms: **indolent, listless,** and see **phlegmatic**). [91]

levity, *n.* joking around, silliness, esp. at inappropriate moments. [63, 64, 279]

liable, *adj.* likely to experience something unpleasant or unfortunate. [264]

licentious, *adj.* lacking **moral** restraint, esp. in sexual conduct. [219]

listless, *adj.* showing no interest or effort, lacking energy (synonyms: **indolent, lethargic,** and see **phlegmatic**). [91]

litany, *n.* a long list or recitation. [111]

literacy, *n.* the ability to read and write. [205]

literally, *adv.* actually, in the strict or primary sense of a word or expression, not **metaphorically** (cf. **figuratively**). [92, 97, 104, 152, 155]

litigious, *adj.* of or pert. to *litigation,* lawsuits or legal proceedings. [142]

loath, *adj.* unwilling (synonym: **reluctant**). [175, 200]

loathe, *v.* to dislike intensely, hate, detest (synonym: **abhor**). [96, 248, 313]

loathsome, *adj.* disgusting, revolting (synonyms: **abhorrent, appalling, distasteful, odious, offensive, repugnant, repulsive**). [291]

locomotion, *n.* the ability to move from place to place. [230]

★ **lofty,** *adj.* 1. of great or impressive height. 2. noble, grand, high-minded (synonym: **exalted**). [25, 134, 196]

loiter, *v.* to hang around a place with no obvious aim or purpose. [183]

long-standing, *adj.* existing or lasting a long time. [143]

loom, *v.* to come into view, esp. in a distorted, **indistinct,** or **imposing** way. [2, 60, 82, 155, 165]

loophole, *n.* a small, narrow opening or slit in a wall (of a castle or fortification) through which an enemy can be observed and weapons can be discharged. [153]

loquacious, *adj.* talkative, esp. excessively (synonyms: **garrulous, voluble**). [119, 136, 419]

lucid, *adj.* 1. easily understood, clear, plain (synonym: **distinct**[2]; cf. **elucidate**). 2. **luminous** or transparent. [123, 285]

lucrative, *adj.* profitable, making money, creating wealth. [54, 83, 245]

ludicrous, *adj.* laughable, hilarious, ridiculous (synonyms: **absurd, farcical, preposterous**). **ludicrously,** *adv.* [9, 16, 134]

lugubrious, *adj.* **mournful,** gloomy, dismal, esp. in an exaggerated way. [243]

lull, *n.* a temporary period of quiet, calm, or decline in activity: a *lull* in sales; a *lull* in traffic (cf. **hiatus, respite**). [4, 110]

lumber, *v.* to move in a heavy or clumsy way. [27, 135]

luminous, *adj.* giving off light, shining, glowing, bright (synonym: **radiant**[1]). [20, 84, 169, 204, 224, 321]

lummox, *n.* a clumsy and stupid person, an oaf. [171]

lure, *v.* to attract or tempt (synonym: **entice**). [218]

lurid, *adj.* shocking in an exaggerated, overly dramatic way (synonym: **sensational**). [137, 216]

lurk, *v.* 1. to lie in wait, lie hidden in ambush. 2. to exist unseen and unsuspected. [169, 325]

lush, *adj.* 1. characterized by luxury, **opulent.** 2. appealing to the senses, sensuous. [25, 95]

luxuriant, *adj.* showing thick and **abundant** growth: *luxuriant* vegetation. [2, 174]

M

machination, *n.* (usu. in pl. *machinations*) a crafty scheme, cunning maneuver, **artful** design or plot to accomplish a **sinister** purpose. [111]

maelstrom, *n.* 1. a violently powerful whirlpool. 2. something as **turbulent** and **tumultuous** as a maelstrom (synonym: **turmoil**). [9, 276]

magnanimous, *adj.* noble and generous, high-minded, unselfish. [5, 233]

magnate, *n.* a person of great importance, influence, and power, esp. in business. [153, 245]

magnitude, *n.* greatness in size, extent, or significance: the *magnitude* of his **offense.** [299]

majestic, *adj.* grand, possessing majesty, having a **lofty** or **imposing** appearance or bearing (synonyms: **august, stately**). [1]

maladroit, *adj.* awkward, clumsy (synonyms: **incompetent, inept**). [172]

malevolent, *adj.* wishing or doing evil to others, showing ill will (synonym: **malicious**). [11, 52, 123]

malfunction, *v.* (of a machine or device) to fail to work or work improperly. [198]

malicious, *adj.* deliberately mean or nasty, desiring to hurt or harm, spiteful (synonym: **malevolent**). [47, 151]

malodorous, *adj.* having a disagreeable odor, stinking, foul-smelling (synonyms: **fetid, putrid, rancid**). [72, 117, 281]

mandatory, *adj.* ordered or commanded by authority, required, obligatory (synonyms: **indispensable, requisite**). [218]

mania, *n.* excessive enthusiasm or interest. [166]

manifest, *v.* to show plainly, display, reveal, make evident or clear. [86, 123, 150–51, 162]

manifest, *adj.* clear, apparent, obvious, easily seen or understood. [155]

★ **manipulate,** *v.* 1. to handle, operate or control by hand. 2. to alter or tamper with, usu. for personal advantage. 3. to manage, influence, or control cleverly and dishonestly for personal gain. **manipulation,** *n.* [57, 167, 202, 207, 226, 228]

mannerism, *n.* a **distinctive** and often **habitual** and unconscious way of behaving (synonym: **idiosyncrasy**). [64]

mar, *v.* to spoil, make imperfect, do damage to. [119]

★ **mass,** *adj.* 1. consisting of a great amount or number. 2. done or occurring on a large scale: *mass* production, *mass* destruction. [16, 84, 206, 217]

★ **mass,** *n.* a large body of matter without definite shape. [175]

masses, *n.* (preceded by *the*) the common people, working classes, proletariat. [207]

massive, *adj.* 1. unusually or impressively large and heavy: *massive* boulders (synonyms: **bulky, cumbersome, ponderous**[1]). 2. unusually or impressively large in scope, scale, or amount: a *massive* effort; a *massive* helping of food (synonyms: **colossal, gargantuan, immense, monumental**[1]**, prodigious**[2]. [xiii, 9, 20, 30, 85, 153, 245, 286, 322]

material, *adj.* consisting of matter, physical as opposed to spiritual, **palpable** as opposed to **intangible**. [74, 197]

maternal, *adj.* of or pert. to a mother. [247]

matron, *n.* a **dignified** old married woman or widow. [12]

maudlin, *adj.* foolishly or tearfully sentimental, esp. as the result of drinking alcohol. [221]

maxim, *n.* a **concise** expression of a general truth or rule of conduct (synonyms: **adage, aphorism, axiom**). [99, 145]

meager, *adj.* small or limited, insufficient, inadequate (synonym: **scanty**). [250]

meander, *v.* 1. to wind and turn, follow an indirect course. 2. to ramble, wander aimlessly. **meandering,** *adj.* [148, 223, 289]

★ **mechanism,** *n.* 1. a machine or mechanical device. 2. a process or means by which something is accomplished. [54, 198, 305]

meddle, *v.* to interfere, intrude where one is not wanted or does not belong. **meddling,** *n., adj.* [73, 301]

mediate, *v.* to bring about a settlement between disputing parties, act as a peacemaker or go-between. [188]

★ **medieval,** *adj.* of or pert. to the Middle Ages, the period in European history between the fall of the Roman Empire and the Renaissance, lasting from A.D. 478 to about 1450. [205]

meditation, *n.* **reflection** or **contemplation**, esp. in the form of an extended **discourse**. [233]

★ **medium,** *n.* a means or channel for **conveying** or expressing something. [210, 216]

melancholy, *adj.* 1. sad or gloomy, causing or feeling sadness or depression (synonyms: **mournful, plaintive, somber**[2]). 2. given to sad or gloomy thoughts, **pensive. melancholy,** *n.* [5, 20, 172, 203, 221, 287, 300]

melodious, *adj.* sweet-sounding, agreeable to the ear. [238, 285, 309]

memorable, *adj.* worth remembering (synonyms: **notable, noteworthy**). [97, 125, 163]

menacing, *adj.* threatening, showing an intention to do harm (synonyms: **forbidding**[2], **ominous, sinister**). [9, 29, 175, 261, 280]

mentor, *n.* one who acts as a wise and trusted guide or teacher; a counselor, **sage,** esp. for a person who is young or inexperienced. [23, 100, 126]

mercenary, *adj.* greedy, **avaricious,** spec. motivated by a desire for money, done only for reward or personal gain (synonym: **venal**). [245]

merciless, *adj.* without mercy, cruel, ruthless, pitiless (synonym: **remorseless**). **mercilessly,** *adv.* [115, 161, 272]

mercurial, *adj.* quick to change moods or change one's mind, **unpredictable** in behavior or **temperament** (synonyms: **capricious, volatile**). [2, 140]

★ **merit,** *n.* excellence. **merits,** *n.* pl. 1. **inherent** qualities, good or bad. 2. superior or praiseworthy qualities. **merit,** *adj.* [31, 58, 130, 232]

★ **merit** *v.* to deserve, earn, receive as one's due or gain because of one's effort. [257]

mesmerize, *v.* to fascinate, capture and hold the attention of, bind as if in a spell. **mesmerizing,** *adj.* [191, 235]

★ **metaphor,** *n.* a figure of speech that suggests a likeness between two otherwise unlike things, an **implied** comparison: "The road was a *ribbon* of black" and "Love is a *rose*" are *metaphors.* [229]

★ **metaphorical,** *adj.* expressing one thing in terms of another, using **metaphor. metaphorically,** *adv.* **figuratively,** not **literally.** [154]

methodical, *adj.* carried out in an orderly or **systematic** way: a *methodical* search. [189]

methodology, *n.* a **bombastic** word for "methods" or "rules and procedures." To **paraphrase** Mark Twain, you could start building a very expressive vocabulary just by leaving *methodology* out. [169]

★ **meticulous,** *adj.* extremely (often excessively) careful about details (synonyms: **conscientious**[2], **fastidious, painstaking**). **meticulously,** *adv.* [xiii, 3, 72, 173, 284]

mettle, *n.* spirit, courage, strength of character: show your *mettle* under pressure. [253]

microcosm, *n.* a miniature version or representation; a little world. [221]

★ **mimic,** *v.* to imitate, esp. to copy the speech or behavior of. [134, 293]

minimal, *adj.* 1. small in amount or degree. 2. the least amount possible or acceptable. [86, 189, 198]

minuscule, *adj.* very small, tiny (synonym: **minute**). [228, 266]

minute, *adj.* extremely small, tiny (synonym: **minuscule**). [60, 75, 104, 234, 282]

mirth, *n.* lightheartedness, often accompanied by laughter. [237, 298]

misanthrope, *n.* a person who hates or deeply distrusts other human beings. [172]

misanthropic, *adj.* having an **aversion** to the human race. [305]
misanthropy, *n.* hatred of humankind, spiteful **pessimism** about the human race. [150]

★ **misconception,** *n.* a misunderstanding, mistaken thought. [228]
misdeed, *n.* an illegal or **immoral** act (cf. **deed**). [184]
misguided, *adj.* mistaken, misled, based or acting on error. [196, 314]
mishap, *n.* an unfortunate accident, unlucky turn of events. [229, 323]
misinterpretation, *n.* a misunderstanding, incorrect **interpretation.** [131]
misinterpret, *v.* to misunderstand, **interpret** incorrectly. [77]
mitigate, *v.* to make less severe, intense, or serious (synonyms: **alleviate, assuage, mollify**). **mitigating,** *adj.* [184, 260, 319]
mobility, *n.* movement or the ability to move. [200]

★ **mock,** *v.* to make fun of, **ridicule,** show laughing **contempt** for (synonyms: **deride, taunt**). [11, 96, 293]

★ **mock,** *adj.* pretended, not real but made to look so: *mock* remorse. [26, 28, 53]
mockery, *n.* ridicule, making fun of, showing laughing **contempt** for (synonyms: **derision, taunting**). [47]
mode, *n.* method, type, means. [84, 199]

★ **modest,** *adj.* 1. not proud, boastful, or self-important; not wanting to call attention to oneself (synonym: **humble**[2]). 2. simple, plain, not **elaborate**[2] or **pretentious**: *modest* accommodations. 3. limited in scope or size: a *modest* proposal. [xii, 5, 78, 119, 187, 219, 317]
modicum, *n.* a small amount. [234]
modulate, *v.* to adjust to an appropriate level, adapt to fit the circumstances. **modulated,** *adj.* [164]

★ **molecule,** *n.* the smallest chemical or physical particle of an element or compound. **molecular,** *adj.* [197, 198, 209]
mollify, *v.* to soothe, appease, pacify; make less intense or severe (synonyms: **alleviate, assuage, mitigate, placate**). [159, 188]
momentous, *adj.* of great importance and significance. [205]

★ **monarch,** *n.* historically, the hereditary ruler of a state (e.g. a king); hence, a person with supreme power or the leader in some **domain.** [223, 256]

★ **monarchy,** *n.* government led by a **monarch,** a hereditary ruler. [204, 217, 256]
monolithic, *adj.* made of or resembling a single large block of stone; hence, solid and **massive** in appearance or character. [25]
monopoly, *n.* a group exercising exclusive control over the production and sale of a **commodity.** [84]
monotonous, *adj.* sounded or spoken in a tone that does not change or vary. [85]
monument, *n.* something built to honor or remember a person (synonym: **tribute**). [155]
monumental, *adj.* 1. huge or great (synonyms: **colossal, gargantuan, immense, massive**[2]**, prodigious**[2]). 2. hugely important or significant. [155, 218]

★ **moral,** *adj.* 1. affecting the mind or will, having a psychological influence: *moral* support. 2. showing or teaching right behavior or the difference between right and wrong. 3. concerned with right and wrong, affecting the conscience. **morally,** *adv.* [98, 130, 131, 202, 209, 219]

moral, *n.* a **moral**[2] or practical lesson. [33]

moralistic, *adj.* 1. concerned with **morality,** choosing between right and wrong. 2. controlling or regulating **morality,** esp. in a narrow-minded and excessively strict way. [110, 213]

★ **morality,** *n.* the standards of, or the distinction between, right and wrong behavior. **morality,** *adj.* [31, 207]

mortify, *v.* to humiliate, embarrass, injure one's pride or self-respect. **mortified,** *adj.* [35, 37, 41, 43, 244, 286]

★ **motivation,** *n.* a reason or cause to act. [109, 130, 162, 195, 203]

★ **motive,** *n.* something (an emotion, desire, need, etc.) that makes a person behave in a certain way. [33, 62, 126, 182, 275]

mournful, *adj.* full of sorrow or grief (synonyms: **melancholy, plaintive**). [5, 56]

muffled, *adj.* dulled or deadened in sound, lowered in volume as if by being wrapped in something. [116, 138, 158, 303, 322]

multifaceted, *adj.* having many aspects or elements. [159]

multiplicity, *n.* a large number (synonym: **multitude**[2]). [226]

multitude, *n.* 1. a great number of people gathered together, a host, army. 2. a great number of something (synonym: **multiplicity**). [57, 221]

★ **mundane,** *adj.* common, everyday, ordinary: *mundane* affairs (synonyms: **commonplace, pedestrian**). [25, 54, 83, 211]

munificence, *n.* great generosity. **munificent,** *adj.* [88, 153]

murky, *adj.* made dark or cloudy by sediment. [235]

mute, *adj.* silent, not speaking or making sound. [1, 263]

mutual, *adj.* shared, common. [235]

myriad, *adj.* consisting of a very great but indefinite number (synonym: **innumerable**). **myriad,** *n.* [1, 25, 96, 134, 201, 221, 306]

—*Usage note*: Some people **assert** that the noun *myriad* should be avoided, but there is no reasonable basis for the objection. In fact, the noun is more than two hundred years older than the adjective and has been used by many **reputable** writers. The choice between the adjective and the noun, says *Garner's Modern American Usage,* "is a question of style, not correctness."

mystique, *n.* an aura or special quality of mystery and power surrounding a person. [301]

mythic, *adj.* of the nature of a *myth,* a story or legend involving gods or heroes. [150]

mythologize, *v.* to make the stuff of *myth,* turn into a heroic or godlike figure. [175]

N

★ **naive,** *adj.* simple, innocent, and childlike (synonym: **guileless**; antonym: **disingenuous**). [137, 229]

narcissistic, *adj.* admiring or loving oneself excessively. [40]

★ **navigate,** *v.* to steer a course, sail, make one's way. [114, 185, 237]

negligence, *n.* a failure to exercise appropriate care or concern. [178]

negligible, *adj.* too small or unimportant to be worth considering (synonyms: **inconsequential, trivial**). [196]

nemesis, *n.* a **formidable**[3-4] opponent, enemy, or **rival**. [100, 169, 255]

neoclassical, *adj.* of or pert. to a revival of classical (ancient Greek and Roman) style, form, and **aesthetic** concerns. [147, 153]

neophyte, *n.* a beginner or recent convert (synonyms: **apprentice, novice**). [228]

nomad, *n.* a member of a group of people who do not have a permanent place to live and instead wander from place to place. [204]

nonchalantly, *adv.* in a cool, offhand, or unconcerned manner. [263]

nondescript, *adj.* without any **distinctive** qualities, having no special character, utterly ordinary and uninteresting. [88]

★ **norm,** *n.* a widely accepted standard; the typical behavior or beliefs of a group. [130]

nostalgia, *n.* a bittersweet longing for one's home or for something in the past. [126]

notable, *adj.* 1. worth pointing out or taking note of (synonyms: **memorable, noteworthy**). 2. important, outstanding (synonyms: see **distinguished**). [88, 109, 188, 204]

noteworthy, *adj.* deserving attention, worthy of notice (synonyms: **memorable, notable**). [205]

★ **notion,** *n.* 1. an idea (synonym: **concept**). 2. an opinion or belief. [31, 54, 87, 99, 127, 140, 192, 219, 229, 241, 299, 317, 325]

notoriety, *n.* the state of being **notorious**. [142]

notorious, *adj.* widely known, esp. unfavorably (synonym: **infamous**). [27, 150, 175, 289]

novel, *adj.* completely new, different from anything seen or done before: a *novel* approach (synonyms: **innovative, unprecedented**). [x, 141, 198]

novice, *n.* someone new to a task or situation, a beginner (synonyms: **apprentice, neophyte**). [210]

noxious, *adj.* harmful to a person's health or **morals**: *noxious* smoke; *noxious* influences (synonyms: **deleterious, detrimental, pernicious**; antonym: **wholesome**). [83]

nullify, *v.* to cancel, wipe out, **deprive** of value or force. [208]

nurture, *v.* to care for, help to grow and develop, provide with physical or **intellectual** nourishment (synonym: **cultivate**). [152, 256, 257]

O

★ **objective,** *n.* a goal, aim, purpose, something one strives to accomplish. [196]

oblige, *v.* 1. to be gratefully in another's debt for a service or favor given. 2. to do a service or favor for, yield to a request (synonym: **accommodate**). [70, 107, 189]

obliterate, *v.* to wipe out completely, destroy, remove any trace of: The storm *obliterated* the village (synonyms: **annihilate, eradicate**). [200, 302]

★ **oblivious,** *adj.* 1. forgetful, unable to remember. 2. unaware, not conscious or mindful. [65, 70, 136, 325]

obscenity, *n.* a word or expression, or certain words and expressions, considered indecent, insulting, lewd, or **profane**; a swearword or cursing in general. [213, 258]

★ **obscure,** *adj.* 1. not well-known: an *obscure* poem. 2. not plain or clear in meaning (synonyms: **ambiguous, vague**). 3. hard to understand; confusingly mysterious, strange, or complicated: an *obscure* message. 4. far off, at a great remove, remote. 5. not easily seen or heard, hard to **perceive, indistinct**: an *obscure* sound. [xiv, 22, 55, 74, 77, 87, 96, 148, 152, 277]

obsequious, *adj.* too eager to please, flatter, or obey (synonyms: **fawning, servile, sycophantic**). [257]

obsolescence, *n.* the process of becoming **obsolete.** [79]

obsolete, *adj.* no longer in use, out-of-date. [199]
—*Antiquated, outmoded, archaic,* and *obsolete* all refer to that which is old and out of general use. *Antiquated* and *outmoded* both mean no longer in style, out of fashion, but *antiquated* emphasizes a lack of suitability because of age or an inappropriate adherence to the past, while *outmoded* emphasizes that something is no longer practical or useful because of age: *antiquated* ideas; *outmoded* technology. *Archaic* suggests another **era,** a time long past: an *archaic* custom. *Obsolete* describes that which has been discarded or has long since fallen into disuse: an *obsolete* word.

obstinate, *adj.* stubborn, unyielding, inflexible, esp. in the face of argument, attack, or criticism (synonyms: **adamant, intractable**). **obstinately,** *adv.* [196, 223]

obstreperous, *adj.* 1. stubbornly resisting control, unruly (synonyms: **defiant, disorderly, intractable, recalcitrant**). 2. loud and unruly, **boisterous, clamorous** (synonyms: see **vociferous**). [68, 288]

obtuseness, *n.* stupidity, mental dullness. [230]

odious, *adj.* hateful or disgusting (synonyms: **appalling, distasteful, loathsome, offensive, repugnant, repulsive**). [163, 209]

offense, *n.* 1. an insult or **affront,** something that angers or wounds the feelings. 2. a violation of a rule, law, or **moral** code (synonym: **transgression**). [13, 44, 109, 125, 178, 185, 227, 319]

offensive, *adj.* 1. shocking to one's sense of decency, **morally** objectionable, crude and tasteless: *offensive,* off-color jokes. 2. insulting; causing anger, **resentment,** or extreme annoyance: *offensive* remarks. 3. disgusting, highly disagreeable to the senses: an *offensive* odor (synonyms: **appalling, distasteful, loathsome, odious, repugnant, repulsive**). [12, 32, 68, 130, 294]

officious, *adj.* overly forward in offering unasked for help or unwanted advice. [147]

★ **offspring,** *n.* a child or the children of a particular parent or parentage. [238]

olfactory, *adj.* of or pert. to the sense of smell. [27]

★ **ominous,** *adj.* threatening or foretelling evil, harm, or disaster (synonyms: **forbidding**[2], **menacing, sinister**). **ominously,** *adv.* [56, 152, 192, 248, 288]

omnipotent, *adj.* all-powerful, having infinite or unlimited power. [145]

omnipresent, *adj.* present everywhere at once (synonym: **ubiquitous**). [29]

omniscience, *n.* knowledge of everything. [57–58]

opaque, *adj.* characterized by **obtuseness**. [103]

opportunist, *n.* someone who takes advantage of any opportunity to get what he or she wants, without **scruples** and regardless of the **consequences**. [46, 255]

★ **oppression,** *n.* the cruel and unjust exercise of authority or power. [131, 218]

oppressive, *adj.* burdensome or depressing to the senses or spirit. [1]

optical, *adj.* of or pert. to the eyes or the sense of sight; visual. [191]

★ **optimism,** *n.* a cheerful and hopeful outlook on life, belief that the good always outweighs the bad and things tend to work out for the best (cf. **pessimism**). [188]

★ **optimistic,** *adj.* characterized by or full of **optimism** (antonym: **pessimistic**). [240]

★ **opulent,** *adj.* indicative of great wealth, very rich, costly, expensive: *an opulent* estate; *an opulent* lifestyle (synonyms: **extravagant, sumptuous**; cf. **lavishly**). [1]

★ **oral,** *adj.* using or consisting of speech; involving or done by the mouth. [120]

oration, *n.* a speech, esp. a formal or ceremonious one. [23, 208]

orator, *n.* a person who gives a speech, esp. a long, formal one. [7]

★ **organism,** *n.* an individual life form (e.g. an animal, plant, bacterium, etc.) [60]

ornate, *adj.* highly and often excessively decorated; fancy, showy. [2, 297]

★ **orthodoxy,** *n.* established belief or practice; also, the people who embrace and adhere to established belief and practice. [195]

ostensibly, *adv.* apparently, seeming to be so on the surface. [209, 216]

ostentatious, *adj.* showy or flashy in an attempt to impress, making a **conspicuous** display to attract attention (synonyms: **affected, grandiose, pompous, pretentious**). [1, 295]

outcast, *n.* a person rejected as unacceptable or inferior. [132]

outlandish, *adj.* strange, unfamiliar, strikingly different or odd: *outlandish* clothing; *outlandish* ideas (synonym: **bizarre**). [320]

outmoded, *adj.* old-fashioned, no longer useful or practical (synonyms: see **obsolete**). [199]

outrage, *n.* fierce anger caused by something wrong, insulting, or unjust (synonyms: **indignation, resentment**). **outraged,** *adj.* [11, 219, 275, 313]

outspoken, *adj.* spoken without reserve or restraint, **straightforward**. [292]

overt, *adj.* done or shown openly, not concealed, not **covert**. [130]

P

painstaking, *adj.* done with great effort and careful attention to detail (synonyms: **conscientious**[2], **diligent, fastidious, meticulous**). **painstakingly,** *adv.* [xi, 31, 189]

palliative, *adj.* serving to **alleviate,** helping to make less severe or intense. [170]

pallid, *adj.* pale; lacking color or liveliness: *pallid* skin; *pallid* prose (synonym: **wan**). [94, 127]

palpable, *adj.* capable of being felt or touched; hence, easily seen or **perceived** (synonym: **tangible**). [272, 419]

panacea, *n.* a cure-all, remedy for all ills or evils, solution for all troubles. [317]

paragon, *n.* a model of excellence or perfection: a *paragon* of virtue. [22, 41, 153, 230]

paramount, *adj.* 1. of the highest rank (synonym: **preeminent**). 2. of supreme importance. [78, 313]

paranoia, *n.* in general, extreme distrust and suspicion of others; spec. a mental disorder in which one sees oneself as a victim of **persecution** and imagines that other people have **hostile** intentions. **paranoid,** *adj.* affected with or exhibiting **paranoia**. [159, 258]

paraphrase, *v.* to put what someone else has expressed into different words, reword, restate. [47]

★ **passively,** *adv.* without reacting or responding. [257]

pastime, *n.* an amusement, such as a sport or hobby; any activity that gives pleasure and makes the time pass pleasantly (synonym: **diversion**). [220, 282]

patently, *adv.* plainly, obviously, **blatantly.** [164]

pathetic, *adj.* pitiful; **arousing** either sympathetic pity or **contemptuous** pity. **pathetic fallacy,** *n.* in literature, giving human qualities or feelings to **inanimate** objects or nature, as in *O sweet spontaneous earth* (E. E. Cummings). [40, 53, 103, 135, 257]

patron, *n.* a customer or paying guest. [169, 264]

pedantic, *adj.* scholarly in an **ostentatious** way; making an inappropriate or **tiresome** display of knowledge by placing **undue** importance on **trivial** details. [167]

pedestrian, *adj.* dull, ordinary, uninteresting (synonyms: **commonplace, mundane**). [112, 195]

★ **peer,** *n.* a person of equal standing, usu. a **colleague** or coworker. [151]

penchant, *n.* a strong liking or **inclination**: a *penchant* for gourmet food. [31, 119, 275]

penetrating, *adj.* quick to discover, recognize, or understand: a *penetrating* mind (synonyms: **astute, keen, perceptive, perspicacious, sagacious, shrewd**). [25]

penitent, *adj.* deeply sorry for one's sins or **misdeeds** (synonyms: **contrite, remorseful**). [19, 109]

pensive, *adj.* deeply thoughtful, often in a sad or dreamy way (synonym: **contemplative**). **pensively,** *adv.* [2, 86, 276]

penurious, *adj.* poor, living in poverty. [207]

perambulate, *v.* to walk around or about; stroll, roam. [112, 257]

★ **perceive,** *v.* to become aware of through the senses, esp. the sight; to observe, take notice of; to grasp mentally, understand (synonym: **comprehend**; cf. **detect, discern**). [31, 33, 71, 154, 155, 206, 234]

★ **perception,** *n.* 1. knowledge or ability to know, comprehension, **insight.** 2. a way of **perceiving** something. [103, 155, 195, 286]

perceptive, *adj.* quick to understand or see the true nature of something (synonyms: **astute, keen, penetrating, perspicacious, sagacious, shrewd**). [xiv, 11, 22, 42, 99, 138]

perfidious, *adj.* deliberately betraying another's trust or confidence. [265]

perfunctory, *adj.* 1. showing little interest or enthusiasm, careless, halfhearted: a *perfunctory* effort (synonym: **apathetic**[1]). 2. done in a routine manner, with little interest or care, as if merely to get finished (synonyms: **cursory, superficial**). [195, 216]

perilous, *adj.* dangerous, involving great risk (synonyms: **hazardous, treacherous**). [207, 217]

periphery, *n.* a boundary or the area just outside a boundary: the *periphery* of town. [304]

permutation, *n.* a thorough change in form, character, or condition; transformation, alteration. [226]

pernicious, *adj.* harmful, destructive (synonyms: **detrimental, deleterious, noxious**). [106, 228]

perpendicular, *adj.* being at a right angle to, like the vertical and horizontal lines of the capital letter L. [191, 262]

perpetrator, *n.* a person responsible for carrying something out, esp. a **misdeed.** [31]

perpetual, *adj.* lasting or continuing forever. [133]

perplexed, *adj.* puzzled, confused (synonyms: **baffled, bemused**[2]**, bewildered**) [51, 68, 76, 92, 305]

perplexing, *adj.* puzzling, confusing, **baffling** (synonyms: **cryptic, enigmatic, inscrutable**). [141]

perplexity, *n.* a state of confusion, puzzlement, or troubled **uncertainty**[2]. [12]

perquisite, *n.* a benefit, something received in addition to one's salary or wage: Use of the company gym is a great *perquisite* of the job. [218]

persecution, *n.* constant bothering or annoyance (synonym: **harassment**). [164, 165]

persevere, *v.* to persist or show **persistence,** continuing despite hardship or discouragement. [27]

persistent, *adj.* continuing in spite of difficulty or opposition, **persevering** (synonyms: **dogged, tenacious, undaunted**). **persistence,** *n.* **persistently,** *adv.* [6, 102, 113, 165, 255, 274, 291]

persona, *n.* public personality, the image one presents in public. [175]

personification, *n.* in literature, representing an idea or an **inanimate** object as having human qualities or human form: She is the *personification* of sweetness. [150]

perspicacious, *adj.* having a powerful and **penetrating** mind, quick to see and understand (synonyms: **astute, keen, perceptive, sagacious, shrewd**). **perspicacity,** *n.* [xvii, 25, 217]

pertinent, *adj.* connected in some way to the matter at hand, to the point, appropriate (synonyms: **applicable, relevant**) [xix, 176]

perturbation, *n.* the state of being **perturbed**, agitation, disquiet, uneasiness. [234]

perturbed, *adj.* made anxious or uneasy, disturbed, upset, agitated, disquieted, (synonym: **disconcerted**; antonym: **imperturbable**). [191]

peruse, *v.* to read or examine closely and carefully: *perused* the contract before signing (synonym: **scrutinize**). [xi, 16, 22, 85, 217]

pervade, *v.* to spread or be present throughout. [116]

pessimism, *n.* a gloomy and negative outlook on life, a belief that something bad is going to happen and that things tend to go from bad to worse (cf. **optimism**). [188, 220]

★ **pessimistic,** *adj.* characterized by or full of **pessimism** (antonym: **optimistic**). [126]

petty, *adj.* of little importance, minor: a *petty* disagreement; a *petty* complaint (synonym: **trivial**). [44, 319]

phantasm, *n.* a fantasy, creation of the imagination, **illusion**. [286]

★ **phenomena,** *n.* pl. (sing. *phenomenon*) observable events or circumstances. [124]

philanthropy, *n.* charitable giving, contributing money to help others or support a worthy cause. [39, 126]

phlegmatic, *adj.* not easily excited or moved to action, calm, unemotional. [xi, 92, 305]
    —*Sluggish, listless, lethargic,* and *languid* suggest a lack of energy and a lack of desire to act. *Apathetic, dispassionate, impassive,* and *indifferent* suggest a lack of emotion, interest, or concern. *Phlegmatic* suggests a lack of both emotion and energy.

phobia, *n.* an overwhelming fear or hatred of something. [313]

picturesque, *adj.* visually charming and attractive, resembling a painting or picture. [1]

pious, *adj.* deeply religious (synonym: **devout**). [31]

placate, *v.* to soothe the feelings of, pacify, appease (synonym: **mollify**). **placating,** *adj.* [61, 159, 309]

placid, *adj.* calm, peaceful, quiet: a *placid* lake (synonyms: **serene, tranquil**). [174]

plagiarize, *v.* to use someone else's words or ideas without permission or acknowledgment. [255, 257, 258]

★ **plague,** *v.* to bother, pester, annoy in a **persistent** manner. [123]

plaintive, *adj.* expressing sorrow, grief, or longing (synonyms: **melancholy, mournful**). [203]

plaudit, *n.* (usu. used in pl. *plaudits*) enthusiastic praise or approval. [266]

★ **plausible,** *adj.* seemingly true, honest, or reasonable; appearing worthy of belief or trust on first glance: a *plausible* excuse for arriving late. [51, 193, 246, 275]

plentiful, *adj.* existing in **ample** and **abundant** supply. [86]

plethora, *n.* an excessive amount or a very large number (synonyms: **abundance, profusion**). [xii, 89, 122, 419]

ploy, *n.* a crafty and **devious** maneuver performed to frustrate or gain an advantage over an opponent (synonyms: **ruse, stratagem**). [167]

plummet, *v.* to fall or drop sharply and suddenly. [271]

plunder, *v.* to take wrongfully or by force, steal, loot. [196, 257]

poignant, *adj.* affecting the emotions, touching, intensely or painfully moving: a *poignant* reunion. [31]

poised, *adj.* positioned, in a position to. [259]

pompous, *adj.* puffed up with self-importance (synonyms: **affected, grandiose, ostentatious, pretentious**). **pompously,** *adv.* [230, 257, 260, 314]

ponder, *v.* to weigh in the mind, reflect upon, think carefully or deeply about (synonyms: **contemplate, ruminate**). [26, 89, 118, 306]

ponderous, *adj.* 1. large and heavy (synonyms: **bulky, cumbersome, massive**[1]). 2. dull, boring, labored. [66, 112, 169]

pontificate, *v.* to express oneself in a **pompous** or **dogmatic** way. [122, 313]

★ **portray,** *v.* 1. to describe in words. 2. to represent in a picture or by acting out (synonym: **depict**). **portrayal,** *n.* [11, 31, 132, 174]

posit, *v.* to present as a fact or suggest as an explanation (synonym: **postulate**). [100]

★ **posterity,** *n.* future generations. [83]

postulate, *v.* to **assert** as a fact or truth, assume without proof, esp. as a basis for reasoning or argument (synonym: **posit**). [154, 226]

practicable, *adj.* doable, possible, capable of being accomplished. [260]

pragmatic, *adj.* practical as opposed to **theoretical**. [17, 39]

precarious, *adj.* characterized by risk or danger, not safe or secure, subject to chance. [189, 283]

preceding, *adj.* coming before in time or sequence. [103]

precocious, *adj.* showing marked ability, talent, or development at an unusually early age. [21, 151, 210, 419]

precept, *n.* a rule for guiding conduct or action. [xvii]

★ **predator,** *n.* a creature that hunts other creatures for food. [177]

predatory, *adj.* like a **predator**; **plundering**; living by feeding on other creatures (**literally** or **figuratively**). [170, 262]

predicament, *n.* a troublesome, unpleasant situation that is difficult to fix or get out of (synonyms: see **quandary**). [71, 229, 261]

preeminent, *adj.* supreme, chief, outstanding, **notable** above all others (synonym: **paramount**[1]). [202]

preening, *adj.* dressing and grooming oneself in an excessively careful way. [76]

★ **preoccupation,** *n.* 1. something that absorbs the mind or attention, that makes one **preoccupied**. 2. the state of being **preoccupied**. [162, 207]

preoccupied, *adj.* completely absorbed in thought or in doing something (synonyms: **bemused**[1], **engrossed, immersed**). [146, 211]

preposterous, *adj.* senseless, foolish, ridiculous (synonyms: **absurd, farcical, ludicrous**). [141, 311]

presciently, *adv.* with or as if with knowledge of what is to come, with **foresight.** [50]

prescribed, *adj.* laid down as a rule or guide to conduct. [137]

preside, *v.* to rule, control, exercise authority. [222]

prestigious, *adj.* having fame or importance based on reputation or achievements; honored, respected (synonyms: **esteemed, distinguished**). [15, 192]

presumptuous, *adj.* overly bold or forward, taking liberties, going beyond the limits of good sense or proper conduct. [73, 93, 135, 136]

★ **pretentious,** *adj.* 1. making a pretended or exaggerated outward show to attract attention (synonyms: **affected, grandiose, ostentatious, pompous**) 2. making exaggerated or unjustified claims to superiority or **merit,** putting on airs (synonyms: **arrogant, haughty, supercilious**). [39, 76, 96, 295]

prevail, *v.* to win, triumph, be victorious. [253]

prevailing, *adj.* widely accepted, currently in fashion. [86]

prevaricating, *adj.* lying, fibbing, playing fast and loose with the truth. [214]

★ **prey,** *n.* something hunted, esp. an animal hunted for food; the victim of a **predator.** [266, 283]

primordial, *adj.* primitive, original or ancient, primeval. [11, 272]

★ **principal,** *adj.* first, foremost, chief. [21]

★ **principle,** *n.* 1. a basic law, rule, truth, or **assumption**: a *principle* of physics; the *principles* of a democratic society (cf. **doctrine**). 2. a rule, standard, or code of conduct. 3. **ethical** conduct: a woman of *principle*. [78, 154, 184, 208, 218]

pristine, *adj.* pure, clean, fresh, unspoiled, not polluted or **corrupted.** [189, 319]

privy, *adj.* having knowledge of something private or secret. [221]

probability, *n.* likelihood, likely chance of happening. [145]

probe, *v.* 1. to search, explore, investigate. 2. to explore with a device or instrument. **probing,** *adj.* [60, 107, 234, 242]

problematic, *adj.* being or presenting a problem; difficult to figure out. [177, 184]

prodigious, *adj.* 1. marvelous, amazing, exceptional, phenomenal. 2. huge, enormous, monumental; extraordinary in size, extent, or degree (synonyms: **colossal, gargantuan, immense, massive**[2]**, monumental**[1]). [2, 151, 198, 322]

prodigy, *n.* someone, esp. a child, with exceptional talent or extraordinary ability. [21]

profane, *adj.* disrespectful of what is considered sacred or holy; spec. consisting of or pert. to abusive, **irreverent** language (synonym: **blasphemous**). [213]

proficiency, *n.* expert skill or ability, expertise. [26]

proficient, *adj.* highly capable, expert, skilled (synonyms: **adept, dexterous**). [103]

★ **profound,** *adj.* 1. deep. 2. having or demonstrating deep understanding or intelligence: *profound* ideas. 3. great, intense, or intensely felt: *profound* error; *profound* disgust. 4. sweeping, extensive: *profound* changes.

profoundly, *adv.* [xii, 55, 67, 116, 175, 201, 203, 206, 217, 219, 277, 325]

profuse, *adj.* done freely and **extravagantly,** given in great supply. **profusely,** *adv.* [3, 302, 322]

profusion, *n.* a great quantity, outpouring (synonyms: **abundance, plethora**). [56]

proliferate, *v.* to increase or spread rapidly. [218]

prolonged, *adj.* drawn out, extended (synonym: **protracted**; cf. **interminable**). [322]

★ **prominent,** *adj.* 1. important and widely known, usu. favorably (synonyms: see **distinguished**). 2. sticking out, projecting, noticeable: a *prominent* chin (synonyms: **conspicuous, salient**). **prominence,** *n.* [39, 63, 92, 96, 139, 207, 221]

promulgate, *v.* to make known formally or officially, publish, circulate. [202, 216]

prone, *adj.* stretched out face downward (synonym: **prostrate**). [9]

proponent, *n.* a supporter or follower, one who adheres to a cause or **doctrine** (synonyms: **advocate, champion**). [205]

★ **proportions,** *n.* size, dimensions. [304]

proposition, *n.* a proposal, plan, or offer. [145, 292]

propriety, *n.* socially acceptable behavior, proper conduct. [4]

prose, *n.* ordinary written or spoken language, as opposed to poetry or verse. [169, 205]

prospect, *n.* a chance, possibility, **expectation.** [83, 113, 144, 234]

prospective, *adj.* possible, expected, or likely. [43]

prosperous, *adj.* wealthy, well-to-do (synonym: **affluent**). [153]

prostrate, *adj.* lying facedown or flat on the ground (synonym: **prone**). [323]

prototype, *n.* an original or early model on which later versions are based. [83]

protracted, *adj.* drawn out in time, lengthened (synonym: **prolonged**; cf. **interminable**). [18, 200]

protrude, *v.* to stick or push out, extend, project. [10, 32, 70, 87]

proverbial, *adj.* commonly known and mentioned, as a **cliché** or **adage.** [98, 246]

provocative, *adj.* tending to **arouse,** as by making one curious, angry, or interested. [97]

★ **provoke,** *v.* 1. to give rise to, call forth, bring about (synonym: **stimulate**). 2. to make angry, stir up (synonyms: **goad, incite, instigate**). [131, 204, 317]

proximity, *n.* nearness, closeness. [60, 99, 148]

    —*Usage note*: Avoid the phrase *close proximity,* which is redundant.

★ **prudent,** *adj.* using good judgment or common sense; wise and cautious in handling one's affairs (synonyms: **circumspect, discreet, judicious, tactful, vigilant, wary**). **prudently,** *adv.* [xii, 29, 98, 118, 145, 271, 285]

pseudo-, a combining form used in compound words to mean "false," "fake," "pretended," as in *pseudoscientific* and *pseudointellectual.* [96]

pugilist, *n.* a boxer, fighter. [189]

punctiliousness, *n.* strict attention to detail and formality in conduct; an intense and precise concern for **propriety.** [240]

punctuate, *v.* 1. to interrupt occasionally. 2. to **emphasize,** give additional force to. [96, 136, 310]

pundit, *n.* a **learned** person, esp. an expert or **critic** who issues opinions. [224]

pungent, *adj.* sharp or biting to the smell or taste: *pungent* spices. [2, 72, 111, 271]

purloin, *v.* to steal, take dishonestly, commit theft. [54, 192, 272]

purposeful, *adj.* having a specific purpose or goal. **purposefully,** *adv.* [175, 227, 245]

purveyor, *n.* someone or something that provides, furnishes, or supplies. [272]

putrid, *adj.* stinking, foul, rotten (synonyms: **fetid, malodorous, rancid**). [15, 281]

Q

quandary, *n.* a state of difficulty and **uncertainty**[2] about what to do, a **perplexing** situation, a jam, fix, pickle. [167, 176, 248]
—*Predicament, dilemma,* and *quandary* all apply to situations or conditions that are difficult and **perplexing.** A *predicament* is a situation that is especially unpleasant or unfortunate: Losing his job left him in a *predicament. Dilemma* is often used loosely of any difficult problem or troublesome situation, but in the best usage *dilemma* is used only of situations in which one faces a choice between equally undesirable **alternatives:** When you're "damned if you do and damned if you don't," that's a *dilemma.* A *quandary* is a state of **uncertainty**[2] or confusion that **renders** one unable to act. To be "in a quandary" means to be puzzled, full of doubts, and not sure what to do.

★ **quarrel,** *n.* an angry argument, heated or **hostile** dispute (synonym: **altercation**). [188]

quarrel, *v.* to fight, engage in a **quarrel. quarreling,** *adj.* [271]

quarry, *n.* a hunted animal (synonym: **prey**). [161]

★ **quest,** *n.* the act of seeking something, pursuit of a goal, a mission. [113, 161, 196, 209, 245]

quiescent, *adj.* in a resting state, quiet, not active. [197]

quiver, *v.* to shake or tremble slightly. [132]

quixotic, *adj.* foolishly impractical and high-minded, inclined to pursue noble but unreachable goals or **far-fetched,** unworkable schemes (synonyms: **idealistic, visionary**; antonyms: **pragmatic, utilitarian**). [196]

R

radiant, *adj.* 1. glowing, bright, shining (synonym: **resplendent**). 2. glowing or shining with love, joy, confidence, etc. [87, 102, 321]

★ **radically,** *adv.* in an extreme, thoroughgoing, or **fundamental** way. [201]

ramifications, *n.* pl. the far-reaching effects, related developments, or **consequences** of something (synonym: **implications**). [199, 229]

rancid, *adj.* having a disgusting smell or taste, as of rotting oil or fat (synonyms: **fetid, malodorous, putrid**). [16, 117]

rancorous, *adj.* full of *rancor,* bitter and long-lasting **hostility** or ill will. [188]

random, *adj.* 1. without order, method, or design; having no definite pattern or purpose. 2. unplanned, unexpected, unintentional. **randomly,** *adv.* [xviii, 60, 85, 88, 95, 148, 197, 227, 229, 246, 282]
—*Random, haphazard, fortuitous,* and *desultory* all apply to that which is unplanned or accidental. *Random* suggests a lack of organization, pattern, or purpose. *Haphazard* suggests a careless leaving to chance. *Fortuitous* may be applied to chance events with good or bad outcomes; today it is often used of happy accidents. *Desultory* suggests an aimless shifting from one thing to another.

rapturous, *adj.* full of delight or joy (synonym: **ecstatic**). **rapture,** *n.* [102, 242]

rarefied, *adj.* of a highly refined or sublime nature, **lofty**[2] and **esoteric**. [156]

rascal, *n.* 1. a low, dishonest, **unscrupulous** person (synonym: **scoundrel**). 2. a mischievous person. [122, 138, 265]

★ **rational,** *adj.* 1. sane, not crazy. 2. founded on or guided by reason: a *rational* decision. **rationality,** *n.* reliance upon reason; the state of being *rational.* [64, 118, 163, 306]

rationalize, *v.* to attempt to make one's actions or **motives** appear reasonable or proper when they are not. [184]

raucous, *adj.* loud, noisy, disagreeably harsh or grating in sound (synonyms: see **vociferous**). **raucously,** *adv.* [93, 133, 212]

ravenous, *adj.* extremely hungry, greedy for food, starving, famished (synonyms: **insatiable, voracious**). **ravenously,** *adv.* [84, 170, 180]

readily, *adv.* with ease, promptness, or willingness. [22, 205]

★ **realm,** *n.* a region or province, spec. a royal kingdom (synonyms: **domain, dominion**). [74, 113, 123]

rebuff, *n.* a blunt rejection or refusal. [105, 157]

rebuke, *v.* to criticize sharply, express strong disapproval of. [49]

recalcitrant, *adj.* actively or stubbornly resisting authority or control, impossible to work with or manage (synonyms: **intractable, obstreperous**[1]). [124, 283, 323]

reckless, *adj.* acting without any concern for **consequences,** rash, heedless (synonyms: **foolhardy, impetuous**). **recklessly,** *adv.* [10, 56, 76, 89, 141, 250]

reclusive, *adj.* living alone, apart from the world; preferring solitude or isolation. [230]

recoil, *v.* 1. to shrink back, as in fear or disgust. 2. to spring or bounce back. [62, 263]

reconvene, *v.* to gather or come together again, reassemble. [147, 292]

★ **recount,** *v.* to tell or relate the details of, narrate. [151]

rectify, *v.* to correct, fix, solve, set right: *rectify* a mistake; *rectify* an injustice. [139, 179]

recurring, *adj.* happening again and again. [165]

redeem, *v.* to save (as from sin), change for the better, free from guilt or blame. [315]

redolent, *adj.* giving off a smell or odor: *redolent* of roses; *redolent* of onions. [17]

redoubtable, *adj.* **arousing** awe or **dread,** fearsome, **formidable**; hence, worthy of or commanding respect. [58, 74, 194, 255]

★ **reference,** *n.* 1. direct mention, citation, the act of referring (*usage note*: see **allusion**). 2. something one **cites** or refers to, a source of facts or information. [xi, 17, 22, 228]

★ **refinement,** *n.* 1. a small improvement. 2. appreciation of higher learning and culture. [30, 172, 282, 419]

reflection, *n.* 1. serious thought, **contemplation.** 2. a serious thought or observation. [32, 202, 272]

refuge, *n.* a place offering shelter, privacy, and protection (synonym: **haven**). [25]

★ **refute,** *v.* to prove to be untrue or **erroneous**: *refute* a claim (synonym: **repudiate**). [176]

regal, *adj.* royal, kingly or queenly (synonyms: **majestic, stately**). [256]

regimen, *n.* a regulated way of living (e.g. a diet or exercise program) that one follows to promote health or gain some other benefit. [291]

regrettable, *adj.* unfortunate, causing or deserving regret. **regrettably,** *adv.* [31, 47, 120, 167]

relegate, *v.* to assign to an inferior or insignificant position or condition. [242]

relentless, *adj.* not letting up in intensity, severity, or pace; steady, unyielding (synonyms: **inexorable, remorseless**). **relentlessly,** *adv.* [26, 27, 161, 281]

★ **relevant,** *adj.* bearing upon the point or matter at hand; to the purpose (synonyms: **applicable, pertinent**). [xii, 91, 277]

relinquish, *v.* to give up, let go of (synonyms: **abandon, forsake**). [45, 200]

relish, *v.* to enjoy, take special pleasure in, savor. [147]

★ **reluctant,** *adj.* unwilling, hesitant, disinclined (synonym: **loath**; *usage note*: see **reticent**). **reluctantly,** *adv.* [7, 107, 146, 234, 251, 269]

remnant, *n.* something remaining, a surviving trace; a small piece or scrap. [201, 285]

remorseful, *adj.* full of *remorse,* deep and painful regret for doing something wrong (synonyms: **contrite, penitent**). [108]

remorseless, *adj.* showing no pity or mercy, cruel (synonyms: **merciless, relentless**). [161, 257]

★ **render,** *v.* to make, cause to be. [199, 208]

rendition, *n.* a performance (as of a piece of music or a role in a play). [103, 289]

renown, *n.* fame, widespread reputation. [162]

★ **renowned,** *adj.* famous, well-known, acclaimed (synonyms: see **distinguished**). [150]

repartee, *n.* conversation full of quick, witty replies; playful sparring with words (synonym: **banter**). [222]

replete, *adj.* thoroughly or **abundantly** full, well-stocked. [203]

repository, *n.* a place where things are stored, esp. for safekeeping. [140]

★ **reprehensible,** *adj.* deserving strong disapproval, harsh criticism, or blame. [xii, 12, 109]

reprieve, *n.* temporary relief from harm or punishment. [261]

reprimand, *n.* a formal and often severe expression of disapproval. [264]

reprisal, *n.* retaliation for an injury or wrong suffered, esp. by inflicting as much or more injury in return. [18, 261]

reproach, *n.* criticism or disapproval. [275]

reproachful, *adj.* full of or expressing disapproval or disappointment: a *reproachful* look. [76]

repudiate, *v.* to reject as groundless or untrue (synonym: **refute**). [176]

repugnance, *n.* disgust, loathing, extreme distaste (synonyms: **antipathy, aversion**) [148, 239]

repugnant, *adj.* disgusting, objectionable, repellent (synonyms: **appalling, distasteful, loathsome, odious, offensive, repulsive**). [27, 79]

repulsive, *adj.* causing **repugnance** or **aversion** (synonyms: **appalling, distasteful, loathsome, odious, offensive, repugnant**). [28]

reputable, *adj.* having a good or worthy reputation, respectable. [219]

requisite, *adj.* required, necessary, obligatory (synonyms: **indispensable, mandatory**). [179, 280, 306]

resentful, *adj.* full of **resentment** (synonym: **disgruntled**). [152]

★ **resentment,** *n.* deep-seated anger, bitterness, or ill will (synonyms: **indignation, outrage**). [187]

residue, *n.* something that remains, esp. after a physical or chemical process. [254]

resolute, *adj.* firm, determined, strongly set (antonym: **indecisive**). [256]

★ **resolve,** *v.* 1. to decide, determine, come to a definite decision. 2. to work out, settle, find a solution to (e.g. a problem or conflict). [87, 145, 196, 202, 215]

resonant, *adj.* having a full and rich tone or sound (synonym: **sonorous**). [256]

resonate, *v.* to **resound**, be **resonant**. [59, 135]

resort, *v.* to turn to or make use of, usu. **reluctantly** or as a final option. [63, 166, 261, 296]

resound, *v.* to echo, roll, or ring loudly with sound. **resounding,** *adj.* [40, 115]

respective, *adj.* individual, particular: their *respective* careers. [115]

respite, *n.* an interval of rest or relief: a *respite* from work (cf. **lull, hiatus**). *Pronunciation*: Take care to stress this word on the first syllable (RES-pit). [37]

resplendent, *adj.* splendid or brilliant in appearance: *resplendent* jewelry (synonym: **radiant**[1]). [239]

reticent, *adj.* unwilling to speak freely, reserved, keeping one's thoughts to oneself (synonym: **laconic**). [xii, 182]
    Usage note: Though you increasingly hear people use *reticent* to mean *reluctant,* in careful usage these words are not synonymous. *Reluctant* means unwilling, hesitant, disinclined. *Reticent* means reluctant to speak.

Thus, you can be *reluctant* to answer a question, and you can be *reticent* when someone asks you a question, but you cannot properly be *reticent* to answer or *reticent* to talk.

retort, *v.* to give a quick, pointed, or witty reply. [37, 53]

retort, *n.* a sharp or quick-witted reply. [292]

retribution, *n.* punishment given in return, payback, revenge. **retributive,** *adj.* [154, 256]

revelation, *n.* 1. the revealing or communication of an important or **divine** truth, great **enlightenment.** 2. a moment of **profound** understanding or **insight.** [123, 276, 420]

revel, *v.* to party or celebrate in a **boisterous** way, engage in rowdy merrymaking. [299]

revelry, *n.* rowdy, noisy partying; **boisterous** merrymaking. [146, 265]

reverberation, *n.* a loud, **resounding** noise, or one of a series of loud, echoed sounds. [115]

revere, *v.* to look upon with deep respect, awe, and devotion; to treat with **reverence,** regard as **venerable.** [v, 163, 313]

reverence, *n.* a feeling of deep respect and awe mingled with affection. **reverent,** *adj.* [188, 193, 195, 232]

reverie, *n.* a daydream, **contemplation,** musing. [223, 306]

revile, *v.* to attack with abusive and **contemptuous** language. [163]

★ **rhetoric,** *n.* the skillful, persuasive, and elegant use of language. [123]

rhetorical question, *n.* a question asked only for effect, and not meant to be answered. [61, 69, 176, 200, 208, 303]

★ **ridicule,** *v.* to make fun of, laugh at, insult humorously (synonyms: **deride, mock**). [131]

rife, *adj.* widespread, common, prevalent. [220]

★ **rigor,** *n.* strictness and inflexibility in opinion or judgment. **rigorously,** *adv.* in a strict, disciplined, and precise manner. **rigors,** *n.* pl. difficulties, challenges, harsh reality. [77, 119, 213, 274]

riled, *adj.* upset or angry, highly irritated or annoyed. [133, 317]

rite, *n.* a ritual. [xvii, 146]

★ **ritual,** *n.* a ceremonial act, formal procedure, or **customary** practice (cf. **tradition**). [264]

★ **ritual,** *adj.* of or pert. to a **ritual.** [286]

★ **rival,** *n.* a competitor; a person who strives to equal or outdo another. [100, 151, 216, 244]

robust, *adj.* strong, hearty, rich and full-bodied (synonyms: **animated, vibrant, vigorous, vital, vivacious**). [240]

★ **romanticize,** *v.* to make something seem romantic, adventurous, noble, or **idealistic.** [228]

rouse, *v.* to awaken from sleep or bring out of an inactive state (synonyms: **arouse, stimulate**). [190, 306]

rudiments, *n.* pl. the basic techniques, elementary **principles,** or **fundamental** laws. [26, 197, 210]

rueful, *adj.* filled with sorrow and regret. [285]

ruminate, *v.* to turn something over in the mind (synonyms: **contemplate, ponder**). **rumination,** *n.* [167, 202, 306, 325]

rummage, *v.* to search, esp. by moving things around roughly. [184]

★ **rural,** *adj.* belonging to or characteristic of the country as opposed to the city. [31, 77, 205, 207]

ruse, *n.* a crafty trick or plot designed to mislead (synonyms: **chicanery, deception, hoax, ploy, stratagem, subterfuge**). [25, 250]

rustic, *adj.* 1. **rural**; of or pert. to country life. 2. crude, backward, **unsophisticated.** [11]

S

safeguard, *v.* to protect, guard, keep safe. [185, 307]

sagacious, *adj.* wise, exercising **sound** practical judgment (synonyms: **astute, keen, penetrating, perceptive, perspicacious, shrewd**). **sagacity,** *n.* [25, 189, 232]

sage, *n.* a wise and experienced person, respected for having **sound** judgment. [121]

salient, *adj.* standing out, attracting attention, easily seen, noticeable (synonyms: **conspicuous, prominent**[2]). [9, 99, 174]

salubrious, *adj.* favorable to health, healthful (synonyms: see **wholesome**). [210]

salutation, *n.* an expression of greeting. [99, 273]

sanction, *v.* to approve of, authorize as appropriate or permissible. [97]

sanguine, *adj.* cheerful and confident, **optimistic.** [15, 111, 187, 419]

★ **sarcasm,** *n.* the use of sharp, biting language to make fun of or wound. [95]
  —*Sarcasm* and *irony* are related in meaning. *Sarcasm* refers to sharp, sneering language meant to hurt or insult. *Irony* suggests the use of more subtle language (spec. language that **implies** the opposite of what it literally says) to make fun of in a milder way.

sated, *adj.* satisfied completely: The delicious meal left them *sated.* [215]

satirical, *adj.* of or pert. to the art of exposing human **folly** or vice with wit (synonym: **ironic**; cf. **irreverent**). [7, 130]

saunter, *v.* to walk in a leisurely way, stroll. [103, 190]

savor, *v.* **literally,** to taste or smell with pleasure; **figuratively,** to enjoy, take delight in, appreciate fully, relish: to *savor* a victory; *savored* the wine. [27, 121, 187]

savory, *adj.* tasty, flavorful, appetizing, appealing to the taste or smell. [89, 126]

savvy, *adj.* knowledgeable, experienced and informed. [227]

scamper, *v.* to run or go hastily with light, rapid steps (synonym: **scurry**). [273]

scandal, *n.* the public exposure of an **offense**[2] or disgraceful action that damages the reputation of someone or something. [216]

scanty, *adj.* inadequate, insufficient, not enough to fill the need (synonym: **meager**). [219]

scatterbrained, *adj.* incapable of orderly or serious thought, flighty. [305]

scenario, *n.* 1. a possible situation or sequence of events. 2. the design or scheme of things. [126, 193, 207]

scheme, *v.* to plot or plan secretly, esp to do something **devious. scheming,** *adj.* [253, 307]

scintillate, *v.* to **emit** sparkles or twinkles of light, shine brightly. [202]

scintillating, *adj.* lively, clever, or witty: a *scintillating* discussion. [222]

scoff, *v.* to make fun of, show **contempt** for, dismiss with **mockery** or **derision.** [75, 140, 251, 311]

★ **scorn,** *n.* a display of intense dislike or disrespect (synonyms: **contempt, disdain**). [274]

scoundrel, *n.* a dishonorable person, villain, rogue, knave (synonym: **rascal**). [68, 271]

scruple, *n.* the pricking of one's conscience; an uneasy feeling that stops one from doing something that may be wrong or evil. **scruples,** *n.* pl. **moral principles** or a code of conduct that restrains action. [183]

scrupulous, *adj.* 1. honest, having **scruples:** *scrupulous* behavior (synonyms: **upright, virtuous**). 2. extremely careful and precise: a *scrupulous* report. **scrupulously,** *adv.* [xi, 184, 188]

★ **scrutinize,** *v.* to examine carefully and closely (synonym: **peruse**). [xiv, 18, 22, 55, 58, 88, 158, 254, 276, 298]

scurry, *v.* to rush, move briskly, step lightly and quickly (synonym: **scamper**). [8, 265, 268]

scurrilous, *adj.* foul-mouthed; using coarse, indecent, or abusive language. [213]

secluded, *adj.* far off, remote, away from the mainstream or general activity. [231]

secrete, *v.* to hide, conceal, stash. [189]

secretive, *adj.* keeping secrets, not open or **frank.** [159]

secular, *adj.* concerned with or pert. to things of this world rather than the next one; not religious or spiritual (antonym: **ecclesiastical**). [205]

sedulous, *adj.* extremely hardworking, **persevering** until the job is done (synonyms: **assiduous, diligent, industrious**). [xi, 150]

self-absorbed, *adj.* excessively concerned about or **preoccupied** with oneself. [135, 186]

self-effacing, *adj.* making light of oneself, making oneself appear unimportant or unworthy (synonyms: **humble**[2], **modest**[1]). [121]

self-indulgent, *adj.* giving in to one's every desire, passion, or whim; tending to **indulge**[1] oneself excessively (synonym: **decadent**). [84]

self-righteous, *adj.* convinced that one is right and others are wrong; unwilling to accept or listen to other opinions; **smug** and **moralistic**[2]. **self-righteousness,** *n.* [44, 84, 131]

self-serving, *adj.* looking out for one's own needs and interests, serving only oneself. [84]

sensational, *adj.* intended to thrill, excite, startle, or **arouse** curiosity (synonym: **lurid**). [85, 137]

sensationalism, *n.* expressing or presenting something in a **vulgar** way that is calculated to thrill, excite, startle, or satisfy curiosity. [216]

sensibility, *n.* awareness, appreciation, esp. of high culture. [172]

sensor, *n.* a device that transmits a signal. [89, 93]

sensual, *adj.* pert. to or **arousing** physical appetites or desires, esp. sexual desire. [101, 238]

—*Sensual* and *sensuous* are similar but *not* synonymous. *Sensuous* refers favorably to things experienced through the senses: *sensuous* music; *sensuous* colors; the *sensuous* aroma of fine food. *Sensual* refers, usu. unfavorably, to the **gratification** of the senses or physical appetites, esp in a **self-indulgent** or sexual way: the *sensual* excesses of the **glutton**; the *sensual* nightlife of the city. If you mean lovely, pleasurable, or experienced through the senses, use *sensuous*. If you mean self-**gratifying** or pert. to physical desires, use *sensual*.

★ **sentiment,** *n.* a feeling, opinion. [121, 290]

serendipity, *n.* the lucky, accidental discovery of things unsought. [148, 277, 285]

★ **serene,** *adj.* calm, quiet, peaceful, undisturbed (synonyms: **placid, tranquil**). [xii, 22, 127, 190]

serpentine, *adj.* like a snake; hence, winding, curving, twisting (synonym: **sinuous**). [289]

serviceable, *adj.* useful, helpful, being of service. [124]

servile, *adj.* like a slave: i.e. submissive, obedient, and **abject** (cf. **fawning, obsequious, sycophantic**). [242]

shabby, *adj.* showing signs of wear or **slovenly** in appearance (synonym: **threadbare**). [152, 251]

shameless, *adj.* feeling or showing no shame or embarrassment when one ought to; hence, disgraceful, shocking, outrageous. **shamelessly,** *adv.* [59, 184, 219]

sheepish, *adj.* showing embarrassment, esp. for doing something wrong or foolish. **sheepishly,** *adv.* [36, 260, 301]

shrewd, *adj.* 1. highly aware and intelligent in dealing with practical matters: a *shrewd* lawyer (synonyms: **astute, keen, penetrating, perceptive, perspicacious, sagacious**). 2. tricky, cunning, crafty, **artful**: a *shrewd* lawyer. [188, 250, 253, 419]

shrill, *adj.* having a harsh, high-pitched, piercing sound; annoying, grating. **shrillness,** *n.* [18, 29, 138, 161, 302]

shroud, *v.* to hide, cover, conceal. [2, 287]

shrouded, *adj.* hidden, concealed, covered: *shrouded* in shadow. [123]

sibilant, *adj.* hissing; producing or characterized by the sound of *s* or *sh*. [213, 275]

siege, *n.* an attack, esp. a **prolonged** effort to capture a fortified place. [153]

signify, *v.* to mean, apply to, denote. [76]

simplistic, *adj.* overly simple or simplified, lacking sufficient information or intelligence: a *simplistic* explanation. [216, 229]

simultaneous, *adj.* happening, existing, or operating at the same time. **simultaneously,** *adv.* [10, 58, 199, 215, 226]

sincere, *adj.* genuine in feeling, honest, real; without exaggeration or **deceit** (synonyms: **candid, forthcoming**[1], **frank, straightforward**). **sincerely,** *adv.* [12, 36, 77, 102, 320]

single-minded, *adj.* having a single purpose or goal. [21]

sinister, *adj.* evil; causing fear or **apprehension**; threatening trouble or disaster (synonyms: **forbidding**[2], **menacing, ominous**). [94, 172, 246]

sinuous, *adj.* having curves or turns, wavy, winding, snakelike: a *sinuous* road (synonym: **serpentine**). [174, 289]

★ **skeptical,** *adj.* 1. tending to question or doubt, disbelieving. 2. feeling or showing doubt or disbelief (synonyms: **dubious, incredulous**).
    ★ **skepticism,** *n.* [55, 61, 65, 98, 123, 165, 169, 176, 206, 220, 241]

skulk, *v.* to sneak, creep, slink, move in a stealthy and **furtive** way; also, to **lurk**[1]. **skulking,** *adj.* [175, 213]

slovenly, *adj.* messy, untidy, unclean (synonym: **squalid**). [15, 172]

smirk, *v.* to smile in a self-satisfied or artificial way; simper: He *smirked* when John gave the wrong answer. **smirking,** *adj.* [45, 97, 259, 295]

★ **smug,** *adj.* self-satisfied to an annoying or irritating degree (synonym: **complacent**; cf. **self-righteous**). [46, 105]

sneer, *n.* a facial expression of **scorn** and **contempt,** usu. made by slightly raising a corner of the upper lip. [45]

sneer, *v.* 1. to smile or laugh with a sneer. 2. to speak to in a **condescending, contemptuous** way. [101, 261, 293]

sober, *adj.* 1. serious, **solemn**[1]. 2. not under the influence of alcohol or drugs. [241]

sociable, *adj.* friendly; fond or full of good companionship and pleasant conversation (synonyms: **convivial, gregarious**). [169]

sojourn, *n.* a temporary stay, visit. [30, 71, 319, 419]

solace, *n.* comfort or relief, esp. from anxiety or trouble. [190]

★ **sole,** *adj.* being one in number; the only. [7, 221, 227]

solely, *adv.* to the exclusion of all else. [119]

solemn, *adj.* 1. deeply serious and earnest (synonym: **grave**[1]): a *solemn* expression. 2. of great, sacred, or ceremonial importance: a *solemn* vow. 3. impressive and awe-inspiring in its seriousness: a *solemn* occasion. [77, 140, 174, 232]

solicitous, *adj.* concerned, worried, or anxious about someone or something: *solicitous* about her welfare. [51, 93, 132, 147, 276]

somber, *adj.* 1. dark, gloomy, dismal: *somber* furnishings (synonym: **dreary**[1]). 2. sad, unhappy, downcast, glum: a *somber* look (synonym: **melancholy**[1]). [1, 155, 299]

somnolent, *adj.* sleepy, drowsy. **somnolently,** *adv.* [90, 272]

sonorous, *adj.* rich and full in sound: a *sonorous* bassoon solo (synonym: **resonant**). [135, 232, 274]

sophisticated, *adj.* 1. cultured and refined (a *sophisticated* group) or suited to the taste of cultured and refined people (a *sophisticated* drama). 2. knowing and worldly-wise, socially polished, "cool" (synonyms: **chic, suave, urbane**). 3. highly advanced: *sophisticated* technology; *sophisticated* knowledge. **sophistication,** *n.* [11, 68, 217, 227, 237]

soporific, *adj.* **inducing** sleep. [20, 56, 208]

soporific, *n.* something that causes sleep. [208]

sound, *adj.* 1. healthy, strong, in good shape. 2. undamaged, free from
    defects. 3. sensible, reasonable (synonym: **valid**). [31, 279, 291]

spartan, *adj.* simple in a severe or stern way, completely without luxury
    (synonym: **austere**). [175]

★ **species,** *n.* a distinct sort or kind, esp. the basic category of biological
    classification. [80, 92, 136, 152, 219]

specimen, *n.* a typical example; a part representing the whole. [230]

spectrum, *n.* broad range, full extent. [202]

speculate, *v.* to reason and form **assumptions** based on evidence that is
    inadequate or not **conclusive** (synonyms: see **surmise**). [62, 84, 140, 227]

★ **speculation,** *n.* 1. the act of thinking or reasoning, esp. based on evidence
    that is incomplete or not **conclusive**. 2. something supposed or thought
    to be true, an educated guess (synonyms: **conjecture, surmise**; and see
    surmise, v.). 3. risky business deals or investments. [140, 216, 231]

★ **spontaneous,** *adj.* 1. occurring naturally or without practice or forethought
    (synonym: **impromptu**). 2. acting according to one's inner nature rather
    than being prompted by external forces; guided by instinct or **impulse**.
    [11, 118, 133, 163, 230, 260, 264, 289, 306]

spurious, *adj.* false; not genuine, legitimate, or **valid** (synonyms: **counterfeit,
    fraudulent**). [132, 258, 291]

spurn, *v.* to reject with **contempt** and **disdain**. [294]

squalid, *adj.* miserably filthy and rundown, esp. because of poverty or neglect
    (synonym: **slovenly**). [22]

squander, *v.* to use or spend foolishly and wastefully. [191]

stagnant, *adj.* inactive, not advancing or developing: a *stagnant* economy.
    [209]

staid, *adj.* proper, conservative, strait-laced, uptight (synonyms: **dignified**[2],
    sober[1]). [11, 195, 222]

★ **stamina,** *n.* the strength to keep on going; endurance, staying power.
    [119, 282]

stanza, *n.* an individual section or division of a poem, often having a
    particular pattern of rhyme and rhythm. [95, 203]

staple, *n.* a basic item of food; a regular or necessary part of the diet. [180]

stately, *adj.* impressively formal and serious in style, proportions, or bearing
    (synonyms: **august, majestic, regal**). [15, 147, 153, 256]

★ **static,** *adj.* not moving or active, still, at rest. [175, 197]

★ **status,** *adj.* 1. social standing; a person or group's position in relation to
    others. 2. condition, state of affairs. [170, 189, 217]

steadfast, *adj.* faithful, constant, loyal, firm: *steadfast* in his determination.
    [113]

★ **stereotype,** *n.* a fixed mental image or way of thinking about a person, thing,
    or event. [172, 228]

★ **stimulate,** *v.* to make active or more active; excite (synonyms: **arouse, rouse**).
    stimulation, *n.* [20, 115, 131, 194]

stimulating, *adj.* interesting, serving to **stimulate** the mind. [101, 156, 282]

stimulus, *n.* something that **stimulates** or **incites** to action. [73, 195]

stoic, *adj.* not affected by or showing emotion, esp. pain or distress; calm, unmoved (synonym: **impassive**; and see **phlegmatic**). [108]

straightforward, *adj.* honest and direct, not roundabout or circumlocutory (synonyms: **candid, forthcoming**[1]**, frank, sincere**). [78]

stratagem, *n.* a trick or scheme used to outwit an enemy, gain an advantage, or achieve a goal (synonym: **ploy, ruse**). [165, 261]

stratum, *n.* (pl. *strata*) a level, layer, or rank. [242]

strident, *adj.* loud and **shrill**; harsh and grating to the ears (synonyms: see **vociferous**). [138, 155, 212, 301]

strife, *n.* struggle, conflict. [107]

stupefy, *v.* to put into a *stupor,* a state of mental numbness or paralysis, a daze. [131]

suave, *adj.* smooth and courteous, well-mannered and polished in social situations (synonyms: **chic, sophisticated, urbane**). [68]

★ **subdued,** *adj.* toned down, reduced in force or intensity, **suppressed.** [130, 177]

★ **subjective,** *adj.* 1. personal, individual, of or pert. only to a particular person. 2. based on personal feelings or opinions. [130]

subliminal, *adj.* below one's level of awareness; coming from the subconscious mind. [162]

subordinate, *adj.* occupying an inferior position or rank; secondary or second-class. [187, 207]

subscribe, *v.* to approve of, follow the **doctrine** of, support, **endorse.** [180]

subside, *v.* to become quiet or less active, settle down to a lower level. [5, 190, 281]

subsist, *v.* to live or remain alive, esp. under difficult or harsh conditions. [204]

★ **substantiate,** *v.* to support by proof or reliable evidence (synonyms: **confirm, corroborate, verify**). **substantiation,** *n.* [xii, 93, 122, 164, 176, 192, 302]

substantive, *adj.* having considerable substance (importance or practical value). [216]

subterfuge, *n.* a trick, underhanded scheme, **deception** (synonyms: **chicanery, deception, hoax, ruse**). [165, 253]

subterranean, *adj.* underground. [152, 173]

★ **subtle,** *adj.* 1. indirect, not obvious, difficult to see or understand: *subtle* changes. 2. delicate, refined, or faintly mysterious: a *subtle* smile. 3. sly, crafty, cunning: a *subtle* plot. **subtly,** *adv.* [x, 26, 30, 37, 99, 101, 124, 165, 218, 226, 296, 419]

subversive, *adj.* trying to overthrow a government or destroy an established order. [205]

succinct, *adj.* brief and to the point; expressed in a precise and compact way, without wasted words (synonyms: **concise, terse**). [xiv, 202]

succumb, *v.* 1. to yield, surrender, submit to an overpowering force. 2. to die. [18, 135]

★ **suffrage,** *n.* the right to vote. [217]

suffuse, *v.* to spread through or over, as with light, color, or emotion (synonym: **imbue**). [127, 203]

sullen, *adj.* silent and **resentful.** [109, 293]

sully, *v.* to make imperfect or unclean; soil, stain, tarnish, taint. [201]

★ **summit,** *n.* the top, highest point, peak (synonyms: **apex, zenith**). [1, 56, 153]

sumptuous, *adj.* exceptionally rich and luxurious (synonyms: **extravagant, opulent;** cf. **lavishly**). [3]

supercilious, *adj.* looking down at others or treating them in a proudly superior way (synonyms: **arrogant, haughty, pretentious**[2]). [45, 96, 252]

★ **superficial,** *adj.* shallow, lacking in depth or substance (synonyms: **cursory, perfunctory**). [131, 216]

supernatural, *adj.* not of this world, otherworldly (synonyms: see **uncanny**) [212, 301]

supplant, *v.* to take the place of, replace, displace. [143]

supple, *adj.* 1. flexible, easily bent. 2. quick to adapt and respond. [8, 194]

supplication, *n.* humble and earnest pleading, **beseeching, entreaty.** [274]

★ **suppress,** *v.* to hold back, stifle. [4, 6, 72, 117, 231]

★ **supremacy,** *n.* superiority, supreme power. [151]

surfeited, *adj.* overly, excessively, or nauseatingly full (cf. **cloying**). [249]

surmise, *n.* an **assumption** based on limited evidence, an educated guess (synonyms: **conjecture, speculation**). [113]

surmise, *v.* to conclude or **infer** from incomplete evidence. [155, 173]
   —*Surmise, speculate,* and *conjecture* all mean to make an educated guess, to form an opinion or reach a conclusion based upon uncertain or insufficient evidence. To *surmise* means to come to a conclusion by using one's intuition or imagination. To *speculate* means to make an **initial,** inconclusive judgment based on observation and reasoning. To *conjecture* means to take whatever evidence is available and quickly construct an opinion based on one's knowledge and experience.

surpass, *v.* to go beyond, exceed (synonyms: **eclipse, transcend**). [196]

surreal, *adj.* having the strange and unreal quality of a dream. [276]

surreptitious, *adj.* secret and stealthy, not **overt** or **conspicuous** (synonyms: **clandestine, covert, devious, furtive**). **surreptitiously,** *adv.* [52, 118, 159, 237, 265]

swagger, *n.* a superior attitude, **arrogant** and **haughty** manner. [96]

swindle, *n.* a scam, confidence game, **fraudulent** scheme. [217]

swindler, *n.* the **perpetrator** of a **swindle.** [111, 253]

swoon, *v.* to faint or be overwhelmed to the point of losing consciousness. [113, 199]

sycophant, *n.* someone who tries to win favor or gain advancement by flattering influential people (synonym: **toady**). **sycophantic,** *adj.* like a **sycophant** (synonyms: **fawning, obsequious, servile**). [44, 69, 255, 290]

★ **systematic,** *adj.* following a system or plan, done in a step-by-step way (synonym: **methodical**). [205]

T

tacit, *adj.* unspoken, silent; understood without being expressed in words. [8, 192, 252]

tactful, *adj.* having or showing *tact,* skill and grace in dealing with delicate or difficult situations, the ability to say or do the right thing to avoid giving **offense**[1] (synonym: **discreet**). **tactfully,** *adv.* [12, 71, 238, 286, 322]

tangible, *adj.* 1. having substance, capable of being touched, formed of matter (synonym: **palpable**). 2. real, actual, concrete, definite. [74, 234]

tantalizing, *adj.* intensely tempting, **arousing** great interest or desire for something that seems unreachable or unobtainable (synonym: **alluring**). [27, 101, 178]

taunt, *v.* to make fun of in a **sarcastic** and insulting way (synonyms: **mock, deride**). [261]

taunting, *n.* **sarcastic,** insulting language (synonyms: **mockery, derision**). [47]

taut, *adj.* drawn or pulled tight. [94]

tawdry, *adj.* tastelessly showy, cheap, sleazy (synonyms: **garish, gaudy**). [110]

tedious, *adj.* tiresome and boring: a *tedious* assignment (synonym: **dreary**[2]). [x, 169, 419]

tedium, *n.* a boring, tiresome quality or state; **tedious** nature. [119]

teem, *v.* to be full of (e.g. people or things), to abound or swarm with. **teeming,** *adj.* [6, 161]

telling, *adj.* revealing or striking; having great importance or weight. [183, 192, 298]

telltale, *adj.* indicating or revealing something intended to be secret: a *telltale* remark. [244]

temperament, *n.* one's personal nature, an individual and characteristic way of thinking and behaving (synonym: **disposition**). [2]

★ **temperance,** *n.* moderation or **abstinence,** esp. in drinking alcohol. [222]

temperate, *adj.* having moderate temperatures, without extremes of hot and cold. [203]

tenacious, *adj.* stubborn, **persevering,** holding firmly and refusing to let go (synonyms: **dogged, persistent, undaunted**). [165]

tenacity, *n.* the quality of being **tenacious.** [147]

★ **tentative,** *adj.* hesitant, uncertain, unsure of oneself (synonym: **timid**). **tentatively,** *adv.* [29, 55, 60, 177, 186, 213]

tenuous, *adj.* thin, flimsy, having little substance: a *tenuous* thread. [219]

terse, *adj.* brief and to the point: a *terse* manner of speaking (synonyms: **concise, succinct**). **tersely,** *adv.* [97, 253]

theological, *adj.* of or pert. to religion. [205]

★ **theoretical,** *adj.* of, pert. to, or based on *theory,* a system of knowledge or a general set of **assumptions** or **principles**[1]. [58, 197]

therapeutic, *adj.* having healing powers, curative. [17]

★ **thesis,** *n.* 1. an opinion or proposition to be proved by argument. 2. a **dissertation** developed from original research, esp. one presented by a candidate for an academic degree. [122, 148, 149, 162, 275, 277, 279]

thrall, *n.* slavery, bondage, servitude. [220]

threadbare, *adj.* so frayed that the threads show, old and worn out (synonym: **shabby**). [26, 87]

★ **thrive,** *v.* to be successful, do very well, prosper (synonym: **flourish**[1], *v.*). **thriving,** *adj.* [204]

throng, *n.* a crowd, host of people, **multitude**[1]. [46]

★ **thwart,** *v.* to frustrate the plans of, prevent from accomplishing, oppose and defeat (synonym: **baffle**). [162, 177, 229]

timid, *adj.* lacking courage or self-confidence, hesitant and shy (synonym: **tentative**). [186, 242, 312]

timorous, *adj.* fearful, scared (synonym: **apprehensive**). [186]

tinge, *v.* to apply a small amount of color to, tint, shade. [190]

tirade, *n.* a prolonged and angry speech (synonyms: **diatribe, harangue**). [213]

toady, *n.* someone who flatters others hoping to gain favors, an **obsequious** follower, bootlicking servant (synonym: **sycophant**). [44]

tolerable, *adj.* able to be put up with, capable of being **endured**[1]. [91]

tolerably, *adv.* fairly, moderately, somewhat. [30]

★ **tolerance,** *n.* 1. endurance, capacity to deal with difficulty, pain, etc. 2. acceptance. [4, 44]

tome, *n.* a large, weighty book, usu. a scholarly one. [16, 22]

torment, *v.* to annoy or upset greatly, distress deeply, torture (synonyms: **harass, vex**). **tormentor,** *n.* [138, 163]

torpor, *n.* a state of inactivity, inertia; mental or physical sluggishness or dullness; apathy, lethargy. [18]

torrent, *n.* a rapid and violent flow, as of water; a raging stream. [136, 213]

torrid, *adj.* passionate, heated (synonyms: **fervid, vehement**). [112]

★ **toxic,** *adj.* harmful, poisonous. [112, 199]

★ **tradition,** *n.* a long-standing custom or **customary** practice (cf. **ritual**). [146, 207]

★ **traditional,** *adj.* 1. of, pert. to, or following beliefs, styles, or practices that have been passed down from one generation to the next (synonym: **conventional**). 2. done according to **tradition** (long-established practice or mode of thought or behavior). [21, 197]

★ **trait,** *n.* a personal feature, quality, or characteristic, esp. a **distinctive** one (synonym: **attribute,** *n.*). [102, 111, 150]

★ **tranquil,** *adj.* calm, quiet, peaceful (synonyms: **placid, serene**). **tranquillity,** *n.* [22, 187]

★ **transcend,** *v.* to rise above, go beyond the limits of, be greater than, exceed (synonym: **surpass**). [179, 197, 220]

transfixed, *adj.* made motionless with awe and amazement (or often terror). [191, 198]

transgression, *n.* a sin; a violation of a law, **moral** code, rule, command, etc. (synonym: **offense**[2]). [179, 184]

★ **transient,** *adj.* temporary, passing away with time, lasting only a short while. [xix, 92, 270, 325]

—*Transient, transitory, evanescent, ephemeral,* and **fleeting** all mean passing, temporary. *Transient* refers to anything that lasts or stays only for a short while: a *transient* occupant, a *transient* event. *Transitory* refers to something that by nature must pass or come to an end: life is *transitory,* and sometimes so is love. *Evanescent* refers to that which appears or exists briefly and then quickly fades or vanishes: *evanescent* joy, the *evanescent* bloom of a rose. *Ephemeral* means **literally** lasting only a day, but in a broad sense it refers to anything **conspicuously** short-lived: youth is *ephemeral. Fleeting* is used of that which happens rapidly and then is gone: *fleeting* fashions, a *fleeting* interest.

transitory, *adj.* passing away, not permanent or **enduring** (synonyms: see **transient**). [92]

treachery, *n.* deliberate betrayal of trust or confidence. [111]

treacherous, *adj.* full of hidden or **deceptive** danger (synonyms: **hazardous, perilous**). [114]

treatise, *n.* a **systematic** and usu. lengthy and scholarly discussion of a subject in writing: a *treatise* on modern poetry. [xiv, 205]

trepidation, *n.* agitated fear or alarm (synonyms: **apprehension, dread**). [183]

trial, *n.* a test of endurance, patience, or belief. [147]

tribulation, *n.* (often used in the pl.) trouble, suffering, distress, affliction. [147]

★ **tribute,** *n.* a formal display or expression of **esteem** (respect, gratitude, praise, etc.) (synonym: **monument**). [155]

trifle, *n.* a small or insignificant amount. [75]

trifling, *adj.* worthless or insignificant (synonym: **trivial**). [91]

★ **trivial,** *adj.* of little value or importance, not worth noticing or caring about (synonyms: **inconsequential, negligible, petty, trifling**). [103, 112, 208]

trustworthy, *adj.* reliable, dependable, worthy of trust or confidence. [13, 31, 140]

tumultuous, *adj.* wild and disorderly, riotous (synonym: **turbulent**). [276, 322]

★ **turbulent,** *adj.* violently agitated, tempestuous; also, marked by unrest and disorder, unruly, **chaotic** (synonym: **tumultuous**). [190, 204, 267, 276]

★ **turmoil,** *n.* great confusion, commotion, agitation, or disturbance. [202, 266, 275]

U

ubiquitous, *adj.* existing or seeming to exist everywhere at the same time: The cockroach is a *ubiquitous* creature (synonym: **omnipresent**). [218]

unadorned, *adj.* not decorated or dressed up, not **adorned.** [153]

unadulterated, *adj.* pure, at full strength, not watered down or diluted. [311]

unbecoming, *adj.* socially inappropriate, unseemly (synonym: **indecorous**). [285]

uncanny, *adj.* mysterious and extraordinary in a strange, almost **supernatural** way. [13, 111, 148, 277]

—*Uncanny, eerie,* and *supernatural* are all used of things that are strange, unearthly, and sometimes frightening. *Supernatural* means beyond what can be explained by the laws of nature; hence, not seeming to be of this world. It is often used to mean miraculous or superhuman: a *supernatural* gift. *Eerie* is the most frightful of these words; it usu. refers to things that are **unsettling**, creepy, or **sinister**: the old house was full of *eerie* noises. *Uncanny* may refer to something that is strange in an unnatural or unearthly way, or it may mean beyond what is normal or expected, strange in a remarkable or marvelous way: an *uncanny* resemblance; *uncanny* ability.

★ **uncertainty,** *n.* 1. **unpredictability**; indefinite character or nature. 2. doubt; not knowing for sure (cf. **certainty**). [26, 63, 113]

uncharted, *adj.* not yet explored or known. [85, 242]

★ **unconventional,** *adj.* not bound by accepted custom or practice, not ordinary, not **conventional** (synonym: **unorthodox**). [x, 11, 26, 59, 212]

uncultivated, *adj.* not **cultivated,** *adj.* [11, 31]

undaunted, *adj.* fearless and determined, not discouraged or dismayed (synonyms: **dogged, persistent, tenacious**). [162, 316]

underdog, *n.* the candidate or contestant who is expected to lose. [45]

★ **undermine,** *v.* to weaken or ruin slowly or in small degrees: The constant criticism *undermined* his self-confidence (synonyms: **corrupt, debase, vitiate**). [xii, 55]

undeterred, *adj.* not discouraged or prevented from going on; not **deterred.** [311]

undue, *adj.* unwanted, inappropriate, or excessive. [213]

undulate, *v.* to move in a wavelike fashion, move with a smooth up-and-down or side-to-side motion. **undulating,** *adj.* [167]

unduly, *adv.* in an **undue** manner. [167]

unethical, *adj.* not **ethical** (synonym: **corrupt**). [183, 228, 229, 233, 245]

unfettered, *adj.* free, liberated, not restricted in action or opinion (synonym: **uninhibited**). [222]

unforeseen, *adj.* unexpected, not seen beforehand. [228, 276]

uninhibited, *adj.* free and unrestricted; not hindered, hampered, or restrained (synonym: **unfettered**). [200]

★ **universal,** *adj.* 1. existing or operating everywhere: a *universal* need for shelter. 2. including, covering, or involving all: a *universal* belief. **universally,** *adv.* [21, 123, 194, 224, 265]

unkempt, *adj.* messy, untidy; (of hair) uncombed (synonym: **disheveled**). [15, 152]

unnerving, *adj.* upsetting, distressing, spec. depriving one of strength or self-control. [191]

unobtrusive, *adj.* not obvious or **conspicuous**; quiet and in the background. [184]

unorthodox, *adj.* not **customary,** not conforming with **orthodoxy** (synonym: **unconventional**). [195]

unparalleled, *adj.* without parallel or equal, matchless, peerless (synonym: **incomparable**). [127]

unprecedented, *adj.* never before seen or known (synonym: **novel**). [177, 209]

unpredictable, *adj.* 1. difficult or impossible to predict or know in advance. 2. likely to do something unexpected; changeable, variable (synonyms: **capricious, erratic, fickle, volatile, wayward**). [112, 125, 229, 253, 272]

unpretentious, *adj.* not **pretentious.** [180]

unravel, *v.* to figure out, solve, explain: a problem to *unravel.* [78, 178, 304, 305]

unrefined, *adj.* lacking **refinement**[2]; showing a lack of culture, elegance, good manners, and good taste (synonym: **boorish**). [30, 69, 79]

unremitting, *adj.* not letting up, constant (synonyms: **continuous, incessant**). [164, 165]

unrequited, *adj.* not returned in kind. [221, 274]

unruffled, *adj.* not upset or agitated; calm, cool, and collected. [4, 99]

unsavory, *adj.* **literally,** disagreeable to taste or smell; **figuratively,** undesirable, objectionable, morally **offensive:** an *unsavory* reputation. [82]

unscrupulous, *adj.* not controlled or restrained by conscience, dishonorable, **unethical,** not **scrupulous**[1]. [110, 183]

unsettling, *adj.* disturbing; causing uneasiness, confusion, or dismay. [166, 284]

unsophisticated, *adj.* simple, plain, ordinary, not fancy or refined. [59, 180]

unswerving, *adj.* fixed, unchanging, steady, constant: *unswerving* loyalty. [306]

unwarranted, *adj.* uncalled for, unjustified, without good reason. [185]

unwary, *adj.* not **wary,** not cautious and watchful. [177]

★ **unwitting,** *adj.* 1. not intentional, unintended. 2. unconscious, not aware or knowing. **unwittingly,** *adv.* [77, 227, 228]

upheaval, *n.* violent or disorderly change. [205]

uphold, *v.* to support, maintain, and defend. [184]

uplifting, *adj.* serving to raise to a higher **moral** or spiritual level. [21]

upright, *adj.* honest, doing what is **morally** right or just (synonyms: **conscientious**[1], **ethical, scrupulous, virtuous**). [11, 31]

uproar, *n.* noisy excitement or disturbance (synonyms: **clamor, din**). [300]

uproariously, *adv.* very loudly. [298]

urban, *adj.* of or pert. to a city. [88, 205]

urbane, *adj.* extremely polite and polished in manner (synonyms: **chic, sophisticated, suave**). [68]

usurp, *v.* to seize and hold by force or without proper right or authority. [256]

utilitarian, *adj.* concerned with or intended for ordinary, practical use; not **aesthetic** or recreational. [83]

utilization, *n.* this and the verb to *utilize* are **bombastic** words for *use,* the all-purpose noun and verb. To **paraphrase** Mark Twain, you could start building a very expressive vocabulary just by leaving *utilize* and *utilization* out. [169]

utterance, *n.* something expressed (either spoken or written); a statement. [97]

V

vacillate, *v.* to sway between one opinion and another, waver mentally, be **indecisive.** [186]

vacuity, *n.* emptiness, absence of matter or intelligence. [230]

★ **vague,** *adj.* not clear or plain in meaning or form, not **distinct**[2], indefinite (cf. **ambiguous**). [127, 169, 325]

vaguely, *adv.* slightly, somewhat. [285]

★ **vain,** *adj.* 1. overly concerned with or proud of one's appearance or achievements (synonyms: **conceited, egotistical**). 2. unsuccessful, **fruitless, futile.** [76, 77, 95]

vain, in (*idiom*) without success, uselessly, to no avail. [1, 61, 115, 235]

valedictory, *adj.* expressing a farewell. [321]

★ **valid,** *adj.* right, well-founded, reasonable, just: a *valid* argument (synonym: **sound**). [245]

vandalism, *n.* **willful** or **malicious** destruction of property. [206]

vanguard, *n.* the forefront, leading position, or that which occupies it, the leader. [100, 232]

vanity, *n.* 1. that which is **vain**: worthless, useless, empty, or **futile.** 2. excessive pride in one's reputation or appearance. [220, 223, 317, 325]

vanquish, *v.* to conquer, defeat, overcome, subdue: *vanquish* the foe. [263]

vapid, *adj.* lacking spirit or flavor, without **zest** (synonyms: **bland, insipid**). [219]

vapor, *n.* mist, steam, or smoke. [186, 300]

★ **vast,** *adj.* very great in size, amount, extent, or number (synonyms: **boundless, immense, infinite**). [xii, 16, 75, 138, 198, 201, 207, 245]

vastly, *adv.* hugely, greatly. [xiii, 230]

vault, *n.* an arched structure forming a ceiling or roof. [134]

veer, *v.* to turn aside or change direction suddenly, swerve. [263, 280]

vehement, *adj.* characterized by intense emotion, passion, or energy (synonyms: **fervid, torrid**). **vehemently,** *adv.* [55, 164, 206, 275]

venal, *adj.* capable of being bribed or bought off, able to be obtained for a price (synonym: **mercenary**). [245]

venerable, *adj.* deserving respect because of age, accomplishments, character, standing, etc. (cf. **dignified, distinguished**). [135, 217, 232, 256]

vengeance, *n.* revenge; punishment in return for a wrong. **with a vengeance:** with great violence or energy. [152, 312]

vengeful, *adj.* seeking **vengeance** (synonym: **vindictive**). [53]

veracity, *n.* truthfulness, correctness. [184, 241]

verbatim, *adj.* word for word, expressed in precisely the same words. [163, 255, 420]

verbose, *adj.* overly wordy, long-winded, containing more words than needed. [136, 201]

verify, *v.* to prove the truth or accuracy of (synonyms: **confirm, corroborate, substantiate**). [xv, 142, 183, 192, 241, 255]

vernacular, *n.* the common, everyday spoken form of a language. [31]

versatility, *n.* the quality of being *versatile,* capable of performing many functions or serving various purposes. [199]

vestige, *n.* a slight trace, tiny bit or amount (esp. of something no longer present or in existence). [213]

vestigial, *adj.* being a **vestige.** [255]

vex, *v.* to bother, pester, worry, annoy (synonyms: **harass, torment**). **vexation,** *n.* [73, 115, 147, 220]

vexatious, *adj.* troubling, disturbing, annoying, irritating. [138, 161]

vibrant, *adj.* filled with energy, lively, bustling: a *vibrant* performance (synonyms: **animated, robust, vigorous, vital, vivacious**). [218]

★ **vigilant,** *adj.* on the alert, watchful (synonyms: **circumspect, discreet, prudent, tactful, wary**). **vigilance,** *n.* [113, 154, 177, 232, 251, 265]

vigorous, *adj.* healthy and energetic, strong, forceful (synonyms: **animated, robust, vibrant, vivacious**). **vigorously,** *adv.* [11, 25, 155, 178, 264, 312]

vile, *adj.* 1. disgusting: depraved, **morally** objectionable (synonyms: **despicable, loathsome, offensive**[1]). 2. disgusting: highly disagreeable to the senses (synonym: **offensive**[3]). [28, 248, 260]

vindictive, *adj.* motivated by a desire for revenge, unforgiving and spiteful (synonym: **vengeful**). [37]

virile, *adj.* masculine, manly, showing manly strength and spirit. [95, 188]

virtuosity, *n.* the skill of a **virtuoso**. [274]

virtuoso, *n.* a person of extraordinary skill, esp. an outstanding musician. [226]

virtuous, *adj.* pure and good, righteous, characterized by **moral** excellence (synonyms: **conscientious**[1], **ethical, scrupulous**[1], **upright**). [87, 175, 319]

visceral, *adj.* of or pert. to the gut or belly; hence, guided by instinct or **intuition** rather than by the mind or reason. [156, 163, 243]

visionary, *adj.* 1. dreamlike, imaginary, unreal, like a vision. 2. given to fanciful, impractical ideas and the pursuit of unworkable projects or impossible schemes (synonyms: **idealistic, quixotic**). [95, 196]

★ **vital,** *adj.* full of life and energy (synonyms: **robust, vibrant**). [209]

★ **vitality,** *n.* energy, liveliness, pep. [xiii, 119]

vitiate, *v.* to spoil, reduce the value or quality of, make faulty or ineffective (synonyms: **corrupt, debase, undermine**). **vitiating,** *adj.* [208, 245]

vituperative, *adj.* characterized by harsh, abusive language: a *vituperative* editorial. [xi, 213]

vivacious, *adj.* filled with lively spirit, sprightly (synonyms: **animated, robust, vibrant, vigorous**). [8]

★ **vivid,** *adj.* 1. strong, intense: a *vivid* feeling (synonym: **keen**[2]). 2. brightly or intensely colored: *vivid* hues. 3. consisting of or producing clear, sharp images: a *vivid* description; a *vivid* memory. 4. having the appearance of life: a *vivid* portrait. [56, 97, 129, 133, 164, 215, 283, 292, 319]

vociferous, *adj.* shouting, crying, or calling out loudly. **vociferously,** *adv.* [9, 41, 286]

—*Boisterous, raucous, strident, obstreperous, clamorous,* and *vociferous* all mean strikingly, insistently, or unpleasantly loud. *Vociferous* applies to any noisy outcry, esp. a loud and **vehement** one: their *vociferous* demand. *Clamorous* suggests noise that is loud and **continuous**: *clamorous* music coming from next door. *Obstreperous* suggests noisiness accompanied by unruly behavior: an *obstreperous* child; the *obstreperous* mob. *Strident* applies to noise that is disagreeably loud, harsh, and **shrill**; a piercing scream, screeching brakes, and the whining of a power tool are all *strident. Raucous* may suggest the noisy unruliness of *obstreperous* (*raucous* laughter, a *raucous* crowd) or the harshness and roughness of *strident* (a *raucous* voice). *Boisterous* suggests the noise that comes from being rowdy or having fun: a *boisterous* party.

void, *adj.* useless, ineffective, having no force. [208]

volatile, *adj.* changeable, unstable, inconstant; likely to change or shift suddenly, or erupt with violence or anger (synonyms: **capricious, mercurial, unpredictable**). [113, 175]

voluble, *adj.* extremely talkative, releasing a steady flow of words (synonyms: **garrulous, loquacious**). [84, 147]

voluminous, *adj.* very large; of great volume, number, or extent. [112, 158, 173]

voracious, *adj.* extremely hungry (synonyms: **insatiable, ravenous**). [36, 137]

vulgar, *adj.* lacking **refinement** or taste; coarse, crude, **crass, profane**: *vulgar* gestures. **vulgarity,** *n.* [11, 32, 88, 222]

★ **vulnerable,** *adj.* open to injury, attack, or harm; having insufficient defenses. **vulnerability,** *n.* [83, 185, 189, 227]

vying, *adj.* competing, **contending**, striving for superiority (from *vie, v.*). [270]

W

wallow, *v.* to completely devote oneself to or take unrestrained pleasure in, like an animal rolling about in water, mud, or dust. [286]

wan, *adj.* pale and sickly looking (synonym: **pallid**). [291]

wane, on the (*idiom*). gradually receding or fading away, diminishing. To *wane* means to fade away, diminish gradually. **waning,** *adj.* [221, 282]

★ **wary,** *adj.* watchful and cautious, suspicious, distrustful, leery (synonyms: **circumspect, discreet, prudent, tactful, vigilant**). [113, 206, 250]

wayward, *adj.* unpredictable (synonyms: **capricious, erratic, fickle, volatile**). [263]

whelp, *n.* a young person, esp. one who is **impudent**. [110]

whet, *v.* to sharpen or **stimulate**. [216]

★ **whimsical,** *adj.* oddly fanciful and playful; arising from *whimsy*, **fickle** humor. **whimsically,** *adv.* [27, 299]

wholesome, *adj.* promoting well-being, healthful, **beneficial**[1]. [208]
　　—*Wholesome* and *salubrious* both mean good for one's health. *Wholesome* refers to that which benefits or builds up the body, mind, or spirit: a *wholesome* diet; *wholesome* recreation. *Salubrious* refers to that which promotes physical health: a *salubrious* climate.

wield, *v.* to exercise, have and use: *wield* authority. [207]

wiles, *n.* pl. trickery, **artful** and seductive behavior. [110]

willful, *adj.* 1. intentional, deliberate. 2. stubbornly insisting on getting one's own way. **willfully,** *adv.* [156, 165, 196]

wily, *adj.* sly, cunning, crafty, full of **wiles**. [124]

windfall, *n.* sudden and unexpected good fortune. [285]

wistfully, *adv.* with sad and wishful longing. [27, 59, 116]

withering, *adj.* overwhelming, esp. in a harsh and bitter way (synonym: **devastating**). [163, 221, 274]

witticism, *n.* a joke, quip, funny or witty remark. [12, 420]

wrath, *n.* anger, esp. righteous anger. [174]

wreak, *v.* to inflict or bring about. [177]

writhe, *v.* to twist and squirm, contort oneself as if in pain. [11, 107, 252]

wry, *adj.* cleverly and **deviously** humorous: a *wry* commentary. [124]

Y

yearn, *v.* to long for deeply, desire earnestly. [113, 163, 203]

Z

zeal, *n.* intense enthusiasm, passion, or devotion. [30]
zealous, *adj.* filled with great passion or devotion, extremely enthusiastic
       (synonyms: **ardent, avid, fervent**). [196, 256]
zenith, *n.* the highest point, peak (synonyms: **apex, summit**). [263]
zest, *n.* an enjoyable or interesting flavor. [82]

Acknowledgments

Writers may write in solitude, but they never work alone. I am **emphatically** grateful to my two marvelous editors and literary midwives: Jen Charat, for **invaluable** prenatal coaching; and Elizabeth Parker, for heroic assistance with labor and delivery. Thank you both for your **sanguine** support and splendid deskside manner.

I am also grateful to my colleagues on *A Way with Words*—Richard Lederer, Jill Fritz, and Stefanie Levine—for holding the fort during my **sojourn** on Planet Book; my parents, Reinhardt and Nancy Carr Elster, my sister, Judith Williams, and Barbara Wallraff for their suggestions and encouragement; John Uphouse, for technical assistance that saved me hours of **tedious** labor; Miriam Breyer, for procuring a **plethora** of SATs and ACTs; Steve Hayes, for **shrewd** guidance and **subtle refinements**; my agent, Deborah Schneider, for the spondulicks; Holly Kuemmerlin, who, like "Time's wingéd chariot," was always at my back; my big girl, Carmen, for her **precocious** suggestions; my little girl, Judith, for her delightfully **loquacious** company; and my wife, Myrna Zambrano, for her capacity to love and for standing, in more ways than one, the test of time.

My visit to Mark Twain's remarkable house in Hartford and Hal Holbrook's brilliant impersonation of Twain helped make the man **palpable** to me as a character. Justin Kaplan's

engrossing and beautifully written biography *Mr. Clemens and Mark Twain* was a source of many **revelations,** and Shelley Fisher Fishkin's *Lighting Out for the Territory: Reflections on Mark Twain and American Culture* helped me understand Twain's **legacy** and inspired me to incorporate the real-life George Griffin and Warner T. McGuinn into my story. Caroline T. Harnsberger's *Mark Twain at Your Fingertips* provided **verbatim witticisms** and **insights** from Twain that I mixed in with my **fabricated** ones; Twain's autobiography and William Dean Howells's *My Mark Twain* were excellent sources of **anecdotes** and details; and the comprehensive edition of *The Adventures of Huckleberry Finn*, which has a fascinating foreword and addendum by Victor Doyno, was **indispensable.**

Finally, I'm grateful to Carol Beales and Ron Vanderhye of the James S. Copley Library in La Jolla, California, for their **amiable** cooperation and **alacrity** in sharing with me the section about George Griffin in Twain's unpublished "Family Sketch." I couldn't have done justice to the man without it.